Register for Free Membership to

solutions@syngress.com

Over the last few years, Syngress has published many best-selling and critically acclaimed books, including Tom Shinder's *Configuring ISA Server 2000*, Brian Caswell and Jay Beale's *Snort 2.0 Intrusion Detection*, and Angela Orebaugh and Gilbert Ramirez's *Ethereal Packet Sniffing*. One of the reasons for the success of these books has been our unique **solutions@syngress.com** program. Through this site, we've been able to provide readers a real time extension to the printed book.

As a registered owner of this book, you will qualify for free access to our members-only solutions@syngress.com program. Once you have registered, you will enjoy several benefits, including:

- Four downloadable e-booklets on topics related to the book. Each booklet is approximately 20-30 pages in Adobe PDF format. They have been selected by our editors from other best-selling Syngress books as providing topic coverage that is directly related to the coverage in this book.

- A comprehensive FAQ page that consolidates all of the key points of this book into an easy to search web page, providing you with the concise, easy to access data you need to perform your job.

- A "From the Author" Forum that allows the authors of this book to post timely updates links to related sites, or additional topic coverage that may have been requested by readers.

Just visit us at **www.syngress.com/solutions** and follow the simple registration process. You will need to have this book with you when you register.

Thank you for giving us the opportunity to serve your needs. And be sure to let us know if there is anything else we can do to make your job easier.

SYNGRESS®

HOW TO CHEAT AT MANAGING

Windows Small Business Server 2003

Susan Snedaker

KEY	SERIAL NUMBER
001	HJV764VBB8
002	PO5FGVB623
003	829KM8NJH2
004	87655GHVBN
005	CVP3JFDW33
006	VBP5JMLLP9
007	HJWD3E3288
008	298MKNMCC6
009	62TVBHWAS7
010	I5T6TVBJ93

PUBLISHED BY
Syngress Publishing, Inc.
800 Hingham Street
Rockland, MA 02370

How to Cheat at Managing Windows Small Business Server 2003

ISBN: 1-932266-80-1

Publisher: Andrew Williams   Page Layout and Art: Patricia Lupien
Acquisitions Editor: Jaime Quigley   Copy Editor: Amy Thomson
Technical Editor: Daniel H. Bendell   Indexer: Julie Kawabata
Cover Designer: Michael Kavish

Distributed by O'Reilly Media, Inc. in the United States and Canada.
For information on rights and translations, contact Matt Pedersen, Director of Sales and Rights, at Syngress Publishing; email matt@syngress.com or fax to 781-681-3585.

Acknowledgments

We would like to acknowledge the following people for their kindness and support in making this book possible.

Syngress books are now distributed in the United States and Canada by O'Reilly Media, Inc. The enthusiasm and work ethic at O'Reilly is incredible and we would like to thank everyone there for their time and efforts to bring Syngress books to market: Tim O'Reilly, Laura Baldwin, Mark Brokering, Mike Leonard, Donna Selenko, Bonnie Sheehan, Cindy Davis, Grant Kikkert, Opol Matsutaro, Steve Hazelwood, Mark Wilson, Rick Brown, Leslie Becker, Jill Lothrop, Tim Hinton, Kyle Hart, Sara Winge, C. J. Rayhill, Peter Pardo, Leslie Crandell, Valerie Dow, Regina Aggio, Pascal Honscher, Preston Paull, Susan Thompson, Bruce Stewart, Laura Schmier, Sue Willing, Mark Jacobsen, Betsy Waliszewski, Dawn Mann, Kathryn Barrett, John Chodacki, and Rob Bullington.

The incredibly hard working team at Elsevier Science, including Jonathan Bunkell, Ian Seager, Duncan Enright, David Burton, Rosanna Ramacciotti, Robert Fairbrother, Miguel Sanchez, Klaus Beran, Emma Wyatt, Rosie Moss, Chris Hossack, Mark Hunt, and Krista Leppiko, for making certain that our vision remains worldwide in scope.

David Buckland, Marie Chieng, Lucy Chong, Leslie Lim, Audrey Gan, Pang Ai Hua, and Joseph Chan of STP Distributors for the enthusiasm with which they receive our books.

Kwon Sung June at Acorn Publishing for his support.

David Scott, Tricia Wilden, Marilla Burgess, Annette Scott, Andrew Swaffer, Stephen O'Donoghue, Bec Lowe, and Mark Langley of Woodslane for distributing our books throughout Australia, New Zealand, Papua New Guinea, Fiji Tonga, Solomon Islands, and the Cook Islands.

Winston Lim of Global Publishing for his help and support with distribution of Syngress books in the Philippines.

Author

Susan Snedaker (MBA, BA, MCSE, MCT, PM) is Principal Consultant and founder of VirtualTeam Consulting, LLC, a consulting firm specializing in start-ups and companies in transition, particularly technology firms. VirtualTeam works with technology start–ups to develop viable business plans in preparation for debt/equity funding or due diligence with venture capital firms. VirtualTeam also provides IT consulting, design, and implementation services to companies of all sizes. The firm assists companies with strategic planning, operations improvement and project management. Through its team of subject matter experts, VirtualTeam also offers financial analysis, change management and operations improvement services.

Prior to founding VirtualTeam Consulting in May 2000, Susan held various executive and technical positions with companies including Microsoft, Honeywell, Keane, and Apta Software. As Director of Service Delivery for Keane, she managed a division with 1200+ technical support staff delivering phone and email support for various Microsoft products including Windows Server operating systems. She has contributed technical chapters to six Syngress Publishing books on Windows (including *The Best Damn Windows Server 2003 Book Period*, ISBN: 1-931836-12-4) and security technologies, and has written and edited technical content for a variety of publications. Susan has also developed and delivered technical content from security to telephony, TCP/IP to wi-fi and just about everything in between (she admits a particular fondness for anything related to TCP/IP).

Susan holds a master's degree in business administration and a bachelor's degree in management from the University of Phoenix; she also holds a certificate in project management from Stanford University. She is a member of the Information Technology Association of Southern Arizona (ITASA).

Technical Editor

Daniel H. Bendell (BA, CNE) is the founder and President of Assurance Technology Management, Inc. (ATM), a full-service consulting practice specializing in providing complete business technology guidance to small and medium companies. ATM's unique consulting approach takes a company's technology systems into consideration, combined with a clear understanding of the client's business goals and practices.

With over twenty years of experience in the IT industry, Daniel combines his breadth of technical knowledge with an ability to understand his clients' business needs. He is widely published on a number of topics, including technical systems documentation and remote systems management. He also delivers customized presentations and educational seminars to organizations and groups of small business owners on how to better manage the technology systems they have invested in.

Prior to founding ATM, Daniel worked as a senior-level consultant for CSC Consulting, where he specialized in client/server technologies, and as a Healthcare Information Systems Consultant with Superior Consultant Company.

Daniel lives in Framingham, MA with his wife Phyllis and daughters Melissa and Jessica.

Contents

Contents

Foreword

You're holding this book in your hands at the local bookstore, or maybe viewing it online. Better yet, you're sitting at your desk with a cup of coffee looking at this foreword. You're wondering if you bought the right book.

You're probably expecting to find some serious shortcuts to managing Microsoft Windows Small Business Server 2003. And that's exactly what this book is about. It's focused, concise and to-the-point. Don't you wish you could say the same about your weekly meetings?

This book will give you the essential information you'll need to install, configure and manage your Windows Small Business Server 2003 network. It provides step-by-step instructions along with focused technical background for those of you who are *not* full-time IT professionals. In fact, we're assuming that most of you reading this book are from some other career field (accountant, office manager, mechanic, warehouse manager, monkey wrangler, etc.) and were tasked with implementing or managing your small business's network. For many of you, managing the network comes under that catch-all phrase often found in job descriptions "*and other duties, as assigned*."

This book cuts to the chase and lets you know exactly what you need to do. It guides you through key server tasks with explanations and screen shots. It provides additional resources on many topics so you can continue to learn after you've mastered the concepts in the book. We don't drown you in arcane technical detail or go on and on about the subtleties of Internet Protocol addressing (though that's a particular passion of mine, I held myself in check). This is a no-nonsense reference that is comprehensive in all the right places.

If you were starting to wonder how you would actually manage to do your job *and* manage your network, this book is the answer. You can read it from cover to cover (only recommended if you have strong geek tendencies) or you can read chapters as you need them. The information, solutions and recommendations are easy to find and easy to use. Now get going, you've got a network to manage.

Chapter 1

Essentials of Windows Small Business Server 2003

- Features of Windows Small Business Server 2003

- Components of Windows Small Business Server 2003

- Restrictions of Windows Small Business Server 2003

- Determining Which Operating System Package is Best for You

The End Result

By the end of this chapter, you'll have a thorough understanding of what makes up Windows Small Business Server (SBS) 2003, including features, components, and restrictions. You'll know what SBS can do for you and you'll understand, at a high level, the different components involved in the two different editions. You'll also understand the restrictions to be aware of when implementing SBS, though for most small businesses, these are relatively minor issues. You'll also understand the differences between Windows Server 2003 and Windows Small Business Server 2003, and you'll be able to decide which one is right for you. If you're new to managing Windows Small Business Server 2003, don't skip this chapter. You'll come away with a strong foundation on which the rest of the book is built. Besides, you don't want to miss this snappy start.

Features of Windows Small Business Server 2003

The features of Windows SBS 2003 make this version of the SBS operating system the best one yet. Earlier versions (4.5 and 2000) were shaky at times, but Microsoft has put quite a bit of thought and effort into this new version, and users (and industry critics) are giving this one high marks. In this section, we'll look at the features that will help simplify your administrative life. There are other useful features you'll learn about throughout this book, but the ones highlighted in this section really stand out in the "makes life easier" category.

Simplified Administration and Management

There's a reason this feature is listed first. Many people managing a network for a small business are not seasoned IT professionals, but rather are people with an interest and aptitude for managing the network (and sometimes those unsuspecting few who missed the meeting where this task was assigned). SBS 2003 simplifies the most commonly used network management tasks. Since managing a network (users, groups, devices) is what takes up a majority of a network administrator's time, the simplification and streamlining of these tasks is one of the most important improvements to SBS 2003 and one of its most compelling features.

Microsoft has created a number of wizards, which are simply small automated programs, that help you configure, schedule, monitor and manage a wide variety of network admin tasks. We'll look at the various wizards throughout this book.

Enhanced Security

Another area of major concern for anyone involved in managing a network, whether experienced or novice, is security. It seems there's a new virus or worm or spyware program making the rounds every day. SBS 2003 includes an internal firewall, which protects your network. It also supports the use of external firewalls. If you purchase the Premium Edition (see the section "Components of Windows Small Business Server 2003" later in this chapter), you'll also get Internet Security and Acceleration (ISA) Server, which provides both improved security and usability.

Easy Internet and E-mail

Most companies can't live without e-mail these days, and access to the Internet is also a vitally important element of networking. As mentioned earlier, SBS 2003 comes with many helpful wizards, so Internet and e-mail setup is greatly simplified with the Configure E-mail and Internet Connection Wizard.

Instant Intranet

Many small businesses want to set up an intranet (a website available only internally to people logged onto the network) because it can be a great way to share information quickly, easily, and efficiently. However, these same small businesses also usually lack a dedicated IT staff that can create, configure, and maintain an intranet. Enter SBS 2003. A pre-built website for an intranet is included in SBS 2003 and is based on Windows SharePoint Services (see the section "Components of Windows Small Business Server 2003"). The sample website has all the commonly used features pre-configured all of which can be easily added to, removed, or edited.

Painless Remote Access

Remote access is often a dreaded topic because it involves allowing employees access to your corporate network when they're not in the office. This is like swimming in shark-infested waters—you're not sure exactly when or how, but you know sooner or later you're going to feel pain. The good news is that with SBS 2003, remote access has become painless. A feature of SBS 2003 is the

Remote Web Workplace, which allows any device that can connect to the Internet to connect to a dynamically created website using an Internet address. Users can then read e-mail, access shared files on the corporate network, or access the intranet.

Simplified User Management

Another area of network management that can take up an admin's time is adding, configuring and managing user and computer accounts on the network. With the Add User Wizard, this problem is simplified. The wizard basically sets up everything.

Manage Data More Easily

If your company depends on managing large amounts of data—inventory, e-commerce, customer information, etc., the Structured Query Language (SQL) Server 2000 component included in the Premium Edition will make your life easier. SQL Server is a robust database solution that can scale up as your company grows. Many small companies build databases using Microsoft Access, which is fine for small databases, but as your company grows, or if you need to manage access to the data in the database, you need SQL Server.

SOME INDEPENDENT ADVICE

If you're not an experienced IT pro and you're not sure which direction to take your company's network, SBS 2003 has some very compelling features that will have your network running as if it *was* managed by a seasoned IT pro. SBS 2003 is not the cure-all, but its impressive list of capabilities, combined with its ease-of-use, make this an operating system that small businesses should consider. If you've heard not-so-good things about SBS in the past, well, that was then. Earlier versions (4.5 and 2000) did have some issues that made it a temperamental operating system. However, SBS 2003 has moved beyond that and has grown into a solid, stable, feature-rich product for small businesses.

Components of Windows Small Business Server 2003

You may already be managing a Small Business Server-based network or you might be trying to figure out if it's right for you and your company. Let's look at the various components of SBS 2003 so you can make an informed decision. SBS 2003 (we'll refer to it as just SBS from here on out) is built upon the Windows Server 2003 operating system. It's got all the features of Windows Server 2003—with a few limitations, which we'll discuss in the next section. SBS comes in two flavors—standard or premium. The components of each are show below and we'll talk about what they each mean in just a moment.

The components of SBS Standard Edition are:

- Microsoft Windows Server 2003
- Microsoft Exchange Server 2003
- Microsoft Outlook 2003
- Microsoft Shared Fax Service
- Microsoft Windows SharePoint Services

The components of SBS Premier Edition are:

- All the components of SBS Standard Edition
- Microsoft ISA Server
- Microsoft SQL Server 2000
- Microsoft Office FrontPage 2003

If these components only sound vaguely familiar (or completely foreign), don't panic. We're going to talk about each of them briefly in this chapter and we'll take a more in-depth look at them throughout the remainder of this book.

Windows Server 2003 (Standard, Premium)

This is the foundation of SBS—Windows Server 2003. It's a very secure, stable operating system with more features than you can shake a stick at. As a result, we're going to focus on the features you really need to know and use in SBS to make sure your network runs well and stays secure. Later in this book, you'll learn about the features of Windows Server 2003 used in SBS that you'll need.

For now, what you need to know is this is where everything starts. Users, groups, printers, file storage, routing, remote access, and security (to name a few) all are managed through the Windows Server operating system, and we're going to spend quite a bit of time working with the most commonly used (and needed) elements in the chapters that follow.

Exchange Server 2003 (Standard, Premium)

Exchange Server 2003 is the latest version of Microsoft's messaging (e-mail) server. Combined with Outlook 2003 (only included in the Premium version, see the section entitled "Outlook 2003"), these two programs give you all the tools you need to manage e-mail and messaging for your organization. If you're not familiar with Exchange Server, stick around. We've got a whole chapter on Exchange Server 2003 that will take the mystery out of managing your corporate e-mail server.

Outlook 2003 (Premium)

Outlook 2003 is included in the Premium and Standard version. Outlook is the desktop application that is often used in conjunction with Exchange Server. You're probably familiar with Outlook since it's a pretty popular part of the Microsoft Office application suite. It includes e-mail, calendar, tasks, notes, and contacts, along with a lot of very useful features that your users will take full advantage of. We'll discuss Exchange Server and Outlook together in more detail later in the book.

Shared Fax Service (Standard, Premium)

Earlier versions of SBS had a shared fax service that left much to be desired. In fact, a lot of companies opted to use a third-party faxing program because the one built into SBS was unreliable. However, Microsoft put some muscle behind improving this service for SBS 2003 and this version of the shared fax service is a great tool. Some companies live and die by the fax, while others have moved more toward e-mail with attachments for many transactions. Faxing is still an important function for many businesses, and we'll look at this feature in more detail later in the book.

Windows SharePoint Services (Standard, Premium)

Even if you're experienced with Windows and server operating systems, you may not be familiar with Windows SharePoint Services (WSS). WSS is, essentially, a collaboration application. It allows people in your organization to work together more easily and effectively. One of the features you don't see emphasized much is that WSS has a document management feature that can save your organization time and money. Many document management systems are a bit too "big" for a small organization in terms of cost and capabilities. However, the document management feature that WSS provides is a useful tool for many small businesses. We'll look at WSS in more detail later.

Internet Security and Acceleration Server (Premium)

ISA Server is something you may be completely unfamiliar with, but it's not as spooky as it sounds. ISA is Microsoft's industrial-strength firewall, caching, and Internet-related security software. If you've purchased (or are considering purchasing) the SBS Premium Edition, this functionality will certainly help you justify the additional cost of the Premium Edition. While the firewall built into Windows Server 2003 via Routing and Remote Access Server (RRAS) works just fine, ISA has additional features and capabilities you won't find in RRAS. If security, especially Internet-related security, is a major concern for you, read the chapter on ISA later in this book to better understand what ISA is and what it can do for you. You'll find this capability alone may be worth the additional cost of the Premium Edition for your company.

SQL Server 2000 (Premium)

SQL Server 2000 is also included only in the Premium Edition of SBS. SQL is the database software used by many organizations and applications. SQL Server 2000 allows you to use the robust features of SQL Server for your company's database needs. We've dedicated a whole chapter to SQL Server in this book, so if databases are important to your company, you should consider the SBS Premium Edition for the SQL Server software that's included.

Office FrontPage 2003 (Premium)

FrontPage is the software application used to build and manage websites. There are a number of these types of programs available on the market and many web developers have very strong opinions about the pros and cons of each. If your company has an intranet or an Internet presence, or if you're thinking about creating one, FrontPage gives you the tools to create and manage it. We'll look at this feature in depth later in the book.

BEST PRACTICES ACCORDING TO MICROSOFT

- Consider using SBS Standard Edition if you're running a very small outfit that doesn't require more robust email management and additional security features.
- If messaging, database management or extra security features are important to your organization, you should consider using the Premium Edition.
- Don't skimp on the operating system. Purchase the version best suited to your organization—the extra investment will quickly pay for itself.

SOME INDEPENDENT ADVICE

At this point, you may be feeling comfortable with the different elements that comprise SBS Standard or Premium Edition—if so, that's great. If you're feeling a bit overwhelmed because much of this is new to you, don't worry. Microsoft has put a lot of thought and effort into making SBS 2003 even more user-friendly than previous versions. The installation and setup process is actually easy and doesn't require a tremendous amount of technical knowledge to complete. This software uses a To Do List and a multitude of Wizards that will make your installation and setup as smooth as butter.

Now, if you're an experienced admin, the only complaint you might have is that it's not quite as easy to get "under the hood" of this version of Windows. This is on purpose. A good friend of mine always says, "I don't have to know how the engine works to drive my car." His point is that he should be able to use and manage his computer without having a PhD in computer science—and he's right. SBS doesn't require that PhD, so if you're a real techie, you might find that the ubiquitous wizards feel like they're keeping you from the nuts and bolts. For non-techies, that's probably the best news you've had since you were assigned the task of managing your company's network.

Restrictions of Windows Small Business Server 2003

SBS has a lot of features that many small businesses can really use. However, it's not appropriate for all companies. There are several very significant restrictions you need to be aware of so that you don't end up with the wrong operating system for your needs.

Location of Installed Components

One of the most notable restrictions of SBS is that the components that come bundled with SBS (the ones we just reviewed) must be installed on the same computer on which SBS is installed. For instance, you cannot install the SQL Server software on a separate computer. The only exception to this is that you can install FrontPage (which comes with the Premium edition) on another computer. The assumption is that you'll have one server hosting all of the functions that come with SBS. For a small company (the target market for this product), this works just fine, assuming your server hardware is up to the task.

Client Limitations

In addition to the limits of domains and domain controllers, SBS also restricts the number of users that can access the network at one time to 75. SBS will simply not allow more than 75 users (or computers) to connect at any given time. This limitation does not apply to printers, network storage devices or other network devices. So, you can have 50 users and 30 printers on the SBS network if you want, but you cannot have 76 users. It just won't happen. Keep in mind that this means a maximum of 75 users actually logged on to the network. You can have more than 75 users defined in Active Directory, but only 75 can be logged on at any given time. If your organization currently has 50 or 60 users and the company is growing, you may want to consider Windows Server 2003 right off the bat. SBS works best with about 50 users maximum. When you start approaching the 75-user limit, you may find the network slows down due to the load on that single server. If you have fewer users but think you might outgrow SBS in a year or two, there is an SBS migration kit that allows you to upgrade from SBS to Windows Server 2003 without losing your settings so that you don't have to start from scratch.

Remember, too, that the number of users does not always equal the number of employees. There are many small businesses that have employees in warehouses, in manufacturing facilities, or out in the field that don't regularly use computers. So, you might have a company with 200 employees with only 28 people using computers. If this is the case, SBS may be a great choice for your company. Also, if your company runs two or three shifts and your users are spread over a 12 or 24-hour period where no more than 50 (or so) users are logged on at any given time, SBS might also be a good choice. Look at the actual number of users during your operating hours to determine which operating system makes the most sense for you.

Client Access Licenses

SBS comes with five *client access licenses* (CALs). This is a very important point to remember when estimating your costs. Although you're allowed to have up to 75 users (up from 50 in SBS 2000), you must purchase additional CALs for all users beyond the first 5. That means you'd need to purchase 70 additional CALs in order to run at the specified 75-user limit. For more information on client licensing for SBS, visit the Microsoft website at: www.microsoft.com/windowsserver2003/howtobuy/licensing/default.mspx.

SOME INDEPENDENT ADVICE

Microsoft has made purchasing CALs a lot easier. You can purchase SBS CALs online directly from the SBS server via the Internet. You can manage licensing in SBS via the **Licensing** link in the Server Management console. We'll review this later in the book, but don't make the mistake of thinking that you can run up to 75 users on SBS without purchasing additional licenses. Out of the box, you can run 5 users on an SBS network.

Client Operating Systems

SBS supports a number of Windows operating systems, which means the computers on your network can run a variety of operating systems. You can use Windows XP Professional (not the Home Edition), Windows 2000, Windows ME, Windows NT Workstation 4.0, Windows 98, and Windows 95.

SBS, like the Windows Server 2003 operating system it is built on, provides only limited support for other operating systems including Windows NT version 4.0 and earlier, Windows for Workgroups, Windows 3.x, Macintosh, UNIX workstations, and LAN Manager Clients. SBS doesn't work at all with OS/2 clients.

SOME INDEPENDENT ADVICE

If you're running Windows ME on any computer, upgrade as soon as possible. Windows ME was a mistake from the start and even Microsoft grudgingly admits it was an operating system that should never have hit the streets. ME is not particularly stable and you'll save yourself a lot of time and aspirin if you just upgrade to Windows XP Professional. If you're running Windows 98 Second Edition, you actually have a fairly stable operating system and you could consider running that for a while longer, if needed.

Microsoft has everyone on a steady diet of upgrades – sometimes that's a good thing and sometimes it's not. If you're still running the older operating systems for which SBS has limited support, you might want to consider upgrading those computers, if possible. Of course, there is the cost of hardware and software to consider, but if you don't have a really good reason for running those older systems, start budgeting for some newer equipment—it will make your life (and that of your users) much easier.

Single Domain

Another important limitation you should be aware of is that SBS only allows one domain. You might know that a domain is a logical grouping of computers, users, and devices for security and administration. The SBS installation must be the root domain controller in Active Directory. A domain controller computer controls access to the network by checking user credentials and passwords (among other things). Active Directory is the database in Windows Server products that stores information about everything on the network from users to devices to protocols and more. The computer on which SBS is installed becomes the root domain controller in Active Directory and the domain becomes the root domain. You cannot have more than one computer running SBS in that domain. If you're not sure what all this means, just remember that you can only have one computer running SBS in your office and everyone in that office will be on the same domain or logical grouping. SBS will walk you through the process without any trouble.

Since only one domain is supported, if you're thinking of using SBS for a branch office, for example, think again. SBS is designed for small businesses (hence the catchy title) and as such, it's assumed that the company is contained in one building and has one domain. And, if you're the type who's inclined to try a hack or two, you should also rethink that. SBS cannot be modified to run in a multi-domain model. The SBS domain lacks the ability to create trust relationships between domains. If you need multiple domains, stick with Windows Server 2003.

The computer running SBS is configured (and required) to be the domain controller for the network. You can implement a second domain controller (DC), but most networks are so small that there's really no need for a secondary DC in SBS. If you're new to Windows, domain controllers and Active Directory, you don't really have to worry about it because the SBS wizards will walk you though everything you need to do to set the network up properly.

Don't get confused here—you can install as many servers, often called *member servers* or *application servers*, as you want. Application or member servers are servers that host applications or simply store user files and are not actively involved in the management of the network the way a domain controller is. It's usually a good idea to have one or more member servers on the network to host applications and store files. This helps to even out the load among servers on the network and makes sure users can use the files, folders, and programs they need without waiting after every mouse click.

Determining Which Operating System Package Is Best For You

After reading through the preceding material, you probably already have a good idea of which way you need to head. However, just to summarize for you, Table 1.1 shows the comparison of SBS to Windows Server 2003. If you need more technical detail, you can visit the Microsoft Small Business Server 2003 website at www.microsoft.com/windowsserver2003/sbs/default.mspx for more information. Remember, SBS includes Windows Server 2003, so it has most of the features of Windows Server 2003. Your choice, really, is whether you can work within the restrictions of SBS. If you cannot work within the restrictions of SBS, you'll need to get the full-blown version of Windows Server 2003 and purchase the additional software components separately.

Table 1.1 Small Business Server 2003 and Windows Server 2003 Compared

	Small Business Server 2003	Windows Server 2003
Users	Up to 75	Unlimited*
Client licenses included	5	5
Client license max	75	Unlimited*
Domains	1	1 or more
Domain controllers	1	1 or more
Includes Windows Server 2003	Yes, with restrictions	Yes, unlimited
Includes Exchange Server 2003	Yes	No
Includes Outlook 2003	Yes	No
Includes Shared Fax Service	Yes	Yes
Includes SharePoint Services	Yes	Yes, as free add-in feature
Includes Internet Acceleration and Security (ISA) Server	Yes – Premium edition only	No
Includes SQL Server 2000	Yes – Premium edition only	No

Continued

Table 1.1 Small Business Server 2003 and Windows Server 2003 Compared

	Small Business Server 2003	Windows Server 2003
Includes FrontPage 2003	Yes – Premium edition only	No

For all practical purposes, the number of users and licenses you can attach to Windows Server 2003 is unlimited. Is it truly infinite? Of course not. But it can accommodate many (thousands) users and computers, and can be configured in multiple domains to create a forest, which essentially makes your options unlimited.

If your company is small and you're not going to need multiple domains or more than 75 licenses, take a good look at SBS. It's got the robust (that's a favorite Microsoft word you'll see thrown around a lot here and in the industry) features of Windows Server 2003 and the ability to use some of the advanced products like Exchange Server and SQL Server (Premium Edition only) that will make your network function like a large multi-national corporation without the expense or headache.

One More Time

Microsoft Windows Small Business Server 2003 has a multitude of features that make this operating system a great product for small businesses. It comes in two flavors: Standard and Premium. Standard comes with Windows Server 2003, Exchange Server 2003, Outlook 2003, Shared Fax Service and Windows SharePoint Services. The Premium Edition comes with all that plus ISA Server, SQL Server 2000 and Office FrontPage 2003.

SBS can only have one copy of SBS running on the network, it can only have one domain and one root domain controller. All the software components (with the exception of FrontPage 2003) must be installed on the same computer running SBS. You can run up to 75 users or devices on the network at any given time, but SBS only comes with 5 licenses. You must purchase additional CALs in order to increase the number of users or devices permitted to log onto the network at once.

☑ SBS 2003 is really driven by wizards, which walk you through just about every step of installation, configuration and management.

☑ Consider SBS Premium Edition if you need more robust security than standard Windows Server 2003 security (which is quite robust on its own).

☑ Consider SBS Premium Edition if you will use the database capabilities provided by SQL Server 2000.

☑ Consider SBS Premium Edition if you want to create and manage intranets or an Internet web presence using FrontPage 2003.

☑ SBS lets you use a variety of operating systems on computers connected to the network. If you're running Windows ME, upgrade as soon as you can.

☑ Don't forget to include the cost of additional CALs in your budget. SBS supports 75 licenses, but they must be purchased separately.

☑ If your company is growing and you expect to exceed the 75 user limit within the next year or so, you probably should consider stepping right into Windows Server 2003.

☑ SBS has a migration kit that makes upgrading from SBS to Windows Server 2003 fairly painless. It preserves your settings and configurations.

Chapter 2

Understanding and Designing Your Network

- Understanding Computer Basics
- Understanding Network Basics
- Designing Your Network
- IP Addresses, Firewalls and Network Address Translation

The End Result

When you finish reading this chapter, you'll understand the basics of a network. You'll also be able to design your network or review your existing network so you can prepare to install the Windows Small Business Server 2003 (SBS) software. If you're familiar with networks, you can use this chapter as a quick review. If you're not, this chapter will help you understand networking enough for you to make informed choices about how to configure your network infrastructure.

Understanding Computer Basics

If you already understand some of the basics of the computer world, you can skip this section and jump right into the next one. We're going to quickly review some terminology so you don't get lost in the jargon.

Server A computer that provides vital services to the network, which can include security, file sharing, applications, and printing, among other things. Servers run a network operating system to provide networking capabilities. This includes Windows NT 4.0, Windows 2000 Server, Windows Server 2003, and Windows Small Business Server 2003 (which is Windows Server 2003 with a few limitations and bundled with other applications).

Client A computer that uses the services provided by servers. Client computers are also called *user computers, workstations* or *desktops*, and are used for daily tasks such as word processing, spreadsheets, e-mail, or Internet access by users. Clients run a workstation or desktop operating system to provide user capabilities. This includes Windows 95, Windows 98, Windows ME, Windows 2000 Professional, and Windows XP Professional.

Printer Most printers these days are laser or inkjet printers, though older printers are still widely in use (they typically use inked ribbons). Printers can connect to desktop computers and can be shared across the network. Printers can also be connected to the network via a print server or they can be connected directly to the network.

Hubs and switches Equipment used to connect multiple devices to a single network connection. Switches are often "smarter" and faster than hubs.

Routers Devices used to send (route) network traffic to the correct destination. Routers are often used for security purposes and can also improve network performance (speed of response). They can also filter traffic and prevent unauthorized traffic from entering or leaving a network.

Firewalls Devices used to protect a network by monitoring and filtering information flowing into or out of the private network to the Internet. A firewall looks at the network traffic and determines whether or not it meets a specific set of criteria (determined by how the firewall is configured). By comparing network traffic to these established rules, only legitimate traffic can flow through. A firewall can also be configured to trap viruses and spam.

Internet Service Provider (ISP) A company that provides access to the Internet for a fee. ISPs will provide the Internet connection to your office, and it's your job to connect safely to the Internet from that single connection point.

IP address All computers on a network (and the Internet is one giant network) must have a unique address called an Internet Protocol (IP) address. This address is comprised of four sets of numbers in *dotted decimal* notation. An example is 192.168.64.5. Each of the four sets can range from 0 to 255. There are very specific rules about IP addressing and we'll cover what you need to know to install, configure, and manage your SBS server throughout this book.

Network Address Translation (NAT) A process that usually runs on a router or firewall that will automatically provide a valid *public* (one that can be used on the Internet) IP address for any communications to devices outside the local network.

Domain Name System (DNS) A system used on the Internet that allows you to use "friendly" names rather than IP addresses. For instance, it's easier to remember www.microsoft.com than it is to remember its 12-digit IP address. DNS is used on internal networks in the same way. This is a service provided by the SBS server.

Dynamic Host Configuration Protocol (DHCP) A service provided by a designated server to automatically assign unique IP addresses (and related configuration information) to client computers. This is a service provide by the SBS server.

SOME INDEPENDENT ADVICE

All IP addresses must have four sets of numbers separated by a dot, each set ranging from 0 to 255. These cannot simply be picked at random; they must follow very stringent rules for network addressing, which is why you should let SBS do the work for you.

Part of the IP address indicates what *network* the device is connected to and part of the address indicates the specific *device*. Therefore, you cannot simply create numbers at random. If you do so, there's a very high likelihood (close to 100%) that none of the devices will be able to communicate with one another. The topic of IP addressing is extensive and could fill an entire volume itself, so we'll only discuss enough about IP addressing in this book for you to install and manage SBS.

If you're really interested in the topic of TCP/IP and IP addressing (one of my personal favorites), there are plenty of resources on the Internet that will help you learn more. For a very thorough (and technical) discussion of the topic, check out "IP Addressing & Subnetting, Including IPv6" by Syngress Press (ISBN: 1-928994-01-6) or online, visit www.learntcpip.com or www.learntosubnet.com. Both sites have free web-based tutorials (or you can purchase a CD version) that provide great information on TCP/IP and IP addressing.

Understanding Network Basics

A computer network is comprised of computers and some method of connecting them together. Up until a few years ago, it was safe to say a network was comprised of computers and wires connecting them together, but with the growing popularity of wireless technologies, that's no longer a true statement. The method of connecting them together may vary from cabling to dial-up phone lines to wireless connections. Devices on a network communicate through their *network interface cards* (NICs) using a variety of protocols (standards) including *Transmission Control Protocol/Internet Protocol* (TCP/IP), a suite of protocols used across the Internet. Most corporate networks also use TCP/IP for their network communications as well. Each device on a network must have a unique IP address.

Who's In Charge?

If a network doesn't have a computer that manages activity on the network, it's considered a workgroup. Workgroups are not supported in SBS. A network that has one or more computers managing activity is called a *domain*. A domain is a logical grouping of computers organized primarily for managing security, including who is allowed on the network and what they can access once admitted to the network. The computer with SBS installed manages the domain and that SBS server becomes the *domain controller.*

In a domain, there must be at least one computer designated as a domain controller. That computer manages things like the list of authorized users, the list of what areas of the network each users can access, what services will be available on the network, and more. In a domain, there must be a computer designated as the DNS server, which is used to resolve domain names to IP addresses. A DHCP server must also be present to manage the automatic configuration of IP addresses for the domain. While not theoretically required (you could assign a permanent, or *static,* IP address to every computer in the domain), a DHCP server is a practical requirement on most networks. In an SBS network, both the DNS and DHCP server functions are supplied by the SBS server.

Connecting Computers Together

When you create a way for two or more computers to communicate, you have a network. Most corporate networks have computers connected together via some sort of cabling. You also have other devices such as routers, switches, and hubs that, when connected together, form your network.

By far, the most popular type of cable used in networking today is CAT5 cable. CAT5 stands for *Category 5*, which refers to a technical specification for how the cable is manufactured. Faster versions include CAT5e and the latest, CAT6. CAT5/5e/6 cabling uses RJ-45 connectors, which look like big phone jack connectors. If you hire a company to come in and wire your office, that's what they'll use. It's an easy cable to install and use, it's relatively inexpensive, and the connectors are easy to connect/disconnect. It also is compatible with Ethernet NICs used in PCs. If you hire an outside contractor (and you should if you have any cabling to do), don't just use your local electrician unless he/she is also low voltage certified. If possible, select a cable installer that is BICSI RCDD certified.

You can also connect computers to the network via phone lines. Many companies provide the ability for employees who are not in the office to connect to the network via a dial-up phone line or via the Internet. Don't confuse this with using your existing phone lines in your building for your computer network. This is something that can be done at home, but not in a business environment. In addition, some companies provide the ability for employees to connect to the network using wireless technologies. We'll explore these methods later in this book.

Network Communications

Once all the components are in place and are properly connected and configured, computers and users can communicate with one another. The following explanation, though greatly simplified, will help you understand how your e-mail gets from your computer to a computer a few hundred feet away or a few hundred miles away. We'll use the example of an e-mail, since it's one everyone can understand.

Each device on a network requires a unique address. In addition to the unique IP address, other configuration information is required, which is one reason most networks use DHCP to automatically provide this configuration information. Each device also requires a subnet mask and a default gateway. The *subnet mask* looks similar to an IP address and is used to tell the network which computers are on the local network and which ones are not. *The default gateway* is the IP address of the computer to which information is sent when it does not belong to a device on the local network. It acts as a router to send the packet to the correct destination. When setting up the SBS server, we'll show you how to configure this information.

When a message is sent to another computer, it contains the address of that other computer. Based on your computer's IP configuration (IP address, subnet mask, and default gateway) and the IP address of the destination, the information is routed to the proper computer, whether on the local network or on the Internet.

Network traffic is in the form of small units of data called *packets*. These packets are sent out the network interface card along the network cable and are either sent directly to their destination or to an intermediate destination such as a router, default gateway or firewall. These devices inspect the packets, ensure they meet requirements (which vary depending on the function of the device), and in most cases, pass the packets along. If the packets do not meet the requirements, the packets are simply discarded. Once passed along, the packets may go through many intermediate devices until they reach their final destination. They are received at the destination by the NIC and passed along to the appropriate part of the computer operating system or application for use. Although this is an over-simplified explanation, having this basic understanding will be useful as you learn more about installing, configuring, and managing SBS.

IP Addresses, Firewalls and Network Address Translation

Before we head off into configuring your server, it's important to understand a few concepts about IP addressing. Don't worry, we're not going to get heavy into IP, but you will need to understand how to configure your addressing so your network works. The information that follows is not an exhaustive look at IP addressing and it skips over big chunks of information about IP that are beyond the scope of this book. However, you will get all the information you need to successfully configure and manage your SBS network. We'll talk about specific configurations in later chapters; this chapter gives you the fundamental concepts.

IP Addressing Basics

There are three classes of IP addresses; Class A, B, and C (there are actually two other classes and there are classless, but we don't need to go there). Each class defines how many maximum networks and devices you can define through available IP addresses in that class. Table 2.1 shows an example of how this works. The numbers listed in the millions are rounded for ease of understanding. Notice that Class A addresses allow far fewer networks and far more devices per network than a Class C network, which allows just the opposite—many more networks each with far fewer possible devices.

Table 2.1 IP Address Class Example

	Maximum Possible Networks (Network IDs)	Maximum Possible Devices (Device IDs)
Class A	126	16 million
Class B	16,384	65,000
Class C	2 million	254

There are a finite number of total IP addresses available because we're using 12 digits for all classes of IP addresses (there are more advanced ways around this limitation, but we won't discuss those in this book). Also notice that the more digits you use for your network ID, the less that are available for your devices. That's why there's an inverse relationship between the two. Figure 2.1 shows how the network and device addresses work in an IP address. This is not exactly how an IP address looks—it's used to represent the general concept.

Figure 2.1 Network and IP Addresses in Class A, B, and C Networks

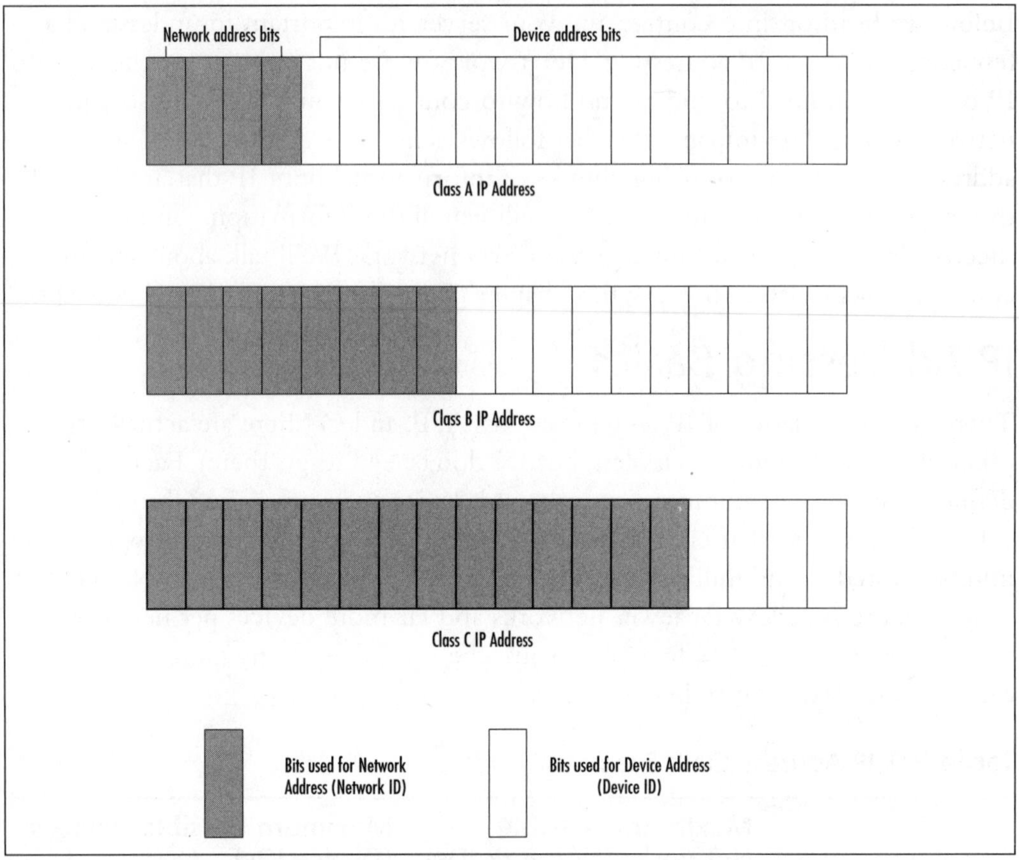

Network address bits — Device address bits

Class A IP Address

Class B IP Address

Class C IP Address

Bits used for Network Address (Network ID)

Bits used for Device Address (Device ID)

Subnet Masks

The way the network portion of the IP address is identified or separated from the device address of the IP address is through the use of a *subnet mask*. Essentially, it "blocks out" or masks the network address and whatever isn't blocked out is the specific device ID. This is important to know because if you use an incorrect subnet mask with your network, it will cause major problems because some (if not all) devices will be unable to communicate. However, even though a subnet mask identifies the portion of the IP address that is the network ID, the entire IP address is used for the device (and each must be unique on that network). So, even though only one section of the IP address points to the specific device, the entire IP address is the device's IP address—you can't just lop it off and use only the device portion. It's similar to a postal address, you can't just lop off the city, state and postal code and just leave the street address if you expect the package to arrive at its proper destination.

Class A networks, by default, use a subnet mask of 255.0.0.0. The Class B default subnet mask is 255.255.0.0. The Class C default subnet mask is 255.255.255.0. Notice that we're "blocking out" more and more of the 12 digits as we go from A to C. This is why we can have more networks in a Class C network because we're blocking out or masking 9 of the 12 digits. That only leaves three digits left for device IP addresses.

The reason we're using the number 255 is because, when translated into binary notation, 255 looks like this: 11111111. Using all 1s is how you mask out a portion of the IP address. However, any number can create a mask, such as 255.248.0.0, but using custom subnet masks requires a solid understanding of IP addressing including binary to decimal conversion.

SOME INDEPENDENT ADVICE

If you're interested in learning more about IP addressing basics and how to configure custom subnet masks (as well as other basic IP topics), take a look at the Knowledge Base article 164015 on the Microsoft website at http://support.microsoft.com/default.aspx?scid=kb;EN-US;164015. Cisco also has a good basic tutorial on IP addressing located at www.cisco.com/warp/public/701/3.html.

Another important thing to understand about IP addresses is that some addresses are *public* and can be used to communicate across the Internet and some are *private* and cannot be used on the Internet. This is an important distinction because private IP addresses can be duplicated in different companies. For instance, Companies A, B, and C can all use the same private IP addresses. This is because those IP addresses (private IP addresses) cannot travel across the Internet—the computers on the Internet responsible for forwarding packets will simply not forward those. The reason private IP addressing is a great option is because most of the communication required on a network is internal—it occurs between local devices, such as a user requesting a file from a local server.

Recall the requirement that all IP addresses be unique on the network. If a company has a private network not connected to the Internet, it can use any addressing it wants as long as the IP addresses within *that* network are unique. Now, most companies these days want to connect to and communicate across the Internet in some manner. So, using only private addressing doesn't really work since it won't allow your users to send e-mail across the Internet or browse to web pages on the Internet. You essentially have two choices if you want to communicate across the Internet. Use public IP addressing for your entire network or use private IP addressing for your network and have one IP address that can go across the Internet. That one address can be shared by all the devices on the private network, essentially swapping a single public address for any internal private address. How does that work, you ask? Enter *network address translation* (NAT).

Network address translation allows private (corporate) networks to still use private IP addresses and allows users to communicate across the Internet. It does this by translating those private IP addresses into IP addresses that are unique out on the Internet. Figure 2.2 shows a diagram of this concept. All information sent to the Internet from the internal network passes through the device running NAT. The private address is translated into a public, routable address that is sent out to the Internet. NAT keeps track of the translation so when data comes back in response, NAT knows where to send those packets on the internal network. To the Internet, it appears that there is one IP address—the public IP address assigned to the computer running NAT services. All internal network addresses are hidden because they never go out on the Internet—they are always translated before going public.

Figure 2.2 Network Address Translation Conceptual Diagram

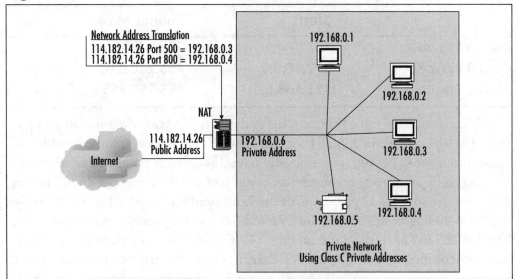

One of the interesting things about NAT and what makes it a powerful tool for small businesses is that NAT only allows in data packets that were originally requested from an internal client. This means that random or malicious packets sent to the NAT server will be discarded if the information was not first requested by an internal computer. In addition, the address of the requesting computer is never sent out on the Internet, providing another layer of security. Keep in mind that if a user on the network requests information from a questionable source out on the Internet, it may still get in—but unsolicited information will not be allowed in.

Public and Private IP Addresses

Now that you understand public and private addresses as well as NAT, let's look at it in a bit more detail. Public addresses include almost all possible combinations of addresses in Class A, B, and C networks with the following exceptions (again, this is not an exhaustive list). Table 2.2 shows the range of private addresses in each of the three classes.

Table 2.2 Private Addresses in Class A, B and C Networks

	Start	Subnet Mask
Class A Private	10.0.0.0	255.0.0.0
Class B Private	172.16.0.0	255.240.0.0
Class C Private	192.168.0.0	255.255.255.0

If you wanted to use a private Class A network ID, you could use anything from 10.0.0.1 to 10.255.255.254 for your device's IP addresses. Most small businesses use Class C because you can only have 254 devices attached and if you're running SBS (which is the assumption here), you can only have 75 computers or users anyway, so Class C gives you all the headroom you need. Most small companies, including home offices, use 192.168.0.0 and the default subnet mask of 255.255.255.0. This is the configuration we'll use for the remainder of the book when discussing addressing and NAT. Larger companies may opt for Class A or B private addresses, but they would have to run an operating system that permits more than 75 users/devices (such as Windows Server 2003 instead of SBS).

You can pick any of the private IP address ranges available for your internal network, but we suggest sticking to one of the generally acceptable 192.168.X.0 ranges. The public address or range of public addresses you use will likely be assigned to you by your ISP. A range of public addresses can be used for mapping to a specific device inside your network, such as a mail or web server that you do not want people to be able to access from the outside. However, it's also possible to simply have all internal addresses translated to a single assigned public address.

Firewalls and NAT

A firewall is a computer, dedicated network device (appliance), or software program that filters IP packets coming into or leaving the network. The firewall can be configured to allow or disallow very specific kinds of data. NAT, as you just learned, only lets in packets that were requested from a computer on the internal network. When used in conjunction with firewall software, you can create a pretty secure network because NAT only lets in packets you requested and a firewall keeps an eye on even those packets to make sure nothing too ugly sneaks in. One thing to keep in mind is that there's always somebody trying to devise new ways to get in, so you'll have to stay on top of the latest tricks to keep your network safe.

We'll discuss firewalls in various chapters of this book. What's important to understand at this point is that a firewall can be a computer running two network cards or it can be a device like a router with special firewall software running on it. There are several different flavors of firewalls, but the two main categories are hardware and software-based.

SBS provides a software-based firewall in both the Standard and Premium editions. To use this built-in function, you have to have two NICs installed in the computer. One connects to your internal network and one connects to the Internet connection (the ISP's modem or other device). The NIC connected to the Internet intercepts all incoming traffic and passes it off to the firewall software that is part of SBS. The firewall software then examines the incoming packets and compares them to the rules set up in the firewall software (something we'll discuss later in this book). Specific types of data can be specifically allowed or disallowed. For instance, to allow users to browse the web, you'll need to allow HTML through the firewall. If the packet matches a rule on the allowed list, it's allow to pass through to the NIC connected to the internal network. If it's on the disallowed list, it is discarded and that's as far as it gets. The same is true of traffic trying to leave the network. It goes into the SBS NIC attached to the internal network and is passed off to the firewall software. If it matches the rules for traffic that's allowed out onto the Internet, away it goes, off to the Internet-connected NIC and out onto the Internet. If it's on the *disallowed* list, it's toast. That's why configuring your firewall is a very important element in securing your network and how, in conjunction with NAT, it can help keep out the riffraff.

Designing Your Network

If you've read the preceding pages, you should have a basic understand of the fundamental concepts of networking. That should be enough to start planning your network. Once you've planned out how things should be configured, you can get down to the job of installing, configuring, and managing SBS.

Many people are often anxious to just get down to business and start installing software. Some even consider *P-L-A-N* a four-letter word. The time you spend on planning and designing your network will payoff tenfold in the end. Chasing down strange and intermittent network problems or troubleshooting why a particular computer won't connect to the network can be time-consuming and frustrating. Many of those problems can be avoided with a little planning on the front end.

In this section, we're going to walk through making several different lists. These lists will serve as the foundation for your network design, so don't skip this section, or you'll find yourself redoing a lot of work later on.

In this next sections, we'll:

- Inventory equipment
- Review hardware and software specifications
- Create a network diagram
- Connect and protect your network
- Create connection, location, and user lists
- Decide domain and computer naming conventions

Inventory Equipment

Begin with taking a physical inventory. Create a list of all computers connected to the network including servers and client computers. The list should include:

- Equipment type (server, workstation, router, printer, etc.)
- Location
- Computer specifications (processor speed and amount of memory)
- Installed operating system (for computers)
- Printers, faxes, scanners (list type and speed, whenever possible)
- Other devices connected to your network such as wireless access points or switches, hubs and routers

Make a note of equipment manufacturers on all equipment when taking inventory. Particularly with networking components and wireless technologies, it often is helpful to stick with one manufacturer so you don't run into strange compatibility issues down the road. Also make a note of any equipment so old it would serve better as a door stop. Use this list to make your case for getting funds approved to replace those relics.

SOME INDEPENDENT ADVICE

Old hardware and software can often be donated to charities for a tax write-off. Look for local organizations in your area that accept computer donations. Remember to either remove hard drives from the systems or use a software program to wipe out the data on the hard drive before you donate the equipment. Search for "disk wiping tools" on your favorite search engine—there are many reputable products available, including one from CyberScrub (www.cyberscrub.com) that meets stringent Department of Defense (DoD) requirements. Simply reformatting the drive (or even running the *fdisk* utility) does not guarantee that the data cannot be later recovered and read—including account names and numbers, passwords, and other sensitive data. You can reload the operating system (OS) once you've wiped the disk if you want to help out the charity, just remember to provide the original OS software media (typically CD-ROM) with the computer so the licensing remains valid and legal. If you want to keep the OS for a new computer installation, that's fine, just don't install it on the computer to be donated.

Hardware and Software Specifications

If you're going to be upgrading your computer to SBS, look at the server you've selected for SBS. If it's not relatively new (last 2 years, maximum), consider purchasing a new server. If you're building a network from scratch, purchase the best server you can afford. The investment you make in the SBS server hardware will pay off quickly. Remember, if you skimp on your server hardware, it will cost you later in downtime, poor system performance, user frustration, and headaches. Remember, too, that the specifications Microsoft publishes are typically the bare minimum, not the optimal specs.

Server Hardware

Given today's technology, the following list is a good starting point, but technology always changes, so be sure to look for top of the line processing power, RAM (Random Access Memory) and hard drive capacity when shopping for server hardware.

- Pentium 4 processor, 2.8 MHz or better
- 512MB – 1GB RAM

- 100 GB (or more) hard drive capacity, preferably two SCSI (Small Computer System Interface) drives

- 100Mbps Ethernet network cards (typically you'll need 2 NICs)

- Internal tape drive

- CD/RW drive (Read/Write CD-ROM)

- Monitor capable of running at least 800 x 600 resolution

SOME INDEPENDENT ADVICE

One way to get more computer for the money is to purchase a refur-bished computer from a reputable company like Dell or HP. These com-puters typically come pre-configured, so you don't have the flexibility of creating your own configuration (which can sometimes be a good thing), but you'll save money on these types of systems. Things to watch for: pur-chase only from a very reputable company, make sure the system meets *your* requirements, compare the price of this system to a new system to make sure you *are* saving money, buy the best computer you can afford, and make sure the system comes with the same manufacturer's warranty as a new system. And whatever you do, don't purchase a refurbished system from your cousin Billy. That's a disaster waiting to happen.

Also, consider purchasing the manufacturer's service contract on a new computer. If available, consider the extended warranty (typically a pretty affordable add-on) as well as the option for fast, on-site service. If your server goes down and you're not a hardware guru, the service con-tract will save you time, headaches, and money. Some vendors also pro-vide SBS product support, either contractual or for a per-use fee, which you might find useful as your "go to" resource if you get stuck.

SBS Server Specifications

In an SBS network, you can only have one computer running the SBS operating system. That computer will provide all of the important services your network will need and will be the server upon which the network relies for managing users, groups, security, and more. As mentioned earlier, the SBS computer becomes the domain controller for the domain formed when SBS is installed.

This is a built-in function of SBS that cannot be modified. We'll see how that works later in this book.

You may choose to install, configure, and use other types of servers on your network. For instance, an *application server* is a computer that provides access to a specific application or function on that server. If you choose to run other servers (sometimes referred to as *member servers*) on your network, they will have to run a network operating system *other than* Windows Small Business Server 2003. SBS can only be installed on one computer in a domain. Other acceptable operating systems for member servers could include Windows NT (if existing servers are still running that operating system), Windows 2000 Server, or Windows Server 2003.

One of the restrictions of SBS is that the applications that come bundled with it (SQL Server, Exchange Server, ISA Server, etc.) must be run on the SBS server. In a pure Windows Server 2003 environment, you could (and in many cases, would) run Exchange Server or SQL Server on a separate server to balance the load. However, because SBS only allows 75 users, load balancing is not an issue. Nevertheless, make sure your SBS server has enough horsepower to do the job.

SBS Client Specifications

As mentioned earlier, client computers (also called *workstations* or *desktops*) can run a variety of operating systems from Windows 95 to Windows XP Professional. Two important notes: First, you cannot run Windows XP Home edition with SBS. Well, technically you can, but the computer can't join the domain, which means it misses out on all the security features SBS provides, which means you really should avoid this if at all possible. Make sure all your installations of Windows XP are the Professional, not the Home, edition. Second, if you're running any computers on Windows ME, consider upgrading immediately. Windows ME is a very unstable operating system and even Microsoft admits it probably never should have been released. So, it's really worth the time and cost of an upgrade to remove all traces of Windows ME.

SBS, like Windows Server 2003, does not support the IBM OS/2 operating system and it provides limited support for Linux, Unix and Macintosh client operating systems.

Client computers don't have to be the latest and greatest, but if they're slower, older machines, you should have a retirement schedule in place so that the oldest computers are replaced occasionally. Older computer can't run newer operating systems, which can cause compatibility issues, security holes, and user frustration.

Other Network Devices

You'll need hubs, switches, and/or routers for your network. If you're not completely familiar with these components, it might be worth your money to hire an outside firm to come in and set them up for you. Sometimes the company that installs cabling will also install (or at least design) the configuration of these components. A good resource for figuring all this out can be the manufacturer of the equipment—often they'll provide useful information on their websites about designing, configuring, and managing their network components. As stated earlier, this is one of the reasons for choosing networking components from a single manufacturer (rather than mixing and matching).

Switches are the most commonly used and most versatile network devices. Devices can connect directly to them (see Figure 2.3 and Figure 2.4 later in this chapter) and they, in turn, are connected to the network. This provides network connectivity to the devices connected to the switch. Devices connect to switches using Ethernet (CAT5/5e/6) cabling. Switches have different numbers of ports (places for devices to connect), depending on the switch. They typically come in groups of 4, so switches typically will have 4, 8, 16, or 24 ports, for example. Another nice feature of switches is that they can have different speed devices connected to them. You can run a 10MB device, a 100MB device, and a 1GB device all on the same switch. This is not true of hubs. Switches cost a bit more than hubs, but it's well worth the extra cost for all the extra benefits.

Hubs are like switches in that devices connect into the hub and the hub connects to the network. However, hubs are "dumb" devices, where switches are considered "smart." Hubs do not allow different speeds of devices to be connected and they lack other capabilities that switches have. Hubs have been known to be "flaky," so if you want to avoid problems, stick with switches whenever possible.

Create a Network Diagram

Create a diagram of the layout of the network; not a diagram of your building and where every cable is (we'll do that in a moment), but a simple diagram of how the network is laid out. Figure 2.3 shows a sample network diagram. Yours will certainly differ, but this should give you a good idea of what we're aiming for here.

Figure 2.3 Sample Network Diagram

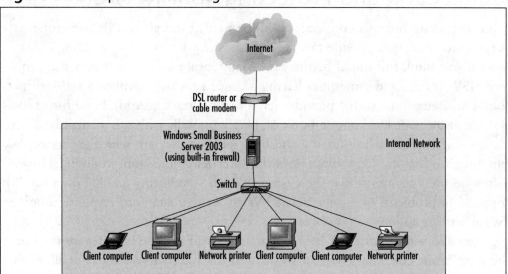

SOME INDEPENDENT ADVICE

There is a tremendous amount of terminology related to computers, networking and information technology. Even seasoned pros can be left in the dust if they don't keep up on the ever-changing language. For definitions of common computer, networking, and Internet terminology, try the user-friendly website at www.webopedia.com.

Some of the network components your diagram should account for are:

- Internet connection
- DSL (digital subscriber line) router or cable modem
- Firewall
- Internal network
- Perimeter network (if any)

These are critical components to getting your network safely connected to the Internet. If your network diagram doesn't look anything like the sample or if you don't yet have a network, make sure you read the next section.

Connecting and Protecting Your Network

Your corporate Internet connection will be made through an ISP. Sometimes large office buildings provide this capability, so check with your building manager if you think this might be the case. Many local phone companies also provide ISP services and sometimes having a single provider for phone and Internet can make sense (unless that provider has a terrible track record). For a list of local ISPs, consult your local phone book or, better yet, talk with other small businesses and find out who they use and how satisfied they are with the service. Ask the tough questions: How often does the Internet connection go down? How often do users complain that their connection is slow? How quickly does the ISP respond to problems or service tickets? What is the guaranteed response time? What service options are available?

You also want to evaluate how important e-mail and the Internet are to your business. Some companies don't use e-mail or the Internet very much at all, while others live and die by e-mail and the Internet. You should assess the importance of these two services to your company's business so you can implement the appropriate plan. For instance, if you live and die by e-mail, you'll want to have a service plan that provides for high availability and perhaps redundancy (more than one available connection point to the Internet). If you hardly use e-mail at all, you can save a bit of money and not worry if the connection goes down for 5 minutes or 5 hours. Talk with your ISP about your needs.

The Internet connection will come into your office via a cable of some sort. The ISP often provides the router or cable modem. If not, they'll provide specifications on the proper equipment to purchase. It's typically very affordable. From your DSL router or cable modem, you should go directly into a firewall. A firewall prevents unauthorized access to or from the network and can be implemented with hardware (a firewall device) or software (firewall software running on a computer). Typically, a firewall filters data at the packet level, allowing or blocking data based on the rules used to configure the firewall. SBS provides a firewall function in both editions of the product. It can easily be configured via one of the SBS wizards, as you'll see later in the book.

At this point, you have three main options. You can use the firewall that comes with SBS, which is a good, reliable firewall. You can use a third-party firewall or computer with a corporate-strength firewall program installed (you'd have to go out and purchase those), or you can use the firewall that comes with the SBS Premium edition called *Internet Security and Accelerator (ISA) Server*. For the money, ISA is your best bet, though many small companies may decide they're safe enough behind the standard firewall provided in SBS Standard edition. Regardless of which way you go, do not think for even one nanosecond that you can connect your corporate network to the Internet without a firewall. It's an absolute requirement in today's environment.

As shown in Figure 2.4, the internal network should be on the "inside" of the firewall and the Internet connection should be on the "outside" of the firewall. This means that all traffic to and from the Internet passes through the firewall—the network watchdog that keeps the riffraff out.

Some companies find a perimeter network is useful in some situations. A perimeter network, also shown in Figure 2.4, is situated between the firewall and the internal network. One good example of this type of network is a café that offers wireless Internet access. It's likely they have these access points installed on a perimeter network. That prevents public users from accessing their corporate network but it keeps those public users somewhat safe while they're surfing the Internet because they're behind the firewall. A perimeter network is sometimes referred to as a DMZ (*demilitarized zone*). Figure 2.4 shows a sample network diagram with a perimeter network.

Figure 2.4 Sample Network with Perimeter Network

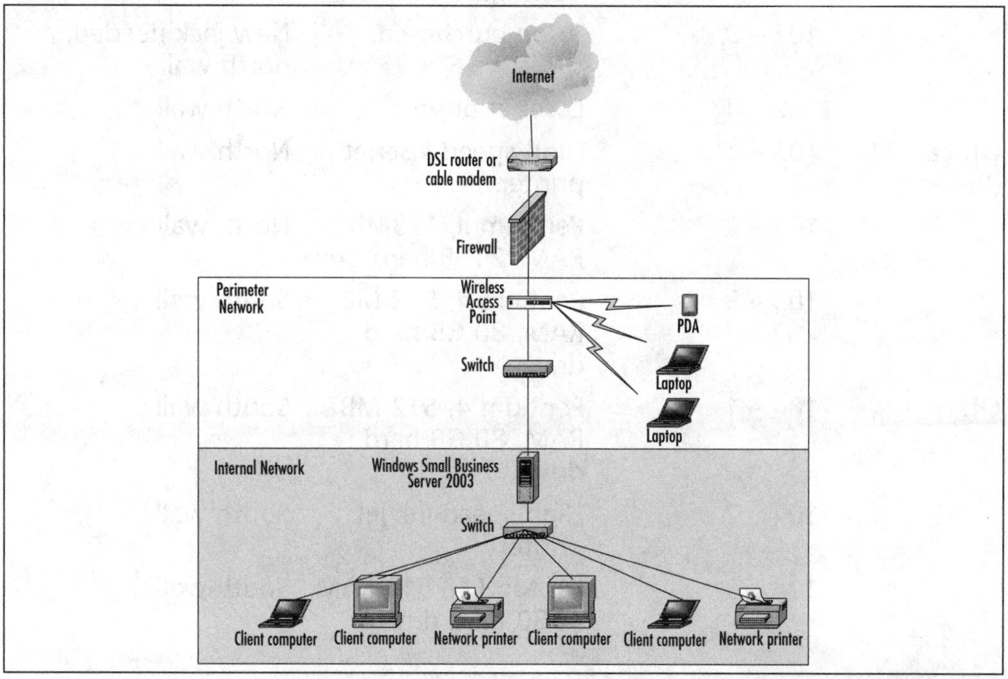

Connection, Location, and User Lists

The next step in your planning process is to create lists of where there are existing network connections, where computers are to be located, and all the users that will need access to the network.

Connections and Locations

Make a list of all existing and proposed computer connections and locations. For this you might create a spreadsheet showing the room number, jack number, computer type, and location. If desired, you can create a floor layout and locate jacks, wiring, and/or equipment on the diagram. The point is to figure out how many existing jacks or connections you have, how many more you'll need, and where they need to be located. Table 2.3 shows a sample list.

Table 2.3 Sample List of Cabling and Jacks

Location	Jack Number	Computer Type	Comment
Office 102	102 – 1	Pentium 2, 256 RAM, 20GB hard drive.	South wall
	102 – 2	Laptop PIII, 512 RAM, 40GB hard drive.	South wall
	102 – 3	To be purchased.	New jack needed, north wall
	102 – 4	Laserjet printer.	North wall
Office 103 (Reception)	103 – 1	High speed laserjet printer.	North wall
	103 – 2	Pentium II, 128MB RAM, 20GB hard drive.	North wall
	103 – 3	Pentium 4, 512 MB RAM, 80 GB hard drive.	South wall
Office 104	104 – 1	Pentium 4, 512 MB RAM, 80 GB hard drive.	South wall
	104 – 2	High speed ink jet printer.	South wall
	104 – 3	Laptop PIII, 512 RAM, 40GB hard drive.	South wall

Continued

Table 2.3 Sample List of Cabling and Jacks

Location	Jack Number	Computer Type	Comment
	104 – 4	Pentium 4, 512 MB RAM, 80 GB hard drive.	North wall
	104 – 5	Pentium III, 2562 MB RAM, 40 GB hard drive.	North wall

The next step is to identify where servers are currently located and where new servers (if any) should be placed. Give strong consideration to security and locate servers in secure areas or locked rooms with controlled access, if possible. Ideally, servers should also be in areas that have a stable climate and are relatively clean and dust-free. A server room is ideal, but many companies place servers wherever they can find room. Avoid placing the server in hot locations or where the temperature fluctuates wildly. Make sure the servers are out of the way so no one trips over the cabling and accidentally disables the network.

You can also create a map of your offices showing existing and new computer (and printer) locations. An example of this type of map is shown in Figure 2.5. You can use a program like Microsoft Visio to create a very polished map or you can use a pen and paper to simply note where things are located.

Figure 2.5 Example of Computer Location Map

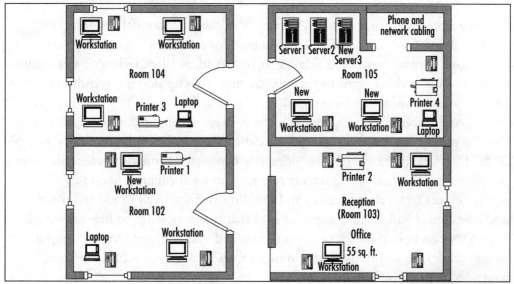

User lists

Create a list of all users in the organization. Include their name, title or position, phone extension, corporate email address, office location, department and, if desired, the computer equipment they use. You can then organize your users into logical groups based on their common network needs. For instance, you might group your finance staff together because their files may need to be more secure. You might want to group all your executives in order to provide greater network privileges. We'll discuss organizing users in more detail later in the book.

Cabling

Some newer buildings are pre-wired, while others have older cabling that should not be used (more on that in a moment), and still other offices have no existing network wiring. Cabling can be tricky, so if you're not up to the task of reviewing, testing, installing, and connecting network cabling, you should consider hiring an outside firm to do this for you. Sometimes office buildings retain cabling experts you can use. If not, talk to other small businesses to get a good referral.

Ethernet networks these days use CAT5, CAT5e, or CAT6 cabling. Unless you're planning on installing a very fast network, CAT5e should be fine. CAT6 will support speeds in the gigabit range. Many small businesses don't need that kind of speed but if you can afford it, faster is always better. It's good, too, to plan for future growth, so getting the fastest you can afford today will typically allow you to use it farther into the future than if you purchase just enough speed to meet today's requirements.

One note about older existing wiring: if it's *thinnet* (coaxial Ethernet) or *CAT3* cabling (also known as UTP or *unshielded twisted pair*), don't even try to use it. Your network will be unreliable at best. And, as all experienced net admins know, you really don't want to spend your time chasing down intermittent cabling problems if it can be avoided.

Ethernet cabling is configured in a star pattern—it all radiates out from one point. Typically this is a wiring room (or closet) in an office. All the cables converge in this location and all devices are ultimately connected through this location.

Keep in mind that if you decide to run your own cabling (not advised), you're subject to local ordinances and building codes related to electrical wiring and safety, etc. Most small companies find that it makes sense to hire an outside expert for this task. If cabling is already installed and you need to re-configure things, that's fine. Just don't start running cables through your office—leave that to trained professionals.

Network Switches and Hubs

Switches and hubs can be used to run multiple devices on a single wire run. For instance, if you have three computers and a network printer in one office, you may want to run one cable to the office then connect these four devices to that wire via a switch or a hub. Though hubs can be used, switches are much less troublesome devices and should be used whenever possible. The only reason to use a hub to service multiple devices is when the cost to run cabling to individual devices is prohibitive. Keep in mind, however, that hubs are just notorious troublemakers—so if you use them and you begin noticing problems with computers connected through hubs, suspect the hubs first.

SOME INDEPENDENT ADVICE

Your best bet for the money is to go with switches. They're smarter and faster than hubs, so you get more bang for your buck. Switches offer superior performance and you can usually use different speeds of devices on the same switch. For instance, if you have an old laser printer attached to the network, it might only run at 10Mbps (mega, or million, bits per second). However another newer device might run at 100Mbps and yet another device at 1 Gbps (giga, or billion, bits per second). A switch can often handle all of those (check the specs to make sure it can), whereas a hub typically can only handle one speed.

As with network cabling, if you're not sure how to connect all these devices, you can hire an outside firm to come in and set things up for you. That will make your job of installing, configuring, and managing Windows Small Business Server 2003 that much easier.

Wireless

We will spend time in a later chapter talking about wireless, and we've already broached the subject earlier in this chapter. Although we're focusing on wired networks, wireless connections can be considered in locations that are difficult or impossible to run Ethernet cabling, or in places like public cafés and coffeehouses where you want to provide easy Internet access to your customers. Otherwise, don't plan to install a completely wireless network for your corporate network just yet. In a few more years wireless technology may catch up, but until it does, it's not your best choice. Ethernet is faster and more secure.

Wired and Wireless Network Speeds

Table 2.4 shows different options for your network. Using this chart, you can determine the best choices for your particular situation. Many businesses use wired networks with some combination of *wireless access points* (WAPs), to provide access where wiring just won't go.

Table 2.4 Network Connection Options

Connection type	Advertised Speed	Actual Speed	Range	Other
Ethernet – CAT5 wire	10 Mbps	8.5 Mbps	328 feet from switch or hub.	Ethernet switch or hub.
Fast Ethernet – CAT5e wire	100 Mbps	94 Mbps	328 feet from switch or hub.	Fast Ethernet switch or hub.
Gigabit Ethernet - CAT6 wire	1000 Mbps (1Gbps)	327 Mbps	328 feet from switch or hub.	Gigabit switch or hub.
802.11b (WiFi) - wireless	11 Mbps	4.5 Mbps	Up to 150 feet indoors, rated at 1800 feet (if used in an un-obstructed area).	802.11b or 802.11g wireless access point (WAP). Up to 32 users per AP.
802.11a (WiFi5) - wireless	54 Mbps	18 Mbps	Up to 100 feet indoors, rated at 1650 feet.	802.11a WAP, up to 64 users per AP.
802.11g - wireless	54 Mbps	12 Mbps	Up to 150 feet indoors, rated at 1800 feet.	802.11g WAP, up to 32 users per AP.

SOME INDEPENDENT ADVICE

Bits and bytes. What's the difference and why do you care? Bits are literally the 1's and 0's the computer uses to do everything it does. Each 0 or 1 is a bit. Eight bits make a byte. Why do you care? Cables are rated in *bits* per second. Hard drives and Internet download speeds are typically rated in *bytes* (and bytes per second). Understanding bits and bytes makes doing some of the math a bit easier. Plus, it's a great conversation starter at geek events.

Domain Naming Conventions

We've talked about IP addressing and how each IP address must be unique. The same holds true for domain names. You're familiar with domain names like Microsoft.com and Syngress.com. These names are required to be unique on the Internet, just as their IP addresses are required to be unique.

Typically, companies separate their Internet presence from their internal network by using a different extension (the letters to the right of the dot in a domain name). If your company already has an Internet presence (website), you can use that domain name with the *.local* or *.office* extension. For example, if your website address is www.syngress.com, your network domain could be *syngress.local* or *syngress.office*. A quick note: if you have Mac OS users, don't use the *.office* extension—it conflicts with the Mac OS. Use *.local*, *.lan*, or even *.here*.

If you don't already have an Internet presence, you should consider a domain name that is somewhat descriptive of your business and easy to remember. Once you select an appropriate domain name, make sure to register it with an Internet domain registrar to prevent others from using that domain name. The typical cost for registration of a single domain name ranges from $10 to $30 annually.

BEST PRACTICES ACCORDING TO MICROSOFT

When selecting a domain name, follow these practices for best results.

- The domain name should contain a maximum of 15 characters (not including the extension such as .com, .net, etc.). Longer domain names don't work with some operating systems.
- The 15 characters should have only letters, numbers, the underscore or hyphen. Using other characters may make the name incompatible with certain name resolution functions on the Internet or on your internal network.
- The name should be unique—ensure no other company is already using it on the Internet.

SOME INDEPENDENT ADVICE

When choosing a domain name for use on the Internet, make sure the chosen domain name does not infringe on another company's copyrights or trademarks. If your chosen domain name ends up causing confusion with consumers, you might find yourself in legal hot water. If in doubt, go the safe route and if still in doubt, you can always consult with a trademark attorney to ensure your choice will not cause problems down the road. These days, it's usually more difficult to find a suitable domain name that's available than it is to inadvertently infringe on a competitor's trademark, but it's always good to keep this in mind, since changing domain names later is can be a real chore.

Computer Naming Conventions

All the computers, including the servers, require unique names on your network. Some small companies like to get creative with computer names, relying on eso-teric lists of galaxies and stars, scientists, or philosophers, for example. That might work for a small company with three employees, but it might cause problems later on. You might consider using descriptive names like "Reception," "Server1," or "Admin1." Boring? Sure, but sometimes boring is good. When someone's looking for the departmental budget file, are they more likely to remember "Finance" or "Copernicus"? If you really want to get creative, assign original names for user computers since they don't typically store files that are in demand by network users. Then, remembering if a file is on "Einstein" or "Uhura" won't be an issue.

One More Time

You now have a solid understanding of network concepts needed to successfully set up your SBS network. You also should have several lists and/or diagrams describing your network equipment, locations, and connections. If you read those steps but didn't actually *do* them, take time now to go back and make those lists and diagrams—they'll come in handy when we begin SBS installation and setup in the next chapter.

- ☑ Networks are comprised of servers, clients and other network devices all connected together to share resources and to manage access to the network (security).

- ☑ The most common ways to connect computers is using network cabling, phone lines, or wireless connections.

☑ A logical grouping of network resources, including computers and users, is a domain.

☑ Each domain has at least one domain controller to manage network resources.

☑ To design a new network or review an existing network, begin by taking a physical inventory.

☑ List all computer hardware and software, including manufacturers, versions, and capabilities (speed, ports, memory, etc.).

☑ Use existing cabling only if it's fairly new and in good shape. Cabling problems can waste a lot of time and effort.

☑ Wireless networks provide some great benefits, but at the cost of both speed and security. Implement with care.

☑ Domain and computer naming conventions require unique, descriptive names that don't conflict with others on the Internet.

☑ Develop a computer naming scheme that will growth with the organization.

Chapter 3

Installing Small Business Server 2003

- Preparing for Installation

- Installing Small Business Server 2003

- Upgrading to Small Business Server 2003

- Migrating to Small Business Server 2003

- Completing the To Do List and Other Post-Installation Tasks

The End Result

At the end of this chapter, you'll have a fully installed version of Windows Small Business Server (SBS) 2003, whether you're performing a clean installation, upgrading from a prior version of SBS (or other upgradeable versions of Windows), or migrating to a new server. You'll also understand how to work with the To Do List and how to complete other post-installation tasks.

Preparing for Installation

Chapter 2 walked you through most of the planning phases needed to get ready to install SBS 2003. However, there are a few more things we need to cover before we insert the CD (or DVD) and start the install.

There are essentially three ways to install SBS:

1. You can install SBS on a new server or install it on an existing server overwriting any previous operating system (clean install). All previous settings are lost, which is why it's called a clean install even when it's not on a brand new server.

2. You can upgrade from a previous version of SBS or other upgradeable Windows operating systems (upgrade). We'll review which operating systems can be upgraded to SBS 2003 in the upgrade section of this chapter.

3. You can move your existing domain onto a new server (migrate). This is typically done in conjunction with upgrading from an older operating system to SBS 2003, particularly when the older operating system is one that cannot be directly upgraded to SBS 2003.

In this section, you'll learn more about each of these three methods so that you can choose which is the right path for your organization.

SOME INDEPENDENT ADVICE

If you purchased a server that has Windows Small Business Server 2003 pre-installed, you will need to step through the Windows Small Business Server Setup Wizard. See "Windows Small Business Server Setup Wizard—Phase II" later in this chapter.

Important Note for Pre-installed SBS Users

If you purchased a server that has SBS pre-installed, please note that your installation steps may vary from those described here. In some cases, not all steps included here are shown or the steps you see may appear in a different order. Do not be concerned that something is going wrong. The pre-installed version has a few less steps and they may appear in a different order. If you need information on any of the steps in your installation, simply refer to the appropriate steps delineated in this chapter.

Clean Install

A clean installation means the operating system is installed on a new computer that does not have an existing operating system or on a computer that has an operating system that you're going to overwrite. This type of installation is the most stable and offers the best performance because all settings are set to default values. If you're installing over an older operating system, it can still be considered a clean installation because all previous settings are overwritten. In that case, errors made in prior configurations (such as inadvertent security holes) are overwritten and you start with a clean slate. Clean installations can require more configuration after installation, but they offer the best method of ensuring the system is properly configured once you've finished. Figure 3.1 depicts this type of installation.

Figure 3.1 Clean Installation

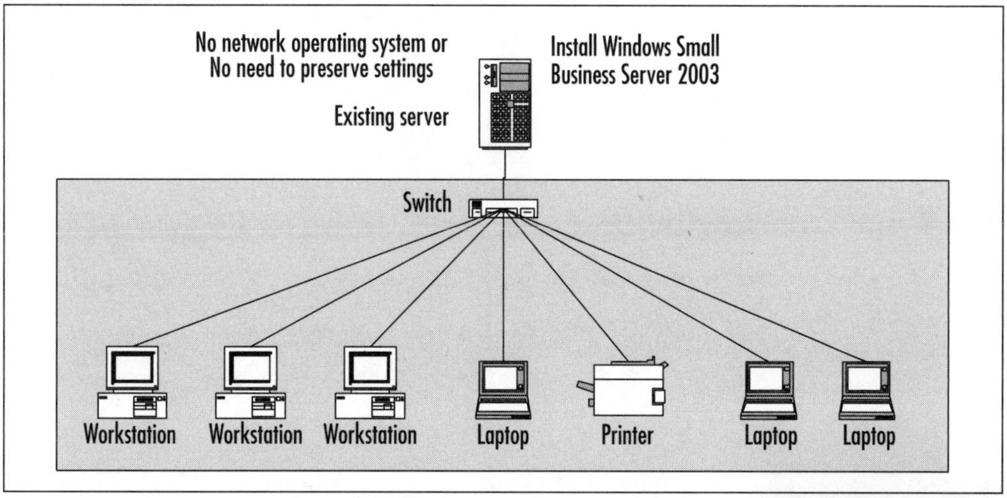

Upgrade

If you're running a prior version of SBS or other Windows operating systems that can be upgraded to SBS 2003, you may choose to upgrade. You might do this for a number of reasons, but the majority of people that choose to upgrade do so because they want to take advantage of improvements to the operating system and they don't want to perform a clean install because they *do* want to preserve existing settings. An upgrade will preserve your settings including users, groups, security settings, and more. However, any problems that exist in the current system's configuration may be preserved, which isn't always a good thing.

An upgrade is performed on a server, so if the hardware on that server doesn't meet minimum (or optimal) specifications, you should upgrade the server hardware first, if possible. An upgrade type of installation is good when you have a prior version of SBS (or other Windows operating systems) and server hardware that is still useable (with or without upgrading it). If your system has a shady past, you might want to consider a clean install. If your server needs to be replaced to meet performance specifications and preserving your network settings is vital, you'll need to perform a migration.

You can perform an upgrade to SBS 2003 from Windows Small Business Server 2000, Windows 2000 Server and Windows Server 2003. These three operating system versions are the only ones that can be directly upgraded to SBS 2003. If you are running any other version of the Windows operating system (such as Small Business Server 4.5 or Windows NT), you'll need to perform a migration instead.

Figure 3.2 shows an upgrade installation.

Figure 3.2 Upgrade Installation

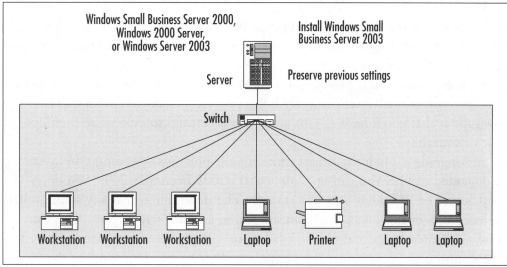

Migration

Migrating to a new server is a lot of work, but if the situation warrants it, the effort you put in will be well worth it. If you're running an older operating system that cannot be directly upgraded to SBS 2003 or an older server that won't meet the minimum (or optimal) requirements for running SBS 2003, you will need to migrate to a new server. Figure 3.3 is a diagram of a migration showing movement to a new server with prior domain settings.

Figure 3.3 Migration Installation

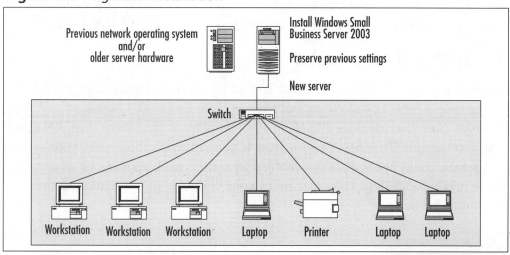

Deciding on Your Installation Path

We've looked at the three ways you can approach installing SBS, so you might already know which direction makes the most sense for your organization. If not, let's talk about it for a moment.

A clean installation is ideal because all your settings start from a known point. This can correct inadvertent security holes created by incorrect settings. The downside is that you'll have to configure all the settings to customize them for your organization.

An upgrade is often the easiest route if your previous operating system can be upgraded to SBS. You can upgrade to SBS 2003 from SBS 2000, Windows 2000 Server or Windows Server 2003 only. The downside is that any settings that are incorrect (or no longer used and still sitting around) stay in place. This can cause security holes or odd network behavior if incorrect settings are preserved. One option is to go in before the upgrade and try to clean up some of those old, unused settings and review your security settings.

A migration is your best choice when you need to move your existing settings to a new server and/or if your existing operating system is *not* SBS 2000, Windows 2000 Server, or Windows Server 2003. If you don't care about your existing settings or you're willing to start from scratch, a clean install is a better way to go. You must migrate if you want to keep your previous settings AND either your old operating system cannot be upgraded to SBS or you want to use a new server (or both). The downside is that migration is probably the most challenging of the three methods. A migration is not for novice- or intermediate-level network administrators (net admins). If this is the method you think is best for your situation and you are not an advanced net admin, you should hire an expert consultant to assist you in this process.

Pre-Installation Tasks

Before you do your installation, check to make sure you've completed the following tasks: *Create an Installation and Recovery Plan for Install, Upgrade, or Migration, Back Up Your Data, Plan Disk Partitions, Prepare Your Server, Verify Network Configuration*, and *IP Address Configuration*. If you fail to do these tasks, your server or network could become totally disabled after the install, upgrade, or migration. There may be additional tasks specific to your company or configuration that also should be done.

Create an Installation and Recovery Plan for Install, Upgrade, or Migration

The plan should include when you're going to do the installation, how you will notify users, and how long you expect installation to take. Whatever estimate you have for how long the installation will take, double it and you should be safe. The recovery portion of your plan should include what you'll do if the installation doesn't go as planned. This should include information on how to recover your system using backups, how to restore system state data, as well as at what point you will implement the recovery plan. For instance, you may estimate the installation will take 4 hours, doubling that, you're allowing 8 hours. At 7 hours and 30 minutes, you should begin preparing for your recovery plan. When you hit 8 hours, you automatically implement your recovery plan. This eliminates second-guessing yourself when you're running into trouble and will help ensure the network is up and running when users need it.

In the unlikely event you have to implement your recovery plan, spend time (once the network is back up) to analyze what went wrong. Create a new installation plan, taking into account the information you learned from analyzing the install-gone-bad. Keep in mind, however, if you've taken time to plan before your installation, things will likely go just fine.

You may want to identify an outside consulting firm that can assist if things go wrong. You can choose to have that company come in before the install and review what you've done to make sure you're on the right track or you could contract them for the entire installation (especially if it's a migration and you're not comfortable with your skill level). This book is intended to help you manage your SBS network; there's no rule that says you have to do the install, upgrade, or migration yourself if you feel an outside firm could do it faster, better, and more efficiently than you can. You can also use that type of firm for your emergency backup—if things go wrong, you can call them in to help bail you out. Remember, though, it often costs more to bring someone in to fix the problem than to bring them in before the problem and have them do the entire install, upgrade, or migration project for you.

SOME INDEPENDENT ADVICE

Here's a useful rule of thumb—every hour of planning results in a net savings of four hours on the other end. Fixing, re-doing, and troubleshooting will chew up your time quickly. And, planning is typically done when you have time for it—troubleshooting is done under pressure when things are broken, which rarely happen at convenient times.

Back Up Your Data

Make sure your user files, data files, and system files are all properly backed up. Also make sure that your registry is backed up. There are several ways to do this, so check your operating system's Help files for specifics on how to accomplish this. Make sure you have ready access to information on how to restore your system from your backups. Review the Help files of whatever operating system you're running right now to get instructions on backing up and restoring your system, should that be necessary. Print these Help files out or load them onto a computer that will be available if the server is down. If necessary, spend time taking inventory of your files to make sure your backups do include all critical files.

Plan Disk Partitions

Your server has one or more hard disk drives to store your system and data files. It's often helpful to figure out how to section off (partition) your disks before you install the operating system. If you are upgrading, your disk(s) is already configured and you'll probably just use that configuration. If you have a new server (clean install or migration), you should give some thought to this.

NOTE

Although this section contains some information on disks, if you're not sure exactly how you should configure your disks for your network, be sure to read Chapter 5 on Disk Management before proceeding with your installation. Some of the decisions you make at the outset cannot be easily reconfigured, so it's better to take a bit of time on the front end and make sure your disk configuration is exactly how you want it right off the bat.

A disk partition is simply a section of the disk drive designated as a single useable segment. This section of the disk is logically separate from the rest of the disk. A drive can have up to four partitions. Only one partition can be designated as the *active partition* at any time. The active partition is the one the computer boots up from. You may be familiar with dividing a disk drive into Drive C: and Drive D:, a common configuration for larger disk drives. This is partitioning and can increase the speed and efficiency of the drive.

In addition to the active partition, there can be up to three other partitions. Partitions can be further divided into logical volumes. So, if you have a second partition of 10GB, you could create two logical volumes of 5GB each within that partition. For the purposes of installing SBS, if you have a partition and log-ical volume plan, that's fine. Otherwise, create three partitions—the first for the operating system of about 8GB, the second for installing applications and pro-grams (files that rarely change) and the third for data and other files that change frequently. This will help when you design your backup and recovery plan (we'll step through that later in the book). Thus, if you have an 80GB disk, the three partitions could be 8GB, 30GB and 42GB. Within the 30 or 42GB partitions, you can later create logical volumes to further subdivide those partitions.

During installation, you'll have the option of creating partitions. During the initial portion of the installation, create a partition for the operating system and log files that is at least 8GB to ensure you have enough room on the system volume for these critical files. It's also recommended that you create two addi-tional partitions by following the on-screen prompts. Select an unpartitioned seg-ment and press the letter **C** to create a partition. Enter the size of the partition and press the **Enter** key. Typically these sizes are not even numbers, but you can enter even numbers such as **20000** for 20GB. The system will determine the exact size (perhaps 20003) and subtract that from the unpartitioned space. The remainder is still unpartitioned until you create another partition. If you don't have specific size requirements in mind, you can take the remaining unpartitioned space and divide it evenly between the two partitions. For instance, after creating an 8GB partition, you might have 72GB left. Create two partitions of approxi-mately 36GB each. For the first partition, type in **36000** and press **Enter**. The size will be modified slightly, that's ok. Next, select the last unpartitioned space and partition it using whatever default value the computer enters for you—that is the exact size of the remaining space and should be around 36GB.

Redundant Array of Inexpensive Disks

If you're unfamiliar with disk drives and disk management, you should read through Chapter 5 prior to installing SBS so you're familiar with the disk management options you'll be presented with during installation. It's easier to select some of the desired options during setup than to reconfigure after installation is complete.

Using a *Redundant Array of Inexpensive Disks* (RAID) is a way of creating disk storage from two or more disk drives. It uses inexpensive drives that you can buy off the shelf at most computer stores (as opposed to very large, expensive, specialized drives). They are considered an array because they work together as a unit. There are different levels of RAID, based on how the data is written to the drives (RAID always involves two or more drives). SBS supports RAID-0, RAID-1 and RAID-5.

RAID-0 is called a *striped set* because data is written across two or more drives. This speeds up performance but provides no fault tolerance. If one drive fails, the only way to recover is to replace the drive and restore from backup. RAID-0 can be implemented as a software solution through the built-in features of SBS.

RAID-1 is called a *mirrored set* because two drives are mirror images of each other. Performance can be a bit slower, but you have good fault tolerance. If one drive fails, the other has an exact copy of the data on it and kicks in automatically. You can connect each drive to a separate disk controller to increase performance and to remove the disk controller as the single point of failure. This type of configuration is called *disk duplexing*. Like RAID-0, RAID-1 can also be implemented as a software solution through the built-in capabilities of SBS.

RAID-5 is a *striped set with parity*. This means that one of the stripes of data contains parity information. Parity is a mathematical calculation performed on data to provide error correction. This parity stripe is used in the event one of the drives fails. Using the parity data, the information can be reconstructed and the system can continue to run—the users will never know a drive failed. This provides a good balance between performance and fault tolerance, but requires a bit of know-how to configure. One important note is that RAID-5 cannot recover from two or more drives failing. In that case, the drives must be replaced and the system restored from backups. RAID-5 is best implemented as a hardware solution, meaning that the disk controller provides the RAID functions. Although it can be implemented via software, it is much slower and a less desirable configuration than hardware-based RAID.

Hardware RAID

If you're using hardware-based RAID, you must create the volume for the operating system using the hardware manufacturer's tools *before* you start your installation. If you're installing a new server, you'll know if you have hardware-based RAID or not because you will have had to specifically order that when you ordered the server. If you're planning on using RAID-5, you should use hardware-based RAID, as it provides superior performance over software-based RAID-5.

Software RAID

If you're using software-based RAID, you create the volumes after the setup process is complete. One thing to keep in mind is that hardware RAID is really the best choice (some would argue the only viable choice) for implementing RAID-5. For a more in-depth discussion of RAID and disk concepts, refer to Chapter 5, "Disk Management."

BEST PRACTICES ACCORDING TO MICROSOFT

For a quick tutorial on disk basics, visit Microsoft's website and search using the phrase *basic disks and volumes*. Select the link that shows *Windows Server 2003* in the URL.
   The link is:
   www.microsoft.com/resources/documentation/WindowsServ/2003/
   standard/proddocs/enus/dm_basicvol_overview.asp

Prepare Your Server

If you're using an older server, you'll need to make sure the hardware is supported in Windows Server 2003. Microsoft used to call the list of supported hardware the *Hardware Compatibility List* (HCL). It's now called the *Windows Catalog*. Make sure your server hardware is supported *before* beginning the installation. SBS will check compatibility during Setup and will halt or notify you if there are problems. It's much easier to square things away before you begin Setup. Here are a few more server tasks that should make your life easier:

- Make a note of any unusual or important settings before you take the server down.

- It's also a good idea to upgrade the system BIOS (Basic Input Output System) before upgrading the server. Check the manufacturer's website for any updates to the BIOS. If you have no idea what this is, you'll probably get by fine without it, but if you're up for it, it can help create a more stable server environment. If the system is older, you *should* spend time figuring out how to do this and install any available updates.

- Set the boot order in the BIOS to boot first from the CD-ROM/DVD (if it's not already first in the boot sequence) so that when you start up the SBS CD, it will install from the CD-ROM/DVD. Refer to the server manufacturer's documentation on how to do this (as well as how to update the BIOS).

- Locate any custom hardware drivers or files needed for the system. Check the manufacturer's website for updates. Copy these to removable media or burn them to a CD so they're available during or after the install.

- Disconnect the server from the Internet.

- Remove the UPS (Uninterruptible Power Supply) management cable from the server, if installed.

- Read the release notes on the SBS CD (or DVD). These notes contain important and helpful information that will make your install, upgrade, or migration go smoother and help you avoid problems during the process.

SOME INDEPENDENT ADVICE

Check your hardware and software for compatibility by checking out the Microsoft Catalog at www.microsoft.com/windows/catalog/default.aspx.

Verify Network Configuration

Chapter 2 discussed network configuration in some detail. Additional information on a secure network configuration can be found in Chapter 4. If you're not sure if your network is properly configured, review these two chapters for a more detailed explanation.

Make sure your network will be properly configured once you complete installation. The primary methods of securing the network from the Internet are either using the SBS firewall (in either the the Standard or Premium Editions), an actual firewall device, or a router with firewall capabilities. You'll notice we keep mentioning the firewall—and that's because it's a critical element in securing your network from the Internet.

If you're going to use the SBS firewall, you must have two network interface cards (NICs) installed in the SBS server. One will attach to your internal network and one will connect to your Internet Service Provider's (ISP's) device (cable modem, router, etc.). If you're using an external firewall device (external to SBS), you will only need one NIC in the SBS server to connect to the network.

Ensure you have either two NICs installed in your SBS server if you're using that as the firewall or that you have a firewall device connected to your Internet connection. Don't leave your network exposed to the Internet.

When we go through the To Do List later in this chapter, we'll set up our firewall by configuring Internet Protocol (IP) according to how you're connecting your network to the Internet.

IP Address Configuration

If you haven't already figured out your IP addressing configuration, you should do so before installing SBS so you have all the information at your fingertips once you get underway. Your ISP can be a great source of information. Incorrect IP configuration will prevent users from using the network and/or connecting to the Internet, so it's important to make sure every detail is correct.

Private IP Addressing

In most cases, it's best to use private IP addressing and network address translation (NAT) to go out to the Internet. Private addressing gives you more flexibility, and using NAT provides another layer of security. You can use one of the three private address ranges discussed in Chapter 2. However, we recommend using the Class C range because it allows for up to 254 devices; plenty for a small company. We'll get into NAT configuration later in the book.

The IP configuration you'll use should be some variation of the private Class C network 192.168.X.Y. The X indicates you can use any number (1 through 255) in this position. *All* devices on your network will use this *same* number. The

Y is the unique number for each network device. Each device on your network must have a *different* number in the Y position. We'll talk about assigning IP addresses for network devices later in the book, after we discuss setting up the server. The subnet mask for this configuration is 255.255.255.0 and will be used for *all* devices on the internal network. Thus, the internal NIC should have the following addressing. Choose a number for X between 1 and 255.

- IP address: 192.168.X.1
- Subnet mask: 255.255.255.0

Using a Broadband Connection

If you're using your SBS computer as the firewall, it should have two network interface cards installed in it. Each will have its own IP address. Even though the computer is one device, each NIC must have a unique address. This is how the SBS computer acts as the firewall. Traffic is sent to one NIC, the firewall intercepts and evaluates the traffic then sends it on to the address of the second NIC, if appropriate.

The NIC connected to your Internet connection will use a public IP address provided to you by your ISP. Ask your ISP to provide you with the following information so you can configure the Internet settings when you go through your To Do List.

- IP address
- Subnet mask
- Default gateway
- Preferred DNS Server IP address
- Alternate DNS Server IP address

These will either be provided to you because you have been assigned a static IP address or your ISP will tell you to use DHCP (SBS can utilize DHCP and we'll cover that later in the book). You may want to request a static IP address, especially if you are hosting an external website that requires a set, public IP address. Your ISP can help you figure out the best way to go on this solution based on your specific needs.

Using a Router Connection

If your server uses a local router for the Internet connection, your server will have one NIC and it will connect to the internal network. If this is your configuration, *the default gateway address for the server should be set to the IP address of the router.*

If you are using a router/firewall to connect to the Internet, the router will have either one or two network interfaces. If it has one NIC, the NIC will connect to a switch or hub on your internal network (and another connection goes to the Internet). If the router has two NICs, they will connect to your SBS server and to the Internet. You'll need to check your router documentation and talk with your ISP to configure the router properly.

Public IP Addressing

If you are going to use public IP addressing on your *internal* network, you will need to configure your internal addressing based on strict public IP rules. Discussing all the variations of public IP addressing is outside the scope of this book. Typically, the ISP will provide you a range of IP addresses to use. This will likely entail using a custom subnet mask to identify your network as a unique segment of a larger ISP network. However, this will vary depending on your unique configuration. Contact your ISP if this is the direction you've decided on and they can help you determine the correct settings. Once you have them, you can enter them into the appropriate screens during the Internet setup.

One Last Check

Okay, before we get down to the business of installing SBS, we'll go through a quick checklist to make sure everything's set.

1. Network is ready for the new server—devices (workstations, printers, server, etc.) can all run with SBS 2003 and all devices and cabling are set, IP address configurion has been determined.

2. Server hardware is certified for use with Windows Server 2003 (includes SBS).

3. BIOS is updated, updated drivers for any special hardware is backed up on removable media (burn them to a CD, for instance).

4. System and data files are backed up.

5. Installation and recovery plan is in place and accessible.

6. Release notes have been read.

SOME INDEPENDENT ADVICE

Regardless of the installation type you choose, you should read the release notes, which contain information you might need before, during, or after installation. To access the release notes, place the SBS CD or DVD in any computer running a Windows operating system. From the **Autorun** menu, select **Read Release Notes**. If the CD does not automatically start, you can browse the CD and open the file **Sbsrelnotes.htm**. Reading release notes is vital to a successful install, upgrade, or migration. Release notes are best served with coffee and doughnuts.

IMPORTANT NOTE FOR PRE-INSTALLED USERS

If you purchased a server that has SBS pre-installed, please note that your installation steps may vary from those described here. In some cases, not all steps that are included here are shown or the steps may appear in a different order. Do not be concerned that something is going wrong. The pre-installed version has a few less steps and they may appear in a different order. If you need information on any of the steps in your installation, simply refer to the appropriate steps delineated in this chapter.

Installing Small Business Server 2003

Windows Small Business Server 2003 comes on CD and DVD. If your server has a DVD drive in it, you won't be prompted to swap CDs—all the files needed are on the DVD media. If you don't have a DVD drive in your system, you'll need to use the CDs instead and you will have to swap them out when prompted. More advanced network administrators might want to copy the CDs to the server hard drive (create flat file copies) to avoid the CD swap and allow the installation to proceed with less user intervention. If you don't know that any of that means, don't worry, just be ready to swap a few CDs during the install.

The installation has two major phases—the installation of the system files and the setup of the SBS specific elements (Active Directory, Exchange Server, etc.). The first major phase is also divided into two phases—*text mode* and *graphical user interface (GUI) mode*. In text mode, the system boots from the SBS CD Disk 1. You select the disk partition and then some very basic files are installed that are needed to work with the hard disk and to continue the installation. The computer will reboot into the next phase, the GUI-based setup, which looks like the Windows interface you're familiar with. This phase loads and runs a modified version of the Windows Server 2003 operating system. During this phase, the setup program will detect and install devices, configure the network and install needed files. When complete, the system will restart a second time and boot into Windows Small Business Server 2003. After you log in, you'll launch the Windows Small Business Server 2003 Setup Wizard to complete the second major phase of setup.

Windows Small Business Server 2003 Installation—Phase I

To install Windows Small Business Server 2003, follow these steps:

1. Insert the Windows Small Business Server 2003 Disk 1 into the CD-ROM drive. The CD Disk 1 or DVD should be in the drive when server power is applied so that the system boots directly from the CD/DVD.

2. When prompted, press any key on the keyboard to boot from the CD/DVD.

3. To use a hard disk drive controller for which SBS has no built-in support, press **F6** when prompted (now, aren't you glad you located those drivers and updates before we got here?). Keep in mind, though, that if your disk controller is not supported, you might be walking out on a limb. Double-check that your disk controller is going to work with SBS and if not, take corrective action. The Hardware Abstraction Layer (HAL) screen will be displayed if the install process does not recognize the hardware. If this occurs, you'll be prompted to press **F5**. Check server documentation for more information on this, if needed. Both of these events should raise a red flag for you since these options appear when hardware is not sup-

ported by the installation process. Verify your hardware compatibility if these options appear.

4. The next screen displayed is the text-based Welcome screen. If you want to quit, press **F3**. Otherwise, press the **Enter** key to continue.

5. The next screen displayed is the license agreement. You have two choices, agree and continue or disagree and end setup. Press **F8** to indicate agreement.

6. The next screen will prompt you to select a disk partition. If no suitable partition exists, you can delete a partition or create a new one.

   a. To create a new partition, select some of the free space or unpartitioned space on the disk, press **C**, then specify how large to make the partition and press **Enter.** If this is for the system, remember to make the partition no smaller than 8GB.

   b. To delete a partition, select it using the arrow keys and press **D**. *CAUTION: Deleting a partition is permanent and cannot be undone.* Don't do this unless you're absolutely sure what you're doing.

SOME INDEPENDENT ADVICE

WARNING: If the first partition shown is less than 50MB, it's most likely what's called a *utility partition*. Leave it as you found it—changing or deleting it could cause the system to fail to boot or function.

7. If a suitable partition exists, select the partition or suitable free space where you will install SBS. Press **Enter** to continue.

8. On the next screen, if you selected a new partition or free space (both are unformatted), you'll need to select your formatting. Choose either **NTFS Quick Format**, which is fast but isn't as thorough, or **NTFS Full Format**, which takes quite a bit longer, but is thorough. If the partition is formatted in the **File Allocation Table (FAT) or FAT32 format**, choose to convert the partition to NTFS. Press **Enter** to select the format and, if needed, press **C** to confirm your choice to convert to NTFS to continue. The formatting will be done and if you're converting to NTFS, the system will reboot—don't be concerned, this is normal behavior.

SOME INDEPENDENT ADVICE

FAT and FAT32 are hard disk drive formats. FAT was used in the earlier days of PCs. FAT32 is still used for home systems and is fine in that environment. NTFS (which stands for New Technology File System) is a more sophisticated, secure, and efficient format. It is *required* for the SBS system and it's a better way to go overall.

9. After formatting, some setup files are copied to the server and the server will reboot. Again, this is normal behavior. This time, the computer will display the familiar Windows GUI and installation will automatically continue. If the system attempts to boot from the CD-ROM or DVD, cancel the process and allow the installation to continue from the disk.

10. The next place your input is needed is when the **Regional and Language Options** dialog box is displayed. You can make modifications here, but don't spend a lot of time on this, as these settings can easily be modified in Control Panel once Setup is complete. Choose your settings then click **Next** to continue. There are times during the device installation stage at which the screen may go blank for a period of time and it may do this several times. Don't worry, this is a normal part of the process. If the screen blanks out, just be patient, and the installation will continue. The process can take a while, so have some interesting reading nearby (unless you consider reading the installation splash screens interesting reading...).

11. In the **Personalize Your Software** dialog box, type the **Name** and **Organization** to which the software will be registered.

12. In the **Your Product Key** dialog box, enter the product key from the SBS packaging and click **Next**. Although you probably already know this, you always want to keep your software and the product key in a safe place. The product key is really the only thing that proves you have a legal copy of the software, so guard it carefully.

13. In the **Computer Name and Administrator Password** dialog box, type the computer name in the **Computer Name** text box (we discussed computer and server naming conventions in Chapter 2). Enter the password for the administrator account in the text box labeled

Administrator Password. Enter exactly the same password a second time to confirm it, then click **Next.**

SOME INDEPENDENT ADVICE

The password for the administrator account is the golden key to your system. Make sure you select a password that cannot be easily guessed, but also make sure that YOU remember it. Acceptable passwords are at least 7 characters long and contain a mixture of letters (upper and low-ercase), numbers and special characters. Using acronyms and abbreviations can work well—like *Ih8!2Bla8!* (I hate to be late). We'll talk about complex passwords later in this book. When installing SBS, it's a good idea to write down your password so you remember it. Once it's committed to memory, destroy the paper or store that paper in a very secure location. If you forget the Administrator password, you may have to reinstall the operating system to recover.

If there are problems with your system configuration that will prevent SBS from successfully installing, you'll see a notification screen. Figure 3.4 shows a sample of a screen indicating that the system cannot find a properly configured NIC. Other types of configuration errors can also be displayed in this screen. For further information on the error or message, double-click the requirement or click **More Information**. If you believe you have resolved the issue, you can click **Check Again** to force the system to go back out and re-check the setup requirements.

Figure 3.4 Sample System Configuration Error Message

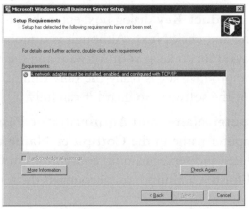

The next step can take 45 to 60 minutes to complete, so if you need to take a break, stretch your legs, clear your head, or fill your stomach, now's the time to do that. When it's complete, the system will reboot and you'll need to log in using the Administrator account and password you selected.

14. If your computer has a modem that the SBS Setup program detects, the **Dialing Location** dialog box will be displayed. You'll need to select your **Country**, type in your **Area Code** and any digits needed to reach an outside line. Click **Next** to continue. If you want to specify additional locations, you can do so via the Control Panel after Setup is complete.

15. The last dialog box to be displayed before Setup completes is the **Date and Time Settings** dialog box. Review and modify any settings here, then click **Next**. These settings can also be modified after Setup has completed. Once you click **Next**, Setup will continue for several minutes.

16. Once Setup is complete, the system will automatically reboot. Again, normal behavior. When the system comes back up, SBS is installed. You'll need to log in using the Administrator password you entered in Step 13. Once you've successfully logged in, the Windows Small Business Server Setup Wizard launches.

Windows Small Business Server Setup Wizard—Phase II

The second major phase of the SBS setup is the Windows Small Business Server Setup Wizard, which launches after you log into the system the first time. The wizard, which is simply a set of automated steps designed to assist you in configuring your system, will step you through setting up the SBS components.

If you purchased SBS pre-installed, this is the only Setup program you'll see (since the Phase I installation was completed for you). We'll walk through the steps in the wizard, but if your software came pre-installed, it might not go through all the steps listed here—that's ok, just follow the on-screen instructions and refer to these steps and you'll be able to set up your pre-installed software.

1. Plug in any UPS devices that you disconnected when you were preparing your server.

2. Ensure your NICs are working and that the proper drivers are installed. If necessary, update the drivers (if you downloaded updates for the drivers before the install).

3. The **Setup Requirements** dialog box will be displayed if the requirements for the SBS Setup are not met. Review these messages and take appropriate action to resolve the issues.

SOME INDEPENDENT ADVICE

If you did your planning, you should not have many (if any) Setup Requirement issues. Some may be "soft" warnings—notifying you that you need to take action after Setup is complete. Others are "hard" warnings that require immediate action before you can continue. Setup can be re-started using the **Continue Setup** icon on the desktop.

4. Enter the **Phone**, **Fax**, and **Address** information for your company in the **Company Information** dialog box, then click **Next** to continue.

5. On the **Internal Domain Information** page, you can change the default DNS and NetBIOS names provided by Setup to the domain name you decided on earlier (see "Domain Naming Conventions" in Chapter 2). The name selected here will be used for your Exchange Server configuration, so it's best to stick with the standard naming conventions discussed in Chapter 2. Click **Next** to continue.

IMPORTANT NOTE FOR NETWORKS WITH MAC OS COMPUTERS

If you're running computers on your network that use the Apple Macintosh operating system, you may run into trouble if you've chosen to use the *.local* extension for your local network (which is the default setting that SBS will use). While it can be used with the Mac operating system, you'll have to configure the Mac to use *DNS name resolution* in addition to the *Rendezvous* resolution native to the Mac.

For more information on this issue, visit the Microsoft Knowledge Base article 836413 or use this link: http://support.microsoft.com/default.aspx?scid-kb;en-us;836413&Product=winsvr2003.

6. Many SBS servers have two NICs installed (one to connect to the internal network and one to connect to the Internet). If your server has two NICs, you'll need to specify which one connects to the local network, then click **Next.** Use care in selecting the right NIC, as changing it later can be tricky.

7. If you have an existing network that has a DHCP server, SBS will detect it and recommend disabling it. SBS is designed to provide DHCP services to the network. If you have another DHCP server, install DHCP on your SBS computer and disable the existing DHCP server. This will make configuring and managing your SBS network easier. If SBS detects another DHCP server, a dialog box will be displayed asking, *"Do you want to install the DHCP server provided by Windows Small Business Server?"* Click **Yes** to install DHCP on SBS. Click **No** if you do not want to install DHCP on the SBS server (make sure you have a good reason for doing this and you know what you're doing). You can click **Cancel** to exit the Setup Wizard or click **Help** for more information.

8. The **Local Network Adapter Configuration** dialog box provides the opportunity to confirm the NIC settings for the local network or to modify them as needed. Click **Next** to continue.

9. Setup will now continue for several minutes configuring SBS components without further input from you. However, the system will reboot several times and each time, you'll need to log in. You can choose to have Setup remember your password by entering it in the **Logon Information** dialog box. This will preserve your password only until Setup is complete. Doing this is not a security risk. However, it's sometimes helpful (if a bit annoying) to have to type in the Administrator password several times during this process to make sure you remember it. Use whichever method suits you.

10. Setup will display a **Component Selection** dialog box. If you've used the Custom installation option with other Microsoft products, this will look familiar. Figure 3.5 shows this screen. By default, all components are selected. You can deselect components as needed. There is a **More Information** button you can click to get more information on any component you highlight. To deselect an item (so that it is not installed), click the arrow next to it. When you're finished selecting (or deselecting) items, click **Next** to continue.

Figure 3.5 Component Selection Screen

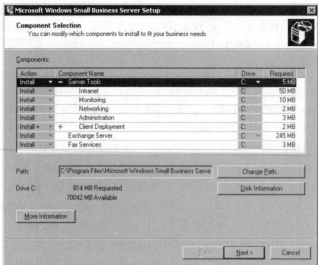

11. In the **Data Folders** dialog box, you have the opportunity to change the path of the folders for the installed components. Make changes here by selecting the item and then clicking the **Change Folder** button and browse to the desired location. It's recommended that you change the path for installing Exchange Server to another partition on your disk for better performance. Click **Next** to continue.

SOME INDEPENDENT ADVICE

It's a good idea to select a different path for your Exchange Server components as well as your SQL Server component. If you configured partitions early on in your installation, choose a different partition (which should now show up as a drive with a letter other than C). If the partition is not formatted with NTFS, you won't be able to redirect these components to it, so make sure you've completed that step prior to installation. Two other default data directories that are created are for user data and company shared folders data. These should also be redirected to a different partition. Ideally, you should install application data (Exchange Server, SQL Server) onto one partition (separate from your system files) and your data files onto another partition. This keeps things tidy and can speed up system performance as well.

12. When you're finished with Step 11, a **Component Summary** dialog box is displayed. Review the selected components and paths, modify as needed, then click **Next** to confirm your choices and complete the Setup Wizard.

13. From here on out, there is no additional input required from you, but you will have to change CDs here and there, so don't go out for a "double tall half caf skinny latte" thinking the install will finish without you. If you're installing from DVD, you won't be prompted for other disks. If the Setup Wizard encounters any errors at this point, you'll see them reported in the **Component Messages** dialog box.

14. The system will reboot one more time and SBS will be fully installed, but not configured. When the system comes up, the To Do List is automatically displayed. This is a list of post-installation tasks that should be completed—some immediately, some at your own pace. We'll take a look at the To Do List later in this chapter. Note that you can access the To Do List via **Server Management**, as shown in Figure 3.6. Congratulations, you successfully installed SBS 2003.

Figure 3.6 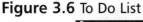 To Do List

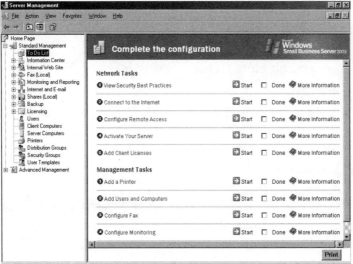

Upgrading to Small Business Server 2003

Just as we did with the installation, we're going to begin with a few things you should do before your upgrade, then we'll step through the upgrade process. Upgrades can sometimes be tricky—they depend on several factors for success, including thorough planning, having all applicable patches, hotfixes, and drivers updated and installed prior to upgrade, and a server that's been properly maintained. If your system has been well maintained and has all applicable updates, patches, and hotfixes applied, you have a better chance of a successful install.

Preparing for the Upgrade

There are several things to do before you actually begin the upgrade process that will make your life easier.

1. Read the release notes. These notes, found on the CD Disk 1 or DVD contain valuable information that will help you avoid or address issues with upgrading. Don't skip this step.

2. Verify that all applications, device drivers, and client computers work with Windows Server 2003.

3. Apply all updates, patches, and hotfixes to your current system, applications, and device drivers.

4. For any updates, patches, or hotfixes you'll need to re-apply, burn these programs and files to a CD (or copy to a removable media) so you have them available once you're finished with the upgrade.

5. Make backups of everything—e-mail, data files, downloads, user files, system files—everything you could conceivably need. Take the time to verify the backups—this ensures the data is written properly *and* readable in case you actually do need to use them. Make two or three sets in case something happens to one of the sets. Do this close to the time of the upgrade so the data is current. After completing the server preparation tasks (see the next section), you should reboot into Safe Mode and save your system state data as well. If you're running Windows Server 2003, you can save system state data without booting into Safe Mode. Read your current operating system's Help files if you're not sure how

to accomplish these tasks or how to make sure you get all the critical files backed up.

6. Make sure your server can run Windows Server 2003 without any problem. It should have at least 2GB of free disk space, should have 1GB of RAM (512MB minimum), and 80 GB disk space (minimum) for starters.

7. Develop your disaster recovery plan. Refer to "Pre-Installation Tasks" earlier in this chapter for details on developing a solid recovery plan.

Prepare the Server

Before you upgrade, there are a number of server related tasks to perform.

1. Gather Internet-related settings. This includes the server's IP address, subnet mask, host name, default gateway, DNS server address, and external mail server address (if any). If there are other settings specific to your organization, gather them now and store them someplace that will be accessible when the server is down (paper, another computer, etc.).

2. Check the Microsoft Small Business Server website for service packs or updates you might need. Download these and copy to a CD or other removable media.

3. Clean up server files. Remove any unused software and delete unused or unnecessary files. Get the server as clean as possible.

4. Remove Windows 2000 Administrations Tools. Don't skip this step. These tools are incompatible with SBS 2003 and you should remove them before upgrading using **Add or Remove Programs** in the Control Panel.

5. Remove Windows Server 2003 POP3 service, if installed, using **Add or Remove Programs** in the Control Panel.

6. Remove remote storage using **Add or Remove Programs** in the Control Panel.

7. Install the latest system BIOS from the system manufacturer's website.

8. Check the Event Viewer log. If there are any errors, address those issues now.

9. Install all applicable updates, patches, hotfixes and service packs to your current operating system. This includes Windows or Windows SBS service packs, ISA service packs, and SQL service packs that may apply to your server.

10. Remove Exchange components that are no longer used in SBS, including:

    ■ Exchange MSMail Connector

    ■ Exchange Chat Service

    ■ Exchange Instant Messaging Service

    ■ Exchange Key Management Service

    ■ Exchange Connector for Lotus cc:Mail

11. Remove trust relationships (if any) with other domains. SBS does not support trust relationships.

12. Remove Client Access Licenses (CALs) by resetting to **5** (the default value). After the upgrade is complete, you can reinstall the CALs. Make sure you have the license information available to you (license numbers, etc.).

13. Ensure all domain controllers in the domain are available during the upgrade. The installation will fail if SBS cannot contact all domain controllers on the network. Remember, the SBS computer rules the network and is the domain controller for the network. It is *possible* to have other domain controllers in the network, but there's usually no good reason for it in an SBS-based network.

14. If you have multiple domain controllers in the network, assign all **Operations Master** roles to the SBS server. Again, this is because the SBS computer will take over as the ruler of the network. Other servers cannot duplicate SBS functions. These servers may exist on your current network, but are not allowed in an SBS-based network.

15. If you have any domain controllers in the network running as Windows NT 4.0 Backup Domain Controllers (BDCs), retire them before performing the upgrade. Not to beat this into the ground, but you only need the SBS domain controller on the network, so you're not going to need the PDC/BDC functions in your SBS-based network. These notes

assume you're upgrading from a network that may have one or more of these functions located on one or more servers in the domain.

16. Break disk mirror sets before upgrading if you want to preserve your original drive data or if mirroring on your system significantly impacts performance. You don't have to break the mirror set, but do so if you want to preserve the original data as your part of your backup plan for a worst-case scenario.

17. Check all hard drives for errors using the command **chkdsk c:** at the command prompt. (**Start | Run | cmd | chkdsk c:**).

18. Run the Disk Cleanup Wizard to remove unused files.

19. Defragment the disk drive.

20. Update the virus program and run a thorough scan (remember to verify that your virus program is compatible with Windows Server 2003. If not, get a hold of the version that is compatible so it's ready to go on the new server).

21. Locate all drivers (on removable media) and your current operating system media.

22. Stop and disable all third-party services on your server. This includes any UPS monitoring software or services, backup applications, anti-virus programs, etc. Nothing should be running on the server except the core system services. All other third-party programs should be disabled. If you're connected to the Internet, disconnect the server from the Internet prior to disabling firewall and virus programs.

SOME INDEPENDENT ADVICE

If any of the steps above seem like they're beyond your capabilities, you have two options. The first is further research to understand the steps involved. For instance, if you have a Windows Server 2003-based network, you may have computers running Operations Master roles that you'll need to address. If researching and understanding these topics is beyond your technical capabilities, you may want to consider hiring an outside expert to assist you with these tasks. Once the system is upgraded (or migrated), you can setup, configure, and maintain SBS yourself. Sometimes these transitional activities are tricky, but managing SBS will be much easier—that's a promise.

Preparing Client Computers

1. If you have any computers running Windows 95 or Windows ME, upgrade them. Although Windows ME is supported, it is an unstable operating system and should be retired.

2. Update Windows NT 4.0 computers so they are running Service Pack 6a and Internet Explorer 6.

3. Any computers running Windows XP Home version should be upgraded to Windows XP Professional. While a Windows XP Home edition computer *can* connect to the network, it won't allow you to take advantage of any of the domain security features available on an SBS-based network. This can potentially create serious security holes on your network.

4. If a computer is NOT going to be connected to the network in any manner, you don't have to be concerned with what operating system it is running. Some companies have stand-alone computers that do not connect to the network.

Preparing Users

1. Create a communication plan to notify users of downtime. This should include checking with department heads or other key staff to ensure the time and date you've selected is acceptable to the company. You wouldn't want to try your upgrade the same weekend you're hosting a demonstration of your new software package for a key client.

2. Notify users well in advance of the upgrade and let them know what to expect, such as how long the server will be down, what they will/will not have access to, etc. Let them know that when the server is ready to come down that the network will come down so they should log off or follow instructions provided.

SOME INDEPENDENT ADVICE

Determining if the upgrade is successful should have some clear parameters such as:

- Users can log on to the network.
- Users have access to applications, data, and user files
- Users can access e-mail.
- Users can browse the Internet.
- The server can run essential services including Backup and anti-virus programs as well as any other critical third-party services or applications.

If you can't answer YES to each of these questions, the upgrade is not successful. Determine what it will take to answer YES to each of these questions, prioritize which functions are most critical and begin resolving issues in order of priority or make the decision to go to your fallback plan. Just because these functions are running, it doesn't mean your network is fully functional. You may have additional tasks required to get your specific configuration fully functional; this is just the bare-bones list.

As you can see, the list of tasks to complete before upgrading is extensive and will take time. Having a thorough plan and adequate time to perform the upgrade will help the process go more smoothly, but be prepared for the possibility of a few bumps in the road. You might also want to identify where you'll go for help should you find yourself needing expert assistance.

SOME INDEPENDENT ADVICE

Planning for the worst-case scenario can help you know what to do if things don't go well. If your upgrade fails to complete successfully and you are unable to restore from backups because the operating system is not operational, you have two failsafe options. You can reinstall the original operating system and restore from backups. You can also reformat your disk drive (thereby essentially wiping out all data), perform a clean install of SBS, and restore needed settings and files using your backups. The first choice gets you back to an operational state on your original operating system, and the second choice gets your server upgraded, though admittedly, the hard way.

Though we don't want to discourage you from upgrading your system yourself, if you're not comfortable with the upgrade process (such as how to determine if all your patches, updates, and hotfixes have been applied or how to troubleshoot error messages that may come up), you may consider hiring an outside consultant with experience in the SBS upgrade process. Once upgraded, you can take over configuring and managing the SBS server. It's up to you and it depends on your current level of expertise, your timeline, and your confidence in your ability to address problems that may arise.

Upgrading Your Server

If you're reading this section, it's assumed that you've completed all the tasks listed earlier. If not, stop and go back now. You'll be really glad you did.

Windows Small Business Server Setup Wizard—Phase I

Use the following steps to upgrade your server.

1. Disconnect any UPS cables from the server.

2. Disconnect the server (or network) from the Internet unless you have a separate firewall in place.

3. Disable all virus software.

4. Notify users that the network will be unavailable and for how long. Use the **net send** command at the command prompt (**Start | Run | cmd**, then type **net send** "*text message*" or type **net send ?** to get a list of commands). For example, **net send "The server will go offline in 10 minutes, please save your work and disconnect from the network. Thank you."** Hopefully, you've scheduled this when there are few, if any, users. If you're in a really small office, you can probably just yell "Server's going down!"

5. Log on to the Administrator account and insert the SBS CD 1 (or DVD). The autorun feature should automatically launch the SBS Setup. If it does not, browse to the CD or DVD and launch the **Setup** program.

6. Click **Set Up Windows Small Business Server.**

7. Click **Next** on the first page to continue.

8. Review the upgrade information in the next dialog displayed and click **Next** to continue.

9. On the **Setup Requirements** screen, review any warnings. If you're prepared to continue (that is, the warnings didn't cause you to stop the upgrade and regroup), click the **I Acknowledge All Warnings** checkbox and click **Next** to continue.

10. The next dialog box displayed is the **Product Key** page. Enter your product key, then click **Next**.

11. The next dialog box is **Required Components.** Click **Next** to continue. After this screen, SBS will begin installing and the computer will reboot several times.

12. When prompted, log on using the Administrator account. Once successfully logged on, the Windows Small Business Server Setup Wizard will launch. In some cases, the wizard will not automatically launch. If this is the case, you should see a **Continue Setup** icon on the desktop. Double-click this icon to continue the upgrade.

13. As with the clean installation, the next step is to review the **Setup Requirements** screen. If there are any issues, resolve them before continuing. Otherwise, click **Next.**

14. Enter corporate information in the **Company Information** dialog box and click **Next** to continue.

15. Ensure you have your Internet configuration information handy now. The next dialog box to appear is **Internet Domain Information** (this screen may not appear in some cases). Enter the requested information including **DNS domain name**, **NetBIOS name** and **Computer name**. Click **Next** to continue.

16. In the next dialog box, **Local Network Adapter Configuration**, select the network adapter (NIC) connected to the internal network. Note: use care in this selection because choosing the wrong one can be tricky to correct later on. Click **Next** to continue.

17. As with the clean installation, Setup will continue and will reboot your computer several times. You can enter your password in the **Logon**

Information screen so you don't have to sit by the computer and log in every time it reboots. This information is deleted once installation is complete and it's safe to use this feature. Click **Next** to continue.

Windows Small Business Server Setup Wizard—Phase II

1. After a period of time (depending on server speed and memory), the **Component Selection** dialog box is displayed. This is similar to other Microsoft software dialog boxes that allow you to customize which components will be installed. To deselect an item, click the arrow next to it. All components are selected by default, and unless you have a reason not to install a component, keep the default settings and click **Next**.

2. The next dialog box, **Data Folders**, provides the opportunity to select alternate folder locations for various components. You can keep the defaults or make changes here, then click **Next** to continue.

3. The last dialog box to be displayed by the SBS Setup Wizard is the **Components Summary** page. Review the information, including any modifications you've made to default settings, then either click **Back** to go back and make changes or click **Next** to complete the installation.

4. The installation will continue without further input from you. Again, the time this takes depends mostly on the speed and amount of memory your server has. If you're installing from CDs, you *will* be prompted to insert different CDs as the installation progresses, so don't go running off just yet. If your server has a DVD drive and you're using the DVD media, you won't be prompted.

5. The **Components Messages** dialog box will display errors related to the installation and configuration of the selected components.

6. Once the computer has rebooted the final time, the To Do List will be displayed. We'll talk about the To Do List later in this chapter.

7. If you're installing the SBS Premium edition and your current server was not running ISA Server or SQL Server, you'll need to install these components separately. The Setup wizard typically looks for installed components to upgrade. If they're not present, these components are not installed. These are found on the Premium Technologies CD.

- Whether you perform a clean install, upgrade or migration, make sure you apply the latest patches, hotfixes and updates by checking the Microsoft website for Window Small Business Server 2003 at www.microsoft.com/windowsserver2003/sbs/downloads/default. mspx.
- Reapply service packs, patches, and fixes that were installed on the server prior to upgrade.
- Scan updates once you've completed Setup.

Migrating to Small Business Server 2003

The migration option is used when you want to upgrade the software from an operating system that cannot be directly upgraded to SBS 2003 and/or you want to use a new server. Since an installation of any Microsoft operating system is specific to the hardware it's installed on, you can't simply back up your data on one system and restore it to another. Well, in some instances, if the original server is completely disabled and the new server is *very* similar (same processor, motherboard chip set, and mass storage controller, among other things), you may be able to get away with it, but you'll almost always run into problems you have to address and there's no guarantee it will work. As with a clean install or an upgrade, migrating requires thorough planning. Review the steps for clean install and upgrade since many of them are relevant to the migration process.

Important Note About Migrations

A migration is a difficult process even for experienced net admins. It is not an appropriate undertaking for novice or intermediate net admins. Errors and/or problems during a migration can make your network and server(s) unusable.

If this sounds dire, it is. If the items in the section that follow sound like a foreign language to you or are in any way beyond your skills, hire an outside expert to assist you. These are critical components to understand if they apply to your server, but explaining what each of these tasks means is outside the scope of this book. You can judge for yourself if you're up to this task. If not, hire an expert to help you—there's really no need to lose sleep over this (or take your entire corporate network down for two weeks) if you don't have to.

Do not attempt a migration if you're not completely confident you can handle the problems that will arise. They will arise, that's guaranteed. Which problems you'll encounter is the only unknown.

SOME INDEPENDENT ADVICE

Microsoft has two helpful documents if you're migrating from earlier operating systems. The documents are titled "Migrating from Small Business Server 4.5 or Windows NT Server 4.0 to Windows Small Business Server 2003" and "Migrating from Small Business Server 2000 or Windows 2000 Server to Windows Small Business Server 2003." These documents provide more detailed information on the migration process and you may want to download and read these. They can be found at www.microsoft.com/windowsserver2003/sbs/techinfo/productdoc/ default.mspx.

Preparing for Migration

Not all settings are migrated when you move to SBS 2003. The following settings are not migrated and must be manually preserved through export or notation (writing them down).

- References to the original server on client computers are not preserved during migration. These include shortcuts, mapped drives, etc. These should be removed from client computers (if practical) and re-created once the migration is complete.

- Group Policy Objects (GPOs) are not migrated and must be exported using the Group Policy Management Console.

- Custom settings, including DHCP scope settings and Exchange server SMTP connector settings, are not migrated.

- If you're hosting custom websites on your server, these are not migrated. Copy the website to the new server and re-create the site in Internet Information Server (IIS) or use the IIS 6.0 Migration Tool.

- Exchange Mailbox rules, the Administrator account mailbox, and Exchange Public Folders are not migrated. These must be exported using the Exchange Mailbox Merge Wizard. You can launch this through Exchange or by locating and double-clicking (running) the **ExMerge.exe** file.

- Other custom settings, including those used with other applications, may need to be manually exported. Review your system thoroughly to determine what additional tasks are required. Note that none of your user data will be moved, so you need to have recent verified backups of all data files (user, application data files, etc.).

Migrating to SBS

It's been said several times already, but it bears one last warning. Before heading off into the migration, verify you are confident you possess both the skills and resources to address issues that will arise, have an idea of what you'll do if things go terribly wrong, and take time to review both the release notes and your entire migration plan. Have your expert on call or better yet, hire someone with the expertise to do this for you and watch over his or her shoulder.

SOME INDEPENDENT ADVICE

The migration process is a tricky process even for experienced network administrators. Consider hiring a qualified expert to come in and perform your migration if you are not an expert network administrator. Even then, working with someone who's done two or three successful migrations can make your life a thousand times easier. Work smarter, not harder.

Use the following steps to migrate to SBS 2003.

1. Disable the DHCP Server service on the existing server.

2. Install Windows Small Business Server 2003 on the new server (see "Installing Small Business Server 2003" earlier in this chapter).

3. Complete the To Do List (we'll look at this in depth later in the chapter).

4. Disconnect the new server from the Internet (if connected) and disable virus software on both the original and new servers.

5. Clean up client computers by removing links, shortcuts, and mapped drives referring to the original server. Remove unused software and make sure the client operating system is supported by SBS.

6. On the new server, use the **Active Directory Migration Tool** (ADMT) to migrate users, groups, and computer accounts to the new domain (remember, when SBS installs, it creates a new domain by default and this behavior cannot be modified).

7. Move shared folders, files, and application data to the new server.

8. Use the **Exchange Migration Wizard** in SBS (on the new server) to migrate Exchange mailboxes to the new server.

9. Use the **ExMerge** function in Exchange (on the new SBS server) to import the Administrator account mailbox and Exchange Public Folders to the new SBS computer. The Mailbox Merge Wizard file, **ExMerge.exe** can be downloaded from the Microsoft website at www.microsoft.com/exchange/downloads/2003.asp.

10. Configure Exchange distribution lists, custom policies, and Microsoft Connector for POP3 mailboxes (if used).

11. Migrate SQL Server databases to the new server. For more information on the specifics of this task, refer to the Microsoft article "How to Move Databases Between Computers That Are Running SQL Server", Article Number 314546, located at http://support.microsoft.com/default.aspx?scid=kb;[LN];314546.

12. Connect client computers to the new domain.

13. Remove permissions used for the migration.

14. Uninstall the Active Directory Migration Tool.

BEST PRACTICES ACCORDING TO MICROSOFT

Whether you perform a clean install, upgrade, or migration, make sure you apply the latest patches, hotfixes, and updates by checking the Microsoft website for Window Small Business Server 2003 at www.microsoft.com/windowsserver2003/sbs/downloads/default.mspx.

SOME INDEPENDENT ADVICE

Remember to install your virus software and update the signature file, if you haven't already done so. It's a step that's sometimes forgotten due to all the other work that must be accomplished during an install, upgrade, or migration.

Completing the To Do List and Other Post-Installation Tasks

Although SBS is now fully installed, there are a few more tasks to complete before everything's fully configured and operational. Regardless of the type of installation you performed (clean, upgrade, or migration), you'll need to complete the tasks in the To Do List. If you performed the upgrade or the migration, you'll also need to migrate users. We'll step through these tasks together in this section.

The To Do List is a comprehensive list of things you need to complete in order to finish configuring and tuning your new SBS server. When the server reboots the last time (when installation is complete) the To Do List is displayed on your screen. If it is not automatically displayed or if you're coming back at a later time to complete your tasks (say, after a good night's sleep), you can access your To Do List via the Server Management console by accessing **Start | Server Management** and selecting the **To Do List**, which is the first item under the **Standard Management** node in the left pane of the console. The Server Management console is divided into **Standard Management** and **Advanced Management**. Figure 3.6 earlier in the chapter shows the To Do List.

SOME INDEPENDENT ADVICE

If you're not familiar with the console layout, it's a lot like Windows Explorer. The left side (or pane) shows available items. Some of those items may have a plus (+) sign to the left indicating that *node* can be expanded to view sub-items. If you click an item in the left pane, the details of that item will be displayed in the right pane.

For now, we'll focus just on the To Do List. As you complete tasks in the To Do List, click the checkbox to the left of **Done** to indicate successful completion. If you're not sure what an item is, you can click the **More Information** link to read more on the selected topic. When you're ready to work on the task, click the **Start** icon to launch the related wizard. Within the To Do List, tasks are divided into *Network Tasks* and *Management Tasks*.

SOME INDEPENDENT ADVICE

A word of caution here: do the tasks in the To Do List in the order shown. Period. Don't monkey around with the order in which you perform the tasks. Working on tasks out of order could cause problems and errors (since some tasks build on previous tasks), so go step-by-step through the To Do List.

View Security Best Practices

Take time to read and understand the Security Best Practices. As we walk through the other tasks in the To Do List, some of the security settings will be configured. Security best practices fall into three general categories—protection from outside attack, protection from internal users (typically errors rather than malicious attack, but a threat nonetheless), and monitoring network security. While external attacks can be devastating to a network and they certainly get a lot of press, the truth is that most security breaches occur from within the corporation. This includes users being given incorrect permissions (such as the ability of a data entry clerk to access the executive salary spreadsheet or users getting into areas of the network they don't belong), or users managing to obtain (through other users or through guesswork) access to Administrator-level accounts. Security is a large topic but SBS makes managing security fairly straightforward. Begin by reading the Security Best Practices.

Connect to the Internet

Connecting your network to the Internet can be a bit tricky if it's something you've never done before. There are excellent Help files available, which you may want to review prior to completing this task. As previously discussed, you should have contacted your ISP for your IP configuration information. If you haven't done so already, contact your ISP technical representative and ask for your IP address, subnet mask, default gateway, primary and secondary DNS servers, and any other relevant information the ISP provides.

When you click **Start** next to the **Connect to the Internet** option, it will launch the Configure E-Mail and Internet Connection Wizard. On the first screen of the wizard, click the link for **Required Information for Connecting to the Internet**. This screen displays Help topics based on the type of connection you're trying to make (dial up, broadband, router, etc.) If you want to print these help files, right-click in a blank area on the screen and select **Print** from the menu. Use this to gather needed information for your configuration before stepping through the configuration. Click **Next** to continue.

As we've discussed, if you are going to use SBS as your firewall, you need to have two NICs installed in the system. If you're using an external firewall device, you only need one NIC. SBS will check your system against your connection choice to make sure you have the proper configuration for your selected option.

SOME INDEPENDENT ADVICE

Often your ISP will be your best friend when trying to set up your Internet connection. Their technical staff should be able to assist you in either answering questions about your specific configuration or even sending out a technician to assist you on-site. ISPs are in the business of providing Internet access, so they thoroughly understand the technical aspects and can be a great (and often free) asset.

SBS supports four types of Internet connections:

- Direct broadband connection (requires two NICs)
- Broadband with a local router (requires one NIC)

- Broadband with user authentication (PPPoE) (requires two NICs)

- Dial-up connection (the only one of the four choices that uses a phone line instead of a network interface)

To complete the Configure E-Mail and Internet Connection Wizard, select your connection type and follow the instructions in the wizard. If you're not sure of your connection type, contact your ISP.

Direct Broadband Connection

After launching the Configure E-Mail and Internet Connection Wizard, you can configure a direct broadband connection using the following steps:

1. On the **Connection Type** screen, select **Broadband**, then click **Next.** The **Broadband Connection** screen is displayed. Select **A direct broadband connection** from the available drop-down list, as shown in Figure 3.7. For more information on this type of configuration, click the **Display a network diagram** link to bring up a diagram of how your network should be configured to use this type of connection. If you select this connection type and do not have two NICs installed, you'll get a warning message (shown in Figure 3.8).

2. On the **Network Connection** screen, verify the ISP network connection and local network connect (both NICs) are working properly, then click **Next.**

3. On the **Direct Broadband Connection** page, enter the IP addresses for the default gateway and DNS servers. Your ISP should have provided these addresses to you. Click **Next.**

4. Follow the steps in the **Configure Your Firewall** section of the wizard (we'll walk through those later in this chapter). Do not skip this step. Connecting directly to the Internet without a firewall is a huge security risk and should not be done. Period. You can skip forward to the section entitled "Configure Your Firewall" later in this chapter.

Figure 3.7 Direct Broadband Internet Connection

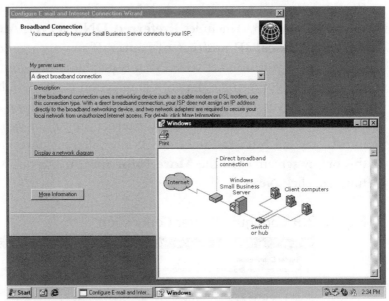

Figure 3.8 Network Interface Card Requirement Warning

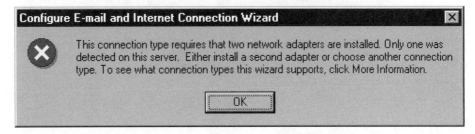

Broadband with Local Router

This configuration assumes you have one NIC and that your SBS server uses a router to connect to the Internet. While your server may have more than one NIC installed, you will connect to the Internet via a local router. You may have other configurations, but the general idea is the same. Follow the steps below to configure this type of connection after launching the Configure E-Mail and Internet Connection Wizard and selecting **Broadband** then clicking **Next.**

1. On the **Broadband Connection** screen, select **A Local Router Device With An IP Address** from the drop-down list provided. Click **Next**.

2. On the **Router Connection** screen, type the DNS server addresses and IP address for the router, then click **Next.** The required information, shown in Figure 3.9, includes **Preferred DNS server**, **Alternate DNS server** and **Local IP address of router**. If any of these settings are unfamiliar to you, contact your ISP for specific information. Notice that the checkbox for a single network connection is selected. If you leave this checked, you'll get a warning from the SBS operating system telling you that you either need to use an external firewall or you need to install a second NIC and use the SBS firewall. For more information on this or any screen, click the **More Information** button. When you are finished, click **Next**.

Figure 3.9 Configure Router Connection

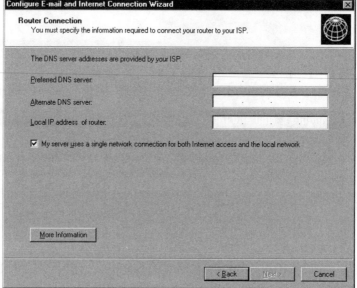

3. On the **Network Connection** screen, select the option indicating the NIC connecting to the router obtains its address from DHCP (assuming it does). If the NIC has a *static* (assigned manually rather than by DHCP) IP address, select **Use The Following ISP Address** and provide the address. Click **Next**.

4. The next screen in the **Network Connection** section asks you to verify the ISP connection and the server's local connection. If they are correct, click **Next**. Otherwise, make necessary corrections before continuing.

5. As with the direct broadband connection, the next step is to configure the firewall. Follow the instructions provided. We'll review this section later in this chapter.

Broadband with User Authentication (PPPoE)

The following steps walk you through configuring a broadband connection that requires user authentication, using Point-to-Point Protocol over Ethernet (PPPoE). This type of configuration requires two NICs as well.

1. From the Configure E-Mail and Internet Connection Wizard, select **Broadband**, then click **Next**.

2. On the **Broadband Connection** screen, select **A Connection That Requires A User Name and Password (PPPoE)** from the drop-down list provided. Click **Next**.

3. On the **PPPoE Connection** screen, select the PPPoE connection from the drop-down list. If the desired connection is not displayed, click the **New** button and enter the name for the service and the connection.

4. Also on this screen, enter the ISP username and password (the one your ISP requires for your connection). If your ISP has assigned a static IP address, click to select the checkbox then enter the IP address as well as the IP addresses for the DNS servers. Click **Next** to continue.

5. On the **Local Network Connection** screen, select the local connection and verify the correct IP address is displayed, then click **Next** to continue.

6. As with the other connections, follow the instructions to configure your firewall. Do not skip this step. We'll review this information in just a moment.

Dial-Up Connection

The fourth and least common method of connecting your corporate network to the Internet is via a dial-up modem. Follow the steps listed to configure this type of connection.

1. From the Configure E-Mail and Internet Connection Wizard, select **Dial-up**, then click **Next**.

2. On the **Dial-up Connection** screen, select the dial-up connection. If the connection does not yet exist, click the **New** button to create a new connection. If you create a new connection, you'll need to enter a name for the connection and the phone number used to connect to your ISP.

3. After selecting the desired connection in the Dial-up Connection screen, enter the username and password associated with your ISP account. If you have been assigned a static IP address for the connection, click to enable the **I have a static IP address with this connection** option, then enter the IP address and the DNS server addresses provided by your ISP. Click **Next** to continue.

4. On the **Local Network Connection** screen, select the local connection, review the IP address, and click **Next**.

5. Follow the on-screen instructions for configuring your firewall, which we'll walk through in the next section.

Configuring Your Firewall

All of the previous selections for connecting to the Internet end with configuring your firewall. Hopefully by now you've figured out this is your last line of defense against the hacking masses on the Internet—so pay close attention to this section.

1. If you've completed the preceding tasks (based on your connection type), you will be prompted to configure your firewall. If you're just coming back to this task, launch the Configure E-Mail and Internet Connection Wizard. You'll be prompted to configure the firewall.

2. On the **Firewall** screen, click the checkbox to **Enable Firewall** and click **Next**.

3. On the **Services Configuration** screen, shown in Figure 3.10, select the services you want to enable, then click **Next**. By selecting one or more services, you are essentially indicating that these are the services you want to be able to pass through the firewall. They include e-mail, VPN, terminal services and FTP (File Transfer Protocol). If there's another type of service you want to be able to pass through the firewall that is not listed, click the **Add** button and follow the on-screen instructions. Note that if you select **VPN**, the system will notify you that the system is not configured for remote access. Click **OK** to close

that warning. We'll walk through configuring remote access in the next section. Only select the services you need—if you're not going to use VPN immediately, for instance, don't enable it. Enable only the services you'll be actively using as a security best practice.

Figure 3.10 Configure Firewall

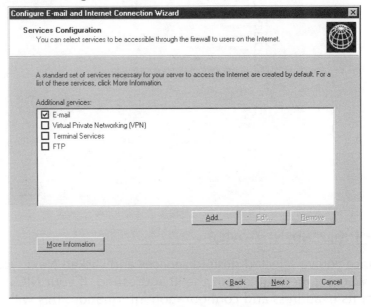

4. The next screen is **Web Services Configuration**, where you can select which of the web services to enable. These are services on your website that users can access from the Internet through your firewall. These options are shown in Figure 3.11.

5. You should only enable services your users will actually use. If some services won't be used until a later date, don't enable them at this time. Find a balance between the highest security (in which none of these services are enabled) and the lowest security (in which all of these services are enabled) by selecting only the needed (and used) services. For more information on these services, review the Help files in SBS or visit the Microsoft website and search for the exact service name. After selecting desired services, click **Next** to continue. If you're just not sure, don't enable any of these services; you can revisit these services later and make changes easily.

Figure 3.11 Web Services Configuration

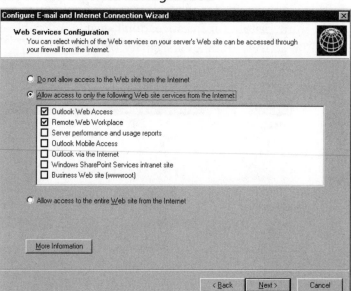

SOME INDEPENDENT ADVICE

Once you've selected desired services and clicked **Next**, you may receive a warning message about the IP addressing. If your NIC is using DHCP for its IP address and configuration information, this will cause problems for users trying to connect to your website via the Internet. Servers, particularly website servers, typically have a *static* (permanent) IP address. You'll need a permanent IP address, so contact your ISP for a static IP address. If you're using DHCP, check with your ISP to see if they support dynamic IP addressing. If not, ask for a static IP address. This is very important for servers that host websites available to the Internet.

6. The **Web Site Server Certificate** screen is displayed next if you selected one or more web services in the prior screen. If you're going to use Secure Sockets Layer (SSL) on your website, you'll need to specify a web certificate. You can't get past this screen without entering your certificate information. If you don't have a certificate, you can go back and deselect web services to bypass this configuration section. You can always come back later to this and add web services once you have a certificate.

SOME INDEPENDENT ADVICE

SSL is a protocol (format) that encrypts data to keep it safe from prying eyes. It's often used on e-commerce websites to protect sensitive consumer information such as account numbers, passwords, credit card information, etc. If you're not sure about SSL or web certificates, you should contact an outside expert to help you through the maze of possibilities. Companies such as Verisign (www.verisign.com), Thawte (www.thawte.com), and GeoTrust (www.geotrust.com) are providers of certificates. If you're doing e-commerce, use a 128-bit (rather than a 40-bit) certificate. Certificates typically cost between $200 and $1000 annually.

Configuring E-Mail

The next step in the Configure E-Mail and Internet Connection Wizard is to configure Internet e-mail. If you're unsure of the correct selections, contact your ISP for more information about how your company manages e-mail. Use the following steps to configure Internet e-mail.

1. On the **Internet E-Mail** screen, enable the **Enable Internet E-Mail to use Exchange for Internet e-mail** option and click **Next**.

2. On the **E-Mail Delivery Method** screen, select how to deliver your Internet e-mail, then click **Next**.

3. On the **E-Mail Retrieval Method** screen, select the method you'll use for retrieving e-mail. Your options are **Use The Microsoft Connector for POP3 Mailboxes** (use this setting if your e-mail boxes are located at your ISP) and **Use Exchange** (use this setting if you're using Exchange).

4. On the **E-Mail Domain Name** screen, enter your e-mail domain name. Remember, this domain name must be unique on the Internet and must be registered (unlike an internal network domain name). Click **Next**.

5. Follow the steps in the remaining screens to determine how often you want mail delivered and what to do with email attachments. In the **Remove E-mail Attachments** screen, you can specify which types of attachments to remove from incoming e-mail. By default, SBS displays and selects a long list of attachment types. These are attachment types

that can harbor worms, viruses, and Trojan Horses, so the default settings are often best. If your firm frequently needs to send and receive files using these file types, you can allow them in by removing the checkmark. You can also choose to remove selected attachment types and save them in a folder. If an e-mail recipient receives an e-mail that's had the attachment removed, there is a note in the e-mail to that effect.

6. The final screen summarizes all the information you've configured throughout the entire Configure E-Mail and Internet Connection Wizard. You can save, print, or e-mail this configuration information, but it's wise to keep a copy of it for future reference. It might come in handy if you need to troubleshoot anything related to email and Internet connections down the road.

Configure Password Policies

Once you've completed configuring e-mail, the system will prompt you to enable password policies. You can work on this task now or you can return to it at a later time. We'll talk about password policies later in this book. For now, however, you should configure password policies. It can be done later through the Server Management console, but it's only one screen, so it's worth doing now while you're thinking about it.

Figure 3.12 shows the single setup screen for password policies that allows you to configure several password requirements that are part of security best practices. By default, none of the options shown in Figure 3.12 is selected. Click the checkbox to select an option and use the up and down arrows to change the default settings. Figure 3.12 shows the default values, which are a good starting point for strong security. Notice the last option, **Configure password policies** and the setting **After 3 days**. This setting determines when the password policies will go into effect. You have several options in the drop-down list. By waiting 3 days to put these policies into effect, you give yourself time to set up client computers without having to use strong passwords, which can greatly simplify the process for you. Once you've configured client computers, you can implement strong passwords and this setting is used to automatically do that for you in the time frame you select.

Figure 3.12 Configure Password Policies

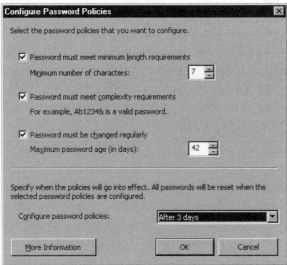

Scan for Critical System Updates

Assuming you successfully set up your Internet connection, the next thing to occur is that your server will connect to the Windows Update website to scan your system for critical updates. You can do this now or later, but it's important to keep the system up-to-date since hackers often exploit newly discovered security holes in systems. By applying updates in a timely manner, you can often avoid being a victim of these types of attacks. If your system is not yet connected to the Internet, you cannot scan for updates. Since your firewall is now enabled, it would be safe to connect to the Internet and scan for updates if you wish to do so. You can always come back to this setting, but don't leave it too long, as critical security updates should be applied as soon as they're made available to protect your server and network.

Configure Remote Access

Remote access is a very useful tool for employees who travel or who work from home on occasion. Clearly, you want to make sure that only users who require remote access have remote access. For instance, it's not likely that everyone in your company needs remote access, so don't grant this ability to all users.

> **BEST PRACTICES ACCORDING TO MICROSOFT**
>
> Follow the security best practices sometimes referred to as *least privilege* or *least access*. Grant users the least possible privileges while still allowing them to freely do their jobs.
>
> Never grant privileges to users that don't need or use them. Doing otherwise creates a security hole.
>
> Never configure or enable services you're not going to use. If you don't have any users that require remote access, don't configure it.

There are essentially two ways to connect to the corporate network remotely. One is via the traditional dial-up line. Using a modem, the computer (at home, in a hotel, etc.) dials a phone number that is answered by the SBS server, which authenticates the user using the username and password. If authenticated, the server allows the user remote access to corporate network resources.

The second way to accomplish this is for the computer to connect to the corporate network via the Internet. In this case, you want to implement Virtual Private Networking to secure the communication across the wild, wooly Internet. Because a dial-up connection is a direct, private connection, your communication back and forth is pretty secure. However, when you connect to the corporate network via the Internet, the data passed back and forth between the computer and the corporate network travels across the very public Internet. As a result, all data is subject to prying eyes and should be secured. This is accomplished by encrypting the data going to and from the network. This is the idea behind VPN. Since the data is encrypted, the communication is as safe as if it was traveling on a private network, hence the name *Virtual* Private Network. We'll discuss remote access later in this book.

If necessary, you can access the To Do List by selecting **Start | Server Management**, then selecting the **To Do List**. Once the To Do List is open, click **Start** to the right of **Configure Remote Access** to launch the **Remote Access Wizard.**

Remote Access via Virtual Private Networking

Use the following steps to configure remote access using VPN.

1. After launching the **Remote Access Wizard**, click **Next** on the **Welcome** screen to continue.

2. On the **Remote Access Method** screen, enable the **Enable Remote Access and VPN (Virtual Private Networking) Access** option and click **Next**.

3. The next screen to be displayed may be the **Client Addressing** screen (if not, don't worry, continue to the next step). If this screen is displayed, specify the DHCP server that assigns IP addresses to remote clients. You can also specify a range of IP addresses to be used by remote clients. Click **Next** to continue.

4. The next screen, **VPN Server Name**, prompts you to type in the full VPN server name. This is the name of the server using your registered Internet domain name, which may or may not be the same name as your local network. An example of a VPN server name is **vpnserver1.microsoft.com**. The local address for that same server might be **vpnserver1.microsoft.local**. Click **Next** to continue. Enter the registered name, not the local name.

5. The final page of the Remote Access Wizard shows a summary of your selections. Click the link at the bottom of the page to save, print, or e-mail this summary for future reference.

Remote Access via Dial-Up Connection

Use the following steps to configure dial-up remote access:

1. After launching the Remote Access Wizard, click **Next** on the **Welcome** screen to continue.

2. On the **Remote Access Method** screen, enable the **Enable Remote Access and Dial-in Access** option and click **Next**.

3. The next screen to be displayed may be the **Client Addressing** screen (if not, don't worry, continue to the next step). If this screen is displayed, specify the DHCP server that assigns IP addresses to remote clients. You can also specify a range of IP addresses to be used by remote clients. Click **Next** to continue.

4. On the **Modem Selection** screen, select the modem(s) designated for remote users. Click **Next** to continue.

5. On the **Dial–Up Phone Numbers** screen, enter the primary and alternate phone numbers that your remote users will use to dial into the network. Click **Next**.

6. The final page of the Remote Access Wizard shows a summary of your selections. Click the link at the bottom of the page to save, print, or e-mail this summary for future reference.

Once the wizard finishes, you may be prompted to enable password policies just as you were at the end of the e-mail setup process. If you haven't already done so, you can continue on to set up your password policies.

Activate Your Server

More recent Microsoft products require activation of the software. This prevents users from installing one copy of software on 3 or 4 or 40 computers without valid licensing. Activation is simple and it's different from registration. Activation simply verifies the software license is valid and not already in use. Registration, which is optional, requires you to provide your name, company, e-mail address, etc.

To activate your server software, use the following steps:

1. From the To Do List, click the **Start** button to the right of **Active Your Server**.

2. The **Activate Windows Wizard** is launched and you have three options for activating your server software (**Activate over the Internet, Activate by calling a customer service representative, or Activate later**).

    Select the first option (unless you want to activate by phone for some reason), then click **Next**.

3. You can choose to register at this time, but that is purely optional. Click **Next** to complete activation. The system will connect via the Internet using the settings you configured during your first To Do List task. If you can't connect, you'll need to go back and figure out what's wrong with your connection. In the meantime, you can activate by phone or activate later.

SOME INDEPENDENT ADVICE

If you don't activate now, you'll have about 30 days to activate your software before you literally become unable to use it. If you can't connect via the Internet immediately, you might want to consider calling to activate the server software—it's fast and easy, even by phone. Although the system will periodically remind you to activate the software, it's often tempting to postpone it—so go ahead and activate it now. It's one more thing to check off your To Do List.

Add Client Licenses

We've reached the end of the tasks that should be done almost immediately upon completing the installation. If you have additional CALs for your server, you should install them now. Recall that SBS comes with 5 CALs, meaning 5 users can connect to the server without additional licensing. If you have 6 or more users, you'll need to purchase additional CALs. If you've already purchased them, you can add them now. After launching the **To Do List** and clicking **Start** to the right of **Add Client Licenses**, use the following steps to add client licenses.

1. On the **Welcome** screen, click **Next**.

2. On the **License Agreement** screen, review the license agreement and click **I Agree** then click **Next**. If you don't want to agree with the licensing terms, you cannot continue.

3. On the **Contact Method** screen, select **Internet** or **Telephone** as your method of connecting. Click **Next** to continue.

4. On the **License Code Information** screen, enter the license codes provided when you purchased SBS or the additional CALs. Double-check the numbers you entered and when you're sure they're correct, click **Next**.

5. If you're connecting via the Internet, the system will connect to the Internet and activate the license codes entered. If you selected to connect by telephone, call the number provided by the wizard and provide the Installation IDs from the **Telephone Information** screen. Write down all confirmation IDs and type them in when prompted.

BEST PRACTICES ACCORDING TO MICROSOFT

If you are transferring licenses from one computer to another, use the Transfer License Wizard (**Start | Server Management | Licensing**). Select **Transfer Licenses** to launch the Transfer License Wizard, which will walk you through the process.

Migrate User Permissions

This section applies only to upgrades and migrations and is located in the **Advanced Management** section of the Server Management tree under **Migrate Server Settings**. You can also change user permissions via the Server Management console under **Standard Management** by selecting **Users**. If you performed a clean install, there are no settings to migrate and you can skip this section. To migrate user permissions, use the following steps:

1. In the To Do List, select **Change User Permissions Wizard** to launch the wizard that will walk you through this process. On the first page, click **Next** to continue. Note that you can only change permissions for one set of users at a time, so you'll need to run the Change User Permissions Wizard multiple times to modify settings for all users in different groups.

2. The **Template Selection** dialog will be displayed, showing several different templates you can use to assign permissions. Select the template you want to use for a group of users (ones you have in mind but that are not yet selected). For advanced users, if you have other templates you'd like to use, you can import them now using the **Add Template** button. Otherwise, select one of the templates displayed. You must also click one of the two radio buttons displayed. By default, the **Replace any previous permissions granted to the users** button is selected. This is a safe way to go because your user settings will be reset based on standard, secure settings. This will overwrite any custom settings you've configured. However, if you've customized user settings and you want to preserve them, you should choose the second option by selecting **Add permissions to any previous permissions granted to the users**. This option will preserve your settings and add any settings related to the selected template. Click **Next** to continue.

3. In the **User Selection** dialog box, select the users whose permissions you want to set according to the template and options selected in the previous screen. After selecting the users, click **Add** then click **Next** to continue.

4. Your selected template, permissions options, and users are displayed in the next dialog, allowing you the opportunity to go back and make changes or accept the settings. Click **Back** to go back and make changes or click **Finish** to complete set permissions for this group of users.

5. Repeat this process as many times as needed to set permissions for all users.

Management Tasks

There are a number of management tasks that must be completed before the server and network are fully functional. The tasks described in the preceding section are the ones critical to complete right after you've finished the installation. The tasks listed in this section are less critical (though some could argue the point). These tasks are related to many topics we'll explore in the remainder of this book. Rather than going into detail here, we'll list the tasks and you can refer to the appropriate chapter in this book if you have any questions. Since each of the tasks in the To Do List launches a wizard, there's a good chance you'll be able to set up many of these features by using the wizards simply by following the on-screen instructions. However, we've got some great information in upcoming chapters, so refer to them as you work through your wizards for tips, tricks and explanations.

Remaining management tasks include:

- Add Printers
- Add Users and Computers
- Configuring Fax Services
- Configuring Monitoring
- Configuring Backup

One More Time

By now you should either be an expert on all the ways you can install SBS (if you read the chapter straight through) or you have a fully installed and functional Windows Small Business Server 2003. Let's recap some of the key points.

☑ A clean install is when there is no existing operating system or you are completely overwriting the existing operating system.

☑ An upgrade is when you upgrade from an earlier version of Windows on the same computer—there are restrictions, so make sure your current operating system can be upgraded. If not, select migration. An upgrade preserves your network settings and most of your configuration.

☑ A migration is when you need to move to new server hardware or your existing operating system cannot be directly upgraded to SBS (or both). This method also preserves existing settings and configurations.

☑ Planning is absolutely critical to a successful installation (clean install, upgrade, or migration). Time spent planning will pay off in time saved on the other end. Planning is also typically done at your own pace, while troubleshooting is an emergency response that rarely occurs at a convenient time.

☑ Review the preparation tasks and complete them before beginning an install.

☑ Have a solid recovery plan in place as well as parameters as to when you'll implement the recovery plan. While solid planning helps avoid many problems, there are always unanticipated problems that could necessitate you rolling back to your original operating system or having other failsafe options. Identify them before the emergency strikes.

☑ If your technical skills are not quite up to the task of installing, upgrading, or migrating, consider hiring an outside consultant for this part. Once installed, you can easily take over the configuration and day-to-day management of SBS.

☑ Once the installation (clean install, upgrade, or migration) is complete, the To Do List steps you through additional post-installation tasks that should be accomplished in the order shown. Doing otherwise could create security and/or administrative problems.

☑ Each item in the To Do List launches a wizard that steps you through configuring the selected item.

☑ Additional management tasks are in the To Do List and those tasks also launch wizards. Additional information on those management tasks is located in other chapters in this book.

Chapter 4

Security

- Overview of Security in Small Business Server 2003

- Review Network Topology and Firewall Configuration

- Secure The Server

- Secure The Workstations

- Secure the User Accounts

- Monitor, Log, and Audit

The End Result

By the end of this chapter, you'll have a solid understanding of what it takes to manage security in Windows Small Business Server 2003 (SBS) environment, as well as how to configure and monitor important security settings. Security is interwoven with all aspects of SBS and this chapter will lay the foundation for you to manage a secure SBS network.

Security best practices are referred to in just about every chapter in this book. This chapter is intended to serve as a guide for approaching security practices. In this chapter you'll learn about the ways an SBS-based network can (and should) be secured, and in subsequent chapters we'll step through how those tasks are accomplished. Refer back to this chapter from time to time (even after you've finished the book and set it on the shelf) to refresh your security best practices.

SOME INDEPENDENT ADVICE

It's often helpful to work with senior management in your company to define rules about network access for the company. Creating written policies can help avoid putting you on the spot, it will increase the consistency of how permissions are granted, and it will create some level of accountability within the organization. Network security is everyone's job and having senior management and your Human Resources department (if you have one) help define and implement secure network policies will help you manage the network.

Overview of Security in Small Business Server 2003

Here's the short version: If you followed the instructions in Chapter 3 and completed the tasks in the To Do List in the order they were shown, you have already established good basic security for your Windows Small Business Server 2003. That's the good news. The bad news is that security is a never-ending task that *cannot* just be done once and forgotten. However, if you set your system up well initially and follow the best practices we'll discuss throughout this book, you'll have a secure network and system.

If you want to guarantee that your network, server, and client computers will be safe all the time, your best option is to unplug everything and turn off the power. There is just no other way to be 100% safe these days. Since that scenario is not an option, the best we can hope for is to *reduce our exposure*, thus reducing the likelihood of a problem. By taking standard precautions, you reduce your risk and by monitoring your network, you can quickly address any problems that do occur before they become major catastrophes.

Types of Security

Security can be discussed on several different levels. If we look at the physical aspects of security, we can define the following security elements:

- Network topology
- Server
- Client computer (workstation)
- Users
- Overall monitoring, logging, and auditing

Network topology refers to the design and physical cabling of your network. There are secure and non-secure (sometimes referred to as *unsecure*) ways to configure your network. Although we talked about designing the network in Chapter 2, we'll look at a few areas of network topology you can review to ensure your network is set up to facilitate strong security.

The **SBS server**, of course, is the big dog on the block. If someone gets access to your server, he or she controls the network. We'll look at a number of different ways to secure the server.

Client computers (workstations, desktops) are also subject to security issues. Since desktops don't control the network, the risk is that they may provide an intruder easy entry to the network that compromises security. We'll look at ways to secure client computers to help avoid these kinds of problems.

Users are a source of security problems as well. From writing down passwords to loading unauthorized software, users can be a source of security holes. However, there are ways to reduce the risk that users create (purposely or inadvertently) without taking draconian measures.

Finally, through regular and targeted **monitoring, logging, and auditing**, you can keep an eye on things. By setting these tasks up to automatically notify you and by reviewing log files and reports regularly, you can spot irregular activities early and take fast corrective action.

SOME INDEPENDENT ADVICE

Security is probably the biggest challenge facing network administrators these days. This chapter is designed to help you understand the various security components. However, SBS does an excellent job, through the various wizards, at establishing good baseline security. If you follow the Setup and To Do List tasks and follow the best practices sprinkled throughout this book, your network will be as secure as can be reasonably expected. It's the philosophy of "hope for the best and plan for the worst—reality will likely be somewhere in between."

Review Network Topology and Firewall Configuration

The first place to begin is to look at your network configuration. If you followed the recommendations in Chapters 2 and 3, you should have a reasonably secure network to start with. Let's take another look to make sure we're working from a secure base.

Network Connections

To protect a network that is connected to the Internet, you must be running a firewall. As we discussed in Chapter 2, a firewall is a device (either hardware or software-based) that filters all data coming into or out of the network. As it filters the data, it decides which packets can pass through and which cannot. This is based on rules established for the firewall. When you configured your Internet connection using the Internet and E-Mail Configuration Wizard in Chapter 3, you set up some of the rules for the firewall that is built into SBS. If you installed Internet and Security Acceleration (ISA) Server, which comes with the Premium edition, you have a more sophisticated firewall in place (we'll walk through installing and configuring ISA later in this book).

In Chapter 2 we also looked at where the SBS server should be placed in your network configuration. In most cases, you should have two network interface cards (NICs) in your server. One connects to the Internet via a cable modem or router and the other connects to your company's internal network. The built-in SBS firewall, when enabled, sits between the two (in a virtual kind of way). Traffic from the Internet comes in through the NIC attached to the ISP's cable modem or router and the built-in firewall in SBS evaluates that traffic. If it meets the rules for incoming traffic, it is passed to the NIC attached to the internal network. If it does not meet the rules, it is thrown away. The same process is in effect for network traffic going out to the Internet. Using private IP addressing on your internal network along with network address translation (NAT) provides an additional layer of security.

Another possible way of connecting is to have an external firewall device (an actual firewall device or a computer running firewall software) that acts as the firewall. In this case, you may only have one NIC in the SBS computer. If you do not have an external device (external to the SBS server) running as a firewall, you *should* have two NICs in the SBS computer and you should have the firewall enabled. If not, go back and review Chapter 3, Phase II installation steps. Figure 4.1 depicts the layout of your network if you're using the internal SBS (or ISA Server) firewall and if you're using an external firewall. Confirm that your configuration meets these general requirements. If not, your network is at risk and you should reconfigure it so it meets these guidelines.

Figure 4.1 Network Configuration Using Internal or External Firewall

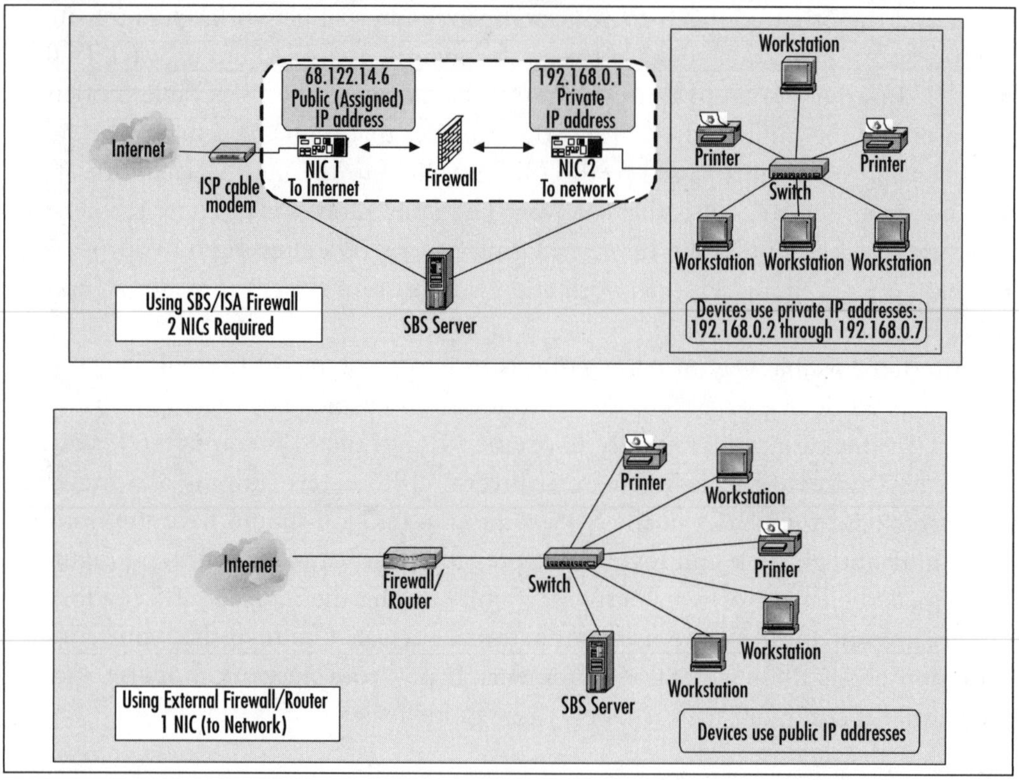

Note that in the second configuration, you *must* use a firewall device because the SBS server has only one NIC, connected directly to the network. If you want to use SBS (or ISA Server from the SBS Premium edition) as your firewall, your server must have two NICs installed and configured as shown in the first diagram in Figure 4.1.

If you are using an external firewall (which is often a router with firewall capabilities), you should verify the configuration of the firewall using the manufacturer's documentation.

Wireless Access Security

Some routers also provide wireless networking access (sometimes called a base station) for wireless devices. If you have no wireless devices, disable the access point. If you do have wireless devices, make sure the router is configured to provide only secure wireless access (refer to manufacturer's documentation).

If you are using a router/firewall device, make sure to secure it using a strong password (to prevent unauthorized access to the router administration features). Do NOT use the default password provided by the manufacturer—make sure you change it before you place it in service. Store a record of the password in a secure location. Also, depending on the router, the wireless access feature should be secured either by Wireless Equivalent Privacy (WEP) or the stronger 802.1x authentication, if supported. The more secure way to provide wireless access is to place the wireless access point outside of the firewall (between the firewall and the Internet) and require users to establish a secure virtual private network (VPN) connection to access the internal network. However, we'll talk more about wireless security later in this book.

BEST PRACTICES ACCORDING TO MICROSOFT

- Use two NICs if using the built-in SBS (or ISA) firewall.
- Enable the firewall in SBS. If using the Premium edition, you can choose to use the ISA Server firewall.
- Disable the internal SBS firewall *only* if using an external firewall.
- If using an external firewall, the SBS server's NIC will connect to the internal network.
- If the external router/firewall provides wireless access, secure the router and use WEP or 802.1x authentication for secure wireless access.
- If the external router/firewall provides wireless access that is not in use, disable that feature. Refer to manufacturer instructions for configuration information.

Secure the Server

There are several important aspects to securing the server. As stated earlier, the SBS server is the big dog on the network and it needs to be well protected to prevent network-wide problems. Securing the server includes physical security, configuration security, and software security.

Physical Security

One of the easiest security steps related to your server is to *place the server in a secure location* where access is controlled. This can be a locked (and well-ventilated) closet, a server room, or someone's office (to which you have the key and 24 x 7 access). Preventing someone from physically accessing the server prevents several different kinds of problems including stealing the server itself, hacking the server to provide administrative rights to the intruder, and connecting cables to the server to download or steal data.

Another aspect of physical security is *restricting the assignment of the Log on Locally* attribute (permission) to the server. Don't provide this administrative privilege to a user unless that person has a specific need to log onto the server directly, such as the person who might perform daily backup procedures or the person who fills in for you when you're on that much-needed vacation. Also, *don't use the server as a workstation,* thinking you'll save money if you just use the server as your computer. While this may be feasible, it's not advisable. Aside from perhaps overloading the server (and slowing down the network for all users), installing user software on a server can create security holes. For the price of a low-cost workstation these days, it's not worth the risk to your network security to employ the SBS server as your own desktop computer.

Best Practices According to Microsoft

- Secure the server in an access-controlled location.
- Do not use the server as a workstation.
- Do not install user software on the server.

Configuration Security

Configuration security, in this context, means looking at the way the SBS server is configured and run. If you stepped through the installation and the To Do List and followed the procedures outlined in Chapter 3, your system is already configured with basic security. Additional ways to configure the server to keep both the server and the network secure are listed below and subsequently described in detail.

- Require strong passwords.
- Rename the built-in Administrator account.
- Don't use the Administrator or Power User account for daily tasks.
- Log out when finished.
- Disable or remove services and applications you're not using.
- Configure your backup.
- Configure remote access to your network.

The first step in configuring a secure network is to *require strong passwords.* We'll cover this again later in this book but you can never hear it too often. As with all types of security, there is always a balance between optimal security and practical security. Finding the balance between a secure network and a useable network is the fine line you have to walk. Strong passwords can be implemented in a way that is still user–friendly, but does not create a security hole. If the requirements for passwords are *too* strong, users will simply write down their complicated passwords, thus defeating the very purpose of strong passwords. Strong password requirements include a password that meets these criteria:

- At least 7 characters long
- Includes upper and lower-case characters as well as numbers and special characters
- Does not include the user's first or last name in the password
- Is not a word found in a dictionary (*tulip* would be against the rules, *21iP* would be acceptable)
- Does not use information commonly known about the user, such as spouse or children's names, birthdays, etc

Another relatively easy security step is to *rename the built-in Administrator account.* Hackers always look first for the account named "Administrator." If you rename it to something you'll remember but a hacker isn't likely to guess, it simply makes things that much more difficult for a would-be hacker. Also, *don't use the Administrator or Power User account for daily tasks* on the server, regardless of what the Administrator account might be called. The Power User account is another account with a lot of network privileges and should also not be used for daily tasks. The best practice is to create regular user accounts for yourself and others who may assist with administration. Have them use the regular user account for normal tasks and have them log on using their more powerful account (Power User or Administrator) only when doing tasks that require that level of permissions. Of course, make sure to *log out when finished* and don't leave the computer unattended while you're logged in with these super-human privileges. You can also set the inactivity timeout function to a reasonable time period (5 or 10 minutes) so that the account is locked after that period of time.

Yet another relatively simple task is to *disable or remove services and applications you're not using.* Remember back in Chapter 3 when you ran through the Internet and E-Mail Configuration Wizard and you selected Web services you wanted to run? We even mentioned only selecting services you were going to use or were already using (on your existing network). It's like locking your house and leaving a window wide open—it's not too hard to get in if you know what to look for. The same holds true for applications and services. If you are no longer using an application (or any software or service), uninstall it from the server. It's good housekeeping and it prevents security holes that you might overlook. If you're not actively using an application or service, you might not think to look for security problems in that area (out of sight, out of mind).

When you set up SBS, certain shares are created automatically and are configured with appropriate permissions. However, to share additional folders or files with users, you'll need to manually configure them for sharing. If you want to create additional shares, be sure to share the file or folder then assign *users* to *groups* and grant those groups the appropriate share permissions. Later in this book, we'll review users, groups, and permissions, but for now, just keep this rule in mind: don't assign permissions to an individual user. Always add users to groups and grant group permissions, even if that group ends up having only one member. This makes managing user permissions much easier and is less likely to create security problems down the road.

Shortcuts

Reviewing Share Permissions

Locate the share you want to review then right-click the name of the share and click **Properties.** Click the **Security** tab and review the list of groups assigned to the share. You can also review the permissions associated with each group. If the share does not have the desired permissions, you can assign groups of users to the share based on your business's unique needs.

For more information on managing shares, you can search for "shared folder permissions" in your server's Help and Support section (**Start | Help and Support**).

Configuring your backup is another vital aspect of security. This security thing is starting to sound a bit easier, isn't it? Setting up security is really a series of fairly easy tasks that together help to create a secure network. Since SBS provides all critical services for the network, it's really important to configure a backup process that will protect your network in the event of server failure, power failure, natural disaster, or theft. We'll look at this in more detail later in the book, but it's important now to understand there are essentially two major types of backup—having redundancy built into the disk hardware (RAID, mirrored volumes, etc.) and backup to removable media. If you have RAID or mirrored volumes, you're in good shape should one drive or one disk drive controller fail, but what if the building floods and your server is on the first floor? Ooops. Backing up data to an internal solution (RAID, mirrored volumes, etc.) is fine for day-to-day redundancy and helps you bring your system back up fast if certain types of problems arise. But, in the event of a more serious problem, you'll also want a complete and current set of backups for your data with at least one set kept off-site in a secure location. If the server is stolen or the building burns to the ground, you want to be able to get your network back up and running as quickly as possible (insurance might ease the financial burden but only backups will ease the operational burden). SBS provides an integrated backup solution that we'll review later in this book. For now, put "configure backups" on your own To Do List.

We saved the best for last—*configuring remote access to your network.* You certainly don't want just anyone accessing your network remotely. The good news is that SBS provides some tools that are easy to configure and manage, and will provide secure remote access for users that require it. There are two main ways to accomplish providing remote access—through establishing VPN connections or through the use of *Remote Web Workplace* (RWW). RWW is easier to configure and use than VPN, but either one can provide secure remote access. We'll review how to configure these options later in the book.

BEST PRACTICES ACCORDING TO MICROSOFT

- Implement strong passwords.
- Rename the built-in Administrator account.
- Do not use the Administrator or Power User accounts for daily work. When possible, use your own login and use the **runas** command as needed.
- Disable or remove unused applications and services.
- Assign permissions to shares.
- Configure the server to perform regular backups, keep one set off-site in a secure location.
- Configure Remote Access to local network using VPNs or RWW.

Software Security

There are various ways the system's software can contribute to (or detract from) network security. This includes keeping the server software up to date, keeping server applications up to date, keeping your virus software up to date, and keeping other software up to date.

Microsoft recognizes that hackers are working 24 x 7 to break into Microsoft products, and for the past several years, Microsoft has increasingly focused on improving security for its products, particularly the critical server products. Windows Server 2003 (and it's close cousin, SBS) is more secure right out of the box than any of its predecessors were. With a focus on improving security, Microsoft is constantly releasing updates, patches, and fixes for vulnerabilities that are discovered in its products. Here's good news: these updates, patches, and fixes are often available *before* hackers figure out there's a hole to exploit. It's only good news, though, if you do something about it before the hackers wise up. You can *configure your system to automatically scan for updates.* Based on your server's software and configuration, the Microsoft website will make these updates available to you for download and installation.

There are three options you can use: *scan and install updates automatically* (not recommended), *scan and download updates automatically, notify me when they're ready to be installed* (recommended), or *notify me before downloading updates and notify me before installing updates* (not recommended). The first option could have your server rebooting when it's not particularly convenient. Some updates require a system reboot, and the update will let you know if this is required to successfully install the update. The third option isn't great because if the download and installation don't occur as updates become available, your system could be a security sitting duck for hackers looking to exploit vulnerabilities. Hard as it is to believe, some hacker types get notified of updates just like you do and then find ways to exploit the vulnerabilities the update is slated to fix. These folks surf the Internet looking for computers that do not yet have the update installed. It's sort of the lazy man's guide to hacking, but it's effective in a warped kind of way.

Looking for updates for server applications that are not built into the operating system is also recommended. In most cases, you'll need to *check periodically for application updates* (server and otherwise). In other cases, the application vendor may have an e-mail list to which you can subscribe in order to be notified when updates and fixes are available. Look for these on the vendor's website or set your calendar to check for updates once a week or twice a month.

OK, here's another simple security measure—*install and configure virus scanning software*. Many software packages also scan for worms, spyware, e-mail viruses (in attachments, typically), and malicious code—get one that meets your company's needs. Remember to get the version that is specifically made to run on *a server* and that is compatible with SBS 2003. It should include the ability to catch viruses on the computer as well as in incoming and outgoing e-mail and e-mail attachments. Configure the software to automatically go out and update the signature file when updates become available. The signature file is the file that provides information to the program about how to recognize the thousands of active viruses floating around the Internet. Without an up-to-date signature file, your system will be vulnerable to the latest viruses even if it's protected from older ones. Virus scanning software programs sometimes release updates every day or two, or it might be a week or two between releases, depending on the malicious activity out there. So, make this easy on yourself and configure the virus software to update itself. Of course, occasionally checking to make sure the automatic update function is working is also a good idea.

BEST PRACTICES ACCORDING TO MICROSOFT

- Configure your server for automatic updates.
- Check for updates for server applications.
- Check for updates for other applications.
- Keep your virus software (especially the signature file) up to date.

SOME INDEPENDENT ADVICE

Security really is a matter of establishing some routine practices that help keep your network secure. Once you've configured your security, you certainly still have to keep an eye on it. But, once configured, monitoring and tweaking the server's security should be relatively easy. The key is to always start with as clean a slate as possible and manage it well. It's always easier to *keep* a server clean than to clean it up after you've created a big mess (sounds like my mother talking about my room when I was a kid).

Secure the Workstations

Now that we've looked at the server's security, it's time to move onto the client computer (workstations, desktops, whatever you like to call them). There are really two primary security issues with workstations. The first is that you should *keep the operating system up to date.* That means upgrading from older, less secure operating systems. As newer operating systems implement better security features, you should consider upgrading away from older operating systems. For example, these days you shouldn't really be running anything older than Windows 98, and that's pushing it. Whatever operating system you're running, make sure you've got the latest service packs, updates, and patches installed on the system to provide the highest level of security possible for that operating system.

You can *install and configure Software Update Services (SUS)* on your SBS network to help collect, review, and distribute updates for operating systems in use on your network. SUS works with Windows XP Professional, Windows 2000 Professional, Windows 2000 Server, or Windows Server 2003. If you're running other operating systems, including Windows 95, Windows 98, Windows ME, or

Windows NT Workstation 4.0, use the Windows Update site to check for critical system updates. We'll review this later in the book.

As with the server, *workstation applications should also be kept up to date.* Again, the vendor of these applications may have an automatic update option or an e-mail list you can join to be notified of updates as they become available.

SOME INDEPENDENT ADVICE

Although most software vendors do a good job of testing their software updates, you might take a cautious approach to updates and install them on one computer and test it. Make sure the update works with the other applications (sometimes updating one application breaks another), make sure the update works with the operating system version you're running and doesn't break anything. Once you're comfortable that it's ok, install and test on a system running another operating system (assuming you've got a mixture of operating systems on your network). The worst thing you can do is download the update, install it on 47 computers, and then be unable to bring any of the systems back up. Test it out first.

Secure the User Accounts

There are several ways to keep user accounts safe and secure. Through ongoing education and requiring the use of strong passwords, you can help users protect their accounts. By adding users to groups to assign permissions and by only providing permissions the user needs, you minimize your risk of users doing things on the network they really shouldn't be doing.

Educate Users

The first and easiest method of keeping user accounts secure is through educating your users. This can be done in a number of ways. Some companies include network security policies in their handbooks, others include this information in employee orientation sessions, and still others post this information on intranets, bulletin boards, or via occasional (and recurring) e-mail reminders to users. Whatever method works best for your organization, keep in mind that continuing education for users about the importance of network security, as well as new security threats that affect users (email viruses, for instance) will go a long way in minimizing risk. What should you educate users on? These are a few suggestions, but your company may have additional requirements.

- Use strong passwords that you will remember, but that are hard to guess.

- Do not write your password down and leave it at your desk.

- Do not give your password to anyone (including friends or co-workers) for any reason, whether it appears legitimate or not. Some people, either inside or outside the company, may try to convince you that giving your username and/or password is a good idea, makes sense, is required, etc. Never give that information out, period.

- Never respond to e-mail by supplying your username and/or password for any reason. If you have accounts with Internet-based companies, log onto your account on their website to manage your account, never respond to e-mail that appears to be from companies with whom you've done business. Unsolicited e-mail requesting your username and password (and often social security number or credit card numbers) is called *phishing* and is a way to obtain logon credentials from unsuspecting users. Legitimate companies will never request this information.

- If you broke the previous rule and gave your password to someone or you think someone has gotten a hold of it, notify your network administrator about changing your password immediately (if this is for an Internet-based company, log on immediately and change your password and/or notify the company).

- Never download and install software that is not approved by the network administrator and that is not signed. Doing so could install spyware and other malicious code including software that records usernames, passwords, and credit card numbers and transmits them to an external location maintained by the hacker.

Keep users informed when new scams, viruses, or worms appear on the Internet. Let them know what the threat is, how it attacks, what users should do to avoid the problem, and what to do if they do get hit. This often is helpful because users can also apply this knowledge to home systems and avoid the problems at home. They can also notify friends and colleagues. The more people who are aware of the threat, the better.

When users understand the different ways their own actions can compromise the network and the security of the company, they usually do a pretty good job of trying to conform to the rules. However, it's human nature to slide back into sloppy or bad habits, so occasional reminders to users are also warranted. Prevention is the best cure in this case.

Require Strong Passwords

In addition to educating users, configuring the server to require strong passwords is also a recommended best practice. There is a hacker attack called a *dictionary attack* where hackers use an automated method of trying every word in the dictionary as the password to gain unauthorized access to an account (this type of attack is also called a *brute force* attack because the attacker just keeps hammering away at the account until it cracks). If a hacker has gotten hold of a legitimate user account name (which can be somewhat easy to do these days), they will often first try to crack the account using a dictionary attack. It's automated and they can fire it up and go out for lunch while it does its work. This is why strong passwords do not allow the user's first or last name in the password, require at least 7 characters and use a combination of characters (uppercase and lowercase, numbers, special characters).

The reason for this is relatively simple. Let's say that you only can use uppercase letters and the password must be two characters long. That means there are about 675 different combinations that can be used as the password. If I create a spreadsheet and begin with AA and go to AZ, then move to BA to BZ, etc., eventually I'll figure out your password. The more character positions you require, the more variations there are. The more types of characters you require, the more variations there are. So, when you require a 7-character password using roughly 176 allowable characters in each character position, the number of combinations grows exponentially, and it is going to take a hacker a really long time to crack (if ever). Remember, though, these are called strong passwords, not impenetrable passwords—given enough time and computing power, just about anything can be cracked, but most hackers look for the easy way in. Also, we'll review monitoring, logging and auditing later in this chapter and again later in the book. Monitoring your server will help you detect someone trying to break in this way so you can take countermeasures to prevent a security breach.

Verify Users Have Only Necessary Permissions

If you set up users during Chapter 3, you added users to groups based on pre-set templates provided by SBS. This is one way that SBS helps you manage permissions. Those pre-defined templates set appropriate levels of permissions, which helps avoid creating security problems when providing permissions to users. Two rules of thumb here (since most of us only have two thumbs anyway):

1. **Use the pre-defined templates whenever possible**. If you need custom permissions, create a group with those defined permissions and add users to that group. Pre-defined templates help configure a standard set of permissions for users that fall into categories such as Users, Power Users, Backup Operators, etc. This helps prevent opening security holes inadvertently through incorrectly assigning permissions to users. We'll discuss templates in more detail when we discuss users and groups in later chapters.

2. **Don't grant permissions to individual users**. It makes it very difficult to track who has what level of permission. If you do experience a security breach, say someone gets into a corporate salary file, you can look at who is a member of the group that has permissions and see if there is someone that doesn't belong in that group. If you didn't use groups, you'd have to look at every single user—not a great way to spend your day.

A corollary of this is to provide remote access only to users that require remote access to do their jobs. Don't provide remote access simply because someone asks for it or because someone feels he or she *should* have the ability to access the network remotely. Create a procedure for requesting and approving remote access. For instance, you might create a policy that says that only department managers can approve remote access for employees in their departments. That keeps some level of accountability and keeps *you* from being the bad guy when the request is denied. It's probably not your job to determine who has a legitimate request (in most cases); it's your job to provide appropriate access for business purposes.

BEST PRACTICES ACCORDING TO MICROSOFT

- Educate users regularly about security practices and Internet risks. When a new scam or virus appears, educate users on how to identify it, how to avoid it, and how to report it.
- When a new scam or virus appears, *spread the word* on how to identify it, how to avoid it, and how to report it.
- Require strong passwords—make the requirements reasonable for users, but difficult enough so hackers can't easily guess or use brute force attacks.
- Use pre-defined or custom templates to assign appropriate permissions for users.
- Grant the minimum permissions to users—enough to get their job done and no more.
- Create policies for remote access and only grant remote access to users that have a legitimate business need.

Monitor, Log, and Audit

After you've configured your security settings, it would be nice if that was that. Unfortunately, security work is never done. So, after establishing a secure network, you need to keep an eye on it. It doesn't have to become an all-consuming task for you, but it should be done consistently and regularly. If you make a habit of checking key areas of your network on a daily basis, you can spend 5 or 10 minutes daily and maintain a secure network. We'll look at all of these practices later in this book, but here are some best practices to keep in mind.

Configure Monitoring and Reporting

If you're not automatically receiving monitoring reports, you should check to see if it's configured or if your e-mail address is in the list of recipients (if you just finished installing SBS, we'll configure this feature later in the book, so stay tuned). SBS includes a number of performance and usage reports that provide valuable information on the health and security of your network and server. Regularly reviewing these reports will help you detect any unusual behavior and take steps to address it in a timely manner. You can configure the system to automatically send you log files with the monitoring reports so that you have all the data you need to keep your network healthy.

Audit Key Events

Auditing is the process of flagging certain events. These events are then automatically added to a log file so you can see what's going on. As with all security practices, your auditing policies and practices must strike a balance between all and nothing. If you audit all events, not only will your system grind to a halt, but you'll be deluged with tons of useless data. Finding the important events then becomes almost impossible. If you don't audit anything, you're not inundated with data, but you also can't see what's going on—it's like driving a car with your eyes closed. Instead, if you configure auditing for key events, you're likely to find problems early and prevent an all-out crisis. By default, SBS enables auditing of *failed logon events* and *account lockouts*.

Audit for Failed Logon Events

Remember our earlier discussion of brute force attacks, including dictionary attacks? Well, here's where you can see if that's occurring. Auditing failed logon events means that every time a user attempts to log on and is not successful, an event will be logged to a log file. There are certainly times when a failed logon occurs because the user had the **Caps Lock** key on or simply mistyped his or her password. However, if you see repeated failed logon events on the same user account, you might suspect a brute force attack. Contacting the user to see if he or she did have those failed logon attempts can verify the logged information for you and you can take additional steps to locate the would-be hacker.

By default, SBS sets the failed logon parameters to 50 failed logon attempts in 10 minutes. After that, the account is locked out for 10 minutes. After 10 minutes, the account is reset automatically so the user can log on. Since it's unlikely that any legitimate user would have 50 failed logon attempts in 10 minutes, lower this default setting to 5 or 6 to help you weed out user error from brute force attacks.

Audit for Account Lockouts

Account lockout occurs automatically when the pre-set logon attempt threshold is exceeded. In this case, if a user attempts 50 times in 10 minutes to get into his or her account, the account will be locked out for 10 minutes. If you configure it to do so, you and the user can also be sent a notification by e-mail of the account lockout event. The lockout is released after 10 minutes, so if a second notification occurs, you can pretty much assume that account is under attack and take counter measures.

BEST PRACTICES ACCORDING TO MICROSOFT

- Configure monitoring so that you receive alerts automatically for critical system events.
- Read log files and reports regularly to look for signs of break-ins or attempted break-ins.
- SBS is configured by default to allow 50 failed logon attempts in 10 minutes before locking the account out for 10 minutes. Note: Most companies will want to lower that threshold to 5 or 6 failed attempts in 10 minutes.
- Keep up to date on the latest security issues. Subscribe to e-mail alerts from Microsoft, virus software vendors, or other reputable security e-mail newsletters. Keep your users informed on the latest threats and countermeasures.

SOME INDEPENDENT ADVICE

Reading log files and reports is a lot like reviewing your credit card statement or bank statement each month. Most of the time everything is just fine and you begin to wonder why you pore over every line each month. Then, two years later, you notice an error on your bank statement or a double charge on your credit card. You save yourself hundreds of dollars in incorrect charges just because you took the time to quickly look things over. Log files and reports are the same—most of the time everything is fine and you can explain any anomalies. But when things go wrong, you'll spot the problem quickly and minimize the disruption to your network. It's worth the 5 or 10 minute daily investment. By the way, log files and reports are best served with coffee and cinnamon rolls.

Microsoft Security Guidance Kit

The Microsoft Security Guidance Kit is a useful tool you can download from Microsoft and learn more about security for your network or individual computer. It runs on any computer running Windows Server 2003 (including SBS), Windows XP, or Windows 2000. Figure 4.2 shows the main screen once you've installed and launched the Security Guidance Kit. Figure 4.3 shows the **Secure Your Server** option selected from the main screen, and Figure 4.4 shows the **All**

Tools selection, also chosen from the options on the main screen. The program is easy to use and navigate. Download it and take a look at it to learn more about security best practices.

Shortcuts

Security Guidance Kit v. 1.0

You can download the Microsoft Security Guidance Kit v. 1.0 (SGKv1) from www.microsoft.com (type in the search term **security guidance kit**). It's a collection of how-to information, software tools, and detailed prescriptive guidance within a small "viewer" application. It's applicable for Windows XP, Windows 2000, and Windows Server 2003 (including SBS). The application is an executable (SGK_v1.exe) that's about 150MB in size. Save it to your system and then double-click to run it. Figure 4.2 shows the main screen displayed after installation, Figure 4.3 shows the options after selecting **Enhance Server Security** and Figure 4.4 shows the list of tools available (**List All Tools** link).

If you download this file, you'll need to allow it to install the .NET framework if it's not already installed, and you'll also have to install the Security Guidance Kit (double-clicking the file opens the initial dialog then prompts you through each of three steps). You can uninstall this file later by accessing **Start | Control Panel | Add or Remove Programs** and selecting **Microsoft Security Guidance Kit**, then clicking **Remove**. Removing this program will not remove the .NET framework from your system. If desired, that has to be removed separately by selecting **Microsoft .NET Framework 1.1**, also found in **Start | Control Panel | Add or Remove Programs**.

Figure 4.2 Main Menu in Security Guidance Kit v. 1.0

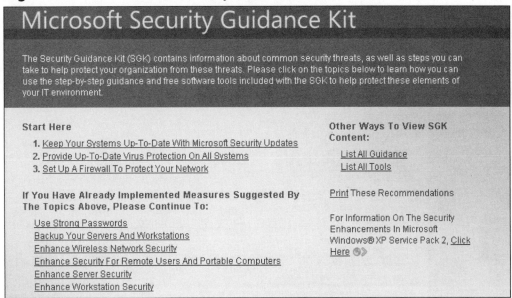

Figure 4.3 Enhance Server Security Recommendations in SGKv1

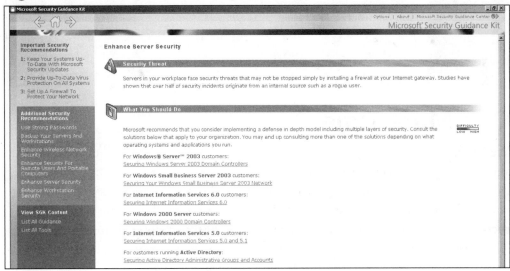

Figure 4.4 List of Tools in SGKv1

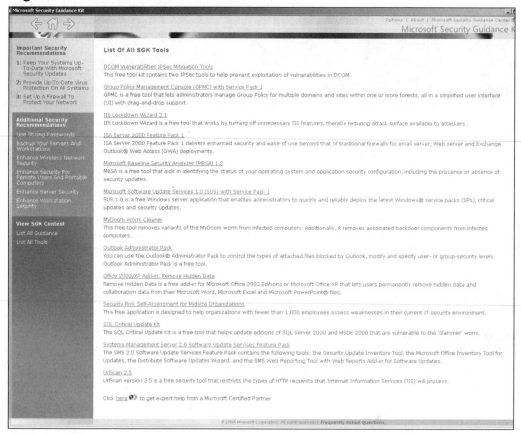

One More Time

Well, you made it through a chapter on security and you should feel pretty good about managing a secure network because you now understand what steps you can take to secure you network and you know those steps aren't as difficult as you might have imagined. As you go through the remainder of the book, keep these security concepts in mind and refer back to this chapter from time to time. This chapter will remind you of security best practices so you can keep your network safe and spend more time in meetings…wait, that's not right.

☑ Security is an on-going project, but one that can be managed through establishing consistent practices, policies, and routines.

☑ Begin by reviewing the way your network, router(s), firewall, and server are configured so you don't create security holes through incorrect configuration.

☑ Take steps to secure the server, including physically, via the configuration, and via upgrades and patches.

☑ Workstations can best be secured by upgrading older operating systems, keeping the operating systems up to date (patches, service packs, fixes), and by keeping software applications up to date.

☑ Educate users about safe practices regarding usernames and passwords.

☑ Keep users up to date about new and developing security threats, especially e-mail viruses, worms, *phishing*, and other Internet-related hacks.

☑ Establish monitoring, logging, and auditing for key events on your network and review those log files and reports regularly for suspicious behavior.

☑ Download and install the Security Guidance Kit v. 1.0 for one-stop shopping on security practices related to managing a Microsoft Windows-based network.

Chapter 5

Disk Management

- Terminology
- Dynamic Disk Concepts
- Managing Server Disks

The End Result

In this chapter, you'll learn about basic and advanced disk terminology and concepts, in case you're not familiar with how disks work, especially in the server environment. We'll also look at specific ways to manage the disks in your Windows Small Business Server 2003 (SBS) server. When you've finished this chapter, you will have an understanding of disk management and your server disks will be configured to meet your organization's needs.

Terminology

Disk drive and disk management concepts range from simple to complex. In this section, you'll learn some of the common terminology and definitions related to disks and disk management. In later sections, you'll learn the basic concepts and a few advanced concepts related to disk management. That will lay the foundation for successfully managing your disk drives in the SBS environment, which we'll discuss later in the chapter. There are a lot of options available today for managing your SBS disks and the choices you make can increase network (or server) performance and provide fault tolerance.

Disk Terminology

Let's begin with a list of disk-related terminology. Be sure you understand these terms and concepts before moving on, since we'll be using them throughout this chapter.

Disk drive or physical disk The physical disk is the actual disk drive itself. Since a drive can be divided into virtual (called logical) drives, where one physical disk holds several logical drives, it's important to differentiate between the physical disk and the logical disk.

Partition The partition is a defined segment of a basic disk drive formatted with a particular file structure; FAT (file allocation table), FAT32, NTFS (new technology file system), etc. On a Windows-based computer, the disk can be divided into a maximum of four primary partitions (see the *Primary Partition* definition below). You can also configure the disk with three primary partitions and one extended partition. A partition must be formatted before it can be used. Figure 5.1 shows various partition configurations for a basic disk (see *Basic Disk*, below).

Volume A volume is synonymous with a partition. It is a defined segment of a disk drive. When using dynamic disks, the segment is referred to as a volume.

Active Partition The active partition is the partition marked as the one from which the computer will boot. Only one active partition can be designated at a time. This partition contains files that allow the user to select which operating system will be started if more than one is present on the computer.

Boot Partition The partition from which the computer boots. In some cases, the boot and system partition are the same, as in cases where there is only one partition on the disk. This partition stores the operating system and associated files. It can be the same as the system partition but does not have to be.

System Partition A system partition is the one on which the operating system resides. The system partition contains hardware specific files for the operating system including files like NTLDR and Boot.ini.

Primary Partition The primary partition is a partition that is identified by the operating system as bootable. This means it could be used to start the computer. However, only one partition can be marked as the partition from which the system will boot (see *Active Partition*). Figure 5.1 shows primary partitions in A, B, and C.

Extended Partition The extended partition is not bootable. It can contain any number of (unlimited) logical drives. A logical drive is assigned a drive letter. Figure 5.1 shows an extended partition with three logical drives.

Basic Disks Used in MS-DOS, Windows 95, Windows 98, Windows Millennium Edition, Windows NT 4.0, or Windows XP Home Edition operating systems. These systems do not support the use of dynamic disks (see *Dynamic Disks*). Figure 5.1 shows three possible basic disk configurations.

Dynamic Disks Supported in newer operating systems including Windows 2000, Windows XP Professional, and Windows Server 2003. Dynamic disks allow for more advanced configurations including the ability to create volumes that span multiple disks and to create fault-tolerant configurations.

Master Boot Record (MBR) A method of formatting the partition information on the physical disk. This is the most commonly used disk partition format or style. This is the method discussed throughout the remainder of this chapter.

Globally Unique Identifier Partition Table (GUID) A more advanced method of formatting the partitions on a disk drive. This method can only be used on Itanium-based computers and supports up to 128 partitions per disk (as opposed to four on an MBR-type disk).

Figure 5.1 Basic Disk Configurations with Partitions and Logical Drives

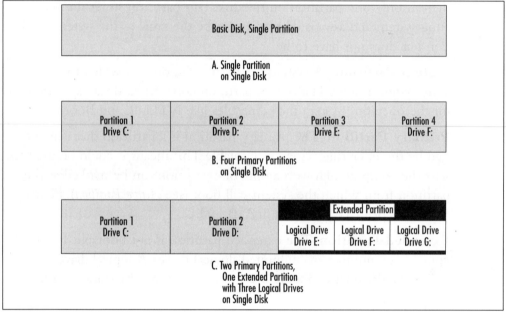

Storage Connection Terminology

There are many different ways to connect disk drives to your server. Before we discuss disk drives themselves, let's look at the technology behind storage devices these days. This is not a comprehensive discussion, but it will give you the basics you need to understand commonly used terminology. There seems to be an ever-expanding vocabulary related to storage connection technology, so we'll really look at two primary categories, *IDE* and *SCSI*, then we'll look at some of the different flavors of each.

Integrated Drive Electronics (IDE) drives are the most common drives used in client computers, including the one(s) you're running at home. They connect to an IDE controller that is often integrated into the motherboard of your computer. You can connect two IDE drives to most systems, the primary and secondary drives, sometimes still referred to by the legacy terms *master* and *slave* drives. Other variations of IDE include Enhanced IDE (EIDE), Advanced Technology Attachment (ATA) and Direct Memory Access (DMA). References to Ultra DMA, ATA, and/or EIDE might all refer to the same drive.

Small Computer System Interface (SCSI, pronounced *skuzzy*) is the other primary type of drive. This uses a completely different disk controller, a SCSI controller, which is not at all interchangeable with IDE controllers or drives. If you go with SCSI, you have to use SCSI all the way. SCSI provides much better performance than IDE and allows you to run up to 13 drives on one controller. The downside is that SCSI is quite a bit more expensive than IDE. The cost is often worth it for servers, but typically not needed for user computers. This is a good choice for server disk drives.

There are many flavors of SCSI on the market now. All are enhancements of the original SCSI specification. These include Ultra SCSI, Wide SCSI, SCSI-2 and SCSI-3. Check with your drive and controller manufacturers for information on interchangeability and drive/controller requirements.

IDE and SCSI are the two most popular options. However, there are two other types of drives you should be aware of: Universal Serial Bus (USB) and Firewire. Drives connecting via USB or Firewire connections are not bootable drives, but are great removable storage options.

For more extensive storage options, you can also use Network Attached Storage (NAS) to connect storage devices to the network for increase capacity. This can be a good option on an SBS-based network, but if you go this route, make sure you purchase an NAS system that is compatible with SBS 2003. These devices attach directly to the network and can be managed via SBS. Finally, a more complex but robust configuration of NAS is the Storage Area Network (SAN). Storage area networks are more difficult to implement and manage and are typically appropriate for large organizations.

Dynamic Disk Concepts

A basic disk is pretty straight forward, as described in the terminology section and shown in Figure 5.1. Dynamic disks are defined volumes comprised or two or more disk drives. In Chapter 3, we briefly touched on RAID-0, RAID-1, and RAID-5. Recall that RAID stands for *Redundant Array of Inexpensive Disks*. These are dynamic disks because the dynamic disk is comprised of space on two or more physical drives. Contrast this with a basic disk that can contain one or more partitions, but is contained on one physical disk drive.

You may want to use dynamic disks on your SBS server. A computer can contain and use both basic and dynamic disks. Each physical disk in a computer can be run as basic or dynamic (assuming the operating system supports it). There are a few limitations regarding the use of dynamic disks. These are highlighted in the "Best Practices According to Microsoft" sections throughout this chapter.

Dynamic disks are made up of volumes. Remember, a volume is the same thing as a partition, but when talking about dynamic disks, we use the term *volume* instead. A single dynamic disk can hold up to 2,000 volumes, but Microsoft suggest limiting it to 32 or fewer. Unlike basic disks, dynamic disk volumes can span multiple physical disk drives. There are different types of dynamic volumes—some increase performance, some provide fault tolerance, some provide a mixture of the two.

Fault tolerance is the ability of disk systems (or anything for that matter) to recover from failure. For instance, if one disk fails, a fault tolerant system will recover by working around the failed drive. Some fault tolerant systems provide the ability to *hot swap* a device so that the system does not have to be stopped, rebooted, or impacted in any way. In these types of systems, you can remove the failed drive, install the new drive, and the system will automatically take care of the rest, incorporating the new drive back into the system.

Fault tolerance often comes at the cost of performance. You usually have to compromise one to get the other. Some configurations provide a balance between fault tolerance and performance, as you'll see in a moment.

Finally, various configurations provide differing degrees of disk utilization—how much disk space is available to use versus how much disk space there is in total. For instance, some configurations use 1MB of disk space for *overhead*, which is virtually nothing on a 40GB hard drive. Other systems use more disk space to manage the fault tolerance elements of the configuration. There is generally an inverse correlation between fault tolerance and disk utilization. The greater the degree of fault tolerance, the more disk space needed as overhead and the less available for data files.

Simple Volumes

Simple volumes are comprised of free space on a single dynamic volume. This can mean space from a single portion of the disk drive or several portions on the disk linked together. This configuration is contained on a single physical disk drive and can help make better use of a single disk drive's space. If the system volume is a system or boot volume, it cannot be *extended* in any way. Simple volumes make good use of disk space but they are not fault tolerant. If the disk fails, you must restore from backups. Figure 5.2 illustrates the simple volume concept.

Figure 5.2 Simple Volume

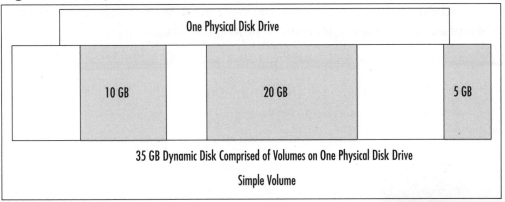

One Physical Disk Drive

10 GB   20 GB   5 GB

35 GB Dynamic Disk Comprised of Volumes on One Physical Disk Drive

Simple Volume

SOME INDEPENDENT ADVICE

Extending a volume is an interesting topic, but not one we'll spend a lot of time on in this chapter. Extending a volume is a method of adding disk space after the volume is already in use and is beginning to run low on available space. Nice concept, but it comes with its own set of challenges. Only *spanned* or *striped* volumes (see following sections) allow you to add disk space to a volume on the fly and because neither configuration provides fault tolerance, you could possibly lose data on the drive(s) when you do this. It beats the alternative of backing up all data, reformatting the drives and restoring data), but it has its own risks, so consider the pros and cons carefully before jumping into extending your disk space.

Spanned Volumes

Spanned volumes are just as the name implies—a volume spans over two or more (up to 32) physical disk drives. Spanned volumes use free space on drives to create a single logical drive and each spanned segment can be a different size. For instance, on Drive 1 it can be 10GB, Drive 2 can contribute 5GB, Drive 3 can contribute 25GB, and so on. Figure 5.3 illustrates this concept.

Spanned volumes, like simple volumes, provide no fault tolerance. If one of the drives in the spanned volume fails, you have to replace the drive and restore from backups. Spanned drives do not enhance performance of your system; they simply allow you to make use of leftover chunks of disk space in a more efficient manner. Keep in mind, however, that using spanned disks does increase your exposure for failure. If any one of the drives in the spanned set fails, your data is, well, toast. Spanning increases your risk of disk failure, but does make better use of unused space across several drives. You can extend spanned volumes on the fly, as discussed earlier, but it does come with its own risks.

Figure 5.3 Spanned Volume

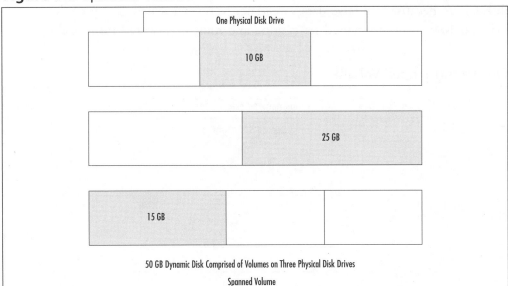

One Physical Disk Drive

10 GB

25 GB

15 GB

50 GB Dynamic Disk Comprised of Volumes on Three Physical Disk Drives
Spanned Volume

Striped Volumes (RAID-0)

A striped volume, also known as RAID-0, requires at least two drives and can support up to 32 drives. A striped set requires that each segment used on each disk be the same size, and the size used will default to the smallest available segment. This is the major difference between spanned and striped. Spanned uses various size segments, while striped requires uniform size segments.

For instance, suppose you have four disks with the following disk space available for your striped volume: 15GB, 11GB, 26GB, 14GB. The striped set will be created using the 11GB segment size, since that's the smallest size available. Using the same example, if you used all four disks, you have a striped set of 11GB x 4 or 44GB. However, you'd be wasting 4GB+0GB+15GB+3GB or 22GB of disk space because your segment size is constrained by the smallest segment used. Match up the available space on your disk drive sizes for optimal utilization (four disks of 20GB each, for example). Figure 5.4 illustrates this concept.

This configuration provides the best overall performance enhancement because data can be written across multiple physical drives quickly. The overhead is about 1MB, so this configuration also provides excellent disk space utilization.

This configuration offers no fault tolerance. If one of the drives fails, the striped volume fails and the data is not available until the striped drive is re-created and the data is restored from backup. This also increases your exposure to disk failure because you have data spread across several drives. If any of those drives fails, your entire striped set is gone and must be restored from backup.

Figure 5.4 Striped Volume

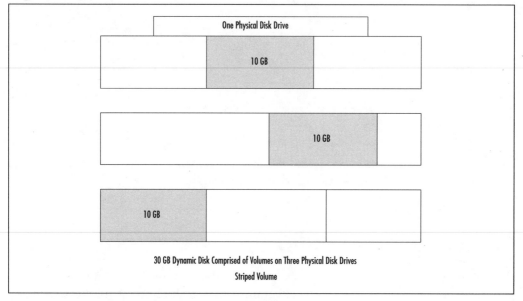

Mirrored Volumes (RAID-1)

Mirroring, or RAID-1, is also as the name implies—two disks (and only two disks) are exact copies of each other. One is designated by the system as the primary mirror and is the "active" drive. Every time some disk activity occurs on one drive, it also happens on the second drive. If a file is saved to the drive, it's simultaneously saved to the second drive. Figure 5.5 illustrates this concept.

If you're going to employ disk mirroring, you really should have drives of the *exact* same size, and it's highly recommended that you have drives of the exact same make and model. Due to subtle differences among drives, you may have quirky problems if you use different makes and models. Mirroring can have an impact on performance because of the time it takes for one disk controller to write to two disk drives on each and every disk access.

To mitigate the system performance degradation, as well as to increase your fault tolerance, you can also have two drives on their own disk controllers. This is called *disk duplexing* and provides a very high level of fault tolerance and performance. If you implement disk duplexing, the SBS system will see the drives as mirrored (in other words, they will not show up as duplexed drives).

Figure 5.5 Mirrored Volumes

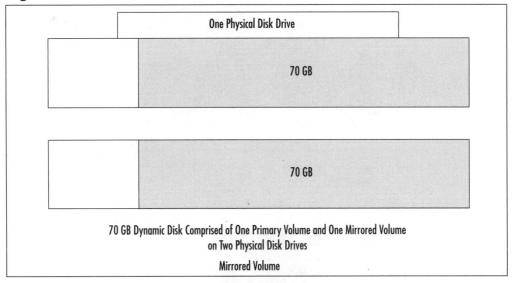

Striped Volume with Parity (RAID-5)

RAID-5 requires three or more disk drives. RAID-5 uses striping, as described earlier, but it uses one of the stripes for parity. Parity is a mathematical calculation used for error checking and correction. All you really need to know about parity is that RAID-5 uses one of the stripes for parity, so it's a fairly large chunk of overhead. Figure 5.6 illustrates this concept. However, RAID-5 gives you top-notch fault tolerance. If one of the drives in a RAID-5 configuration fails, it can re-create the data based on the parity information, and the only way you may know a drive has failed is that you get a notification telling you to replace the failed drive at your convenience. Users may notice a performance decrease if a RAID-5 drive fails—but they may never notice a thing. Be warned, however, RAID-5 cannot recover from two (or more) disks failing. In that case, you'd need to restore from backups. RAID-5 can be implemented via SBS disk management software, but it's really best to implement it using third-party hardware RAID for much better performance and to avoid overloading your server hardware with disk management tasks.

Figure 5.6 Striped Volume with Parity

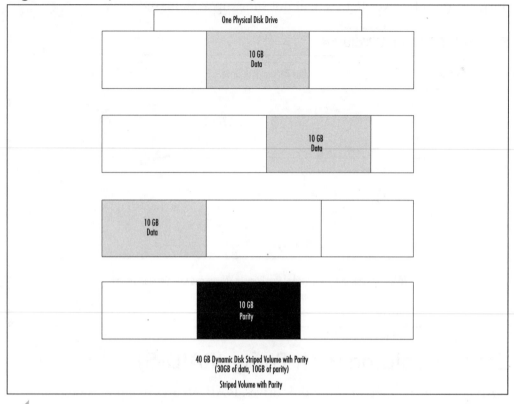

40 GB Dynamic Disk Striped Volume with Parity
(30GB of data, 10GB of parity)

Striped Volume with Parity

BEST PRACTICES ACCORDING TO MICROSOFT

- Dynamic disks cannot be used on laptops, regardless of the operating system being used.
- Removable media and external drives connected via USB or FireWire cannot be converted to dynamic disks.
- You cannot convert a disk to a dynamic disk if it has multiple operating systems installed on it.
- Dynamic disks are not supported by the Windows Cluster Service (an advanced disk feature) in Windows 2000 Server, Windows Server 2003, and SBS.
- Use a maximum of 32 volumes per dynamic disk.

Managing Server Disks

Managing server disks is an important part of keeping the server up and running, but it's typically not a day-to-day type of task. In this section, you'll learn to use various tools to manage your system disks. Configuration takes up the bulk of disk management and the remaining portion is monitoring disk health and making sure your drive(s) are adequately backed up. You may occasionally need to go in and tweak a drive setting, such as user quotas, but that will only be on occasion. Disks in SBS are managed through the **Disk Management** console.

Using Disk Management

To access disk management in SBS, click **Start | Server Management** to open the Server Management console. In the left pane, click the **+** to the left of **Advanced Management** to expand that node. Click the **+** to the left of **Computer Management (Local)** to expand that node. Click the **+** to the left of **Storage** to expand that node, and click **Disk Management** to open that snap-in. This path is shown in Figure 5.7.

Figure 5.7 Accessing Disk Management in the Server Management Console

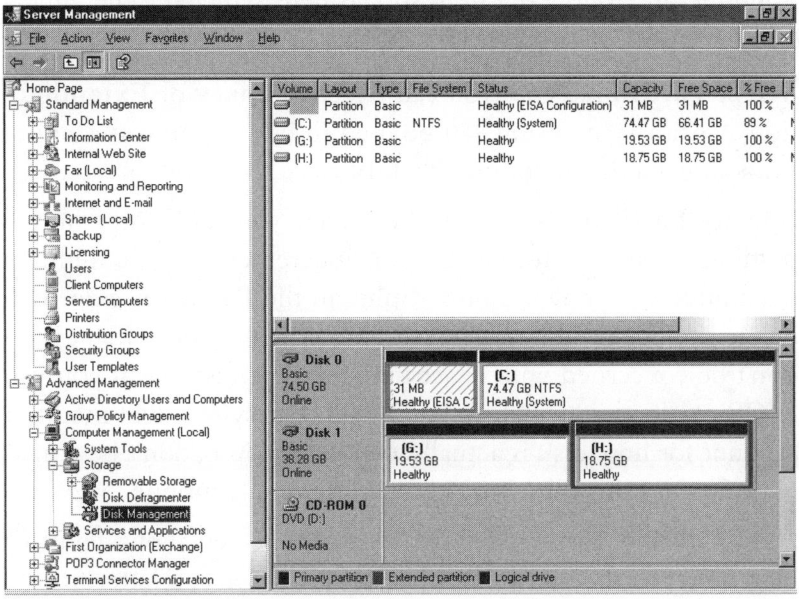

Working with Partitions

If you add a new disk drive, the process of working with partitions is pretty straightforward. Windows will automatically recognize that a new drive has been installed and it will make it available. If you need to partition it or format it, you can do so now. Figure 5.1 (shown earlier) shows two basic disk drives with three partitions, C:, G:, and H. You may wonder why they are not lettered C:, D:, and E:. Windows will provide drive letters in a particular order—from physical to logical disks. The DVD drive and CD-ROM drive in this particular system have the drive letters D: and E:, respectively. There is also a removable USB Flash Drive that was assigned the drive letter F:. Thus, the second physical disk drive has two partitions, which are labeled G: and H:. Don't be concerned about how the drives are lettered, as long as they're all there. You can modify the drive letter when you create a partition or after the partition is created. Refer to Step 3 in the next section for more information.

Creating a Partition

To create a partition, select a section of unallocated space on a drive, right-click and choose **New Partition**. This will launch the **New Partition Wizard**. Click **Next** to continue, and follow the steps shown here, which are the same as the on-screen instructions.

1. **Select Partition Type** You can select **Primary** or **Extended** partition. A primary partition can be used to boot from; you cannot boot from an extended partition. Click **Next.**

2. **Specify Partition Size** On this screen, you can choose how large the partition should be. It must be somewhere between the minimum and maximum sizes shown. Enter a value in the **Partition size in MB** field or use the up and down arrows to increment or decrement the value, so don't be concerned with exact numbers. For instance, if you want a 20GB partition, enter the value **20000**. The system will modify this to account for how disk is actually divided up. Also, don't be concerned if your 20000 turns into 20003. Click **Next** to continue.

3. **Assign Drive Letter or Path** The next screen allows you to assign a drive letter to the partition you're creating. Select a letter from the list. Used drive letters are not included in the list. The second option is to *M*ount **in the following empty NTFS folder** and specify a folder

location. This option allows you to mount the volume in an empty folder rather than assign a drive letter. This reduces the complexity for users by minimizing the number of drive letters displayed. Instead, you can simply place that volume in an empty NTFS folder and make it available to users as "Company Documents" (for example), rather than driver letter M. You can also choose to not assign a letter or drive path at this time. Read the section later in this chapter on mounted volumes for more information on this option, if desired (you can always modify this selection later as well). Click **Next** to continue.

4. **Format Partition** The next screen, shown in Figure 5.8, allows you to format the partition. If you do not want to format at this time, select **Do not format this partition**. To format it, you can select *Format this partition with the following settings* and select the file system, the allocation unit size and volume label. SBS defaults to NTFS, your best choice, so you should stick with this default. Also, accept the default allocation unit size unless you have specific information from the disk drive manufacturer about how this should be set. The **Volume label** is the name you give to the virtual drive. Use a descriptive label to help you and your users make sense of what's what. Your two other choices on this screen include choosing to **Perform a quick format,** which will quickly format the drive but will not perform disk error checking. If you've recently checked the disk for errors, a quick format is ok to use. Otherwise, allow the system to perform a full format. The final option is to **Enable file and folder compression**. This setting allows files and folders on the partition to be compressed. Compression allows more data to be stored on the disk, but it will affect drive performance. You can add or remove compression later, if desired. One note of caution is that if you try to decompress data on a drive that doesn't have enough space, you'll run into problems. Also, don't enable compression on files and folders that are frequently changed – this will definitely lead to performance issues. On files and folders that are rarely accessed and changed, compression may yield acceptable results. Click **Next** to continue.

Figure 5.8 Format Partition

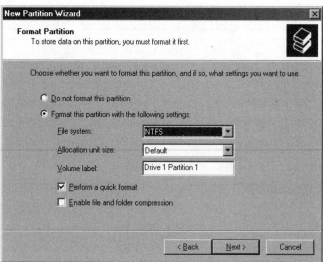

5. **New Partition Confirmation** The final screen in the New Partition Wizard is the confirmation page that displays all the choices you've selected. Once you've reviewed these and clicked **Finish**, the changes you've specified will be put in place. If this includes formatting the partition, the disk management console will simply list "Formatting" in the partition you've selected until it is finished formatting. Then, the label will be displayed and the partition will show up as an NTFS partition.

Some Independent Advice

Volume labels can be a useful tool for you and your users. Rather than using something bland like "New D: Drive," (or "Drive 1 Partition 1" used earlier as an example for clarity) choose a descriptive name such as "UserData" or "Finance." Using descriptive names for the volume label will help you and your users manage disks, volumes and data on your network.

Creating a New Logical Drive on an Extended Partition

If you have an extended partition, you can create a new logical drive within that extended partition. To do so, right-click the free space and select **New Logical Drive**. This will launch the **New Partition Wizard**. The options are the same as those we just went over in the previous section, "Creating a New Partition," with one exception. The only option you'll have on the Select Partition Type screen (Step 1 in the earlier steps) is the **Logical drive**, as shown in Figure 5.9. Click **Next** to continue and follow the steps as delineated earlier for creating a new partition.

Figure 5.9 Creating New Logical Drive

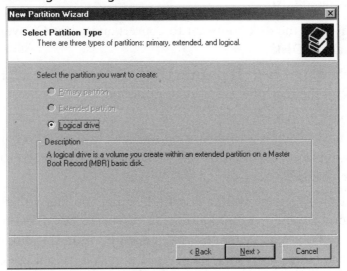

Deleting a Partition or Logical Drive

To delete a partition or logical drive, right-click on it and select either **Delete Partition** or **Delete Logical Drive**. In either case, you'll receive a warning that states that all data on the volume will be lost. If you do not want to wipe out the data, click **No** to exit. Otherwise, if you're absolutely sure you want to delete the partition or logical drive, click **Yes**. If you created a partition or logical drive just to test things out, deleting it is no big deal. If you've got data on a partition or logical drive, you should make sure you have all the data backed up (if it's data you want to preserve) before deleting a partition or logical drive because there is no "undo" function. Also, you can't delete an extended partition that has logical drives on it until you've deleted all the logical drives.

Converting a Basic Disk to a Dynamic Disk

There are a limited number of things you can do with basic disks, as you've just seen. We can create primary or extended partitions, create logical drives within extended partitions, format the partitions, assign drive letters, and add compression to the files and folders on that drive. Now we get into the more fluid, virtual world of dynamic disks. Remember, dynamic disks use disk space on two or more disk drives to create a larger chunk of disk space. The first step in using dynamic disks is to convert your disk from a basic disk to a dynamic disk. Use the following steps from the Disk Management console to convert your basic disk(s) to dynamic disk(s).

1. Right-click the disk you want to convert and select **Convert to Dynamic Disk**.

2. On the **Convert to Dynamic Disk** screen, you'll see a list of basic disks on the machine. Select one or more drives to convert to dynamic disks, then click **OK.**

3. The next screen is a confirmation screen. If you want to convert the disks displayed, click **Convert** to continue. Otherwise, go back and make changes.

4. A warning message will be displayed, letting you know that no other version of Windows can use these drives. Click **Yes** to continue. If you want to boot your system from Windows 98 from this disk drive, for instance (why you would, I'll never know), you cannot use dynamic disks. (See "Best Practices According to Microsoft" earlier in this chapter).

5. If you have no file systems on the drive(s) to be converted, you're done, the drive is converted and off you go.

6. If you have file systems on the drive(s) to be converted, you'll get a warning that the file systems will be dismounted prior to converting. Click **Yes** to proceed. All existing partitions will be converted to simple volumes and from there, you can create various dynamic disk configurations.

Working with Dynamic Disks

We've already talked about how to convert a basic disk to a dynamic disk. Next, we'll look at various ways to configure and work with dynamic disks.

Creating a Volume

This process is very similar to creating a new partition, except now we're working with a disk that has been converted to a dynamic disk. That gives you a couple more options to configure, but you'll see that the process is very similar. Use the following steps to create a new volume:

1. In the Disk Management console, right-click the unallocated disk and select **New Volume** from the menu.

2. When the New Volume Wizard launches, click **Next** to continue.

3. On the **Select Volume Type** screen, select the type of volume you want to create from among the options listed. As we discussed earlier, you can create the following types of dynamic disks in SBS: simple, spanned, mirrored, striped or RAID-5. Spanned, mirrored, and striped disks require two (or more) drives. RAID-5 requires three or more drives. It's recommended that you implement RAID-5 as a hardware solution rather than via software. Click **Next** to continue.

4. The next screen, **Select Disks**, allows you to select which disks you want to include in the type of dynamic disk volume you selected in the previous step. Your options are based upon that earlier selection. Follow the on-screen instructions based on the type of volume you are creating. If you're not sure what you're doing at this point, you can cancel out and go to **Start | Help and Support** and type in the your query (**how to create spanned volume**, for instance) about the type of volume you want to create. However, the on-screen instructions are typically very clear, so you should be able to walk your way through the volume setup using the on-screen instructions.

5. As with creating a new partition, the next step is to **Assign Drive Letter or Path.** You can assign a drive letter, mount the volume in an NTFS folder, or not assign a drive letter or path to the volume. Click **Next** to continue.

6. The next screen is the **Format Volume** screen, where you can choose whether or not to format the volume. If you choose to format the volume, you can select the file system, allocation unit size, and volume label. If you don't want to check for errors, you can perform a quick format, though a standard format is a better choice. You can also set file and folder compression for the new volume at this point. You're probably better off not enabling compression at this point unless you have a clear reason to do so. Click **Next** to continue.

Deleting a Volume

The process of deleting a volume is the same as deleting a partition on a basic disk. Select the volume you want to delete, right-click it and select **Delete Volume**. You'll see a warning message indicating that all data on the volume will be lost. If you have a good backup or if you have no data on the volume you want to save, click **Yes**, otherwise click **No** to exit without deleting the volume. Once you've deleted the volume, the space reverts to "unallocated."

Mounting a Volume

Mounting a volume is a concept borrowed from the UNIX world. Mounting a volume creates a pointer in an NTFS folder (cannot be FAT or FAT32). A volume can be mounted on any empty subfolder of an existing NTFS drive or volume. Although the concept may seem strange to you at first, it can be a useful tool for providing different storage options for users without overwhelming them with drive letters. A mounted volume in a folder called "Finance" might be easier for finance users to find than "Drive K:".

When we created a new partition or a new volume (in basic and dynamic disk sections), the **Assign Drive Letter or Path** screen provided the option to **Mount in the following empty NTFS folder**. This is one way to mount a volume during the partition or volume creation process. You can access that same screen by right-clicking the desired volume and selecting **Change Drive Letter and Paths** from the menu.

Figure 5.10 shows a mounted volume on Disk 1, with a volume label of **MountedVolume1**. This volume is *mounted* on Disk 0 on the volume labeled **Drive 0 Partition 2 (F:)**. Figure 5.11 shows that the mounted volume can be accessed via the F: drive. Figure 5.12 shows that the mounted volume is not displayed in My Computer and can be accessed only via the F: drive pointer.

Mounted volumes are physically located on a particular drive but the pointer or access point to that volume can be located elsewhere. This can be useful in organizing storage for users or applications. If you want to unmount the volume, you need to assign a drive letter to the volume by right-clicking the volume, selecting **Change Drive Letter and Paths**, clicking **Add**, then selecting the drive letter. You can also mount the drive to a different location or add multiple mount points for the same volume so that you can access this volume from several different NTFS folders located on whichever drives you want.

Figure 5.10 Mounted Volume Located on Disk 1

Figure 5.11 Mounted Volume Located on Disk 0 Drive F:

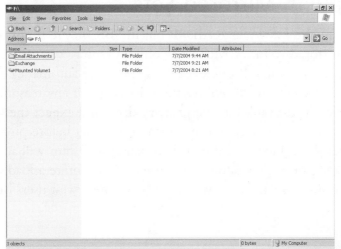

Figure 5.12 Mounted Volume Not Displayed in My Computer

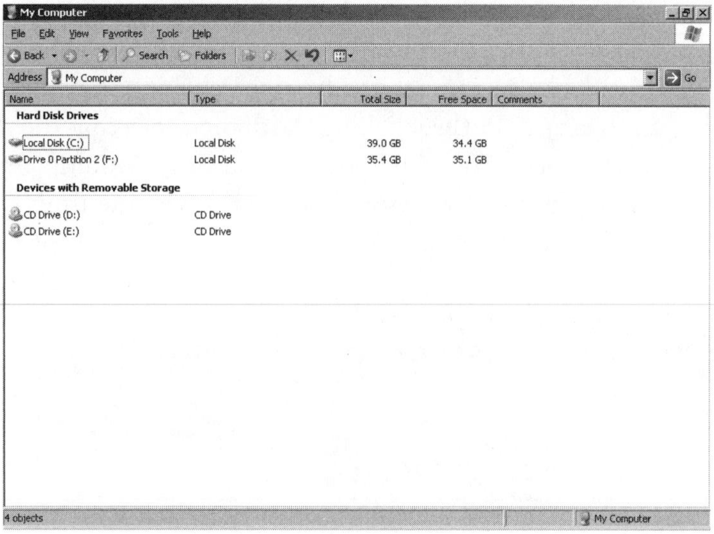

SOME INDEPENDENT ADVICE

Mounting volumes can be a useful tool for helping users access disk space without having to navigate all over the place to find the right location. However, make sure you have a plan for how you're setting all this up and keep it simple. You don't need to create a maze for yourself while trying to simplify things for your users.

Working with Mirrored Sets

Mirrored sets are also known as RAID-1, but in SBS, they're simply called mirrored sets or mirrored volumes. Mirrored volumes require two drives and each is an exact image of the other. If one drive fails, the other automatically becomes the active drive. If you want to remove the mirror set for any reason, keep in mind that you can't just yank out the primary drive and expect the secondary drive to kick in. Instead, you should break the mirror set before physically removing either drive. However, if one drive fails, the system will automatically handle it. Creating or re-generating a mirrored set puts quite a load on the server, so try to do these activities when you have the fewest users on the system.

Creating a Mirrored Set

You must begin with dynamic disks, so if you haven't converted from basic to dynamic, do so now (instructions are found earlier in this chapter). Then, use the following steps in the Disk Management console:

1. Select the volume you want to mirror and right-click it. If a potential mirror is available, the Add Mirror menu item is available. Select the **Add Mirror** command.

2. In the **Add Mirror** dialog box, select the disk that will be the mirror volume. Click **Add Mirror** to create the mirror.

The system will generate a mirror volume on the selected drive. Figure 5.13 shows a mirror set created with a volume on Disk 0 (labeled **Disk 0 Volume 2(F:)**) and Disk 1. The exact same amount of space on the first volume on Disk 0 is allocated on Disk 1 and the remaining segment of approximately 2GB is left as unallocated space.

Figure 5.13 Creating a Mirror Set

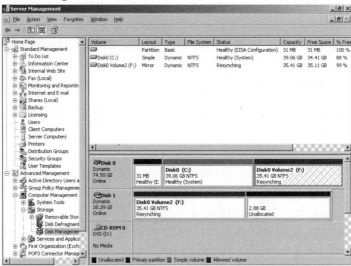

If a mirrored volume fails, the system will continue to operate normally. On the server, you will get a pop-up message indicating your fault tolerance has failed (you can also see this error in **Start | Administrative Tools | Event Viewer | System** log). This message is titled **Windows – FT Orphaning**. Orphaning occurs when a volume fails and the set is no longer complete. Though your system will continue to run, you have no fault tolerance, so you should make sure you have a solid backup and replace the volume as soon as possible.

Removing a Mirrored Set

Removing a mirrored set is a relatively simple process. It will not impact any data on the primary drive and the secondary (mirrored) drive will become unallocated space. Use the following steps in the Disk Management console to remove a mirror.

1. Right-click either mirrored disk (primary or secondary). Select **Remove Mirror** from the menu.

2. In the **Remove Mirror** dialog box, select the disk you want to remove from the mirror set. Click **Remove Mirror** to complete this task. The volume removed from the mirror reverts to unallocated space. The remaining volume contains the original data.

Breaking a Mirrored Set

Breaking a mirrored set occurs if one of the disks in the mirrored set fails. Since you cannot access the disk, you cannot remove the mirror. Instead, you must break the mirror. Use the following steps from within the Disk Management console to break a mirrored set.

1. Right-click either of the mirrored volumes. Select **Break Mirror** from the menu.

2. You will be asked to confirm this selection. Click **Yes** to break the mirror or click **No** to exit without breaking the mirrored set. One of the volumes retains the drive letter of the original mirror and the other is assigned the next available drive letter. Both will contain exact duplicates of the data, but as soon as the mirror is broken, the data will no longer be duplicated on both drives.

3. If you are breaking a mirror due to a problem with one drive, replace the failed drive and re-create your mirrored set using the steps listed earlier.

RAID-5

As mentioned, SBS supports RAID-5 as either a hardware or software configuration. It's best to implement RAID-5 via RAID hardware (which must be purchased separately). The reason is that the necessary data management tasks involved with RAID are best off-loaded to specialized hardware. Otherwise, implementing RAID-5 via the SBS software means placing a fairly heavy load on the server hardware and software. The more time the server has to spend managing RAID-5, the less time it has to do other server tasks. That's why we keep recommending hardware versus software RAID-5. That said, we'll briefly walk through setting up software RAID-5 in SBS in this section.

Many of the tasks you can do with a mirrored volume can also be done with a RAID-5 volume, including creating a volume, assigning a mount point or drive letter, formatting, and using RAID-5 after a single disk failure. However, you cannot add or remove drives from your RAID-5 array. You can remove and replace a failed drive, but you cannot simply opt to keep that failed drive out and run on the remaining drives. To do that, you have to back up your data and completely rebuild your array—no easy task. If you're using hardware RAID-5, it may actually support more dynamic reconfigurations, so check the manufacturer's documentation.

To configure RAID-5 using software in SBS, open the Disk Management console. Next, use the following steps to create a RAID-5 set.

1. Right-click the unallocated space on one of the dynamic disks you want to use for your RAID-5 set and click **New Volume**.

2. In the **New Volume Wizard**, click **Next**, then click **RAID-5** and follow the on-screen instructions (these will vary based on your specific hardware configuration).

Disk Troubleshooting

There are a number of problems that might crop up with your dynamic disks. Typically the problems involve drives not being initialized properly or failure of the drive or controller. If you start physically moving drives around (on or between systems), you'll find there's a whole world of trouble you can get yourself into. Figure 5.14 shows the Disk Management Troubleshooting Help screen. You can access these Help files by selecting **Start | Help and Support** or from the Disk Management console Help. Use this section as well as the Microsoft website if you run into problems with your disks—basic or dynamic. Follow the troubleshooting steps to the letter because you can create a lot of problems for yourself if you start changing things around without having properly determined the root cause of the problem. For instance, a mirror or RAID-5 controller failure might initially look like a drive failure. In this case, you'd be tempted to swap out the drive only to find you still have a problem. Instead, check the troubleshooting steps based on your exact symptoms.

Figure 5.14 Disk Troubleshooting Help Files

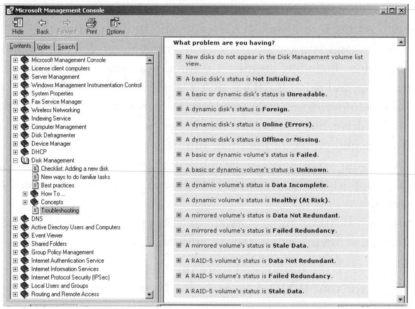

For mirror and RAID-5 drives, you can also use the **Event Viewer** to check the system log. The system log will give you a much more accurate picture of what's gone wrong and will give you a solid foundation upon which to troubleshoot your disk issue. To access the Event Viewer and the system log, click **Start | Administrative Tools | Event Viewer**. Once the Event Viewer is open, click **System** in the left-hand pane and examine disk-related messages in the right-hand pane. You can double-click any event in the right-hand pane to see details of that event or choose **Action | Properties** from the menu (or right-click the event and choose **Properties**).

BEST PRACTICES ACCORDING TO MICROSOFT

- Use Event Viewer to check the system log if a mirrored or RAID-5 drive fails.
- If you have both local disks (in the computer) and Storage Area Network disks, use dynamic disks on either the local disks or the SAN, not both.
- Never break a healthy mirrored set and expect the system to run on the mirrored drive. If one drive fails, the system will make needed changes to allow the mirrored volume to be used. However, this cannot be done manually.
- If Disk Management shows a missing dynamic disk, do not delete the missing disk's volumes or select the **Remove Disk** option unless you intentionally removed the physical disk from the system and do not intend to ever reattach it.
- Don't delete or create a partition on a dynamic disk when the computer has been started from the Recovery Console. Doing so could cause permanent data loss.
- Dynamic disks are not supported for use with Windows clustering. Use a third-party program such as Veritas Software Volume Manager 4.0 to provide this capability.

SOME INDEPENDENT ADVICE

If for some reason you're a big fan of using the command line to do your tasks rather than using the Windows interface, you can manage all of your disk tasks via command line utilities. We won't go into those here, but if you're curious or if you want to use the command line utilities, click **Start | Help and Support** (or **Help** from within Disk Management console) and select **Disk Management** from the contents in the left-hand pane. You can learn about disk management **concepts**, **how to** do various tasks, **troubleshooting** and **best practices**. Within the various **how to** topics, you'll be given the choice between stepping through the task using the Windows interface or the command line. The choice is yours, but the easier way to go is almost always the Windows interface.

One More Time

In this chapter, you learned the basics of disk management from terminology to concepts to step-by-step instructions to accomplish a variety of tasks. You should understand the following concepts about disks and disk management:

☑ Disk drives can be divided into different segments. These are called partitions or volumes.

☑ Basic disks can have up to four primary partitions or three primary partitions and one extended partition.

☑ Extended partitions can have logical drives on them.

☑ Dynamic disks allow you to use disk space across multiple drives to better utilize disk space on the system.

☑ Dynamic disks use segments called volumes, which are the equivalent of partitions on basic disks.

☑ Dynamic disks can be configured as simple, spanned, striped, mirrored or striped with parity, referred to in SBS as RAID-5.

☑ RAID-5 can be implemented via the SBS software but is best implemented using third-party hardware for better performance.

☑ Drives can be roughly divided into two types: IDE or SCSI. Each format has a number of different flavors but they fall within these two general categories. Make sure your drive(s) and controller(s) match each other or you'll run into problems.

☑ You can convert a disk from basic to dynamic but if you have data on the drives and want to convert back, you must back up your data, convert back to basic and restore your data.

☑ All disk management tasks are performed either from the Disk Management console or by using command line utilities. Typically, it's much easier to manage disks using the Windows interface (the Disk Management console) than via the command line.

Chapter 6

Managing File Storage

- Configuring and Managing Disk Quotas
- File Encryption Management
- Disk and File Compression
- Shadow Copy Concepts

The End Result

By the end of this chapter, you'll understand key concepts in managing file storage on your network including how to set and monitor disk quotas, how to enable and manage file encryption, and what shadow copies are and how to configure them. These three tools will help you better manage storage on your network disks and at the end of this chapter, you'll know how to implement and manage these features.

Configuring and Managing Disk Quotas

Disk quotas can be a helpful tool in restricting users from storing hundreds of gigabytes of useless, outdated, or unneeded files. The old adage that things expand to fill the space allotted holds true with users and disk storage. If a user has 10MB or 10GB or 100GB, he or she will likely find a way to use it. Although disk space is relatively inexpensive these days, applications tend to chew up more and more space, so that disk drive suddenly doesn't look so big once you've installed your software. Using disk quotas can be a good way to keep user files in check and help reduce the complexity (and size) of data backups.

Part of storage management is ensuring that old and unneeded files are occasionally weeded out and discarded. Disk quotas can be a good way to get users in the habit of cleaning out their disk storage areas from time to time. As with every management task in SBS, you'll need to find the balance between reasonable disk storage restrictions and heavy-handed restrictions. The network is a tool for users, so you'll need to make sure the quotas you establish are user-friendly. Look at current disk usage (either on network shares or on user's computers) to see how much space is currently being used by the average user. Use this as your foundation for establishing reasonable disk quotas, but allow for growth. For instance, you may establish current usage as roughly 20MB per user. Given the capacity of your server disk drives, you may choose to establish quotas at 50MB per user knowing that you plan on increasing employee headcount by 50% over the next three years. With employee growth and 50MB of storage, you have determined that you still have additional disk space available for user storage, if needed. Now, let's look at how to configure quotas.

Accessing Disk Quota Information

As you recall, you can set disk quotas so that the users who have access to the disk cannot exceed a set limit. To set the disk quota, you right-click the disk and select **Properties** then click the **Quota** tab (shown in Figure 6.1).

Figure 6.1 Access Quota Tab in Disk Properties

1. Enable the **Enable quota management** option to establish disk quotas. If this is not checked, disk quotas will not be enabled.

2. Enable the **Deny disk space to users exceeding quota limit** option if you want to establish hard quotas. If this option is not selected, you are establishing soft quotas. Soft quotas are more like friendly suggestions than actual quotas.

3. Use the following three settings to set the default quota limits for all new users on the volume:

   - **Do not limit disk usage** This setting will not limit usage for new users. If you have selected the setting **Deny disk space to users exceeding quota limit**, only new users will be able to bypass this. It's a strange combination of settings, so use care here.

   - **Limit disk space to** You can set the limit on a per-user basis. If you establish a quota lower than what current users are using, those users will be unable to store any more data until they go below the set limit.

- **Set warning level to** Set the warning level below the quota at a level that will be a useful warning level for users. Don't let them get right to the edge of the quota before notifying them there may be a problem.

4. The next two options are for logging events related to disk quotas. Disk events are logged in the system log, which can be accessed via **Start | Administrative Tools | Event Viewer**. Select the **System** node on the left of the Event Viewer console and the system events are shown in the right pane.

- **Log event when a user exceeds their quota limit** If a user hits their quota limit, whether you've set hard or soft quotas, an event will be logged. This may be helpful in determining if the quotas are too low or if the users are not managing their allotted disk space well. There is no right answer here and only log these events if you're actually going to review them and do something about them. Information you don't use just creates a messy environment.

- **Log event when a user exceeds their warning level** This event will let you know when users reach their warning levels. Again, if you aren't going to do something with this information, there's not much point in logging it.

SOME INDEPENDENT ADVICE

Disk quotas are a useful tool in managing user disk space usage. It's usually best to implement hard quotas since soft quotas will simply nag the user rather than actually limiting the disk space he or she can use. A user should have at least 2MB of disk space available, and much more if they regularly work with large files such as image or sound files.

Users may get an error message when they try to log in stating:

"Windows cannot log you on because your profile cannot be loaded. Check that you are connected to the network, or that your network is functioning properly. If this problem persists, contact your network administrator. Detail – There is not enough space on the disk."

To fix this problem, check the disk quota for the user or group of users and increase it if necessary. If the user's quota is reasonable, the user will have to delete files to free up disk space. Work with your management or Human Resources department in defining and implementing these kinds of policies and make sure users are well aware of them. Information is a great way to avoid user problems, questions and frustration.

Establishing Quotas for Specific Users

As with many other user-related settings in SBS, the first thing that should come to mind is: Avoid creating individual settings whenever possible. When you only have a few users, individualized settings are relatively simple to manage. If you have 50 users, however, you run into more complexity and that's not a good thing—for managing the network or for security. So, while you can set disk quotas for individual users, try to avoid doing this. Instead, set quotas for groups of users via templates (if you're not familiar with using templates, refer to Chapter 7, "Managing Users and Groups" for information on how to use templates—it's important not to alter the pre-defined templates, so make sure you read up on that subject if it's new to you).

For instance, the folks in your Marketing department may have lots of image and sound files that are large and they need more disk space than, say, the folks in the Finance department who primarily work from Excel spreadsheets. In this case, you can provide a larger disk quota to the Marketing group rather than the individuals in that group. You'll learn more about managing users and groups later in this book, so for now just keep in mind that you should manage groups rather than individual users, whenever possible. That said, you may want or need to provide different disk quotas for specific individuals in the organization. If you do so, make sure you document that clearly so you (or another network administrator) can address issues that may arise with those custom settings.

In order to set quotas for groups, you should create a template that implements disk quotas. You can specify the quota in the template and all user accounts based on that template will use the same disk quota. You can set quotas for a disk drive by right-clicking the drive and selecting **Properties** then clicking the **Quota** tab. The quotas you set here will be applied to new users on the volume. You can also choose to log events if users exceed their quota or hit their warning levels.

1. Right-click the drive for which you want to establish specific quotas.

2. Select **Properties**, click the **Quota** tab, then click the **Quota Entries** button.

3. You'll notice a number of built-in groups listed. If you have not added any users yet, that's all you'll see in the Quota Entries dialog box. For this exercise, double-click the **User Template** (or right-click and select **Properties**), as shown in Figure 6.2.

Figure 6.2 Disk Quota Settings for Users

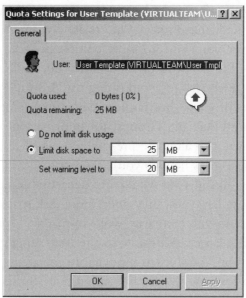

4. Set the disk quota and warning level to an appropriate size for all users. In this example, users are given 25 MB of disk storage and their warning level is set to 20MB.

5. After setting the desired limit and warning level, click **OK**.

6. In the Quota Entries dialog box, the new limit and warning level are now displayed for the **User Template**.

By default, there is no limit set for the Administrators group. That's probably fine, just keep an eye on disk usage by members of this account. The user is "charged" for disk space in cases where the file or folder is not a shared folder. Typically, folders that contain shared files are not limited.

Importing and Exporting Quotas

You can import or export disk quotas. Why, you ask? Well, suppose you've set up different quotas for different groups on one disk and you believe you've found the perfect mix. Rather than re-establishing all those quotas on another disk, you can import them from the original disk. It sounds good in theory, but there are a couple of areas that might bite you. First, if you import quotas, you'll wipe out the quotas you've established on the disk (to which you're importing quotas). Also, if you enable the **Do this for all quota entries** option, you will over-write current quota settings without confirmation or warning. If you import lower quotas than existing users have on the disk, they'll be instantly locked out. Now that you know the pitfalls, you can use the following steps to import or export quotas.

1. Select the volume whose quotas you want to export. Right-click the drive, select **Properties**, click the **Quota** tab, then click the **Quota Entries** button.

2. On the menu, click **Quota** and select **Export**. Browse to the location where you want to save the quota entries file that will be created (this is the file you'll import on the other disk to establish the same quotas).

3. Enter the name for the file and click **Save.**

4. On the target disk, right-click the disk, select **Properties**, click the **Quota** tab, then click the **Quota Entries** button.

5. On the menu, click **Quota** and select **Import**. Browse to the location in you saved the file in Step 3, select the file, and click **Open**.

6. If quotas already exist on the target volume, you'll get the warning shown in Figure 6.3. If you are sure you want to overwrite the settings, click **OK**. Otherwise, click **No** or **Cancel**. Only select **Do this for all quota entries** if you want to overwrite all quotas on the target volume without confirmation (there is no undo function, either).

Figure 6.3 Quota Import Warning

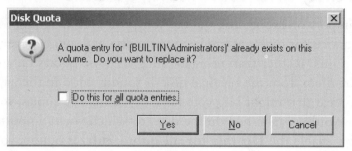

BEST PRACTICES ACCORDING TO MICROSOFT

- Apply appropriate disk quota limits. Some user groups may need more disk space than others. Don't unreasonably limit users' ability to store needed files.
- By default, the Administrator account is not limited. Make sure not to limit the Administrator account, as you may be unable to perform administrative tasks if disk quotas are set.
- Plan for growth. Set reasonable limits and think about how your organization is likely to grow in the next 12-24 months. Based on anticipated growth, set disk quotas accordingly. Constantly re-adjusting quotas is time-consuming and subject to errors.
- Set default limits and modify only those users and/or groups that require greater access.
- Delete users' quotas if they no longer require access to the volume. It will free up disk space.
- Operating system or application installations can require a great deal of disk space during the installation. Install using the local Administrator account or do not set limits on volumes where these installations will occur. Setting limits on these volumes or running the installation from a non-Administrator account could cause the installation to fail due to insufficient disk space, due solely to the quota limit.

Quota Reports

You can create quota reports quickly and easily by opening the Quota Entries dialog box for a given volume and dragging the desired entries into Word, Excel, or another program. The supported file formats include Rich Text Format (RTF) and Comma Separated Value (CSV), used by Word and Excel, respectively. Two other formats supported are CF_UNICODETEXT and CF_TEXT. You can also copy and paste into Notepad, though the column alignment will be off.

SOME INDEPENDENT ADVICE

Disk quotas are a good way to manage those few users who inevitably store thousands of files or who want to store some humongous video file on the disk. However, as with all things SBS, keep it simple. Apply default disk quotas then modify them only for groups of users that really need larger quotas. Also, remember to plan for future growth when establishing quotas. This isn't something you want to have to constantly manage, so establish reasonable quotas that should be good for a year or so. If your company grows faster than you anticipated, that's a good thing and you can make adjustments along the way.

File Encryption Management

The *encrypting file system* (EFS) included in SBS is a great feature for security on the network storage. Encryption is the process of scrambling data so that only those with the 'key' can unlock the data and gain access to it. The nice thing about file encryption in SBS is that it's virtually invisible to the users. This is important because security is strongest when it doesn't require human beings to remember to do something. With SBS encryption, the data will automatically be encrypted if the file or folder in which the file is stored has encryption enabled. No action on the part of the user is required once encryption is enabled. As the network administrator, you may want to designate certain folders for sensitive files and enable encryption on those folders. Simple, easy, no hassle security. Well, that's not *all* there is to security, but it's a very easy component to implement and has virtually no administrative overhead for you.

When file encryption is enabled, the user that created the file (called the *owner* or *creator*) will not notice any difference. Every time he or she opens or saves the file, everything looks normal. If an unauthorized person was to get a hold of that file, though, what they'll see when they open the file will be garbage because the file is encrypted.

Encryption can be done on a per-folder or per-file basis. Typically, it's easier (and recommended) to enable encryption for a folder and store all sensitive files in that folder where they'll be automatically encrypted. As the owner/creator of a file or folder, you can also grant access to that file or folder to others and they'll be able to open, read, modify, and save that encrypted file as well.

One important thing to know about encryption is how encryption works when it's first enabled. If a folder has files and subfolders in it and you, the administrator, encrypt the folder, all *new* files and folders created in the encrypted folder will be encrypted. However, the *existing* files and subfolders will not be encrypted unless you specifically choose this option (see Step 3 in the steps that follow). If you choose to encrypt the folder and all existing files and subfolders in that folder, you will be the only one who can open those files because you enabled encryption on the folder. To avoid this problem with existing files, you should select to enable encryption only for the folder. When encryption for the folder is enabled, all new files and subfolders will be encrypted but existing files can be opened, edited, and saved as before (unencrypted). The key difference is that any file saved with a different name becomes encrypted because it is considered a new file. If sensitive files exist, work with users to identify those files and to encrypt them. If you encrypt them, you become the owner of the file, which is probably not the desired outcome.

To enable encryption, use the following steps:

1. Right-click the file or folder to be encrypted. Select **Properties**, click the **General** tab, then click the **Advanced** button.

2. In the Compress or Encrypt attributes section, select **Encrypt contents to secure data**. Notice that if you click the **Encrypt** option, you cannot also click the **Compress** option. That's because files cannot be both compressed *and* encrypted. Click **OK**.

3. The **Confirm Attribute Change** dialog box will be displayed. You can choose one of two options here. You can apply the change to **this folder only** or to **this folder, subfolders and files**. This dialog box also appears if you choose the **Compress** option instead of the **Encrypt** option. If you browse to the file or folder you just encrypted via Windows Explorer, you'll notice the attributes list contains the letter **E** to indicate the folder is encrypted.

To remove encryption, follow the steps above, ensuring you clear (deselect) the **Encrypt contents to secure data** checkbox listed in Step 2.

File Encryption Recovery Agent

As network administrators, we always have to plan for the worst-case scenario. What if the owner of a very important document places it in an encrypted folder and then suddenly leaves the company or gets ill and doesn't come to work for three months? How can you recover the file?

By default, the Administrator can recover an encrypted file by using a built-in feature called the Data Recovery Agent (DRA). The DRA can open any encrypted file as a fail-safe option for recovering sensitive data. In order to maintain security, however, once the DRA has unencrypted the file, it cannot be re-encrypted by the DRA. This prevents an intruder from unencrypting the file, stealing the data, and then covering his or her tracks by re-encrypting it. A file that has been unencrypted by the DRA remains unencrypted to provide positive proof the file has been compromised and is no longer secure.

To view the Data Recovery Agent for a particular file or folder, select that file or folder, right-click, choose **Properties**, and click **Advanced** on the **General** tab. In the **Advanced Attributes** dialog, click the **Details** button. In the **Encryption Details** dialog box, you can view a list of who has access to the file (to whom the file owner has granted permission to access the encrypted file) as well as the Data Recovery Agent as defined by the Recovery Policy (we'll talk about policies later in this book). The Recovery Policy is a defined set of rules in SBS that determines which accounts or users can act as DRAs.

If an owner wants to grant permission to users to access the encrypted file, he or she can add users in the **Encryption Details** dialog box as well. These users will be able to work with the file as if it was not encrypted. In order to add users, they must have a valid *certificate*. A certificate is a way of verifying, with certainty, the identity of the user so that no one else can pretend to be that user, much like a fingerprint is used to specifically verify a person's identity. We'll talk about certificates in more detail later in the book. If you're not familiar with certificates or with using EFS, you may want to read up on that before you enable EFS. If certificates and recovery keys are mismanaged or lost, a file may not be able to be unencrypted.

BEST PRACTICES ACCORDING TO MICROSOFT

- Create encrypted folders for storing sensitive files before the files are created. This will ensure sensitive files stored in the folder are automatically encrypted.
- Encrypting folders provides better security than encrypting individual files because many programs create temporary files during editing. If the original file is not located in an encrypted folder, the temporary file is not encrypted.
- Use Microsoft Certificate Services to manage EFS and Data Recovery Agent DRA certificates and private keys.
- Encrypt sensitive data on member computers.
- Set encryption on the **My Documents** folder on users' computers and laptops to ensure sensitive data is encrypted. If a laptop is stolen, it will be more difficult to steal the data from the hard drive.
- Encrypt an application's **Temp** folder if the application's files contain sensitive information.
- For very sensitive documents, use Internet Protocol Security (IPSec) to ensure data remains encrypted as it is transmitted over the network.
- Regularly back up the entire server that stores server-based encrypted data. In the event a data restoration is needed, the files and their decryption keys will be restored. Partial backups may not include the needed decryption keys.
- The **RSA** folder on the server is where recovery keys are stored. Do not tamper with this folder in any manner or you could lose your ability to recover encrypted files.

A file that is encrypted remains encrypted when it is backed up and restored. If the file changes ownership, the file remains encrypted and the new owner can open, modify, save, and add users to the encrypted file. If the owner moves the file to a folder that is not encrypted, the file will not be encrypted. If the encrypted file is moved to another disk or computer that does not support encryption, the encryption will be removed. One downside to file encryption is that you can only add individual users to the permissions to access the file. If the entire Finance department needs access to a salary spreadsheet that is encrypted, each individual user must be added. This goes against the commonly-cited best practice of adding groups, not individual users, in order to grant permissions. Keep this in mind as you work with EFS.

Disk and File Compression

Although you cannot use EFS and compression together, there may be files and folders that do not contain sensitive data that are just taking up lots of room. Files and folders (as well as disks) can be compressed to save space. Although disk space is increasingly inexpensive, it seems to go hand-in-hand with applications and operating systems getting bigger and bigger, so your net gain is zero. In order to more effectively manage storage, you can set files, folders, and disks to use compression. Remember, though, you can't use both compression and EFS at the same time.

You can compress files, folders, and programs using one of two compression methods—NTFS (New Technology File System) compression or the Compressed (zipped) Folders feature. If your drives are not formatted using NTFS, you can't use NTFS compression.

To use NTFS compression on a file or folder:

1. Locate the file or folder, right-click it, and click **Properties**.

2. On the **General** tab, click **Advanced**. This is the same place you access to enable encryption and if you recall, the two checkboxes are either/or meaning you can only select one of the two.

3. Click **Compress contents to save disk space**, then click **OK.** When you view the file or folder in Windows Explorer, it will be listed with the letter C to indicate it is compressed.

4. To view encrypted or compressed files and folders with different colors, click **Tools** and select **Folder Options**. Click the **View** tab, scroll down in the **Advanced** settings section to locate the **Show encrypted or compressed NTFS files in color**. Click **OK**.

To compress an entire disk drive:

1. Access the disk, right-click and select **Properties**.

2. Select the **General** tab and select the checkbox **Compress drive to save disk space**. If you make this selection, you'll be prompted to choose to compress only that folder or all files and subfolders as well. Make your selection and click **OK.**

To use Compressed (zipped) Folders (works on both NTFS and FAT formatted drives), open Windows Explorer. From the menu, select **File | New |**

Compressed (zipped) Folder. You can give the folder any name you want, but the extension must remain .zip. Here are a few tips regarding compressed folders using this option. For ease, we'll refer to this option as *zipped*.

- Files and folders compressed using the zipped compression option can be moved from NTFS to FAT file systems and remain compressed.

- Files and folders compressed using the zipped compression are compatible with other compression programs.

- Folders compressed in this manner are identified by a zipper icon.

- Using this option will not decrease system performance.

- To compress individual files, move them to a compressed folder.

SOME INDEPENDENT ADVICE

You can compress individual files and folders, and you can compress folders without compressing the individual contents. You can work with NTFS-compressed files without decompressing them. You can display NTFS-compressed file and folder names in different colors to easily differentiate them.

Here's what you can't do: You can't compress encrypted files, and you can't encrypt compressed files. You might also find decreased performance working with compressed files because when you open a file, Windows will automatically decompress it for you and when you save/close a file, Windows will automatically compress it for you. The work required to compress and decompress a file can slow your system down.

Shadow Copy Concepts

Shadow copies of shared folders is a disk storage feature that provides an extra layer of redundancy to certain folders. Shadow copies of shared folders (which we'll simply refer to as *shadow copies* from here on out) provide snapshots of files in a shared folder. This is useful because you can view, open, or modify shared folders and files as they existed at a particular point in time. You can go back and recover an older version of a file that you mistakenly edited or recover a file you accidentally deleted.

As the network administrator, a fair amount of your time can be consumed by users contacting you for help finding or recovering files they accidentally deleted or changed. Rather than resorting to your backups, shadow copies give you the ability to store up to 64 snapshots of a shared folder. You can recover a deleted file or a file that was accidentally overwritten, or compare versions of two files. In one study, the number of requests to the help desk related to file recovery dropped from 20-30 per month to 1-2 per month after enabling shadow copies of shared folders.

One important limitation is that you must enable shadow copies of shared folders on a per-volume basis. You cannot select specific shared folders and files on a volume for shadow copying and exclude others on the same volume. The shadow copies feature is enabled by default on the volume that holds the *Users* shared folder in SBS. Shadow copies do take up disk storage, so you need to plan in advance how much disk space you're willing to devote to this and how you're going to manage it.

One important note is that you should finish all your disk management tasks before enabling shadow copies. For instance, if you're going to convert from basic to dynamic disks or create new volumes, do so before enabling shadow copies. Making changes to the underlying disk structure can sometimes wipe out shadow copies. Once your users get used to having access to shadow copies, they'll probably come to rely on it and you don't want to suddenly wipe out shadow copies that users have been relying on.

Enabling Shadow Copies of Shared Folders

To enable shadow copies of shared folders, use the following steps from the Computer Management console (**Start | Administrative Tools | Computer Management**).

1. Locate **Shared Folders** in the left pane of the Computer Management console.

2. Right-click **Shared Folders** and select **Configure Shadow Copies.** This will launch the dialog box shown in Figure 6.4.

3. Click the volume on which you want to enable shadow copies and click **Enable.**

4. You'll receive a warning message that shadow copies are not appropriate for servers with high I/O (input/output) loads. If you are sure you want to proceed, click **Yes.** Otherwise, click **No**. Not all operating systems

can work with shadow copies. For more information on the restrictions, click the link provided (also see the next section, *Configuring Clients to Use Shadow Copies* for information on operating system restrictions).

5. To configure the settings for the shadow copy, select the volume you want to configure and click **Settings**. You can specify where you want the shadow copy stored (best practices suggest it be stored on a different volume for better performance). You can specify whether or not there will be a size limit. You can also click the **Schedule** button to specify how often and when the shadow copy is created. By default, a shadow copy is created twice per day. It's a good idea to set a size limit so your shadow copies don't chew up all available disk space. The limit will cause the oldest version to be deleted when a new version needs to be added based on the schedule.

6. To create a new schedule, click **New.** Specify the desired schedule and click **OK.**

7. Use the **Advanced** button to specify more advanced scheduling options including start and end date, and repeat tasks. Click **OK** to accept changes and close the dialog box, or click **Cancel** to exit without saving changes.

To disable shadow copies, right click the target volume and select **Configure Shadow Copies.** Select the shadow copy volume and click **Disable.** Note that disabling shadow copying will delete all previously saved shadow copies for that volume.

Figure 6.4 Shadow Copy Settings

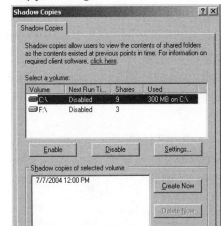

Configuring Clients to Use Shadow Copies

Shadow copies can be accessed by users on computers running Windows Server 2003 because this feature is native to the operating system. Users running Windows XP (Professional and Home editions), Windows 2000 (Service Pack 3 or later) Server, Windows 2000 Professional, and Windows 98 have to have the Shadow Copies of Shared Folders client installed manually to use this feature. The client software can be accessed on the Windows Server 2003 CD or from the Microsoft website at www.microsoft.com/windowsserver2003/downloads/shadowcopyclient.mspx.

To access previous versions (shadow copies) on the client computer, use the following steps.

1. Right-click the network share and select **Properties**.

2. Click the **Previous Versions** tab (note that for the **Previous Versions** tab to be displayed, you must have at least one shadow copy on the server and the client must have the Shadow Copy Client software installed).

3. Select the folder version from the list provided and select one of the available actions (shown in Figure 6.5):

- **View** This will open the selected shadow copy in Windows Explorer. You can open or copy files from there, just as with normal files and folders. You cannot delete files from here, nor can you save files directly to this location.

- **Copy** This will copy the shadow copy of a file to a location you specify. This is useful if you accidentally modify or delete an important file.

- **Restore** This will roll back the shared folder to an earlier point in time based on the snapshot you select. If you've used the System Restore function in Windows XP, it's similar to this feature.

4. Click **OK** to close the dialog box.

Figure 6.5 Using Shadow Copies

To access shadow copies from the server (locally), connect to the shared folder using its Universal Naming Convention (UNC) path, such as **\\sbs2003\Users\JackieB** rather than the local path. There are several ways to do this; one way is to open Windows Explorer and enter the UNC path in the Address bar at the top.

BEST PRACTICES ACCORDING TO MICROSOFT

- Select a different volume on another disk for storing shadow copies. It provides better performance and avoids the possibility that shadow copies will be deleted due to a heavy I/O load on the volume.
- Adjust the shadow copy schedule to fit the work habits of the users using the folders.
- Do not enable shadow copies on volumes that use mount points (mounted on an NTFS folder).
- Do not enable shadow copies on dual-boot computers. The shadow copies may be corrupted or lost when booting into another operating system.
- Do not schedule copies to occur more than once per hour or your users will notice slower performance.
- The upper limit for the number of shadow copies is 64. Once that limit is reached, the oldest copy is deleted.
- The allocation unit size on the disk drive may affect shadow copies, especially if you have to defragment the drive. If this is needed, be aware that you may lose shadow copies that users may be relying upon. For more information, check the Help and Support files on SBS (query phrase: **best practices shadow copies of shared folders**).
- Using shadow copies of shared folders is no substitute for a solid backup procedure.
- Shadow copies do not protect you from disk failure.

SOME INDEPENDENT ADVICE

Shadow copies is a great way to provide a sort of self-service emergency backup system to your users. By allowing them to revert to older versions of files, you'll save yourself a lot of time chasing down important user files that were accidentally modified or deleted. This will certainly reduce the number of e-mails and calls you get requesting help recovering a critical file. Just remember not to set your shadow copy interval to be too frequent or you'll hit your maximum limit much more quickly. To learn more about shadow copies of shared folders, you can download a Microsoft document from www.microsoft.com/windowsserversystem/storage/technologies/shadowcopy/scr.mspx.

One More Time

This brief look at several key storage management features in Windows Small Business Server 2003 included information on managing disk quotas, how they're used, and how they can be helpful in managing user files and folders. You also learned about the Encrypting File System in SBS and how it can be used to keep sensitive files and folders secure. You also learned about shadow copies and how to configure them so users can revert back to older versions of files or recover files that were accidentally deleted, modified, or lost, saving you time and effort because *you* won't have to track down missing files. It's no substitute for a good backup process, but it's a great addition.

- ☑ Configure disk quotes for groups, not individuals, when possible. This makes quota management an easier task.

- ☑ Set a default disk quota amount and provide increases for user groups that need larger disk storage limits.

- ☑ Encrypted files appear as normal files to the owner, but are encrypted so only the owner (and those to whom the owner has granted permission) can access the file.

- ☑ If an intruder manages to open an encrypted file, all that will appear will be random characters—garbage.

- ☑ If an encrypted file is recovered by a Data Recovery Agent, the file will remain unencrypted. This prevents someone from opening the file and closing it back in its encrypted state to cover his or her actions.

- ☑ Users can grant access to an encrypted file to others, but those users must have a certificate. Certificates are discussed later in this book.

- ☑ Files and folders can be compressed to save disk space. Compressing and decompressing files and folders may have an impact on system performance.

- ☑ Compressed files and folders cannot be encrypted, and encrypted files and folders cannot be compressed.

- ☑ Shadow copies create a snapshot of the contents of a shared folder at a frequency and interval specified. This snapshot can be used to recover lost or damaged files.

☑ Shadow copies of shared folders are enabled for an entire volume, not for specific shared folders. When enabled for a volume, all shared folders will have shadow copies enabled. Folders that are not shared will not have shadow copies enabled.

☑ Users can locate shadow copies by connecting to the desired network location, choosing **Properties**, and selecting the **Previous Versions** tab. If this tab is not present, there are no available shadow copies on that volume.

☑ Some operating systems require the Shadow Copy Client to be manually installed. Without this software, these operating systems will not have the **Previous Versions** tab available.

Chapter 7

Managing Users and Groups

- Understanding, Creating, and Managing Groups

- Understanding, Creating and Managing User Accounts

- Understanding and Managing User Profiles

The End Result

At the end of this chapter, you'll understand how to work effectively with groups and users in Windows Small Business Server 2003 (SBS). User accounts and groups provide the framework for security and organization in the SBS network. Throughout this chapter, we'll use the term "user" and "user account" interchangeably, since a user in SBS requires a user account. When you finish this chapter, you'll understand how users and groups are organized and used, and how to manage user accounts and groups so your network remains secure and your users can do their jobs.

Understanding, Creating, and Managing Groups

User accounts and groups form the foundation for managing access to the network. We'll begin by discussing groups because we organize user accounts and assign permissions to users through groups (typically). Once you understand how the groups in SBS are used, we'll look at how groups and user accounts interact.

Understanding Groups

A group is typically a collection of user accounts. While the strict definition of a group in Windows Server 2003 (and SBS) is a bit broader than that, for practical purposes a group is used for managing user accounts. There are two types of groups: security and distribution. Security groups are used to manage (grant and restrict) permissions of users based on group membership. Security groups include built-in groups and custom groups. Distribution groups are not at all related to security groups and are used by e-mail applications to send e-mail to groups of users.

All groups have what is called a *group scope*. The scope indicates the extent to which group permissions are applied in the domain. There are three group scopes: *universal, global*, and *built-in local*. Since SBS only has one domain, the scope is not quite as relevant as it would be in a full Windows Server 2003 installation. If you plan on upgrading to Windows Server 2003 at some point, group scope will become very important.

To view the groups in SBS, open the Server Management console (**Start | Server Management**). In the **Standard Management** section, select **Security Groups** in the left pane to view all security groups in the right pane. To view the scope and other properties of any group, double-click the group in the right pane (or right-click and select **Properties**).

SOME INDEPENDENT ADVICE

Let's talk real estate for a second. SBS Server Management console real estate, to be exact. In Server Management, there are *three distinct areas*. The *left pane* is used to navigate the tree, much like Windows Explorer. The right pane has two regions. The right-most side of the *right pane* contains the specific items under the selected node in the left pane. For instance, when you click **Users** in the left pane, all users are listed in the right side of the right pane. The *left* side of the *right* pane is an area called the *taskpad*. It contains links to tasks specifically associated with both the selected item in the left pane AND the selected item in the right pane (if any). Throughout this book, we'll refer to the three areas of the Server Management console by using the terms *left pane, right pane* and *taskpad*. It's easier when you understand the terminology since it's all about location, location, location.

Built-in Groups

SBS provides a number of built-in groups. These groups are configured around common network tasks that users and administrators perform. As mentioned earlier, these groups can be organized by scope. In SBS, there are eleven built-in universal groups that are used for many of the day-to-day user and account management tasks. There are also four built-in global groups and seven built-in local groups. You can locate these groups by going into Standard Server Management (**Start | Server Management | Standard Management**) and clicking **Security Groups**. All the built-in security groups are listed in the right pane. The taskpad displays several links related to Security Groups.

Built-in Universal Groups

Table 7.1 details the built-in universal groups, the function of each, and the permissions granted to members of that group. When a user account is added to one of these groups, that user gains the permissions granted to the members of that group.

Table 7.1 Built-in Universal Groups

Universal Group Name	Permissions Granted to Group Members
Administrator Templates	Administrators can use templates from this group to create new user accounts.
Domain Power Users	Perform basic network administration including managing user and computer accounts, printers, and Terminal Services. Members of this group cannot log on locally to the domain controller.
Fax Operators	Perform basic fax management tasks including managing fax queues and fax cover pages.
Folder Operators	Manage shared folders in the domain. The Domain Power Users group is a default member of this group.
Mail Operators	Manage Exchange Server mailboxes. The Domain Power Users group is a default member of this group.
Mobile Users	Connect to the server remotely via dial-in or Virtual Private Network (VPN) connections.
Power Users Template	Administrators can use templates from this group to create new user accounts.
Remote Operators	Log on to the server remotely using Terminal Services, but cannot log on locally to the server.
Remote Web Workplace Users	Access the Remote Web Workplace from the Internet.
SharePoint Administrators	Administer the SharePoint website.
Usage Report Users	Access server usage reports.

Built-in Global Groups

Table 7.2 details the built-in global groups, the function of each, and the permissions granted to members of that group. As with all group membership, when a user account is added to one of these groups, that user gains the permissions granted to the members of that group. By default, these accounts have no permissions assigned to them; you must assign all permissions. However, some accounts are already added to these groups by default.

Table 7.2 Built-in Global Groups

Global Group Name	Permissions Granted to Group Members
Domain Admins	The Administrator account is a member of this group by default. This group is also automatically a member of the built-in local Administrators group so that any member of this group can administer any computer on the domain.
Domain Computers	All computers (server and workstations) in the domain are automatically members.
Domain Controllers	The Windows Small Business Server is the domain controller and is the default member of this group.
Domain Users	All domain users are members of this group. This group is automatically a member of the built-in local Users group.

Built-in Local Groups

Table 7.3 details the built-in local groups, the function of each, and the permissions granted to members of that group. As with all group membership, when a user account is added to one of these groups, that user gains the permissions granted to the members of that group. Built-in local groups are created when SBS is installed. These are local groups on the SBS server. These groups cannot be members of other groups and their group scope cannot be changed.

Table 7.3 Built-in Local Groups

Local Group Name	Permissions Granted to Group Members
Account Operators	Account operators can add, change, or delete user and group accounts. The Domain Power Users group is a member of this group.
Administrators	The Administrator account created when SBS is installed is the default member of this group. The Domain Admins global group is part of this group if there are other computers in the domain running Windows XP Professional or Windows 2000 Professional.

Continued

Table 7.3 Built-in Local Groups

Local Group Name	Permissions Granted to Group Members
Backup Operators	Backup operators can log on to the computer to perform backup and restore operations. They do not have permission to change security settings, but can override them, if needed, to successfully perform backup and restore functions.
Guests	The default member of this group is the Guest account. Members of this group have the same access as the Users group.
Print Operators	Print operators have the ability to manage printers and print queues on domain printers. The Domain Power Users universal group is a member of this group by default.
Server Operators	There are no default members of this group. Members can administer servers in the domain.
Users	Users can log on to the computer, access the network, save documents, and shut down the computer. Members cannot install programs or make system changes. If there are computers in the domain running Windows XP Professional or Windows 2000 Professional, the Domain Users global group is added to this group.

Managing Groups

It's a very simple process to create new groups. You can create new security or distribution groups using the wizards. It's always a good idea to see if one of the built-in groups will suit your needs before creating a custom group just so you don't unnecessarily duplicate the permissions of an existing group.

Security Groups

Security groups, as mentioned, are used to manage access and permissions to network resources. The built-in groups delineated in Tables 7.1, 7.2, and 7.3 pretty much cover all the bases in terms of the tasks you're likely to need to perform or delegate on the network. Although SBS provides almost all the types of groups you probably need, you can certainly create new, custom groups to suit your particular needs. To create a new security group, use the following steps:

1. Click **Start | Server Management | Standard Management | Security Groups**.

2. In the taskpad, click the link titled **Add a Security Group** and click **Next** when the Add Security Group Wizard Welcome screen is displayed.

3. In the boxes provided, type in the name of the security group and a description, then click **Next.**

4. In the Group Membership dialog box, click a user or group in the left pane that you would like to add to the new group, then click **Add**. Repeat this process to add all desired users and groups. When finished, the desired list is displayed in the right pane of this dialog box. If you want to remove a user or group, click that user or group in the right pane and click the **Remove** button. When finished, click **Next**.

5. The final screen of this wizard is the confirmation screen showing you the group name and group members. If all entries are correct, click **Finish** to add the group. If not, click **Back** to go back and make changes. To print, save, or e-mail the information, click the link provided.

6. The security group will be added and when complete, the wizard screen will display the message, "*The wizard has completed successfully.*" Click **Close**.

7. In the security group listing of Server Management, you will now see the new group you added. If you do not, click the **Refresh** link in the taskpad to refresh the display.

To view the properties of the group you just created or to modify it in any way, including changing the scope of the group, right-click the group and click **Properties**. The Properties dialog box has four tabs: *General, Members, Members Of,* and *Managed By.* The **General** tab shows information including the name and description of the group as well as its scope and type. The **Members** tab shows which user and group accounts are members of this group. The **Members Of** tab shows which groups this group is a member of and the **Managed By** tab displays information about the person managing this particular group (if any).

To remove a group you've added, simply right-click the group name and click **Remove Security Group**. You'll be prompted to confirm this action, click

Yes to remove it or **No** to exit without removing the group. You can also click the group name and click the red X to the left of the list that says **Remove Security Group.**

SOME INDEPENDENT ADVICE

If possible, work with the built-in groups for a while to see if they'll meet your needs. Since they're based on commonly used sets of permissions, you might find that you can use these groups to manage all your users, groups, and network tasks. If you work with these groups for a while and find they don't cover all your needs, then create new groups.

Distribution Groups

Distribution groups are used solely for the purpose of managing e-mail contacts. For instance, you can create a distribution group called "Marketing" and add all the members of the marketing team. When you address an e-mail to the Marketing distribution group, it will automatically send that e-mail to all members of the group. There is no security provided on distribution groups and the sole purpose of these types of groups is to make sending e-mail to groups more efficient.

Shortcuts

Organizing Groups For Use With Outlook

After you create distribution groups, they'll be dispersed throughout Outlook's Global Address List along with user names. To keep your groups separated from your users so they're more easily located, use a special character as the first character of the name of all groups. For instance, you can use the tilde (~) character as the first character. This will float all the distribution groups to the top of the list and make finding groups much easier.

Adding a distribution group is similar to adding a security group, with a few different options. Use the following steps to add a distribution group.

1. Click **Start | Server Management | Standard Management | Distribution Groups**.

2. In the taskpad, click the link titled **Add a Distribution Group** and click **Next** when the Add Distribution Group Wizard Welcome screen is displayed.

3. Enter the name of the group, a description, and the e-mail alias to be used. An alias is a short name you'll use for the group such as **NetAdmin** or **MarketingStaff**. By default, the name you enter will be used for the alias, but you can modify it later if desired. Click **Next** to continue.

4. In the left pane of the *Group Membership* dialog box, click the user or group you want to add then click **Add**. To remove a user or group you just added, click **Remove**. When finished, the users or groups to be added are displayed in the right pane of the dialog box. Click **Next** to continue.

5. The *Group Manager* screen allows you to add the user or group account that will be able to modify the list of members in this group. Select a user or group, if desired, then click **Next** to continue.

6. In the *Group Options* dialog box, select whether this distribution group can receive Internet e-mail and whether or not these messages should be archived. Click the checkbox to select either or both options then click **Next** to continue.

7. Review the information on the confirmation page. If correct, click **Finish** to create the distribution group with the properties you just defined or click **Back** to go back and make modifications.

8. The *Add Distribution Group Wizard* will create the group and display the following message upon successful creation, "*The wizard has completed successfully.*" Click **Close** to close the dialog box.

As with security groups, you can review and modify the group properties by right-clicking the group and selecting **Properties**. There are a number of properties for distribution groups that differ from security groups. Figure 7.1 shows the properties of the distribution group MarketingStaff. The first four tabs are identical to security groups (*General, Members, Members Of,* and *Managed By*). The next three tabs are unique to distribution groups.

On the *Exchange General* tab, you can manage Exchange-related settings for the distribution group including message size limit (if any) and message restrictions. On the *E-mail Addresses* tab, you can change the default reply address for each e-mail address type. On the *Exchange Advanced* tab, you can change the simple display name, designate the expansion server (if any), hide the group from Exchange message lists, send out-of-office message to originator, send delivery reports (and related settings), and set custom attributes. The wizard will create a Simple Mail Transfer Protocol (SMTP) address for the new group if you configure it to receive Internet e-mail. This default address, however, is often the target for spammers who send bulk e-mail to generic address such as "marketing@mycompany.com." To avoid this, you may want to create slightly different names to try to thwart unimaginative spammers.

Figure 7.1 Distribution Group Properties

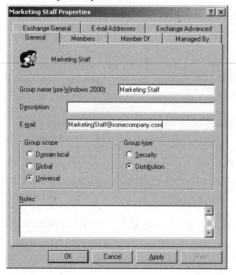

Understanding, Creating, and Managing User Accounts

Now that we've looked at groups, we can focus on user accounts. User accounts are the building blocks of network security. The permissions granted to users (typically through group membership) determine where users can go on the network. As mentioned, it's preferable to add users to groups, which have a defined set of permissions. This is an easier way to maintain user and group accounts and helps prevent inadvertent security holes. If you start granting users individualized permissions, you may find yourself digging through user accounts when you need to troubleshoot problems or make simple changes. Let's look at a brief example. Suppose you have 48 users and over time, you've granted a number of them the ability to make a remote connection to the network. Lately, you've noticed some unusual network behavior on the weekends and you'd like to double-check who has the ability to log in remotely. If you aren't using groups, you're going to have to check all 48 user accounts. However, if you are using groups, you look at the Remote User group, see who the members are and you're done. By assigning permissions to groups and adding users to groups, you'll simplify your administration and avoid problems down the road.

SOME INDEPENDENT ADVICE

Many wizards will auto-enter data for you based on information you type in. For instance, when you add a new user and enter the first and last name, the logon name and e-mail alias are auto-generated. The wizard offers FirstnameLastname by default and provides a drop-down list for three other formats: LastnameFirstname, FirstInitialLastname, and FirstnameLastInitial. The system will remember your chosen format. These can be helpful to use (or just review) because it's a good idea to create a naming scheme for all user names, logon names, and e-mail aliases. You may have noticed that some companies use first name, last initial, others use first initial, last name, and still others use first initial, middle initial, last name. Whatever scheme you use, use it consistently. Using the computer-generated names can provide consistency for you. If you mix and match, you may have trouble spotting errors and attacks in the future.

Understanding User Accounts

A user account is required to access the network. It authenticates the person logging in by requiring a username and password. Once authenticated, it is used to determine what access the user has to network resources. There are only two pre-defined user accounts created by default in SBS: the Administrator account and the Guest account. All other accounts are created by the Administrator. User accounts have two possible types of scope: *valid across the domain* (domain accounts) or *valid on this computer only* (local accounts). Local accounts are created on client computers, not on the SBS server. All accounts created on the SBS server are, by definition, domain accounts.

You can also use the **Add Multiple Users** link in the taskpad to add more than one user account at a time. This is particularly useful when first setting up your server or adding users that all require the same permissions. The main difference you'll see between **Add a User** and **Add Multiple Users** is in the User Information dialog box. In the Add Multiple Users wizard, you'll click **Add** and enter the user's information then click **Add** to enter the next user's information and continue this until you've added all the users.

Creating User Accounts

Creating a user account is a simple task in SBS. Use the following steps to create a new user account.

1. Go to Server Management (**Start | Server Management | Standard Management**) and select **Users**.

2. In the taskpad, click **Add a User** to launch the Add a User Wizard. On the Welcome screen, click **Next** to continue.

3. In the User Account Information dialog box, enter the first and last name of the user, the logon name for the user account and the e-mail alias. Enter the user's telephone number then click **Next**. The logon name and e-mail alias will be entered as you enter the first and last name. You can accept these or enter different text. Often the computer-generated data will be fine.

4. Enter the initial user password and enter it a second time to confirm it. Also, select the appropriate radio button: **Can change password at any time** or **Cannot change password**. For most user accounts, you want the user to be able to change the password. If you are setting up a temporary guest account that will be shared by four people, you may want to prevent the password from being changed. Click **Next** to continue.

5. In the Template Selection dialog box, shown in Figure 7.2, you can choose between two main options—to use the built-in templates or not. If you select one of the built-in templates (recommended), you can also enable the option to **Display selected template's default settings in the wizard**. By selecting this checkbox, you'll be shown the default set-

tings after you click **Next**. This is a good way to become familiar with the default template settings. If desired, you can add a template by clicking **Add Template**. As with other pre-defined settings in SBS, you'll find that the four templates provided cover a lot of ground. Make sure you can't use one of these before defining a new template. For this example, we chose **User Template**. Click **Next** to continue.

6. The next screen, Distribution Groups, allows you to add the user to any of the distribution groups. Click in the left pane to select a distribution group then click **Add** to add it to the right pane. When finished, click **Next** to continue.

7. The next screen allows you to define *SharePoint Access*. SharePoint Services is discussed in detail later in this book. For now, you need to know that SharePoint Services is the engine that allows you to create websites for information sharing and collaboration. SharePoint Services uses four types of user groups: *Reader, Contributor, Web Designer*, and *Administrator*. Each has specific permissions with regard to SharePoint Services sites. Click the group name to see the description on the right side of the dialog box. Select the appropriate group and click **Next** to continue.

8. On the *Address Information* screen, enter the user's address information and click **Next**

9. Define the desired disk quota for this user. The default levels are shown. Avoid changing them if possible, as this will help lend consistency across all users. Click **Next** to continue.

10. The *Set Up Client Computer* dialog box allows you to set up a computer for the user, if desired. Click **Next**.

11. The final screen asks you to confirm the choices you've selected. If you want to make changes, click **Back**. Otherwise click **Finish**.

12. The Add User Wizard will create the user account and configure the group membership settings. When finished, it will display the message, "The wizard has completed successfully." Click **Close**. The new user account will be displayed in the right pane of the Server Management console when **User** is selected in the left pane.

Figure 7.2 Add User Template Selection

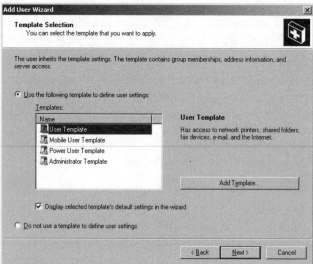

Adding (and Removing) Users to Groups

Once you've created users based on a particular template, you can add those users to groups by locating the desired security or distribution group and adding members. You can do this in two ways – you can add a single user to a particular group or you can access the group and add users. We'll step through both options here.

You can add a user to a security or distribution group using these steps.

1. Select **Start | Server Management | Standard Management | Users**.

2. Right-click the desired user and select **Add User to a Group**. You can also click the desired user and click the **Add User to a Group** link in the taskpad.

3. In the Select Group dialog box, type in the name of the group to which you want to add the user. You can click the **Examples** link to see examples or you can type in part of the name and click the **Check Names** button. For example, if you type in the word **fax** and click **Check Names**, you'll see the Fax Operators group listed. If this is the desired list, click **OK** to add the user to that group. If this is not the group you want, click Fax Operators and press the **Delete** key to remove that group.

4. You should receive an Active Directory notice stating, *"The Add to Group* operation was successfully completed." If the user is already a member of the group, you'll receive an Active Directory notice that the user cannot be added because it is already a member of the selected group.

To *remove a user* from a group via the user properties, right-click the user name, select **Properties**, click the **Member Of** tab, locate the group from which the user is to be removed, click the **Remove** button then click **OK** to exit.

You can also add a user to a security group by starting with the Security Group and adding users with these steps:

1. Select Security Groups in Server Management by clicking **Start | Server Management | Standard Management | Security Groups**. You could select a distribution group instead; the steps are the same.

2. Select the security group to which you want to add user(s). Click the group and click the link **Change Group Properties** in the taskpad or right-click the group and select **Properties** from the menu.

3. In the Group Properties dialog box, click the **Members** tab then click the **Add** button to add users.

4. In the Select Users, Contacts, Computers or Groups dialog box, locate the users, computers or groups you want to add to this group. Use the **Check Names** button to verify the name you entered then click **OK**. For instance, if you have a user **Nick Mammana**, you can simply type **Nick** and click **Check Names**.

5. Click **OK** to close the properties of the group you selected when you are finished adding (or removing) users.

You can remove members using the same steps. In Step 3, select the user to remove and click the **Remove** button instead of the **Add** button.

Managing User Templates

There are pre-defined templates you can use to set up new users. This greatly simplifies your job and it is especially helpful if you're new to all these user and group concepts. The templates provided do a good job of establishing baseline permissions that will help keep your network secure. If you want, you can create new templates and you can also add a template to an existing user account.

If you open Server Management and select **User Templates** (in the Standard Management section), you'll see the four pre-defined user templates provided: *Administrator, Mobile User, Power User* and *User.*

The *User Template* provides permissions needed to access the network, access shared folders, printers, faxes, e-mail, the Internet, and the Remote Web Workplace.

The *Mobile User Template* provides all the permissions of the User template plus the ability to connect remotely to the network through a VPN connection. We'll talk about VPN later in this book.

The *Power User Template* has all the permissions of the Mobile User template plus the ability to perform certain delegated tasks, such as the ability to manage users and groups and manage shared folders, printers, and faxes. The Power User template does not grant permission to delete or do potentially destructive tasks. The Power User can log on remotely to the SBS server but cannot log on locally.

The *Administrator Template* provides unrestricted permissions on the domain and on the local SBS server.

Here's an important concept to keep in mind if you apply a template to a user account: the group membership in the template that's being applied will replace the group membership in the user account. However, permissions previously granted *directly to the user* will remain unchanged after applying the new template. This is important to understand. If you apply a template and the user's account still has some permissions you didn't think it should have, check to see if you (or a Power User) may have applied permissions directly to the user's account. Unexpected permissions create security holes, so this is a great example of how those holes are created by assigning permissions directly to a user account. You assume the user account is using the settings from a template when, in fact, there are additional settings left untouched by the template. If you recall from our earlier discussion, you should add users to groups and grant permissions to groups whenever possible. There are some times it will make sense to customize a particular user's permissions, but doing so creates some risks. It's better to create a group and add just one user to the group than to assign customized permissions to a user's account. This helps you keep track of permissions and keep your network secure.

To manage the template properties, you can double-click any of the templates (or right-click and select **Properties** or left-click and click **Change Template Properties** from the link in the taskpad). However, keep in mind that any changes you make here affect ALL accounts created from here on out. For instance, if you modify the properties of the User Template, all new user accounts you create based on this template will incorporate that modification. All users created from the User Template before you made the modification will not be affected. Avoid making any changes to the pre-defined templates—these are your failsafe option. If you never modify them, you'll always have four templates you can use to create user accounts that adhere to security best practices. Instead of modifying pre-defined templates, you can create a new template using the following steps:

1. Select **Start | Server Management | Standard Management | User Templates**.

2. Click the **Add a Template** link in the taskpad to launch the Add a Template Wizard. Click **Next** on the Welcome screen to continue.

3. In the Template Account Information screen, enter a template name and description. You can select to have the template be the **default option** when you use the Add User Wizard and whether or not **Power users can use this template** when creating users. Click **Next**.

4. The Security Groups screen prompts you to add security groups to this template. Any user accounts created using this new template will become members of the groups added here. You are not required to add any groups in order to continue. Though there wouldn't be much reason for creating a new template without group membership, you may have a specific need. Click **Next**.

5. The Distribution Groups screen prompts you to add distribution groups. Again, users will become members of these groups if their accounts are creating using this new template. You are not required to add distribution groups to the template. Click **Next** to continue.

6. The SharePoint Access dialog box prompts you to add SharePoint Access permissions. You are not required to add SharePoint Access to the template. Click **Next** to continue.

7. The next screen is the Address Information screen. All user accounts creating with this template will use this address information. Click **Next** to continue.

8. The final screen allows you to set disk quotas for all user accounts creating using this template. Click **Next** to review your choices then click **Finish** to create the new template. Click **Close** to close the Add Template Wizard.

You can also change user permissions by applying a template to them. This might be helpful if you create a special template and want to have 5 existing users use the settings in this new template. Rather than recreate these user accounts based on the template, you can apply the template settings to the specified accounts using the steps outlined here:

1. Select **Start | Server Management | Standard Management | Users**.

2. In the taskpad, click the **Change User Permissions** link to launch the Change User Permissions Wizard. Click **Next** on the Welcome screen to continue.

3. In the Template Selection screen, select the template and whether you want to replace or add permissions to users. In the example shown in Figure 7.3, we've selected the **Marketing** template that we've created and we're going to **add to users permissions**. Click **Next** to continue.

4. In the User Selection screen, click users in the left pane for which you want to modify permissions and click the **Add** button. When finished, click **OK**. To remove users accidentally selected, select the user in the right pane and click the **Remove** button.

5. The final screen gives you an opportunity to review your choices. Click **Finish** to complete the change to the selected users' permissions.

Figure 7.3 Change User Permissions Template Selection

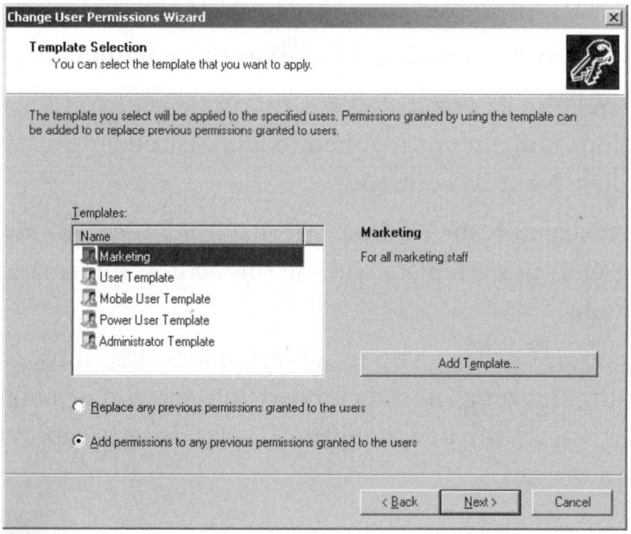

BEST PRACTICES ACCORDING TO MICROSOFT

- Avoid modifying pre-defined templates. Instead, create new templates.
- Test all templates before implementing them across the network. Custom templates may have unexpected results, so test thoroughly before applying them.
- Always assign the least possible permissions. Security best practices dictate that users should have the least possible permissions that allow them to perform their job functions. Never assign more rights and permissions than absolutely necessary.
- Use templates to create user accounts to provide consistent security settings across your network.
- Add users to groups and assign permission to groups whenever possible.
- Add groups to shared resources in order to provide access to that shared resource.

Redirecting My Documents for User Accounts

So far we've looked at user accounts, templates and groups. There is one other important task you'll probably want to do when setting up or managing user accounts, and that is redirecting the location of the My Documents folder. The reason for this is pretty straightforward. Users don't back up their systems. If they store important files in their local My Documents folder and their system crashes, there goes their data. If you redirect the folder to a network location, you can perform backups that will include each user's My Documents folder. A cached copy of My Documents is stored on users' computers so they can work on documents even when disconnected from the network. Every time a user logs on or off, the copy of their My Documents folder synchronizes with the server copy. How nice is that? To avoid users chewing up all your server disk space, use the default disk quota of 1GB. If users exceed that, they're not practicing good housekeeping and they can delete a few files from time to time to free up space.

By default, redirecting the My Documents folder for users will be redirected to a folder called Users Shared Folders on the C: drive. However, the C: drive is going to quickly get overloaded with data (operating system, server applications, etc.) and it's probably best to redirect these folders to a different drive. However, if you do so (which is recommended), you also need to set up additional security.

You can redirect the My Documents folder to either the SBS server or to a network folder. To do so, use the following steps.

1. Click **Start | Server Management | Standard Management | Users**.

2. Click the link **Configure My Documents Redirection** in the taskpad.

3. In the **Client Document Redirection** dialog box, select the desired location, as shown in Figure 7.4. If you want to redirect users' My Documents to a network location other than the default location, you can click the radio button for **Redirect all My Documents folders to a network folder**. **CAUTION**: If you choose this option, you must configure additional security settings. Click the **More Information** button and follow the directions in the Client Document Redirection Help file.

4. Click **OK** to redirect to the chosen location. The Client Document Redirection Wizard will notify you that, *"Client My documents folders will be redirected to the server the next time users log on to their computers."* Click **OK** to close this notice.

Figure 7.4 My Documents Redirection

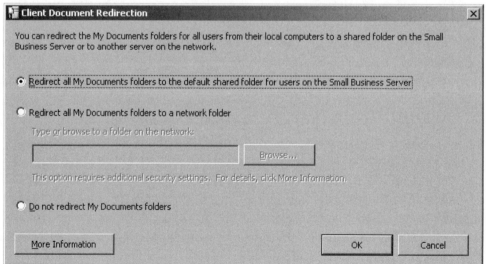

Removing and Disabling User Accounts

When a user leaves the company, his or her account should be disabled as soon as possible to prevent the user from accessing the network when no longer employed by the company. Once you've gotten proper notification from your Human Resources department (or whatever your established practice is), you can go ahead and delete the account. This is a simple matter of selecting the user account and clicking **Remove User** in the taskpad.

If a user is going on vacation or an extended leave, you should disable the account. This will prevent anyone (including the legitimate user and hackers alike) from using the account while it is disabled. This is a good security measure to implement to prevent unauthorized access to the user's account while he or she is out of the office. Don't disable the account for a day or two's absence because you'll probably forget to reactivate it (though you can set a reminder for yourself in your calendar), but do consider disabling the account for absences of a week or more.

There are many more options available in the user account's Properties dialog box. Many of them can be configured by Group Policy, so we won't go into them here. Group Policy and the settings in the user account's Properties dialog box are discussed later in this book. And, as always, you can dig through the Help files on SBS to learn more on any SBS-related topic.

SOME INDEPENDENT ADVICE

Earlier in the book we talked about working with your Human Resources department and/or senior management to define policies regarding access to and use of the corporate network. You should have an established process for disabling and/or removing user accounts when employees leave the company. Unfortunately, not everyone leaves on a happy note and an unhappy user can wreak havoc on a network in a few short unsupervised minutes. Establish a procedure for quickly disabling a user account to prevent problems with the network. It's easier to quickly disable an account than try to recover from a hacked network. And remember to check dial-up and remote access—you don't want someone still having access to your network even after they leave the building.

Understanding and Managing User Profiles

Profiles are small files that store user settings including desktop settings, application data, Favorites, cookies, and more. They're useful because if you have users that log onto different computers or users that share computers, the user's specific settings can be preserved so Lisa doesn't have to look at Nick's Monster Truck screensaver when they share a computer. There are three types of profiles: *local, roaming* and *mandatory*.

A *local profile* is stored on the local computer. The first time a user logs on to a computer, a profile is created and stored locally. If the user logs onto that computer again, the user's local profile is used.

A *roaming profile* is a user profile stored on a network location. The profile is then available to the user regardless of which computer he or she logs onto as long as that computer is running Windows Server 2003, Windows XP Professional, Windows 2000 or Windows NT 4.0.

A *mandatory profile* is a roaming profile that can only be modified by an administrator. If the user wants to change settings in the profile, he or she may be able to make changes, but they will not be preserved. When a user logs off and back on, the mandatory profile settings are reapplied.

Profiles should be set up in a directory on a drive with plenty of disk space and not on the C: drive. Profiles can chew up disk space pretty quickly, so place them where they'll have room to breathe. Also, roaming profiles can impact the user login since the profile has to wind its way across the network before getting to the proper client computer to log the user in. If your network isn't as fast as greased lightning, roaming profiles might be a painful option for users.

To set up a roaming profile for a user, use the following steps:

1. In Windows Explorer, create a shared folder for profiles. For this example, we'll call it **RoamingProfiles**.

2. Select **Start | Server Management | Standard Management | Users**.

3. Right-click the user account and select **Properties**.

4. In the user's Properties dialog box, select the **Profile** tab (shown in Figure 7.5).

5. In the User profile section, enter the **Profile path** in the text box. The
   folder should use Universal Naming Conventions (UNC) such as
   \\SBS2003\RoamingProfiles\%username%. The *%username%* is a
   variable that tells the system to substitute the actual username for the
   variable. If you click **Apply**, the %username% will be changed to the
   user's actual username.

6. If you want to assign a logon script to the user, you can specify it in the
   Logon script text box. If you don't know what logon scripts are or
   why you would use them, that's ok, you don't have to use scripts.

7. You can assign a home folder location here as well. A *home folder* is the
   default storage location used by some programs when a user clicks **File
   | Save As.** Sometimes this is the same location as My Documents,
   sometimes it is different.

8. Click **OK** to accept changes.

Figure 7.5 Creating a Roaming Profile

Once you create a roaming profile for a user, it won't be applied until the
user next logs on. If you specify a home folder, the home folder will be created
immediately. If you want to change the roaming profile to a mandatory profile,
go to the user's profile folder and locate the file named Ntuser.dat. If you don't
see this file, make sure your folder options allow you to see hidden files and

folders by clicking **Tools | Folder Options**. Select the **View** tab, scroll down in the Advanced settings and select **Show hidden files and folders** then click **OK**. Once you locate the file Ntuser.dat, rename it to Ntuser.man. The .man extension indicates to the system that the profile is a mandatory profile. Make sure you're aware of the potential issues you can run into when forcing users to use a mandatory, rather than a roaming, profile. Read the Best Practices section below and also peruse the Help files.

SOME INDEPENDENT ADVICE

You can use logon scripts to manage the user's computer environment as well. Microsoft provides numerous ways to manage the user's environment including profiles, logon scripts, and group policies, among others. Logon scripts are assigned either through profiles (mentioned earlier) or through group policy. These scripts run when the user logs on. Scripts are typically used to set environment variables such as the user's home directory, but can be used for a variety of tasks including setting up non-Microsoft clients. Scripts can be any executable file but are typically .bat (batch) or .cmd (command) files. They can use Windows Script Host (Visual Basic or Java) or MS-DOS commands. For more information on scripting, query **using logon scripts** in the Help and Support on the SBS server or use the same query on the Microsoft website.

BEST PRACTICES ACCORDING TO MICROSOFT

- Allow for different hardware configurations, especially video and display hardware. A mandatory profile set for one hardware configuration may not work well (or at all) on another.
- Create a single mandatory user profile for a group of users *only* if they all use computers with the same video hardware.
- Disable **Offline Folder caching** on roaming user profile shared directories. If it is not disabled, users may experience problems with synchronization of files and folders.
- Do not use the Encrypting File System (EFS) on files in roaming profiles. EFS is not compatible with roaming profiles.
- Set disk quotas high enough for roaming profile users. If set too low, quotas could prevent user profile synchronization.

- Restrict access to roaming profile shared directory. The directory can contain sensitive information, such as confidential documents or EFS certificates. Restrict access to only those that require access (the roaming users only).
- Use Windows 2000 (or later) to host roaming profile shared directories so you can utilize the built-in security features of these later operating systems.
- Always use the New Technology file system (NTFS) for volumes holding user's data. NTFS is more secure than file allocation table (FAT) or FAT32.

SOME INDEPENDENT ADVICE

Some network administrators can get a bit heavy-handed with mandatory profiles. Make sure you work with your company's management team to determine if and when mandatory profiles make sense. The last thing you want is users having difficulty using the network because of settings in a mandatory profile. As with most things in life, moderation is key.

Working with the Administrator Account

As we've mentioned several times, you want to avoid using the Administrator account whenever you're doing routine work on the computer that does not require those privileges. First, you should rename the Administrator account so that a hacker can't start with the account name and begin trying to hack the password. You should also avoid logging on as the Administrator whenever possible. Create a Power User or regular User account for yourself and log in using that. If you need to perform a task that requires administrative rights, you can either log off and then log back on using your Administrator account or you can use the **run as** command. The run as command allows you to perform tasks by *running* the command or application *as* the Administrator. To use the run as command in Windows Explorer or on the Start menu, right-click the program you want to open and select **Run as** from the menu. A dialog box is displayed showing the current user and giving you the option of either running with restricted access (better for security, but the program might behave oddly) or running as a particular user. If you choose the option for **The following user**, you'll have to select the username (in this case the Administrator account name) and the associated password. You can use the run as command not only to run programs using your Administrator account, but you could also use it for any other user account you may have.

One More Time

In this chapter, we started digging into user-specific information including user accounts, groups, and user profiles. While there are a number of other settings that can be configured for users and groups, we've covered the most common tasks in this chapter. More advanced configuration information can be found both in the Help files and online at the Microsoft website. What you did learn in this chapter was:

☑ Groups are used to provide a standardized set of permissions to groups of users.

☑ SBS has built-in universal groups, built-in global groups, and built-in local groups.

☑ In addition to using the built-in groups, you can create new groups to meet your company's needs.

☑ Security groups are used to assign permissions and distribution groups are used to send e-mail to groups of users.

☑ Distribution groups have no security function whatsoever.

☑ Typically, users are added to security groups and permissions are assigned to groups. This helps manage users permissions and maintains better security.

☑ User accounts can be created based on one of four pre-defined templates: User, Power User, Mobile User, or Administrator.

☑ The pre-defined templates meet most companies' needs as-is. You can create new templates to meet your company's needs.

☑ Avoid modifying the pre-defined templates. These provide baseline security and a good failsafe option for you.

☑ You can add users to groups in two ways—by accessing the user account properties and adding the desired group or by accessing the group and adding the specific user.

☑ You can change user permissions by applying a different template to the user account. You can choose to replace or add to existing permissions. Permissions assigned directly to the user will not be modified.

☑ Profiles are small files that hold settings related to a user's computer settings including desktop settings, Favorites, My Documents, and more.

☑ Profiles can be local, roaming, or mandatory.

☑ Local profiles are stored on the local computer and roaming profiles are stored on a network location.

☑ Mandatory profiles are created from roaming profiles by changing the user's Ntuser.dat file to Ntuser.man.

☑ Rename the Administrator account for better security.

☑ Avoid logging on as the Administrator for day-to-day tasks. Instead, use the run as command to run a program or executable with Administrator permissions. You'll need to select the account and enter the associated password to do so.

Chapter 8

Permissions, Shares and Group Policy

- Overview of Permissions
- Configuring and Managing Permissions
- Understanding Group Policy
- Configuring and Managing Group Policy

The End Result

Once your user accounts are created and organized into groups, you need to assign permissions so resources can be accessed. At the end of this chapter, you'll understand share and NT File System (NTFS) permissions and how to configure and manage them in an organized, secure manner. You'll also know how to share resources such as files and folders so they're available to users across the network. Finally, we'll tackle the topic of group policy, which allows you to configure and manage user and computer settings at a very detailed level. By the end of this chapter, you'll understand group policy, group policy objects and how to work with group policies in your domain.

Overview of Permissions

Permissions are the access rights granted to users, groups, computers, and other network resources. These permissions are set in two ways – automatically via default Small Business Server 2003 (SBS) settings and manually via administrator (or other) modifications. We mentioned early in the book that SBS and the underlying Windows Server 2003 operating system was more secure, right out of the box, than any previous server operating system from Microsoft. One reason is that, by default, most settings are locked down in Windows Server 2003 and you must manually "unlock" them to loosen restrictions. Previous operating systems were rather lax by default, and you, the net admin, had to go in and lock everything down. The problem with that approach is that you would probably overlook something and leave a wide opening for would-be hackers. With the operating system locked down by default, you can be confident that your default settings will keep the network reasonably secure. This is a much more secure approach to network security and makes your life much easier right off the bat. Think about it. Users will *always* complain if they lack adequate permission to perform their jobs but they'll almost *never* let you know they have too much access. Human nature at work. Users may not know they have excessive permissions or they may be busy doing things they shouldn't. In either case, it's better to start off restrictive and loosen things up when users notify you they need access to resources. All of this hinges on setting permissions. In SBS, permissions are *share permissions* and *access control* using NTFS permissions.

Access Control Using NTFS Permissions

NTFS is a secure file system introduced by Microsoft in the Windows NT operating system. Earlier in this book, we recommended formatting your disk drives using NTFS to take advantage of the security features of NTFS. NTFS uses a list called an *access control list* (ACL), which contains *access control entries* (ACE) specifying which users and groups have what type of access. The terms *access control* and *NTFS permissions* are often used interchangeably.

NTFS permissions are located on the resource's **Security** tab in the **Properties** dialog box, as shown in Figure 8.1. Notice the list of available permissions: **Full Control**, **Modify**, **Read & Execute**, **List Folder Contents**, **Read**, **Write**, and **Special Permissions**. These can be accessed by right-clicking the resource, selecting **Properties**, then clicking the **Security** tab. You must have formatted your disk drive using NTFS for this tab to be available. Otherwise, only the **Sharing** tab will be available for permissions. The permissions checkboxes in gray indicate the permission was *inherited*, something we'll discuss in just a bit.

Figure 8.1 Default NTFS Permissions

If your disk is formatted using NTFS, your files and folders can use both *share* permissions and *NTFS* permissions, but that's not your best option because combining share and NTFS permissions can yield some odd results (often termed *unspecified results*). If your disk is formatted using a file allocation table

(FAT) or FAT32, you can use *only* share permissions. If you're using NTFS, it's recommended you use only NTFS permissions. It keeps things simple, always a good thing when managing security. The most important reason to not mix share and NTFS permissions is because share permissions, by default, restrict the Everyone group to read-only. If this is not modified and you add full control NTFS permissions for any group, the resource will remain restricted to read-only since all users are part of the Everyone group. Rather than mixing share and NTFS permissions, use NTFS only. NTFS is required on the SBS server and should be used on any disk where NTFS is an option

As you can see in Figure 8.1, you can either explicitly **Allow** or explicitly **Deny** permissions. This is an important concept to understand. If you explicitly allow or deny permissions, those override any inherited permissions. More on inherited permissions in a moment.

SOME INDEPENDENT ADVICE

Any user or group that has full control over a folder can modify and delete any files or subfolders in that folder, regardless of the specific permissions on the individual files and subfolders. That's an important thing to know when organizing files and folders on the network and when assigning permissions. Remember, less is more when it comes to permissions—grant the least possible. Your users won't hesitate to let you know if you've gone too far. Of course, don't go overboard or you'll spend all your time responding to users requesting access to needed resources. Find a good balance, but lean on the side of caution.

Share Permissions

Share permissions are those permissions granted as the result of sharing a file or folder on the network. When you share a folder, the Everyone group is granted read-only access by default, as shown in Figure 8.2. This is a change from previous operating systems (Windows 2000 and prior versions) that set full control permission to the Everyone group by default. Beginning in Windows Server 2003, permissions are always set to the most restrictive, and you may need to go in and loosen some of those restrictions.

The share permissions options are *Read, Change* and *Full Control*. Users and (preferably) groups can be added to the permissions and granted any or all of these permissions. Disks formatted with the FAT or FAT32 operating system can use share permissions. Share permissions apply to all files and folders in the share, meaning that if you set read-only share permissions for a group on the shared folder, that group will have read-only access to all files and subfolders within that shared folder. An important note about share permissions is that they have no effect if someone logs on locally to the computer on which the share resides. The share permissions only apply to users who access the share across the network. Share permissions also have no effect on Terminal Server users that may be connected to that computer (we'll discuss Terminal Server later in the book).

Figure 8.2 Default Share Permissions

Configuring and Managing Permissions

Permissions could fill an entire book, if you really wanted to dig that deep. Our goal is to help you understand how permissions work in SBS so you can manage network resources in a secure manner. If you want to understand the minute details of permissions, query the Help and Support files in SBS or online at the Microsoft website.

Rules and Exceptions

If share *and* NTFS permissions are applied to a resource such as a folder, the share permissions will be used to determine the broadest or greatest access allowed. NTFS permissions can be more restrictive, but NTFS permissions will not grant greater access than share permissions. For example, if share permissions are set to *Full Control* for a particular group and that same group also has NTFS permissions to that resource set to *Read Only*, the group will have read-only access because NTFS permissions will only further restrict access. Here's another example. If a group has *Read Only* access to a share and that same group has NTFS *Full Control* permission, the group will have read-only access because share permissions are used to determine the broadest permissions and NTFS can only restrict access further. Notice that in these two seemingly opposite scenarios, the result is the same. It can get confusing, so it's recommended that you use NTFS permissions exclusively on volumes formatted with NTFS (which should be the drives on the SBS server, at minimum).

Now that you've worked through that logic, let's throw you a curve. There is an important exception to this process. If a user is a member of a group that is granted one set of permissions and that user also has permissions assigned directly to the *user account*, the permissions specifically assigned to the user will be applied. If AnneS is a member of a group, the Marketing Staff group, that has read-only permissions and her account has been granted full control, she will have full control. As you recall, you should avoid assigning specific permissions to user accounts whenever possible and this is another good reason why. If a marketing file is deleted and you're looking for the culprit, you may look at the Marketing Staff group and assume all members have read-only permission and therefore could not be responsible. What you might miss is that AnneS has full control on her user account and can therefore do whatever she wants to Marketing files and folders. Even if the error is unintentional, you're going to spend a lot of time tracking down the problem. To prevent this, avoid granting permissions to individual user accounts unless you absolutely have to, and then, make special note of the information to help you in troubleshooting down the line.

Earlier, we pointed out the checkboxes in Figure 8.1 that allow you to specifically allow or deny a permission. Whenever possible, avoid using the **Deny** feature. It can cause some interesting behavior in the murky world of permissions and it should only be used to specifically override a permission that is already assigned.

BEST PRACTICES ACCORDING TO MICROSOFT

- Use NTFS permissions when possible and use share permissions on FAT or FAT32 volumes only.
- Avoid using both share and NTFS permissions. The results can be confusing, unpredictable, and difficult to troubleshoot.
- Assign permissions to groups, not individual users.
- Assign the most restrictive permissions possible.
- Avoid specifically denying permissions to a shared resource. Only do so if you need to override specific permissions already assigned.
- Limit membership to the Administrators group, as this group has full control permissions by default.
- Avoid changing the default permissions for the Everyone group when possible. The Everyone group includes numerous other groups and your results could be unpredictable.
- Never deny access to the Everyone group because that group includes Administrators. Instead, remove the Everyone group rather than specifically denying the Everyone group.

Principles of Inheritance

When we talk about inheritance in SBS, we're not talking about Uncle Rockefeller or Grandma Hilton remembering us in their wills. We're talking about how permissions trickle down through a folder and file hierarchy. Permissions can be inherited from the folder higher up the ladder. Before we move on, let's talk about hierarchies for a second. In the Microsoft world, hierarchies are formed by *parent* and *child* objects. The child objects are those "underneath" the parent object (as seen from space and Windows Explorer). So, if a folder has three subfolders, those subfolders are child objects. Each of those child objects could be parent objects also, if they contained subfolders within them. This is a good concept to understand when discussing objects in Windows. Now, back to our feature attraction.

There are two types of permissions in this category of inheritance: *explicit* and *inherited*. *Explicit permissions* are the ones you purposely set. *Inherited permissions* are those that are inherited, or handed down, from the parent object. Explicit permissions take precedence over inherited permissions, even inherited deny permissions. By default, when you create a subfolder, it inherits the permissions of the parent. If you don't want this to happen, you can block inheritance at either the parent or the child level. This makes a big difference in how things work out (isn't that always the way with inheritances). If you block it at the parent level, no subfolders will inherit the parent's permissions. If you block it at the child level, then some folders in the parent object will inherit and some will not. Any folders within that child folder will not inherit permissions. Other child folders in that same parent folder will inherit permissions. Sound confusing? It can be. It's often easier to manage inheritance from the parent folder for that reason, but sometimes managing inheritance at the child object level is desirable. For this section, refer to Figure 8.3, which shows the **Advanced** permissions for a folder. This screen is accessed by right-clicking the folder, selecting **Properties**, clicking the **Security** tab, and clicking the **Advanced** button.

Figure 8.3 Advanced Security Settings

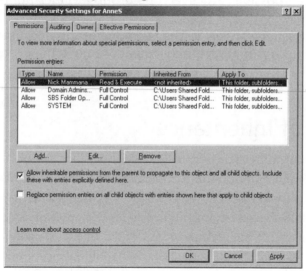

The first checkbox in the Advanced Security Settings dialog box causes child objects to inherit all permissions of the parent. Notice the text: **Allow inheritable permissions from the parent to propagate to this object and all child objects. Include these with entries explicitly defined here**. What on earth does that mean? Recall that we earlier discussed where we can apply permissions—at the parent or child. If a parent has permissions but the parent is set to *not propagate* them, those permissions are not inheritable. Only permissions set to propagate from the parent to the child object are inheritable. Notice in Figure 8.3 that the permissions for Nick are not inherited, but the permissions for the three other entries are inherited.

The second option is to **Replace permission entries on all child objects with entries shown here that apply to child objects.** Some permissions may not apply to child objects and those will be ignored. If you choose this setting, you will reset all permissions on the child objects to those configured in the parent object. Keep in mind that once you select this check box and click either **Apply** or **OK**, you can't go back—there is no undo function.

If you notice, some of the boxes are shaded, indicating the permission was inherited. If the box is shaded *and* checked, it means the permissions are both inherited and explicitly set. There are three ways to change these settings:

- Change the permissions of the parent folder so inheritance changes on child objects.

- Clear the checkbox for **Allow inheritable permissions from the parent to propagate to this object and all child objects. Include these with entries explicitly defined here**. When this option is disabled, you can make changes to permissions or change the users and groups in the permission entries list.

- Select the opposite permission—**Allow** or **Deny**—to override the inherited permission. This can get tricky, especially if you use the **Deny** permission. If you do not select the **Allow** permission, the permission is inherently denied. This is often your better option than to explicitly deny permissions.

Determining Effective Permissions

So, now that you're arrived here, you're probably wondering how you'll ever be able to tell exactly which permissions a user or group has—that is, which permissions are actually in effect. If you can inherit permissions, explicitly set permissions, and use **Allow** and **Deny** to override specific permissions, how can you possibly figure out what the *effective* permissions are? Thankfully, Microsoft provides a tool we can use. Refer back to Figure 8.3. In the Advanced Security Settings dialog box, you'll notice the **Effective Permissions** tab. Click the **Select** button and locate the user or group you want to check on. Type the user or group name in the text box, click **Check Names**, then click **OK**. The effective permissions are displayed. Inherited permissions are indicated by a shaded box and explicit permissions are indicated with a checkmark. The bottom line is this: *Keep permissions simple*. Avoid assigning permissions on child objects, if pos-

sible. The simpler your permissions are, the easier time you'll have troubleshooting when a user complains he or she cannot access a needed resource.

SOME INDEPENDENT ADVICE

The **Effective Permissions** tab can be a handy tool to use—with one
caveat. The results here are not precise and could be considered a ball-
park estimate rather than an etched-in-stone result. Some things that
can impact effective permissions are share permissions and any permissions based on the way the user logs on. Membership in local groups
might also impact the effective permissions. The **Effective Permissions**
tab shows permissions based on membership in global and local groups,
local permissions, and privileges. So, it's a great estimating tool, but
don't rely solely upon these results. If you suspect a problem, dig a bit
deeper to see what might be going on.

About Owners

By default, whoever creates an object (file, folder, etc.) is the owner. The owner
controls access to the resource and can grant or deny access to anyone he or she
chooses. That's fine in most cases, but let's look at a scenario where that could be
a problem. Let's say George has a lot of files he doesn't want people looking at
for whatever reason. He places them in a folder and modifies the permissions so
he's the only one with access. Later, his boss comes to you and says, "There's
been a problem with George, he hasn't been forthcoming about some of his
work and, well, we'd like to know what's going on." As the net admin and a
member of the Administrators group, you can choose to take ownership of
George's folder. Once you take ownership, you can change the permissions to
grant access to George's boss (or whomever). George can still get into the folder
(unless you specifically deny access to him) but he'll soon discover he's not the
only one who can get in and he's no longer the owner. He can go create a new
folder but he cannot take ownership back from you. To take ownership of a
folder, use the following steps:

1. Right-click the folder you want to take ownership of and select
    Properties. Click the **Security** tab. Notice that the **Group or user**

names: box is empty and the **Add** and **Remove** buttons are disabled. The only option available is **Advanced**. Click **Advanced**.

2. In the Advanced Security Settings dialog box, click the **Owner** tab. The current owner is displayed (it might also say, "unable to display current owner"). The box below that, **Change owner to:** lists the possible new owners (Administrative groups). Select the new owner and click **OK**. Once you've taken ownership, you can modify permissions on the folder.

Auditing

The only tab in Advanced Security Settings we haven't yet talked about is the **Auditing** tab. We'll talk about auditing in more detail later in this book, but let's take a quick look at it while we're here.

You can audit events in the folder, such as when someone or some group accesses a file or deletes a file or folder. You can choose to audit both successful and failed attempts. Both are useful in different ways. If someone is trying to access something they shouldn't, you might audit failed attempts. If you suspect someone has access they shouldn't, you might audit successful events. Think carefully about why you want to set auditing and what results you're expecting to see. A log file full of mundane folder access events isn't going to help you. On the flip side, if you have a folder with extremely sensitive corporate data in it and the file is rarely accessed, you might set success and failed audit events for any sort of access to the folder. This might help you spot monkey business before your company becomes the next Enron or Worldcom.

> ### Shortcuts
>
> **Apply versus OK**
>
> Have you ever wondered what the difference is between the **Apply** button and the **OK** button in the Windows dialog boxes you use? If you click the **Apply** button, the action specified in the dialog box is carried out, but the dialog box remains open. If you click **OK**, the action specified in the dialog box is carried out and the dialog box is closed. Clicking **Apply** then **OK** doesn't do anything different than simply clicking **OK**. Same result, one less click.

Understanding Group Policy

Now that you've mastered the intricate details of permissions, let's jump in just a bit deeper and look at Group Policy. First, let's define it. Group Policy is a network management tool that allows you to manage users, computers, and other elements of your network from a global perspective. You can use Group Policy to assign scripts, manage applications, redirect folders, assign permissions, and more. Group Policy is a very powerful tool in Windows Server 2003 (and hence, SBS) and as such, it's a rather complex topic. In this section, we're going to look at some of the basics of Group Policy. You won't become an overnight expert on Group Policy, but you will understand the basics and will be able to use Group Policy to perform a few network tasks. Typically, using Group Policy makes a lot more sense when you're managing thousands of users and computers across various geographic locations. That's when the power of the tool really becomes evident. However, on a smaller scale, Group Policy can make your life a bit easier, as we'll talk about in this section. And, for the faint of heart, the Group Policies created by default in SBS work just fine, thank you very much, and you won't be *required* to jump into Group Policy if you're just not ready. Be sure to read through this section, though, and come back to it later on once you've gained some experience. Understanding Group Policy and how you can use it for good (and not evil) will make your life easier.

When we start talking about Group Policy, the term *object* pops up pretty quickly. An object in the Windows Server 2003 world can be one of several things. An object, such as a file, folder, user account, computer, or printer (among others), has a distinct, named set of attributes. These attributes might include name, location, size, e-mail address, etc. So, when you see the term *object*, you'll understand how it's used in the world of Windows. Now, let's look at Group Policies.

Group Policies are little more than files that store specific information and are then applied to users, computers, and other things on the network based on the rules supplied. Group Policies can be *local* or *non-local*. A local policy only applies to activities on the computer on which is resides. A non-local policy is primarily applied to group objects and typically is applied to all computers or on all users. Some policies are applied to user accounts, others to computer accounts. You can only apply policies to user and computer objects.

User policies affect how user accounts interact with the network and are applied when the user logs on.

Computer policies affect how the computer object interacts with the network and only apply to those computers that participate in Active Directory (some computers may not be able to participate in Active Directory because they lack the ability to communicate with Active Directory. This includes Windows ME and Windows XP Home). In the event there is a conflict between settings in the user policies and settings in the computer policies, the computer policies will override the user policies.

Most settings within group policies (typically called *Group Policy Objects* or GPOs) can be in one of three states: *not configured*, *enabled*, or *disabled*. If a setting in a GPO is not configured, it has no effect whatsoever, it is not defined, and essentially doesn't exist. If it is enabled or disabled, the GPO is applied according to those settings.

Also, group policies are inherited and cumulative. We discussed inheritance earlier in this chapter and we'll revisit it as it relates to GPOs. The cumulative effect means that if several policies are applied, each one builds on the earlier one. And you thought inheritance was tricky.

SOME INDEPENDENT ADVICE

One of the basic functions of a network is to provide access to resources. Part of the network function, then, is to keep a list of all resources and to know how to find those resources. This is a service called *directory services* and is common to all networks. How directory services are implemented is very specific to the operating system. In Windows 2000 Server and Windows Server 2003, the directory service is called *Active Directory* (AD). AD, like all directory services, allows accounts and resources to be organized in a logical, hierarchical way so information can be easily found. The organization of the data is called the *schema*. AD includes a global catalog, which is the list of all available objects. AD also provides the ability to search for (query) and locate objects. Finally, AD provides a mechanism for the global catalog to be replicated, or copied, across the domain or forest (that does not apply in SBS since its limited to one domain).

Administrators can manage permissions, rights, privileges, and other object attributes at a very granular level from one centralized location. For more on Active Directory, check out the overview on the Microsoft website (if the link is impossibly long, simply go to www.microsoft.com and type in **Active Directory** in the search box then select the link that matches this one: www.microsoft.com/resources/documentation/windowsserv/2003/standard/proddocs/en-us/sag_ADintro.asp.

Group policy settings are applied to computers or users. For both computers and users, there are three categories of settings: Software settings, Windows settings and Administrative Templates.

- **Software settings** are primarily used to install, update, or remove software on computers. This section can also be used to configure software settings for specific applications, users or computers.

- **Windows settings** are policies that apply to scripts, security, folder redirection, and Remote Installation Services, among other things. These settings have significantly different results depending on whether they are applied to computer policies or user policies.

- **Administrative templates** are policy settings that contain Registry settings. These contain settings for Windows components such as NetMeeting, Internet Explorer, and Windows Update, as well as settings related to installed applications, services, security, and users.

Let's look at a few examples to put this all in perspective. Group Policy is a useful tool for applying changes on individual client computers in the domain. Password policies, applied via GPOs, can allow the administrator to enforce password history (no repeats in a certain time frame), maximum password age, minimum password length, etc. These are settings found under **Computer Configuration | Windows Settings | Security Settings | Account**

Policies | Password Policies. You can also restrict user rights including the ability to shut down the system or change the system time. These settings are located in **Computer Configuration | Windows Settings | Security Settings | Local Policies | User Rights Assignment.** As you can see, you can configure very specific settings to maintain some semblance of control over the client computers on the network. As we've previously mentioned, you want to avoid getting heavy-handed—is it really important that your users cannot change the local computer's system time? It might be, and that's fine, but if there's no good reason for it, don't set the policy just because you can.

Configuring and Managing Group Policy

Group Policies can be accessed via the Server Management console in the Advanced Management node under Group Policy Management. They can also be accessed via **Start | Administrative Tools | Group Policy Management.** There are a number of commonly used tasks related to managing GPOs including:

- Creating and deleting GPOs

- Managing inheritance order

- Managing implementation order

- Viewing and setting GPO scope

- Backing up and restoring GPOs

- Predicting GPO results

- Using GPOs to update client computers automatically

- Using GPOs to audit events

Although there are many other things you can do with GPOs, we're going to limit our discussion to these commonly used tasks. Keep in mind that you can mangle your network pretty well by applying all kinds of GPOs to it, so keep it simple and use the default GPOs first. If those don't meet all your needs, create custom GPOs and whatever you do, do NOT modify the default GPOs. Those provide your fallback option. If you mess up your custom GPOs, you can simply delete them. If you modify (and subsequently mess up) your default GPOs, well, you're in a world of hurt.

Creating and Deleting Group Policy Objects

When you install SBS, several default group policy objects are created, including a default domain policy, default Domain Controllers policy, and several policies specific to SBS. It's possible you might never need to do anything but use the default policies. If you find you need additional policies, you can create new ones (or delete ones you've created) using the following steps. Avoid modifying the default policies; these are your failsafe option if all else goes wrong. Make it a habit to create new policies rather than modifying the default policies. Note that we'll use a specific example, so your selections will change based on what you're trying to accomplish. Use great care when creating and applying GPOs, you can wreak havoc in no time at all.

1. Click **Start | Server Management | Advanced Management | Group Policy Management | Forest: (***domain name***) | Domains**. From there, expand the domain (by clicking the + to the left of your domain name) and locate **Group Policy Objects**. If you expand this node, you'll see the default policies that were created when you installed SBS.

2. Right-click the **Group Policy Objects** node and select **New** from the shortcut menu.

3. Enter the name you want to give your new GPO. Click **OK**.

4. In the Group Policy Objects node, you should now see the name you just assigned to your new GPO (if not, click the **Refresh** icon at the top of the console or click **Action | Refresh**). Now you have created the "container," but there's nothing in it. A GPO must be configured in order to have any purpose.

5. Right-click your new GPO and select **Edit** from the shortcut menu. This will launch the Group Policy Editor console. Your GPO is listed in the left pane of the console and two nodes, Computer Configuration, and User Configuration are beneath the GPO.

6. Configure the GPO based on the settings you would like to enable for this GPO. In this example, we're creating a new GPO called **New Group Policy Object Example**, and we're going to audit when changes are made to policies. Refer to Figure 8.4. Notice that the **Policy Setting for Audit policy change** field is currently set to **Not Defined**.

Figure 8.4 Creating a New Group Policy Object to Audit Policy Change

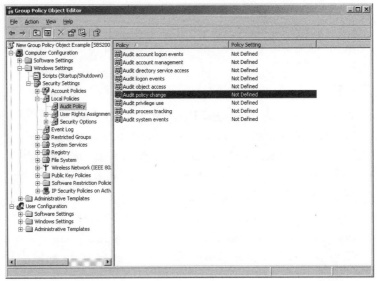

7. Double-click **Audit policy change** to open the Audit policy change Properties dialog box, shown in Figure 8.5 (alternately, you can right-click and choose **Properties** or click **Action | Properties** from the menu).

Figure 8.5 Audit Policy Change Properties

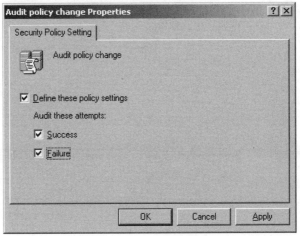

8. To enable the policy, enable the **Define these policy settings** option. Then, define whether you want to audit **Success** or **Failure** events. These settings will vary depending on which attributes you're working with. The checkbox will always be present allowing you to define (enable) the policy settings. The specific settings will vary with the object.

9. In this example, we selected both **Success** and **Failure** events. Click **OK** to accept, or click **Cancel** to exit without saving.

10. When you check the **Audit Policy Change** policy in the Group Policy Editor, you will see that the Policy Settings now shows "Success, Failure" instead of "Not Defined." You may need to click the **Refresh** icon on the toolbar to refresh the display in the right pane.

11. Now that we've created a setting for the GPO container, we have to tell the system how and where to apply these settings. Close the Group Policy Editor to return to the Server Management Console. You can click the **X** in the upper right corner or choose **File | Exit** from the menu.

12. If you click the GPO in the left pane, you'll see four tabs in the right pane: **Scope**, **Details**, **Settings**, and **Delegation.** Click the **Settings** tab and you will see the configuration we just set up in the Group Policy Editor. This is shown in Figure 8.6.

Figure 8.6 Group Policy Settings

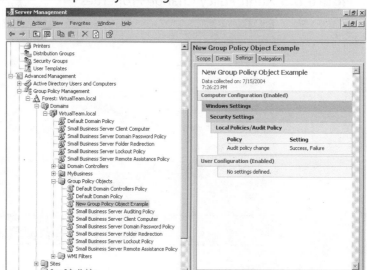

13. To apply this GPO, locate the domain name to be associated with this GPO in the left pane. Right-click the domain name in the left pane and select **Link An Existing GPO** from the shortcut menu.

14. In the Select GPO dialog box, click the GPO you want to link. In this example, we selected **New Group Policy Object Example**. Click **OK** to create the link or **Cancel** to exit without linking.

15. When you click on the domain name, you can now see the new GPO in the right pane via the **Linked Group Policy Objects** tab.

BEST PRACTICES ACCORDING TO MICROSOFT

- Do not make changes to the default group policies. As with other default settings in SBS, this is your failsafe option. If all else fails, you can disable all your custom GPOs and use just the default GPOs – if they haven't been modified.
- Avoid creating a bunch of GPOs. It slows down the server and can cause logins (and logouts) to become painfully slow.
- It's the number of GPOs that affect the login/out time, not the number of settings within the GPO itself.
- As with all things related to security, keep it simple. Creating too many GPOs will confuse you and can create security holes. Even experienced net admins can pull their hair out over unexpected GPO behavior.

To delete a GPO, simply right-click the desired GPO and select **Delete** from the shortcut menu. All GPO links will also be deleted. Note that you cannot (nor would you want to) delete the Default Domain Policy or the Default Domain Controllers Policy.

Managing Inheritance Order

Inheritance of GPOs is a similar process to permissions inheritance, with a few more twists and turns. One major difference is that there is an order in which they are inherited and an order in which they are implemented. Tricky, eh?

In terms of inheritance, when the GPO is applied at the parent level, the child objects inherit the GPO settings…except if the child object has been assigned its own GPO whose settings conflicting with the parental GPO. In that case, kids rule and in one of the only known instances in the universe, the child overrides the parent. If the policies are not contradictory, both can be applied. Policy settings that are not defined are not inherited and policy settings that are disabled are inherited as disabled.

For instance, if you create a GPO that applies at the domain level and you create another GPO that applies to a handful of computers (say, the computers in the Finance department only), the parent is the domain and the children are the computers because the computers are members of the domain. If you create conflicting policies between the domain and the Finance department's computers, you may find some interesting (and unexpected) results. This is why, at the risk of repetition, we suggest keeping GPOs as simple as possible.

Managing Implementation Order

We haven't talked at all about other objects in Active Directory. We'll discuss a few of the relevant ones later in the book, so for now, some of these objects may be unfamiliar to you—that's ok, just be sure to note implementation order for future reference.

Group policies are implemented (or applied) in this order:

1. Local Group Policy Object (remember, that's local to the computer on which the GPO resides).

2. GPOs linked to the site.

3. Domain GPOs.

4. Organizational unit (OU) GPOs from largest to smallest OU.

To see the order of precedence for applying a GPO in a domain, for example, locate the domain in Server Management by clicking **Start | Server Management | Advanced Management | Group Policy Management | Forest: (*domain name*) | Domains | (*domain name*)**. In the right pane, click the **Group Policy Inheritance** tab and view the left-most column. To change the precedence, click the GPO and use the up and down arrows to increase or decrease the precedence for that GPO.

There are a number of other things you can do with GPOs including overriding inheritance, enabling and disabling GPO links, finding GPO links, and disabling a branch of a GPO, but those are more advanced tasks. If you're interested in learning more, use these phrases (the ones we just used) as your query phrases in Help and Support or search the Microsoft website for more information on GPOs.

Viewing and Setting GPO Scope

By default, a group policy applies to all users or all computers in the container with which the GPO is linked. A container can be a domain, an organizational unit, or a site, for example. For our purposes, we'll discuss it as it relates to the entire domain. There may be cases when you want the GPO to apply to a certain subset of users and/or computers in the domain. In this case, you can modify the scope. We'll use the GPO we created in the last exercise as our example. Use the following steps to modify the scope of a GPO at the domain level:

1. Click **Start | Server Management | Advanced Management | Group Policy Management | Forest: (***domain name***) | Domains | (***domain name***) | Group Policy Objects | New Group Policy Object Example.**

2. In the right pane, click the **Scope** tab if it is not already selected. This is shown in Figure 8.7.

Figure 8.7 Scope Tab of Group Policy Object

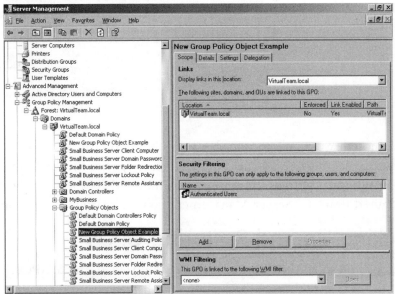

3. In the second section, **Security Filtering**, click **Add** and locate the groups, users, or computers to which you want to apply the policy. After adding the desired groups, users, or computers, click **OK**. Click **OK** again to accept the filter and return to the Server Management console.

4. If **Authenticated Users** is one of the names in the **Security Filtering** section, as shown in Figure 8.8, click it and then click **Remove**. If you leave it in, the GPO will apply, by default, to anyone that logs onto the network (authenticated users). If you want to restrict to whom the GPO is applied, you must remove this entry. Your resulting list will be the only objects to which the GPO will apply, as shown in Figure 8.8.

Figure 8.8 Filtered GPO List

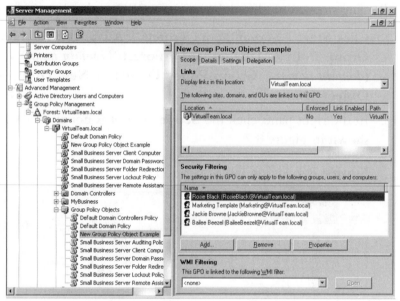

Although we won't go into the details here, you can also set a Windows Management Interface (WMI) filter to further restrict the application of this GPO. Additional settings for the GPO, including delegation, can be viewed and configured from the Server Management console's Group Policy Objects node.

Backing Up and Restoring GPOs

Once you go to all the effort to create customized, detailed GPOs, you definitely want to make sure they get backed up and that you can restore them if need be. In this section, we'll show you how to do just that. Backup up a GPO will save all the information inside the GPO, but it will not save the links, any existing WMI filters, or the Internet Protocol (IP) security policy, which are external to the actual GPO itself. All of the following instructions assume you are in the Group Policy Objects node of Advanced Server Management.

To backup GPOs, use the following steps:

1. To back up a single GPO, right-click the GPO and select **Backup** from the shortcut menu
   OR
   To back up multiple GPOs, right-click **Group Policy Objects** and select **Back Up All** from the shortcut menu.

2. In the Back Up Group Policy Object dialog box, enter the location and description then click **Backup**. The progress of the backup will be displayed.

3. When complete, click the **OK** button to finish.

It's a good idea to create a backup of the default GPOs in SBS right off the bat. Store them in a secure folder with limited access and make sure that folder is included in your normal backup routine. That way if you ever mistakenly tweak to your default GPOs (or mess them up completely), you can restore from your original, untouched GPOs. It's a great insurance policy and it only takes a few minutes to do.

To restore GPOs from backup, use the following steps:

1. To restore a single GPO, right-click the GPO and click **Restore** (you might choose this option if you want to restore the original settings to a GPO that you've modified).
   OR
   To restore multiple GPOs, right-click the **Group Policy Objects** node and select **Restore All.**

2. In the Backup Location dialog box, provide the location of the backed up GPO(s).

3. In the Source GPO dialog box, specify which version of the GPO you want to restore (if multiple versions exist). Click **Next.**

4. In the final screen, review the settings you've selected. To make changes, click **Back**; otherwise click **Finish.**

An alternative to restoring a GPO is to import a GPO. This option doesn't overwrite links and security filtering. To import settings, use the following steps:

1. Right-click the GPO into which you want to import settings and select **Import Settings** from the shortcut menu. This will launch the Import Settings Wizard. Click **Next** to continue.

2. The Import Settings Wizard will prompt you to back up the settings in the existing GPO, since importing will overwrite settings. If you've backed up your GPO, click **Next** to continue; otherwise, click the **Backup** button to save the existing GPO settings.

3. In the Backup location dialog box, select the location of the GPO you want to import. If you want to view the settings of the selected GPO before importing, click the **View Settings** button. Otherwise, select the GPO and click **Next.**

4. In the **Scanning Backup** dialog box, the wizard scans the settings in the backup GPO to see if any security principals or UNC paths need to be transferred. Once the scan is complete, click **Next** to continue.

5. The final screen allows you to review settings before you import. If you're satisfied with the settings, click **Finish** to import the GPO settings into the GPO you've selected. Otherwise, click **Back** to go back and make changes or **Cancel** to bail out without making any changes.

6. If you click **Finish**, the import will proceed and you'll see a progress bar indicating import progress. In the **Status** box, the status of the import will be displayed. When it is completed, it will display "GPO:[Group policy name]…Succeeded." Click **OK** to close the Import wizard.

7. If you want to verify settings, select the GPO in the Server Management console, click the **Settings** tab in the right pane, and review the settings for the GPO.

Predicting GPO Results

Predicting GPO results is about as easy as predicting the outcome of hotly contested election, which is to say it can sometimes be a difficult process. The good news is that SBS provides two very useful tools for working with group policy. The **Group Policy Modeling** and **Group Policy Results** nodes in Advanced Server Management can be used to predict the results of GPOs. Both tools are useful but utilize some of the more advanced features of group policy. For more detailed information on these tools or for help with any of the terminology or features in the tools, query the Help and Support files. Going over every element of these tools is outside the scope of this chapter but we did want to introduce you to the tools.

Group Policy Modeling (also known as *Resultant Set of Policy (RSoP)* for those of you familiar with the concept) is a tool that lets you test out scenarios without actually implementing them. You can use group policy modeling to create "what-if" scenarios and make sure your settings will generate the results you want.

The Group Policy Results tool can be used to determine current group policy settings for a specific user or computer.

To use the Group Policy Modeling tool, locate the node in Advanced Server Management. We'll give the path once here and assume you'll use this path throughout this section as your starting point. Go to **Start** | **Server Management** | **Advanced Management** | **Group Policy Management** | **Forest:** *domain name* | **Group Policy Modeling** (or **Group Policy Results**).

1. Right-click **Group Policy Modeling** and select **Group Policy Modeling Wizard** from the shortcut menu. This will launch the wizard. Click **Next** to continue.

2. The first dialog box prompts you to select the domain controller on which you want to perform the modeling. Since SBS is the domain controller, the drop-down box will default to your SBS domain controller. You can click the box next to the option to **Skip to the final page of this wizard without collecting additional data**. This will jump to the end and skip the configuration dialog boxes. This option is available in all the dialogs in this wizard, so you can skip there anytime.

3. The next dialog box, User and Computer Selection, prompts you to select the user or computer information you want to model. Select the user or computer and click **Next.**

4. In Advanced Simulation Options, you can enter additional options for modeling. Select desired options, click **Next** to continue.

5. The Alternate Active Directory Paths dialog box prompts you to enter new network locations for simulating policy settings. Click **Next** to continue.

6. In the User Security Groups dialog box, you can simulate changes to the selected user's security groups. **Add** or **Remove** groups as desired then click **Next** to continue.

7. The WMI Filters for Users dialog box allows you to select WMI filters in your simulation.

8. The final screen is the Summary of Selections screen, where you can review your selections, go **Back** to make changes or click **Next** to finish. The progress bar at the bottom of the dialog box will advance and when complete, the Completing screen is shown. Click **Finish** to close the Group Policy Modeling Wizard.

9. The results of your query are now listed as a node under the Group Policy Modeling node in the left pane. Click the query to view the Summary, Settings, or Query in the right pane, as shown in Figure 8.9.

Figure 8.9 Results of Group Policy Modeling Query

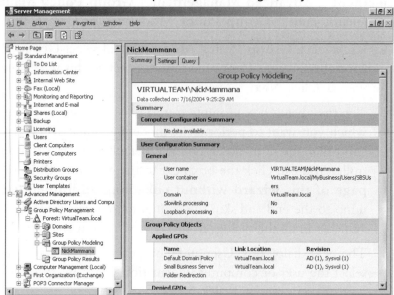

To use the Group Policy Results Wizard, use the following steps.

1. Right-click **Group Policy Results** in the left pane and select **Group Policy Results Wizard** from the shortcut menu to launch the wizard. Click **Next** to continue.

2. The first dialog box, Computer Selection, allows you to specify the computer or to review policy settings only for a user (and not a computer). Make your selection and click **Next.**

3. The User Selection dialog box prompts you to select a user. Make your selection and click **Next.**

4. Summary of Selections is displayed. Click **Next** to continue, **Back** to make changes, or **Cancel** to exit. The progress bar increments until the wizard is finished. Click **Finish** to close the wizard and return to the Server Management console.

5. Under **Group Policy Results** in the left pane, the new results are listed. Click to select and review **Summary, Settings**, and **Policy Events** details in the right pane. An example of results is shown in Figure 8.10.

Figure 8.10 Group Policy Results for User

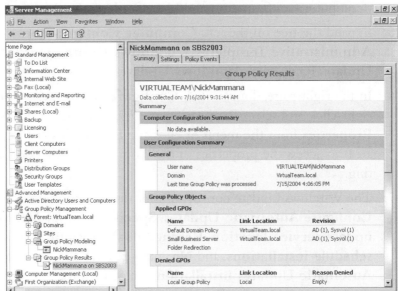

Using GPOs to Update Client Computers Automatically

Did you ever wonder if we'd get to the good stuff—the reason we talked about GPOs at all? Well, you've survived this brief intro to group policy and now we're actually going to put it to work.

One of the continuing tasks for any net admin is keeping client computers up to date. Though we'll talk about using Software Update Services (SUS) in a later chapter, it's relevant here because the easiest way to configure computers to use SUS is to create a new GPO with the appropriate settings and link it to the desired container (in this case, the group of computers to have this GPO applied). To do this, use the following steps:

1. Click **Start | Administrative Tools | Group Policy Management** (an alternate way to get to the Group Policy Management console).

2. Locate your domain and right-click, then select **Create and Link a GPO Here.**

3. Enter the name of the new GPO and click **OK.**

4. Right-click the new GPO and select **Edit** from the shortcut menu. This will launch the Group Policy Editor. Notice the familiar groupings (Computer Configuration and User Configuration) in the left pane.

5. Expand the tree on the left: **Computer Configuration | Administrative Templates | Windows Components | Windows Update**. Right-click **Windows Update**.

6. In the right pane, double-click **Configure Automatic Updates** (or right-click and select **Properties** or click once and select **Action | Properties** from the menu or click the **Properties** link in the taskpad area) to access the properties of the Configure Automatic Updates setting.

7. The Windows Update consists of four discrete configurations: **Configure Automatic Updates**, **Specify intranet Microsoft update service location**, **Reschedule Automatic Updates schedule installations**, and **No auto-restart for scheduled Automatic Updates installations**. Information about each of these can be accessed via the **Explain** tab. Each of these can be **Not Configured** (default), **Enabled**, or **Disabled**.

8. In the Configure Automatic Updates properties dialog box, select **Enabled**, then specify how the updates should be configured. If you're not sure what the settings will do, click the **Explain** tab. This tab provides help and information for each setting and you can scroll forward and back using the **Previous Setting** and **Next Setting** buttons. In our example, we used option 3, **Auto download and notify for install**, the default setting. This is the recommended setting so that updates are automatically downloaded when available, but are not installed until you give the OK. This is to prevent computers from rebooting (required for some updates) when users are in the middle of

critical tasks. You can choose option 4, which allows you to schedule the installation, if you know that users' computers will be on and available at a specified time. This will automate the process and may be a better choice than option 3 for your organization.

9. There are four specific settings you can configure. To configure additional settings, click the **Next Setting** button. When you've finished configuring your settings, click **OK** to close the Properties dialog box. Your chosen settings are displayed in the right pane, as shown in Figure 8.11.

Figure 8.11 Configuring Windows Update Settings

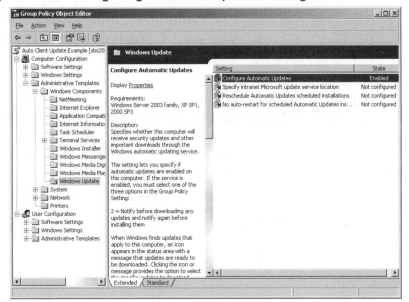

Using GPOs to Audit Events

By default, SBS provides a number of pre-defined performance and usage reports you can use to monitor and manage your network. However, you may also want to use group policy to configure auditing of specific events on your network. We'll talk about performance and usage reports later in the book, so for now, we'll limit our discussion to setting up auditing events via GPOs. However, before you actually configure GPOs for auditing, you may want to review the chapter on monitoring and tuning performance.

You can use the following steps to create a GPO that will create custom auditing based on your needs. Be sure to think through what you're auditing and why, otherwise you'll end up with pages of useless data in your log file. For instance, monitoring successful logons isn't particularly helpful unless you want to monitor a particular account. Conversely, monitoring unsuccessful logons might help detect a hacker trying to get into an account. Think through the auditing to make sure the data you collect will actually help you manage the network. If not, don't audit it. To set up auditing, go to **Start | Administrative Tools | Group Policy Management.**

1. Locate the **Default Domain Controllers Policy** (this will enable auditing on the SBS server), right-click it, and select **Edit** from the shortcut menu. This will launch the Group Policy Object Editor.

2. Expand the following tree: **Computer Configuration | Windows Settings | Security Settings | Local Policies | Audit Policy**, as shown in Figure 8.12.

Figure 8.12 Navigate to Audit Policy in Group Policy Object Editor

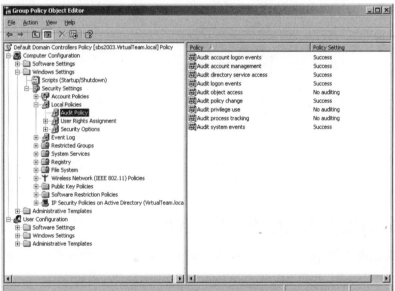

3. Double-click any of the policies to modify the policy settings via the Properties dialog box (you can also access the properties by right-clicking or choosing **Action | Properties** from the menu).

Auditing is now set for these events and will be established through the application of the Default Domain Controllers Policy. If you've been paying attention, this last statement should stop you in your tracks. If so, good catch! We've stated a number of times that you should avoid modifying default group policies, and that still holds true. If you want to make minor modifications to default policies, back up the GPOs first. That way, if you make an error, you have a pristine copy of the default GPOs from which you can restore. However, this is one area that is relatively safe to modify since it turns logging on and off for particular events—a relatively "safe" modification to make. However, if you wanted to follow the rules to the letter, you should create a new GPO for the domain controller (using the steps delineated earlier in the chapter) and establish auditing via the GPO.

Best Practices According to Microsoft

- The fewer GPOs you use, the better. Using many GPOs becomes confusing for you and can create unspecified results.
- Avoid conflicting policies whenever possible (for example, enabling something in one place and disabling it in another).
- Set policies at the highest level possible.
- Avoid non-standard policy processing when possible. That means avoid using **No Override**, **Block Policy Inheritance**, and other special settings that could alter expected results.
- Keep policy object names unique so you can easily tell one from another. It is possible to use duplicate object names, though doing so would be counterproductive.
- Test, test, test. Make sure you know exactly how the GPO will work and what effect it will have before implementing it.

One More Time

This chapter taught you about configuring and managing both share and NTFS (access control) permissions, as well as how to configure and manage Group Policy. Permissions are critical to controlling access to resources on the network and group policy provides a handy tool for managing a multitude of settings across the domain. Group Policy is a powerful tool and we only scratched the surface, but you learned the basics of working with group policies in SBS.

☑ Share permissions are the only access control available on FAT and FAT32 disks and do not apply to users who log on locally.

☑ NTFS permissions provide access control at a more granular (and thus secure) level than share permissions.

☑ If possible, avoid using both share and NTFS permissions. Use only NTFS permissions when possible.

☑ Permissions can be configured for users and groups by either assigning groups permissions to resources or adding groups to resource permissions.

☑ You can specify whether permissions should be inherited by child objects.

☑ You can prevent permissions from overriding child object settings by using the Block Inheritance setting.

☑ Use care in setting custom actions (such as blocking inheritance), as it can cause unexpected results and create security holes.

☑ Group policy is applied to users or computers in the domain.

☑ A Group Policy Object is a small file containing a variety of settings related to computer and/or user configuration.

☑ SBS provides several default Group Policies that should not be modified. Instead, create a new GPO and modify those settings.

☑ Backup default policies to a secure folder location and make sure that folder gets backed up as part of your normal backup routine. Having an untouched copy of the original default GPOs might just save your bacon someday.

☑ Group policies are inherited and the inheritance can be modified. Again, use caution setting custom configurations, which may cause unspecified results.

☑ The order in which group policies are applied (or implemented) may alter the resulting actions.

☑ To test various settings, use the Group Policy Modeling tool, accessed in the Advanced Management section of the Server Management console.

☑ To see the results of settings in place, use the Group Policy Results tool, also available in Advanced Management node of the Server Management console.

☑ Various tasks can be automated using group policy. We reviewed automating client computer Windows updates and setting up auditing of events at the domain level.

Chapter 9

Managing
Client Computers

- Overview of Client Computer Management

- Network Address Translation and IP Configuration

- Adding and Connecting Computers to the Network

- Applying Applications to Network Computers

- Using Windows Update and Software Update Services

The End Result

By the end of this chapter, you'll be able to effectively manage client computers on your network. You'll learn more about client Internet Protocol (IP) configuration using Dynamic Host Control Protocol (DHCP), network address translation (NAT), and how to configure client computers. You'll know how to add computers to the network and how to use Small Business Server 2003 (SBS) tools to apply applications and update software.

Overview of Client Computer Management

So far, you've learned a lot about users and user accounts. Now it's time to turn our attention to computers and computer accounts. Client computers have to be assigned a unique IP address so they can participate on the network. They also have to be configured to be secure. Finally, client computers must also be configured for users' needs. In this chapter, we'll look at these three types of tasks.

Earlier in the book we discussed network address translation as a way of assigning private IP addresses to computers on your network and sending all Internet-bound traffic via one or more public IP addresses. If you stepped through the To Do list in Chapter 3 (as recommended) and used a private address for your server such as 192.168.8.1, NAT and other IP configuration information was automatically set up for you. In the next section, we'll step through checking your IP configuration information, since it must be correct for client computers to connect to the network. Even though this is performed on the server, it directly impacts client computers.

Security needs are managed via joining the domain, managing user and group settings, and configuring the client computer to stay up-to-date with security updates for the operating system and the applications. Windows Small Business Server 2003 provides a number of tools for managing client computers that simplify administration and contribute to network security.

User needs include providing the services and applications users require to perform their jobs. We'll look at SBS features you can use to help manage these tasks.

Network Address Translation and IP Configuration

If you followed the steps provided in this book in Chapters 2 and 3, you have already established the foundation for using NAT. In those chapters, we used a private, Class C IP address for the network interface card (NIC) that attaches to the internal network. The NIC attached to the Internet was assigned the public IP address provided by your ISP. Now that we're ready to add computers to the network, we need to make sure our IP addressing is properly configured. We'll walk through checking NAT configuration. We'll assume you're using NAT since it's both easiest and safest to implement. We'll also quickly look at the Dynamic Host Configuration Protocol (DHCP) options in SBS that are used to automatically assign IP configuration information to client computers.

NAT/Firewall Configuration

Now that you've verified the NAT protocol is installed, the next thing we will do is verify NAT is configured and set to use the DHCP, which automatically assigns IP addresses and related configuration information to client computers. If you are using the built-in SBS firewall, check these settings. If you are using an external firewall, you will not be able to access these settings and you can verify your DHCP settings via the DHCP server interface via Start | Administrative Tools | DHCP. Use the following steps to verify the private IP address configuration when using the built-in SBS firewall. These steps are performed in the Routing and Remote Access management console, via Start | Administrative Tools | Routing and Remote Access.

1. Locate NAT/Basic Firewall under IP Routing in the left pane.

2. Right-click NAT/Basic Firewall and select Properties.

3. In the NAT/Basic Firewall Properties dialog, click the Address Assignment tab to review the IP address and mask. They should be as you originally configured them in the Configure Remote Access wizard (when we went through the To Do List).

4. The checkbox to Automatically assign IP addresses by using the DHCP allocator is selected by default if you are using the internal (SBS) firewall (meaning you have two NICs in your system).. Leave this setting as you found it. For advanced net admins: You can use either the DHCP allo-

cator, which is a mini-version of DHCP, or you can use the DHCP server service if you're using the internal firewall. If you're using an external firewall, you must use the DHCP server service, the allocator will be disabled. It's an either/or selection and the default setting is typically fine.

5. On the General tab of NAT/Basic Firewall Properties, you can enable logging. Choose from one of the four radio buttons. The default is Log errors only, which is a good setting unless you want more information. Click OK to close the NAT/Basic Firewall Properties dialog.

Some Independent Advice

If you have the Windows Small Business Server 2003 Premium edition and are planning on using the Internet Server and Acceleration (ISA) Server firewall (recommended if you do have the Premium edition), the Firewall client (software run on client computers that interface with ISA) must be installed on client computers. If ISA is already installed when you add computers, you'll be prompted to use the ISA firewall client, which you should do. If ISA is not yet installed, your computers will use the standard SBS firewall. Once you install ISA, you'll be prompted to add the Firewall client to the automatically installed client software.

DHCP Basics

Before we go any further, we need to discuss a little bit about the Dynamic Host Configuration Protocol (DHCP) in SBS. DHCP is the method used to automatically assign IP configuration information to client computers. It's a great tool because you can set up just a few parameters and let the server manage client computer IP configuration. Assuming you set it up correctly, your client IP configuration will always be correct.. This is a built-in feature of the Windows Server 2003 operating system (and therefore a native part of SBS as well) and is relatively easy to use. We'll take a look around the DHCP management console and verify the IP configuration information at the same time. The default settings work just fine and you should only make changes if you're very familiar with DHCP, how it works and how it should be configured. The information in this section is only intended to familiarize you with some of the elements of DHCP.

Let's look at some of the elements so you gain a basic understanding of DHCP. DHCP manages client IP configuration. The range of addresses the DHCP server has available to hand out to clients is called the *scope*. Addresses within the scope are automatically assigned to client computers on a first come, first served basis. In Windows Server 2003 networks, you can create multiple scopes, but in SBS you will typically just have one. Under each scope (in this case, the only scope), you'll see the *address pool*, which includes all possible addresses within the scope. SBS automatically sets up the address pool based on your input during the Configure E-mail and Internet Wizard. Although you can modify DHCP settings if you know what you're doing, it's generally best to let SBS take care of it.

Various kinds of network devices should have static IP addresses (servers, routers, and printers, for example) so they're always easily located. These addresses must be *excluded* from the scope so they're not handed out to any other device. These are called *exclusions* and when defined, these addresses will never be offered to a client computer. SBS will automatically create a range of addresses that are excluded so you can use these addresses for that purpose. However, SBS will only create one range of excluded addresses and as you'll see in a moment, you may want to create a couple more. This is generally the only modification you'll make to the DHCP settings on your SBS server.

You can also create *reservations*, which are almost the exact opposite of exclusions. You can *reserve* some IP addresses for permanent lease to specific computers or devices on your network. You should only make DHCP reservations for devices that are DHCP-enabled and that must be reserved for a specific purpose. Typically, you won't need this in SBS and you should avoid using reservations unless you have a specific need and know how to set it up.

You can access the DHCP management console by selecting **Server Management | Advanced Management | Computer Management (local) | Services and Applications | DHCP** or by selecting **Start | Administrative Tools | DHCP**. Either way, you'll end up in the DHCP management section of your server. Once you've opened the DHCP console (for our example, we used the latter method), you'll see a listing in the left pane that will read something similar to *SBSServerName.mshome.net [192.168.16.0]*. If you click that, you'll see two entries in the right pane, the **scope** and **server options**. The description associated with scope will read "Scope configured during Windows Small Business Server setup." When we walked through our Internet setup in Chapter 3 (To Do List), SBS configured this based on the settings we provided.

If you click **Scope** to expand it, you'll see four items listed in the right pane:

- **Address Pool** All possible addresses based on the IP information you provided during setup.

- **Address Leases** The IP addresses currently leased to client computers.

- **Reservations** Any IP addresses reserved for specific DHCP-enabled devices.

- **Scope Options** Advanced options you can configure (but you're better off leaving alone).

Address Pool

The address pool is the range of all possible addresses that can be assigned. This is shown in Figure 9.1. The following addresses are excluded by default: 192.168.16.1 through 192.168.16.9. This is based on the configuration information (Chapter 3) that set the SBS server address to 192.168.16.1. If you set your SBS server address to 192.168.8.1, your excluded range should show up as 192.168.8.1 through 192.168.8.9, for example. Two additional excluded ranges were added. Another listing you'll see is the address range for distribution. Referring to Figure 9.1, you can see that the *range* or *scope* is 192.168.16.1 through 192.168.16.254. Notice that there's overlap—the first 29 addresses are part of the pool, but are excluded from being handed out.

Figure 9.1 DHCP Address Pool

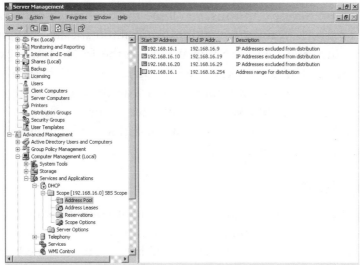

Address Leases

In this section of the DHCP management console, you can review computers' IP leases. Each leased IP address is listed along with the name of the computer and when the lease expires. All computers on the network using DHCP should have leases that will be listed here.

Reservations

As mentioned earlier, reservations are addresses that are reserved for specific computers. The default settings in SBS do not create any reservations. You can add a reservation, but you must have the MAC address for the device, which is a unique address associated with a specific network interface card. In most cases, you can simply assign a static IP address to a device rather than setting it up for DHCP and creating a reservation for it. For more information on reservations and MAC addresses, query the Help and Support files in SBS.

Scope Options

When you click on **Scope Options**, you'll see the configured options for DHCP on your server. Again, these options were automatically configured when you used the E-mail and Internet Setup Wizard in the To Do List back in Chapter 3. **Caution**: Unless you know what you're doing, it's best to leave the default SBS DHCP settings as you found them. The IP address for the router, your DNS servers, and WINS (Windows Internet Name Server) servers are listed here. DNS and WINS are two methods of translating a computer name such as "MonkeyBusiness" to a specific IP address.

Excluding Addresses

Servers should be assigned static IP addresses. Client computers are rarely assigned static IP addresses. If you have servers on your network other than the SBS server, you should assign them static IP addresses. This is done by manually assigning that server an IP address from the excluded range. The server should not be configured to use DHCP if you want to assign it a static IP address. If you manually assign the server an IP address from an IP address in the general address pool, you'll run into network problems with that server as soon as the SBS server tries to hand out the IP address used by the server.

You may want to map out how you'll use address ranges. There are some common configurations, though you can set it up any way that actually makes sense for you as long as it's consistent. These excluded ranges are reflected in the settings shown in Figure 9.1.

One method is:

192.168.X.1 – 192.168.X.9 – Use for network devices such as routers, switches, etc.

192.168.X.10 – 192.168.X.19 – User for servers

192.168.X.20 – 192.168.X.29 – Use for printers

To create new exclusions beyond the default setting, open the DHCP management console (**Start | Administrative Tools | DHCP**) and click the **+** to the left of the server name. Click the **+** to the left of **Scope** and click on **Address Pool**. Click **Action** from the menu and select **New Exclusion Range.** Enter the start and end IP addresses for the new range. For example, you could type in **192.168.16.10** for the start and **192.168.16.19** for the end. This range could be used for static IP addresses for all servers on the network other than the SBS server. Click **Add.** If you make a mistake and want to edit a range, simply delete the range and add a new one with the right IP addresses. To delete a range, select it and select **Action | Delete** from the menu.

You can create new exclusion ranges if you have more devices that need static IP addresses than the default exclusion range allows. If an address within your new excluded range is already in use by a client computer, go ahead and create the new excluded range, then go to the client computer in question and renew the lease. This will assign a new, non-excluded IP address to the client computer. To renew the IP lease on the client computer, click **Start | Run**, type in **cmd** to open a command console, then, type in **ipconfig /renew**. Once the IP lease is renewed, type **exit** and press **Enter** to close the command console. The client computer should now have a new IP address outside of the excluded range.

Now that you've verified that NAT has been installed and configured and that DHCP is configured properly, your client computers will be able to automatically receive their private IP address (and related configuration) from the SBS server. At this point, we're ready to begin adding computers and configuring client computers to connect to the network.

Adding and Connecting Computers to the Network

Adding and connecting computers to the network is the first task related to client computers. Adding and connecting the computers are both easy tasks, so let's get started.

Adding Client Computers

As you know, computers require a unique IP address on a network. They also require a unique name because in some settings, the name can be used to identify and locate the computer. To add a computer, you'll need to assign a unique name. As with other network administration tasks, it's a good idea to create a consistent naming scheme for user accounts, computer accounts, etc. Some companies find it useful to associate the computer name with the user name. Other companies create computer names based on the location or function. Use whatever works best for your company and use it consistently.

To add a client computer to the network, use the following steps:

1. Click **Start | Server Management | Client Computers**.

2. In the taskpad, click **Set Up Client Computers** to launch the Set Up Computer Wizard, then click **Next** to continue.

3. In the Client Computer Names dialog box, enter the **Client computer name**, then click **Add**. When you have finished adding client computer names (you can add multiple computers at one time), click **Next**. If you attempt to add a duplicate name, you will receive an error message stating that a duplicate name exists. Click **OK** on the warning message and remove or rename the duplicate(s).

4. The next dialog box is the Client Applications screen on which you can select the applications to install on client computers. If the application is already installed, it will not be removed even if you deselect the item in this dialog box. By default, the four applications are: **Client Operating System Service Packs**, **Internet Explorer 6.0**, **Microsoft Office Outlook 2003**, and **Shared Fax Client**. Remove the checkbox from any item (all are selected by default) to deselect the item to prevent it from being installed. This dialog box is shown in Figure 9.2.

Figure 9.2 Installing Client Applications

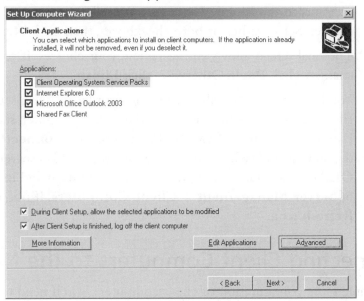

5. There are two additional checkboxes you can select. The first, **During Client Setup, allow the selected applications to be modified**, is used to allow the user who is installing applications to change the default installation location or to deselect applications for installation. The second checkbox, **After Client Setup is finished, log off the client computer**, logs off after installation is complete. This allows you to leave once the installation is started and to make sure no one can access the computer after the Setup is completed. Use the **Edit Applications** or **Advanced** button to modify the default settings. These settings can be modified later by right-clicking on the computer name (in Server Management) and selecting **Assign Applications to this Computer…** from the shortcut menu. Click **Next** to continue.

6. The next screen is the Mobile Client and Offline Use dialog box, which contains two checkboxes. The **Install Connection Manager** checkbox installs Connection Manager on client computers, which configures settings and provides instructions on connecting remotely to the network. The **Install ActiveSync 3.7** checkbox will install ActiveSync on client computers to allow users to synchronize SmartPhones, Pocket PCs, and other mobile devices with their client computers. Note: Before users

can actually make a remote connection, you will have to add the user accounts to the Mobile Users group. We'll cover remote access in a later chapter. Select either or both checkboxes, then click **Next** to continue.

7. The final screen allows you to review your choices. If you need to make changes, click **Back**. Otherwise, click **Finish**.

8. You'll get a message telling you that in order to finish setting up the client computers, you must go to the client computer, start Internet Explorer and type in **http://SBS servername/ConnectComputer** in the address box (where *SBS servername* is your SBS server name). Click **OK**. Your new client computer accounts are displayed in the right pane of **Server Management | Client Computers**. If not, click the **Refresh** icon.

Connecting Client Computers to the Network

To complete the configuration of client computers, you'll need to go to the client computer, open Internet Explorer and type in the following URL (Uniform Resource Locator): **http://SBSservername/ConnectComputer**, where *SBSservername* is the name of your server. Depending on the state of the client computer (formerly connected to network, new computer, etc.), you may have to monkey with the settings to get it to find the server.

SOME INDEPENDENT ADVICE

If you're having connectivity problems with your client computer, you can try a few of these troubleshooting steps.

1. Check to make sure the IP address is set to use DHCP. Check the Network Connection in Control Panel.

2. Open a command window (**Start | Run**, enter **cmd** then press **Enter**). At the prompt, type **ping localhost**, then press **Enter**. This checks TCP/IP on your client computer. If that fails, the problem is on the client computer. If it is successful (per the response on the screen), type **ping 192.168.X.Y**, where the IP address is the SBS server address (do not use the letters, substitute your server's IP address). If this fails, it means the computer cannot locate the server. Check cabling, IP configuration. You can also try **ping** *SBSServerName* to test the name resolution (DNS) function.

3. If you get a message in Internet Explorer (after entering the URL listed at the beginning of this section) that the Internet is not available, click **Connect** (rather than **Work Offline**) and you should connect to the server despite not having an Internet connection.

This isn't a comprehensive troubleshooting list, but it might help you if the client won't talk with the network to get to this URL.

Once you connect to the URL in Internet Explorer, use the following steps to configure the computer on the network. Note: If you chose to apply applications to the client at the time of the connection, you may get additional screens in the wizard. Follow the on-screen instructions if they do not follow step-by-step with these instructions.

1. In the Internet Explorer window, the on-screen instruction prompts you to click the link labeled **Connect to the network now**. Doing so will launch the SBS Network Configuration Wizard. You'll be prompted to install this small application/wizard. Click **Yes** to proceed.

2. When the wizard opens, you'll be prompted for a username and password. Enter the username and password then click **Next.** You can enter the username for the person that will use the computer. If you recall, when we established password policies we set them to not take effect immediately so you could use "simple" passwords during this process. If you're doing this after those policies went into effect, you'll have to use strong passwords, which will require just a bit more work for you.

3. In the first dialog box, **Assign user to this computer and migrate their profiles,** you can add users to the computer. In the left pane, select the user and click **Add**. Continue until all desired users are added. Those names will be added to the list in the right pane. In the lower area of the dialog box, you can preserve previous account settings by using the drop-down list options, as shown in Figure 9.1. Click **Next** to continue.

4. In the Computer Name dialog box, select the computer name that matches the client computer and the computer account added to the SBS server. Click **Next** to continue.

5. On the final screen, you can review your selections, go **Back**, or click **Finish** to complete the task. The computer must be rebooted, so close any other open applications before clicking **Finish**.

Once the computer reboots, you'll briefly see a small dialog box that says Small Business Network Configuration Wizard, the computer will go into Windows, you'll see *sbs netsetup* as the user name, the computer will reboot again, and the logon screen will prompt you for a username and password. This indicates the network connection has been established and if you watch the screen, you'll also notice that security and user settings are being applied, another indication that the client computer has been set up using policies and settings from the SBS server. If you click on **Entire Network**, you will see the domain name of your corporate domain listed.

It's also good to note that once the client computer is connected, you can view the details of the client operating system in **Server Management | Client Computers**, which displays the client computer name, description (if any), operating system, and service pack. This is a great snapshot of the status of your client computers. These same details are available by right-clicking the client computer and selecting **Properties** from the shortcut menu.

Working with Client Computers Running Earlier Versions of Windows

In a perfect (Microsoft) world, all your client computers would be running Windows XP Professional SP2 as the operating system. However, we know that budgets and finances often constrain how often we can upgrade a system, so most companies today are running a mixed environment. We've talked earlier about moving away from Windows 95, 98 and ME because you can't take advantage of the new security features available. Studies have shown that more time, effort, and resources are required to maintain older computers and operating systems than the cost of the upgrade, so make sure you're not fooling yourself by thinking you're saving money by not upgrading. Make sure you're not spending a disproportionate amount of time on older computers. The cost of your time and effort could quickly pay for the cost of upgraded hardware and/or software. OK, you know you should upgrade in some cases, but you may still have older client computers on your network.

You can manage these computers using the SBS interface, but because the different operating systems require different instructions, we're not going to go blow-by-blow through managing different operating systems here. The Help and Support files on this topic are excellent, so go to **Start | Help and Support**. In the search box, type **configure client computers** and click the arrow to start searching. One of the help topics displayed is "Manage client computers running earlier versions of Windows." Click that link in the left pane to display the options in the right pane, which include:

- Configure client computers running earlier versions of Windows.

- Migrate client computers running earlier versions of Windows.

- Install and configure TCP/IP on client computers running earlier versions of Windows.

- Install applications on client computers running earlier versions of Windows.

- Configure e-mail for client computers running earlier versions of Windows.

Each of these links displays details and step-by-step instructions on accomplishing the tasks they reference. Where applicable, the tasks delineate steps for each operating system including computers running Windows 95, 98 or ME or computers running Windows NT 4.0.

Applying Applications to Network Computers

You can apply applications to client computers, either at the time you create the computer account, or later, after the computer account has been created. Either way, a wizard will walk you through the same steps. If you selected applications to be applied to the client computer when you established the client computer account, those applications are installed when you connect the client using the steps outlined in the previous section. If you choose to apply those applications later, in Server Management | Client Computers, locate the computer to which you want to apply applications, right-click and select **Assign Applications to this Computer** from the shortcut menu. This launches the same wizard you saw earlier. Use the following steps:

1. Click **Next** on the first screen.

2. On the Client Applications screen, select the applications you want to apply. If the application is not listed, click the **Edit Applications** button. Click **Advanced** for additional options.

3. In the Mobile Client and Offline Use dialog box, select **Install Connection Manager** to connect from remote locations and/or **Install ActiveSync 3.7** for use with mobile devices. If you choose **Install Connection Manager**, you'll be reminded to set up remote access for the user as well. We configured remote access during our trip through the To Do List in Chapter 3 and we'll cover remote access in a bit more detail later the book as well. Click **Next** to continue.

4. If you've already run the Network Configuration Wizard (we're assuming you have), all that's needed is to log off and back on to the client computer. When you log off, you may notice that a small dialog flashes saying "Synchronization complete" if you're redirected the user's My Documents folder to a network location.

5. Once you log back on, the **Client Setup Wizard** will be displayed. Select **Start Now** or **Postpone** to install (or not) the applications. If the user has something important he or she must get done, the **Postpone** option will allow the user to continue without installing application, but this wizard will appear the next time the user logs on. Click **Start Now.** The Client Setup Wizard will launch. Click **Next** to continue.

6. You'll see a list of the applications you chose to install and a progress bar at the bottom indicating installation progress. This may take a while depending on what you've selected to install. When it's complete, click **Next** to continue. After the applications are installed, click **Finish** to close the dialog box.

There are other ways to roll out applications across the network; this is just one of several options you have. We won't go into other options here, but you can query the Microsoft website for additional methods you may want to explore.

There's one other task in the Server Management | Client Computer section we should cover briefly. If you want to create a diskette to use on a client computer to assist in setting up a remote connection, you can launch the **Create**

Remote Connection Disk Wizard by clicking the link in the taskpad. You'll need to have a diskette drive on your server (some servers these days ship without a diskette drive) in order to use this function.

Using Windows Update and Software Update Services

As you're learned throughout this book, keeping client computers up-to-date is a key feature of a secure network. When security patches are made available, either for the client's Windows operating system or for the applications running on the client, it's important that those patches be downloaded and installed in a timely manner before some enterprising hacker exploits the hole. While the same holds true for the server, we're focused solely on client computers in this chapter, so we'll stick to that topic.

There are two features that work with Windows Small Business Server 2003 to help you automatically update client computers. The Windows Update service can be configured to go out to the Microsoft Windows Update website and locate and install updates for the client computer. The Software Update Services (SUS) is an add-in you can download from the Microsoft website. The updated version of SUS will be called Windows Update Services (WUS) and should be available in late 2004.

Windows Update

The Windows Update function is an online extension of Windows that helps keep your computer up-to-date with the latest patches, fixes and security updates. Use Windows Update to choose which updates to install for your computer based on its operating system, software and hardware configuration. Windows Update will scan your computer to determine which updates are applicable to your computer based on what's currently available and what's already installed on your computer. You'll be prompted to download and install all applicable patches. Some patches require that your computer be rebooted after installation and some do not. Some updates require you to install them separately, but you'll be notified when that's the case.

Using Windows Update Manually

To update a client computer from the client computer, log on (you will need to use a local Administrator account or one with equivalent privileges) and click **Start | Help and Support**. In the Help and Support main screen, select **Keep computer up to date with Windows Update**. Your computer will automatically attempt to connect to the Windows Update website. Once it does, you'll see a link **Scan for updates**. This will prompt the website to scan your computer for appropriate updates. Microsoft specifically states that no personal information is collected during this process and that only information related to the installed software is checked, so this is a safe (and recommended) practice. Once the scan is complete, you'll be shown a list of updates available. They are divided into three categories: **Critical Updates and Service Packs**, **Windows XP** (assuming you're running XP, if not, it will be specific to your version) and **Driver Updates**. Remember that this site won't work with older systems and you'll have to manually check for updates.

You can review and install updates at this point. There may be times when recommended updates are not desired but for the most part, they address important issues in the software and should be installed. If you do not want to install a particular update at this time, you can remove it from your download list and it will re-appear the next time the website scans your computer for updates. Click the **Review and install updates** link once the scan is complete.

After you've reviewed the suggested list of downloads, you can click **Install Now** to download and install the updates. The computer may need to be rebooted and you'll be prompted if this is the case.

You can also connect to the downloads section of the Microsoft Office website by clicking the **Office Update** link on the menu within Windows Update (online). In the left navigation area, you can click the link to **Check for updates**. After appropriate updates have been identified for your computer, you can click **Start Installation** to install the updates.

Automating Windows Update

You can also set client computers to go out to the Windows Update site automatically and download and install the updates using the following steps:

1. Click **Start | Control Panel**, then locate and double-click **System** to access the System Properties dialog box. If the computer is using cate-

gory view, select **Performance and Maintenance** to locate the **System** icon.

2. Click the **Automatic Updates** tab. If the items on the tab are grayed out (disabled), but you can see the check mark is selected for **Keep my computer up to date**, there may be a group policy applied to the computer that has already configured this option. Figure 9.3 shows the options available to you. Once you've selected the checkbox to keep the computer up-to-date, there are three settings you can select.

- **Notify me before downloading any updates and notify me again before installing them on my computer.** This option requires the most interaction and is not the recommended setting.

- **Download the updates automatically and notify me when they are ready to be installed.** This is the recommended setting because it will only install downloads when you tell it. This is important since, as mentioned, some downloads require the computer to reboot after installation. If you allow this process to occur automatically, the system might reboot in the middle of a critical task.

- **Automatically download the updates, and install them on the schedule that I specify.** This option downloads updates automatically in the background (transparent to the user). When downloads are finished, a message appears in the lower status area notifying you of downloads ready for review prior to installation. You can install the updates at that time or allow the updates to be installed on the scheduled time. You must be logged on as the Administrator in order to make any changes or to select to install the updates immediately. Otherwise, if this option is selected, the updates will be installed automatically at the scheduled time. If a user is logged on at that time and the computer requires a restart, the user will be given the option of delaying the restart to a later time. If no user is logged on, the computer will reboot if needed.

Figure 9.3 Automatic Windows Update Options

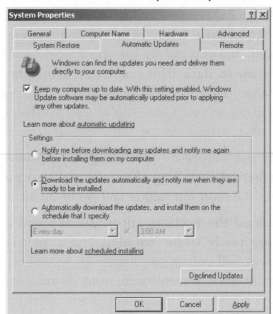

> ## SOME INDEPENDENT ADVICE
>
> You might run into an issue with Automatic Updates on computers where the active user does not have Administrator privileges. The best solution is to add a local account for the main user of that computer and make grant that account local administrative privileges.

Using Windows Update via Group Policy

You've already seen two ways Windows updates can be applied to a client computer. As with many features of Windows, there are usually two, three, four, or more ways to accomplish tasks and the same holds true here. You can also use Group Policy to force client computers to use Windows Update automatically. As with the automatic mode we just discussed, you can set the parameters as to how this will occur. Let's take a look at how to do this (there may be several ways you can approach this as well; we'll show you one way).

1. Open the Group Policy Management console by clicking **Start** | **Administrative Tools** | **Group Policy Management**.

2. Expand the tree in the left pane to locate Group Policy Objects, located in **Forest** | **Domains** | *domainname* | **Group Policy Objects**.

3. Right-click **Group Policy Objects** and select **New** from the shortcut menu.

4. Give the new group policy object (GPO) you're creating a descriptive name. In this example, we're using **Auto Client Update** as the name. After you've created a name, right-click that object and select **Edit** from the shortcut menu. This will open the Group Policy Object Editor.

5. The name of your GPO should be displayed in the top of the left pane. Expand the tree to locate Windows Update, located in **Computer Configuration** | **Windows Settings** | **Administrative Templates** | **Windows Components** | **Windows Updates**.

6. In the right pane, the four settings applicable to Windows Updates can be configured. Recall that in GPOs, settings can be *not configured, enabled* or *disabled*. By default, all four of the following settings are not configured, as shown in Figure 9.4. Click any of the four items in the right pane to view information and settings for that option.

Figure 9.4 Windows Update Group Policy Settings

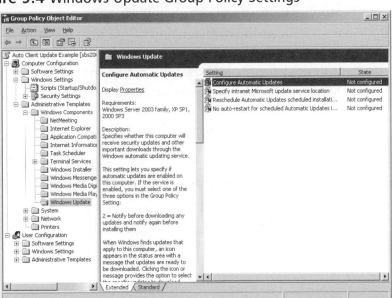

- **Configure Automatic Updates** This setting specifies whether the computer will receive automatic updates. As with the automatic settings discussed earlier, you can select one of three options for downloading and installing (see the previous section "Automating Windows Update").

- **Specify intranet Microsoft update service location** This option allows you to specify a server on your internal network to serve as an update center for Automatic Update clients.

- **Reschedule Automatic Updates scheduled installations** If an installation is missed for any reason, this setting sets the wait time after system start up to re-initiate the installation.

- **No auto-restart for scheduled Automatic Updates installations** This option specifies that the system will wait for the user to log off before restarting the computer automatically (if a user is logged on). This prevents the system from re-booting when the user is in the middle of an important task.

7. For our example, we enabled **Configure Automatic Updates** and **No auto-restart for scheduled Automatic Updates installations**. You can set whatever settings make sense for your company.

8. Click **File | Exit** to close the Group Policy Object Editor to return to the Group Policy Management console.

9. Figure 9.5 shows the configuration of our new GPO, *Auto Client Update Example*. If desired, you can set the security filtering by selecting the GPO in the left pane and selecting the **Scope** tab in the right pane. In the Security Filtering area, remove **Authenticated Users** (the default setting) if you do not want this policy to apply to every user on the system by selecting the entry and clicking **Remove**.

Figure 9.5 Group Policy Settings for new GPO

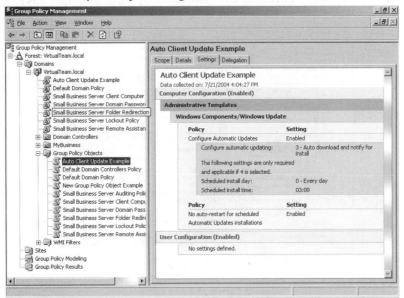

10. Click the **Add** button and enter **domain computers** in the **Enter the object name to select** box, then click **Check Names**, then **OK**. This will set this for all client computers in the domain. A note of caution here—its possible not all computers in the domain should have this applied to them, as older systems are unable to use the automatic Windows Update feature.

11. To apply to specific computers only, click the **Object Types** button, make sure **Computers** is checked, and click **OK**. Enter the name of the computer, click Check Names, then click **OK**.

12. If you don't have the names memorized, you can click the **Advanced** button and query for the computer names based on your naming scheme. Alternately, you can open **Server Management** and click on **Client Computers** to see a list of computer names and enter those (on at a time) into the **Enter the object name to select** box. In this way, you're only selecting computers to which this policy can and should be applied. An example is shown in Figure 9.6.

You may want to apply this to one computer and test the results before applying it to 40 or 50 computers, just to make sure things are correctly configured.

www.syngress.com

Figure 9.6 Security Filtering on Windows Update Group Policy Object

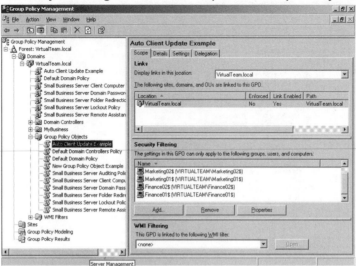

Software Update Services

The Software Update Services application is a free downloadable application from Microsoft. It is used to collect client software updates and store them on the SBS server. You can test configurations before rolling them out to your client computers. Then, client computers can connect to the SBS server and get the appropriate updates. This method does not require client computers to have Internet access.

Windows Small Business Server 2003 does not include Microsoft Software Update Services but it does *support* it. The most current version is SUS 1.0 SP1, which can be downloaded for free, and can be found at www.microsoft.com/windowsserversystem/sus/default.mspx. By the time you get this book in your hands, the newest version of SUS should be available. Rather than going to SUS 2.0, the product will be called Windows Update Services. If you see references to SUS 2.0 or WUS, they're the same thing. WUS should be available for download sometime in late 2004.

You can download the application from the Microsoft website and install it on your SBS server. You'll also need to install the Automatic Updates client component on client computers. Automatic Updates does not have to be installed on computers running Windows 2000 Service Pack (SP) 3 or Windows XP SP1 or later or on any computer running Windows Server 2003. You will need to install the Automatic Update client on computers running Windows XP Home, Windows 2000 Professional, Windows 2000 Server, and Windows 2000 Advanced Server SP2 or later. Users running Windows 95, 98, ME, or NT Workstation 4.0 need to visit the Microsoft Windows Update website or the Microsoft security website periodically to check for updates.

SUS is an advanced feature that might be right for your organization. We won't go into detail in this book, but you should know this option exists. If you want to use SUS/WUS, head up to the Microsoft website (reference the following "Some Independent Advice" section) and download the white paper on how to implement SUS as well as to download the SUS application itself.

SOME INDEPENDENT ADVICE

Software Update Services (SUS) is a great tool when you have to manage many different operating systems on hundreds (or even thousands) of computers. In a small business environment, the effort to use SUS may outweigh the benefits, so you should evaluate the benefit of SUS in your own environment. For instance, in order to use SUS, your client computers must be running Windows 2000 or later. There are also requirements for the computer operating systems to have certain updates and service packs installed. If you have a handful of computers, you may want to simply use the Windows Update feature. If you have less than five computers on your network (other than your SBS server), you shouldn't use SUS—it just won't be worth the effort. Either way you choose to go, make sure you have some process in place for updating client computers. The updates typically address critical security and stability issues and client computers should be kept as up-to-date as possible.

For more information on using the Software Update Services (soon to be Windows Update Services) in Windows Small Business Server 2003, visit this page on the Microsoft website and download the white paper from the link provided there. As with all links referenced in this book, they're subject to change, so if you don't find the material at this link, use the Search function to locate this document.

www.microsoft.com/windowsserversystem/sus/updatingsbswsus.mspx

You can download the SUS application from this location: www.microsoft.com/downloads/details.aspx?FamilyId=A7AA96E4-6E41-4F54-972C-AE66A4E4BF6C&displaylang=en

One More Time

Managing client computers is a relatively easy task in Small Business Server 2003. There are a number of wizards and built-in features that can be used to manage client computers.

☑ Network address translation allows you to use private IP addresses on your internal network for your client computers.

☑ DHCP is used to automatically assign IP addresses to client computers.

☑ You can exclude a range of addresses to use for statically assigned IP addresses.

☑ Servers, printers, and other network devices should have static IP addresses assigned they can always be easily located on the network.

☑ Network address translation is configured in Routing and Remote Access.

☑ The NAT protocol is installed when you use the Remote Access wizard in the To Do List.

☑ Client computers should be configured to use DHCP.

☑ Computers can be added to the network via the Add a Computer wizard in Server Management.

☑ When adding a client computer, you can choose to apply applications to the computer. When the user logs on to the network on the added computer, the applications are installed automatically.

☑ Applications can be applied to computers afterward by using the Assign Applications to Client Computers wizard in Server Management.

☑ The Windows Update feature can be configured on the client computer for manual or automatic scan, download and installation of service packs, patches, and updates for the Windows operating system.

☑ Computers running older operating systems, including Windows 95, 98, ME and Windows NT Workstation 4.0, must be updated manually. Ideally, these systems should be upgraded to a newer operating system for ease of administration.

☑ Windows Update can be configured as a Group Policy so that select client computers are automatically updated. Apply the GPO to the computers that can use this feature.

☑ The Windows Update GPO can be configured with several different settings to customize it to meet your organization's needs.

☑ Software Update Services is a free application that you can download from the Microsoft website to automate the download, configuration, and installation of service packs and updates for client computers. It provides more functionality than the Windows Update feature, but requires additional installation and configuration.

☑ SUS (and the new version due out late 2004, WUS) is a good tool for updating client computers when you have many computers. It's not recommended if you have 5 or fewer client computers on the network.

Chapter 10

Installing and Managing Printers

- **Printer Overview**

- **Installing and Managing Printers**

- **Managing Fax Printers and Shared Fax Services**

- **Group Policy for Printers**

The End Result

In this chapter, we'll focus on managing printers on your Small Business Server (SBS) 2003 network. You'll learn some of the fundamental concepts about printers in a Windows environment. Next, you'll learn how to install and manage network printers, how to audit printer activity, and how to set Group Policy for printers. You'll also learn about the fax features in SBS 2003, since printing and faxing are first cousins.

Printer Overview

Let's start off with a bit of architecture—the software kind (for those of you expecting a tour of medieval castles of Europe, sorry to disappoint you). Printers are connected either to client computers, servers, or directly to the network. As you probably know, printers come in many flavors. The two most commonly used printers these days are laser printers and inkjet printers. Older impact-type printers (those that slam something into a ribbon that slams into the paper to make the characters) are still in use in many companies, though their popularity is waning, as the cost of laser printers has dropped dramatically over the years. Color laser printers are now affordable as well, blurring the once distinct line between high quality black and white output (laser) and high quality color output (inkjet).

Many companies elect to place printers in two ways. In locations where confidential information is frequently printed, it makes sense to install low-end laser or inkjet printers and connect them directly to user computers. For instance, the Chief Financial Officer or the head of your Human Resources department will probably need the ability to print things out and be assured the documents are secure.

A second method is to install a network printer in a central location within a department. For instance, you might install a printer in the Finance department that only people in Finance can use. That way, financial documents can be printed with less chance that someone will (purposely or inadvertently) grab the document and take off with it.

Most companies use a combination of these two methods to provide the easiest, most secure printer access for users. Whatever methods you choose, avoid putting users through the "print and sprint" routine where a user prints a sensitive document then has to run down the corridor to the printer to grab it before someone else sees it or grabs it. It's good for cardiovascular endurance, bad for security.

As you probably know, the small software application that knows how to talk both to the specific operating system and the specific printer is called the *printer driver*. Sometimes the printer driver is referred to as a *logical printer*, as opposed to the *physical printer*. Let's look at the ways these can be configured in a network environment.

Logical and Physical Printers

In the most common configuration, one printer driver (logical printer) manages one physical printer. This is the configuration when a user configures a printer attached to a desktop computer. The printer can be attached to a local computer (a user's desktop, for instance) or it can be attached to a computer whose job is to manage printers (print server). The printer can be attached via a parallel cable or Universal Serial Bus (USB or Firewire) cable to the local computer, or via a USB, Firewire, or network cable (Ethernet) to the network.

Since the printer driver knows how to talk to the physical printer, you can use one printer driver (one logical printer) to talk to several identical printers. This arrangement is shown in Figure 10.1. This is known as a *printer pool* because, to the user, it appears to be one printer. However, since there are multiple printers (each must be able to use the same printer driver), print jobs can be sent (by the driver) to any available printer. This increases throughput and performance. If a printer fails, users are not impacted and the admin can replace the printer without having to reconfigure client computers.

Figure 10.1 One Logical Printer, Multiple Physical Printers

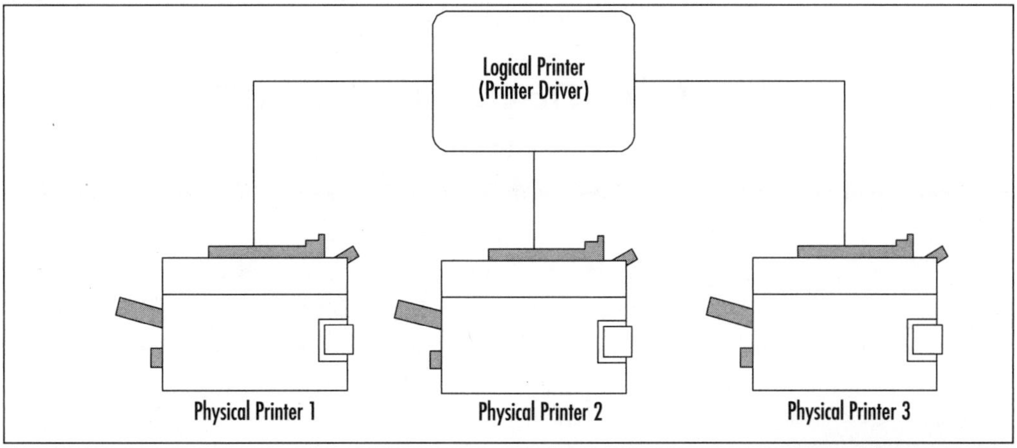

A second configuration is to associate several logical printers (printer drivers) with a single printer, as shown in Figure 10.2. Using this arrangement, you can assign different priorities to the different logical printers. For instance, you may want to set up the Finance folks with the highest priority and the Training department with the lowest priority (no offense to Training folks). You could also simply send a print job to the logical printer that matches the priority of your print job. For instance, suppose you need to print training manuals for a class starting next week. You could probably send those to the lowest priority printer driver, which might schedule that job to print overnight when no one else is printing. You might send the company's cash flow statement to the highest priority logical printer for the Board meeting starting in an hour.

Figure 10.2 Multiple Logical Printers, One Physical Printer

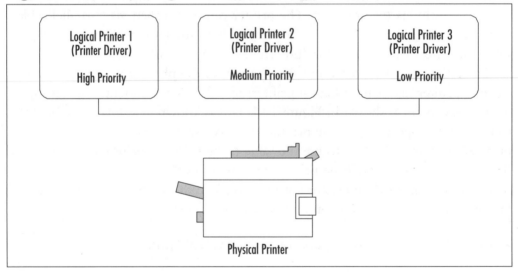

Installing and Managing Printers

There are three primary ways you can add a printer to the network. You can connect a printer directly to a client computer and share it out so other users can use that printer. If the client computer is turned off, access to that printer is terminated, so that's usually not the best configuration. You can physically connect a printer to a server and share it out so users can locate and print to the printer. Since servers are supposed to always be on and available when users are on the network, printers connected to the server will be available as long as the server is functional. This is one common method for connecting shared printers. Finally, you can connect a printer directly to the network via a network interface card. If you use this third option, you can use one of two methods to access and manage the printer. In the first method, users have to add the printer (**Add a Printer** function in **Printers and Faxes** on Windows XP, for example) and install an appropriate printer driver. If you allow users to install their own drivers to access the printer, you can't centrally manage the print queue, since all users have their own separate queue on their own computers. This can lead to problems with the printer and is therefore not the recommended configuration. The second (recommended) configuration is to add the printer to the server and share it out to make it available to users. So, even though the printer is directly attached to the network, a computer (print server) is still managing it. It's best to use a server so that a single print queue is created. Also, there are third-party programs that you can install to allow you to work with printers attached directly to the network.

Adding A Local Printer

There's a good chance you already know how to add a printer to a local computer. It's a fairly easy process. To recap for a Windows XP Professional system, you click **Start | Printers and Faxes** and click **Add a Printer**. In older operating systems, you typically locate the Printer folder in the Control Panel and choose **Add a Printer**. The Add a Printer wizard will launch prompting you through installing and configuring the printer by assigning a name, letting the system know how the printer is installed (local or network), and sometimes prompting you to install the printer driver. With many newer printers, the system automatically locates and installs the correct printer driver. In other cases (as with older printers or specialized printers), you may have to point the system to the location of the driver.

To connect a printer on the SBS server, head to **Start | Server Management | Printers.** Click the **Add a Printer** link in the taskpad and follow the on-screen instructions. You will be prompted to select local or network printer. You'll be prompted to let the system know where it can find this printer and whether or not it should be set as the default printer—all options you're probably familiar with when you've installed other printers on local computers.

If the printer is plug-and-play (PNP) enabled, the system should automatically recognize the printer (as soon as you connect it to the computer). Follow the printer directions as to how to connect cables and when to apply power. If you follow the order specified, the system is more likely to do its job automatically, including installing the appropriate printer driver, sharing the printer, and listing the printer as a network resource in Active Directory. The operative word is *should*. Sometimes the system lacks the proper printer driver to do all this automatically and you'll need to help it find the appropriate driver or even download an updated driver to make everything work smoothly. Most times, though, the printer installs without a hitch.

Adding a Network Printer

The best option for connecting a network printer is to use the Transmission Control Protocol/Internet Protocol (TCP/IP) printer port rather than an LPR (line printer) printer port. An LPR printer port is used for printers that do not natively work in the Windows environment or that cannot use a TCP/IP printer port. These types of printers are not covered in this chapter. You can find more information on LPR printer ports in the Windows Help and Support files by using the search phrase **LPR printer port** and selecting the Help Topic titled **Add an LPR port: Printing**.

Use the following steps to connect a network printer using TCP/IP:

1. Connect the printer to the network and configure the printer's IP configuration. Typically, a printer using TCP/IP will use a static IP address, so it never changes. Select an address from your excluded IP addresses in you DHCP address pool so no other device will be assigned the same IP address. Instructions for doing that are included in Chapter 9 under "DHCP Basics."

2. Click **Start** | **Printers and Faxes** | **Add a Printer** or, alternately, select **Start** | **Server Management** | **Printers** | **Add a Printer**. On the first page of the Add a Printer Wizard, click **Next** to continue.

3. On the Local or Network Printer screen, select **Local printer attached to this computer**, but clear the checkbox for **Automatically detect and install my Plug and Play printer**. Click **Next**.

4. On the next screen, Select a Printer Port, there are two options. If this was a standard printer, you might select the first option **Use the following port:** and select **LPT** for a parallel printer connection or **COM** for a USB printer connection. For this type of printer, however, select the second option, **Create a new port**. In the **Type of port**

drop-down list, select **Standard TCP/IP port**, as shown in Figure 10.3, then click **Next**. This will launch another wizard, the Add Standard TCP/IP Printer Port Wizard.

Figure 10.3 Creating New Printer Port for TCP/IP Printer

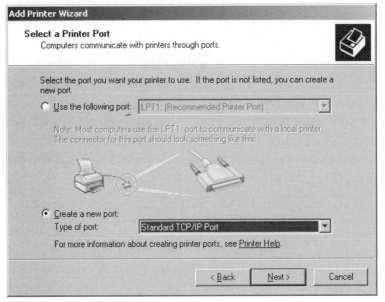

5. Make sure the printer itself is connected to the network and powered on before proceeding. Then, in the first page of the Add Standard TCP/IP Printer Port Wizard, click **Next** to continue.

6. In the Add Port dialog box, enter the printer name or IP address in the first text box. Windows will automatically fill in the second text box, **Port Name**. You can modify this, if necessary, though in most cases, this will not be necessary. For instance, if the IP address for the printer is 192.168.8.15, the Port Name will default to IP_192.168.8.15.

7. If Windows cannot locate the printer with the information you just provided, the Additional Port Information dialog box will be displayed. Select the printer from the list in the drop-down for **Standard** device type or select **Custom** and click **Settings** to configure the printer. Click **Next**.

8. The final screen in the Add Standard TCP/IP Printer Port Wizard is the standard confirmation screen where you can review your choices, go

Back to make modifications, or click **Finish** to apply your choices and close the wizard. Click **Finish.**

9. If Windows does not detect the printer, it will prompt you to install the printer software. Select the printer manufacturer and model from the dialog box or click **Have Disk** if your printer is not shown. The Have Disk option requires you to have the printer driver available (on the hard drive, CD-ROM, diskette, etc.). Click **Next.**

10. The Name Your Printer dialog box allows you to give your printer a descriptive name. For some companies, it makes sense to use the default, which is the printer's make and model. For other companies, it makes more sense to call the printer **Finance High Speed Laser Printer** so users can easily discern which printer this really is. Enter the name, select whether or not this printer should be set as the default printer, and click **Next.**

11. The next screen, Printer Sharing, allows you to share the printer or not. If sharing it, you can give it a descriptive name other than the default name suggested, if you want. Click **Next.**

12. The Location and Comment dialog box allows you to describe the location and add comments that might be helpful to users. If you chose the default name in the dialog box mentioned in step 10, you might use the location and comments here. Click **Next**.

13. The final page allows you to print a test page (or not). It's often a good idea to print a test page from this dialog box, as it can help you immediately verify that your settings are good and that the printer is properly configured and connected. Make your selection and click **Next.**

14. The final screen is the confirmation page. Check your settings, go **Back** to make changes (especially if the printer's test page did not print), or click **Finish** to complete the task. The printer will be listed in your available printers in **Server Management | Printers.**

Managing Installed Printers

Once your printers are installed, you can manage them via **Server Management | Printers** (or via **Start | Printers and Faxes**). You can access, manage and change printer properties by selecting the printer and clicking **Change Printer Properties** in the taskpad area. The Properties dialog box for the selected printer will be displayed. The specific options available in the Properties dialog box will vary depending on the printer driver installed (and by extension, the physical printer installed). Typically, you'll have **General**, **Sharing**, **Ports**, **Advanced**, **Security**, and **Device Settings** tabs. We'll talk briefly about the options on each of these tabs, as shown in Figure 10.4. Keep in mind your options may vary.

Figure 10.4 Printer Properties Tabs

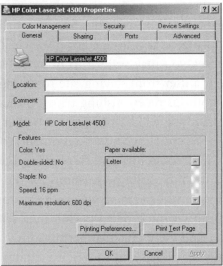

The **General** tab allows you to modify the name, location information, and comments. You can also modify **Printing Preferences** (landscape, portrait, etc.) or **Print Test Page** from here.

The **Sharing** tab allows you to share or not share the printer. You can opt to list the printer in the directory (or not). You can also specify additional drivers for the printer. Each client operating system may require different printer drivers for the same printer. For instance, a driver for a Canon inkjet printer on Windows XP might not work for the same printer in Windows 98. If you are running different operating systems and need specific drivers, click the **Additional Drivers** button. By default, when you add a printer in SBS, it is shared and will be listed in Active Directory. As you may recall, Active Directory is a network directory service provided by the Windows Server operating system that lists network resources, their properties and other related information. By listing the printer in Active Directory, you make it easy for users to locate and use the printer. You can choose not to list the printer in Active Directory by removing the check from the checkbox. If you choose not to list the printer, users will need to know exactly where the printer is in order to print to it because they will not be able to locate it in Active Directory.

The **Ports** tab shows the ports that were available when you were adding the printer. It displays the current port and it allows you to **Add Port, Delete Port**, and **Configure Port**. This is also where you can configure printer pooling, which we'll discuss in a moment.

The **Advanced** tab allows you to fine-tune the printer settings, including scheduling when the printer will be available. Some companies make some printers available only during certain hours. For instance, if you have a very expensive, high-end printer, you may want it to be available only during normal working hours to prevent a user from staying late some night and printing out high-definition photos from his recent fishing trip. On the **Advanced** tab, you can also specify how a print job will be printed – whether or not it is spooled before printing. We'll discuss spooling in just a moment. You can also set **Printing Defaults, Print Processor**, and **Separator Page** settings here.

The **Security** tab is used to assign permissions for the printer. Users and groups can be added or removed, permissions can be customized, and, using the **Advanced** button, you can set more detail permissions, set auditing for the printer, define the owner and view effective permissions.

The **Device Settings** tab allows you to modify settings specific to the physical printer including paper trays, font cartridges and other printer-specific settings.

Setting Up Printer Auditing

As you just saw, auditing can be configured for a printer in the printer Properties from the **Security** tab. On the **Security** tab, click the **Advanced** button to access advanced features, of which auditing is one. Click the **Auditing** tab (from among Permissions, Auditing, Owner, Effective Permissions). Use the following steps to enable auditing.

1. Click **Add** to add a group for auditing.

2. In the Select User, Computer, or Group dialog box, enter the name of the group for which you want to audit printer usage. Click **Check Names** then click **OK.**

3. In the **Auditing Entry for [Printer]** ([Printer] is the printer name), select what this auditing will apply to: **This printer only, Documents**

only, or **This printer and documents** using the drop-down box. You can audit success or failure on the following events:

- Print
- Manage Printers
- Manage Documents
- Read Permissions
- Change Permissions
- Take Ownership

4. Once you have configured permissions as desired, click **OK**. This will return you to the Advanced Security settings of the printer properties. Click **OK** to close this dialog box and click **OK** to close the printer Properties dialog box.

Remember, only audit events that matter to your firm. For instance, in many cases, the only auditing you might select is successful Manage Printers, Change Permissions, and Take Ownership. Every event you audit will end up in a log file you're going to have to review, so choose auditing wisely.

Setting Up Printer Pools

As you learned earlier, printer pools are configured with one logical printer (printer driver) and multiple physical printers. The multiple physical printers appear as one printer to the user since all printers are using the same printer driver (a requirement for setting up a printer pool). For instance, you may have several HP LaserJet printers that all use the same printer driver and that all have the same capabilities. You could form a printer pool with these printers.

Use the following steps to set up a printer pool.

1. Select **Server Management** | **Printers**, select the printer you want to add to the pool, and click **Change Printer Properties** in the taskpad. Alternately, you can right-click the desired printer and choose **Change Printer Properties** from the shortcut menu. Click the **Ports** tab.

2. On the Ports tab screen, select the checkbox labeled **Enable printer pooling**.

3. Select any additional ports you want to add to the printer pool by clicking the checkbox to the left of the port. For instance, you may have

several printers using TCP/IP ports. You can locate and select those printers in this dialog box to add them to the printer pool. When all desired printers have been selected, click **OK.**

Managing Printer Spooling

Spooling is the process of temporarily storing a print job. The reason spooling can be helpful is because if you choose not to spool, the computer may be tied up while the print job is being prepared for printing. Years ago, if you did not spool a job, your computer could literally be unavailable for several minutes while the print job was prepared and sent to the printer for printing. Also, printers have a finite amount of on-board memory and if a print job is larger than the printer's memory, the print job has to be fed to the printer in smaller chunks so it can be properly printed. Spooling allows your computer to shoot the print job off to the spooler and the spooler function manages the rest. You can modify print spooling behavior by locating the desired printer (**Server Management | Printers**) and selecting **Change Printer Properties** link in the taskpad. Alternately, you can right-click the desired printer and choose **Change Printer Properties** from the shortcut menu. In the printer Properties dialog box, use the following steps to modify spooling behavior:

1. Click the **Advanced** tab in the printer's Properties dialog box.

2. In the center section of the dialog box, select either **Spool print documents so program finishes printing faster** or **Print directly to printer**. The **Spool print documents so program...** option has two sub-options. You can elect to either **start printing after the last page is spooled** or **start printing immediately**. If you choose the latter option, the program from which you're printing is freed up quickly and you can get on with your work. The second main option, **Print directly to printer** will slow things down for the user and this is usually not your best option unless you routinely print from an application that does its own spooling. This will decrease the printing time, but may not release the program back to the user quickly enough.

3. In the lower third of the Properties dialog box, there are four checkboxes, each of which can be selected.

   - **Hold Mismatched Documents** This option prevents the printer from trying to print documents that do not match the configuration of the printer. This prevents the printer from hanging up on a print job it cannot print, such as when the printer holds 8.5 x 11 paper and the print job specifies 11 x 17 paper.

- **Print Spooled Documents First** Selecting this option will cause spooled print jobs to be printed before jobs that are partially spooled.

- **Keep Documents After They Are Printed** Documents will remain in the print spooler after they've completed printing. This option is useful for printing the same print job because they don't need to be spooled again. This option will chew up disk space, so use caution if you set this option.

- **Enable Advanced Printing Features** This option, when enabled, allows the document to be rendered using advanced features. If you notice compatibility or printing problems, your first troubleshooting step should be to disable this feature (if enabled).

Managing Printer Priorities with Logical Drivers

As you learned at the beginning of the chapter, you can use multiple logical drivers to manage a single printer. When you do this, you can assign each of the drivers different priorities. You can add groups to these different priority logical printers to provide higher and lower priority for users, or you can allow users to choose printers based on the user's perceived priority for the print job. How you configure this depends upon how your company works and what policies and procedures may be in place for making these kinds of decisions. For now, we'll assume you're going to decide who can print at what priority and the steps that follow will help you configure this. Your settings may vary.

1. In **Server Manager** | **Printers**, double-click the **Add a Printer** icon. Follow the steps in the wizard (which are also described earlier in this chapter) to add a duplicate logical printer.

2. Right-click the first logical printer, select **Change Printer Properties** from the shortcut menu, click the **Advanced** tab and locate the **Priority** selection. Set the desired priority. For this example, we'll select Priority **1**.

3. Click the **Security** tab and select groups to whom you want to provide Priority 1 (lowest) printing on this printer. After you've made desired

selections, click **OK**. Remove groups/users that you do not want to be able to print at this priority.

4. Right-click the second logical printer, select **Change Printer Properties** from the shortcut menu, click the **Advanced** tab and locate the **Priority** selection. Set the desired priority. For this example, we'll select Priority **99** (highest).

5. Click the **Security** tab and select groups to whom you want to provide Priority 99 printing on this printer. After you've made desired selections, click **OK.** Remove groups/users that you do not want to be able to print at this priority.

Managing the Print Server

If you are using a server as a print server, you can configure additional settings that apply to all printers hosted by the print server. These settings include forms, ports, drivers, and advanced settings. We'll review them briefly here. To access the Print Server Properties, click **Start | Printers and Faxes.** In the Printers and Faxes window, click the link **Server properties** or click **File | Server Properties**. Configure the options listed here. For more information, check out the Help and Support files.

■ **Forms** The available forms are listed in the scroll box. You can create new, custom forms (be sure to check all the available forms before creating a new one) by entering the dimensions of the form and clicking **Save Form.**

■ **Ports** This is the same dialog box you've seen before. You can add, delete, and configure ports from this tab.

■ **Drivers** You can add, remove, and reinstall printer drivers from this tab. You can also review driver properties.

■ **Advanced** On this tab, you can log spooler errors, warnings, and information. You can also configure the system to beep on errors of remote documents. You can show informational notifications for local and/or remote printers, and you can also select notification when remote documents are printed.

Best Practices According to Microsoft

- Plan your printing environment so that printers and users are well matched. Productivity can suffer when printers are located too far away from users or if users are waiting for their print job to complete on a shared printer.

- If a user wants to locate and use a particular printer, the fastest and easiest way is to click **Start | Search** and select **Printers**. All printers published in the Active Directory listing for which the user has permissions will be displayed.

- To share a local printer, create a local printer Users group with Print permission then add global groups to the local group.

- Install printer drivers for all the operating systems that will access the printer.

- If security is not an issue, allow other users to manage the printers by delegating the Manage Documents or Manage Printers permission.

- If your network printer will be printing highly sensitive data, you might consider using the Internet Protocol Security (IPSec) to help protect data that is in transit. An alternative is to simply print sensitive material to a locally connected printer.

- If you create a printer pool, physically locate all pooled printers in the same location. You don't want users running around the building looking for their print job if the pooled printers are in far-flung locations. (Ignore this if your company is on a fitness kick and wants users to run around the building rather than doing productive work, your choice).

- Manage printer traffic by creating logical printers and assigning groups to those printers or allowing users to print to different logical printers based on the print job's priority.

- You can audit printers, though you probably want to limit auditing to track changes made by administrators who manage printers.

- Document printer information such as printer make, model, toner or ink cartridge types, interface, etc. Also keep track of who's been granted administrative rights over printers.

- When possible, attach printers directly to the network using a network interface card. They print faster than printers attached to a print server via parallel cable.

- To solve printing problems quickly, use the printing troubleshooter. If the problem appears to be the network connection, use the networking troubleshooter.

SOME INDEPENDENT ADVICE

Troubleshooting printer problems can run the gamut from easy to frustrating. Keep these tips in mind for all troubleshooting:

1. Always check that power and network cables are plugged in properly. Check the printer power to make sure it's actually on. Check cable seating – sometimes cables appear to be connected but are not. Remove and reconnect them if you're not 100% sure. People have wasted hours troubleshooting problems that didn't really exist. Check the easy stuff first.

2. Always ask, "what just changed?" Sometimes the obvious solution is the thing that was just modified. If someone updated a driver and suddenly the printer doesn't work, there's a high likelihood that this is the culprit. If you don't ask what changed, someone might forget to mention it. Also, don't ask someone else what changed in an accusatory voice. Unfortunately, people hate to be wrong and will sometimes fib (OK, tell an outright lie) to avoid taking the heat. Use your best people skills to gather necessary information.

3. Always try to slice the problem in half. If the problem is printing from one user's computer, can another user's computer print to that printer? That immediately tells you whether the printer is ok. Keep trying to cut the problem in half with each troubleshooting step.

4. Avoid changing more than one thing at a time. Making multiple changes could leave you unsure of what fixed the problem or it could create new problems. Changing one thing at a time may be tedious, but it's a sure way to logically attack and resolve a problem.

Managing Fax Printers and Shared Fax Services

SBS provides the ability to implement shared fax services so that all network users can send and receive faxes via the SBS server. The ability to centralize the implementation and management of fax services can greatly increase the efficiency of fax management in your company. We'll look first at the ability of users to fax via the fax printer and then we'll look at shared fax services on the SBS server.

Managing Fax Printers

So far we've focused on regular ol' printers. Now, let's turn our attention to faxes. Some companies have one physical fax machine that's just fine for the three faxes per year they send or receive. Other companies are still heavily using faxes and if your company is one of those companies, you can use the Fax Services in Small Business Server.

SOME INDEPENDENT ADVICE

When you want to send a fax from an application that supports sending faxes, you typically choose **File | Print** and select the fax as the printing device. The process is similar to printing except that the output from the application is formatted so that it can be transmitted as a faxed document. It is directed to your company's shared fax service (typically a modem or two in the server) and the document is sent out via the modem to another computer that can accept fax documents or to an actual, physical fax machine.

Configure Fax is one of the items on your To Do List and you can configure your fax via the To Do List link. When you click this link, it launches the Configure Fax Wizard. Once the wizard is open, use the following steps to configure your fax.

1. In the **Provide Company Information** dialog box, you can review or modify the company information that is populated by default. Once you've made any changes, click **Next** to continue. Make sure you've entered the correct phone number for the fax in this dialog.

2. The second screen, Outbound Fax Devices, allows you to specify the devices for sending faxes. Faxes will be sent via devices in the list in the order shown. Use the up and down arrows to modify the order. This option assumes you have one ore more fax/modems installed in the server. Click **Next** to continue.

3. The Inbound Fax Device dialog box allows you to select which device to use for inbound faxes. You can select to set routing of faxes to be the same for all devices or you can configure specific routing destinations for each device. Click **Next** to continue.

4. On the Inbound Fax Routing dialog box, select the routing methods. As you check an option, the **Configure** link prompts you for the specific routing information. Your options are **Route through email**, **Store in a folder**, **Share in a document library**, or **Print**.

5. The final page of the wizard allows you to check your settings. You can go **Back** and make changes or click **Finish** to apply the settings and close the wizard.

To connect client computers to shared faxes, use the same steps you use from a client computer to connect to a shared printer. One method from the client computer is to click **Start | Run** and type ***SBSserver*** where *SBSserver* is the actual server name. Double-click the fax (or printer) to which you want to connect and click **Yes** to set it up. On the first page of the Add Printer wizard, specify whether you want to be able to print from MS DOS-based programs the click **Next.** If the wizard does not recognize the printer, select the manufacturer and model from the list. If it is not listed, click **Have Disk** and locate the driver for your device then click **Next.** You can enter a descriptive name for the printer or fax and select is as your default device. You can also choose to print a test page. If you elected to connect to the shared fax printer, the first time you send a fax you'll be prompted to install the Share Fax Client so you can monitor faxes as they're sent. Click **Yes** to install the Shared Fax Client. This will crate shortcuts on the Start menu for sending faxes.

Shared Fax Services

You can access the shared fax services in SBS via the Server Management function. Fax (local) is listed in the Standard Management section. By selecting this option, you can access a number of fax options including:

- Device and Providers

- Incoming Routing

- Outgoing Routing

- Cover Pages

- Fax Console

These options are very easy to configure and the wizards walk you through each step. Rather than examine these options in detail, we'll describe them briefly and highlight some of the more notable features.

Device and Providers

Devices are the physical modems that will send and/or receive faxes. These are modems installed on the SBS server. You can install additional fax modems after fax services have been configured (in contrast to older SBS versions) and add them to your pool of fax modems. By default, a fax component is configured for sending but not receiving. Receiving can be enabled by right-clicking the device and enabling receiving. Providers are the installed device providers. By default, the Microsoft Modem Device Provider is the default device provider. For more information on details of configuring the fax device, query the Help and Support files using the query phrase **configuring fax devices**.

Incoming Routing

Once you've configured one or more devices to receive incoming faxes (not configured by default), all incoming faxes arrive in the Incoming queue. Once received and properly routed according to the configured routing information, faxes are moved to the Inbox archive if incoming fax archiving is enabled. In the Fax Service Manager, you can see the incoming routing extensions at a global level by going to **Server Management | Standard Management | Fax (local) | Incoming Routing | Global Methods.** You can elect to have incoming faxes routed through e-mail, stored in folders or printed. You can configure the details of these options by right-clicking the method and selecting **Properties** from the shortcut menu. Once the incoming method is configured, locate it in the right pane, right-click the method and click **Enable** to enable the method or **Disable** to disable the method. To enable archiving, right-click **Fax (local),** select **Properties**, click the **Inbox** tab and check the box for **Archive all incoming faxes to this folder**.

Note that if no method is enabled on a fax device and archiving to the Inbox is not set, the incoming fax will be lost.

Outgoing Routing

You can manage the use of server-based fax services by configuring routing rules for outgoing faxes. You can create rules for a device or group of devices. In the Outgoing Routing section of the Fax (local) in Server Management, you have groups and rules. To create a group, right-click **Groups** and click **New | Group**. Enter the name of the new group. Once the group is created, you must add devices to the group by right-clicking the group and choosing **New | Devices**. Once you have configured the group, you can set rules for that group. To assign rules to groups, right-click **Rules** in the left-pane and select **New | Rules.** In the Add New Rule dialog box, you can specify country/region code and area code as well as the device or group that will use this rule. If you want to assign this rule to a particular fax modem device, you can select it from the list of available devices. If you want to assign this rule to a routing group, you can select the group from the list of available groups. To archive outgoing faxes, right-click **Fax (local),** select **Properties**, select the **Sent Items** tab, and check the box for **Archive all successfully sent faxes to this folder**.

Cover Pages

SBS provides four default cover pages that can be used when you send and receive faxes from the server or when users connect to the fax server via a remote fax printer connection. You can specify that users can only use these predefined templates or ones you create. To create a new cover page, right-click **Cover Pages** and select **New | Cover Page** from the menu. To modify any of the pre-defined templates, double-click the template or right-click and select **Edit.** To require users to use one of the server templates, right-click **Fax (local)**, select **Properties**, select the **Outbox** tab, and clear the checkbox **Allow use of personal cover pages**.

Fax Console

The Fax Console is an SBS server tool you can use to send and receive faxes as well as track and monitor incoming and outgoing faxes and access archived faxes. To access the Fax Console, you can either right-click **Fax (local)** in Server Management and select **Fax Console** from the shortcut menu or click **Start | All Programs | Accessories | Communications | Fax | Fax Console.**

Group Policy for Printers

Since we went through group policy in detail in an earlier chapter, you're probably an expert and we can just skip this section. Actually, if you became an expert in one short chapter, you're probably related to Einstein. For the rest of us mortals, let's go through setting up group policy for printers before we head off into the next scintillating chapter.

To set group policy for printers, use the following steps:

1. Start Group Policy via **Start** | **Administrative Tools** | **Group Policy Management**.

2. Locate the domain. For this example, we're going to create a new GPO in the domain. Right-click the domain and select **Create and Link a GPO here** from the shortcut menu.

3. Enter a name for the new GPO then click **OK.**

4. Right-click the new GPO and select **Edit** from the shortcut menu. This will launch the **Group Policy Object Editor.**

5. Since we're going to apply this to users, we select **User Configuration | Administrative Templates | Control Panel | Printers.** In the right pane, you'll see the options you can configure within this group policy object, as shown in Figure 10.5. The six settings are:

   - Browse a common website to find printers

   - Browse the network to find printers

   - Default Active Directory path when searching for printers

   - Point and Print Restrictions

   - Prevent addition of printers

   - Prevent deletion of printers

Figure 10.5 Group Policy Settings for Printers

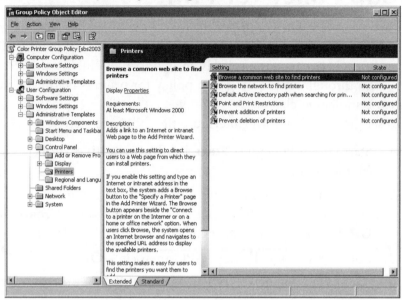

6. Double-click the setting you want to configure. Recall that by default, all options are initially set to *not configured* unless you're modifying an existing GPO. You can leave it not configured or you can enable it or disable it. Some settings may have additional configuration options. If you're not sure what a particular setting will do, you can read the explanation in the taskpad area if you click the setting, or you can double-click the setting, click the **Explain** tab, and read the same explanation. When you've finished configuring your desired settings, click **OK.**

7. Close the Group Policy Object Editor by clicking **File | Exit.** You will be returned to the Group Policy Management console. In the Group Policy Objects list in the left pane, click the new GPO you just created. The properties of the GPO are displayed in the right pane, as shown in Figure 10.6.

Figure 10.6 Group Policy Settings for New Printer GPO

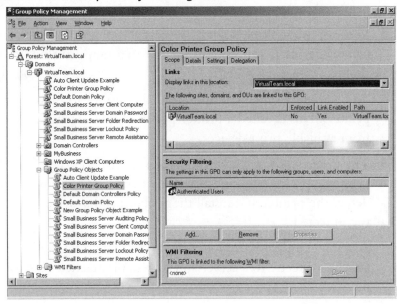

8. The **Scope** tab is selected by default. On this tab, remember to remove **Authenticated Users** from the **Security Filtering** section or the policy will be applied to all users instead of just the user groups you select.

9. In the **Security Filtering** area, click **Add** to add the desired groups to which this policy will be applied. Enter the group name, click **Check Names**, and click **OK**. When you've finished adding user groups, you're finished. Close Group Policy Management. Like other Group Policies, this will be applied the next time group policies are applied to the user and or computers to which it applies.

One More Time

In this chapter, you learned how to manage printers on the network. You learned about how printers are installed and managed, and you learned a couple of interesting ways to configure printers that can increase printer throughput. You also learned about how to connect to a computer from a client computer as well as how to use the fax services in SBS.

☑ Printers require printer drivers that work both with the specific operating system and the specific physical printer.

☑ A printer can be the physical printer or a logical printer, which is the printer driver.

☑ You can use multiple logical printers all pointing to the same physical printer device if you want to be able to assign priorities to different user groups.

☑ You can use a single logical printer that points to multiple physical printers. This is called a printer pool and speeds printing by selecting from available print devices.

☑ The process of installing printers is a relatively easy process. If the printer supports plug-and-play, the operating system may automatically detect the printer and install the proper printer driver when the printer is connected.

☑ A printer can be directly attached to a local computer and shared, attached directly to a server and shared, or attached directly to the network.

☑ A printer attached directly to the network should, ideally, utilize a standard TCP/IP port. If not, check with the Help and Support files, the manufacturer's instructions, or the Microsoft website for more information on how to configure the network printer.

☑ A printer attached directly to the network still requires a print server. Each user's computer can manage the printer individually (not recommended) or a server can manage the printer (recommended). You can also install third-party programs for managing printers directly attached to the network.

☑ Fax printers use drivers that allow the document to be formatted as a fax document and prepared for transmission to a receiving fax machine.

☑ Shared fax services provides a server interface for configuring and managing incoming and outgoing faxes, for archiving sent and received faxes and for managing the use of fax cover sheets.

☑ Group Policy can be set for printers to help manage printers across the domain.

☑ Make sure to remove the Authenticated Users group from the Security Filtering for the group policy object or it will automatically be applied to every single user in the domain.

Chapter 11

Disaster Planning, Backing Up, and Restoring Data

- Disaster Planning

- Backing Up Data

- Restoring Your Server and Data

The End Result

By the end of this chapter, you'll know how to develop and test your disaster plan. You'll also understand backup strategies and be able to implement a backup process that fits the needs of your company. You'll also learn about your restore options and how to use restore processes to recover from small and large failures.

Disaster Planning

We begin this chapter with disaster planning because without a solid disaster plan, backups alone will not secure your network data from loss. If you recall from our discussion earlier in the book, network security takes on many forms. All methods involved keeping data secure. So far, we've focused on preventing unauthorized access to network resources, but physically securing data is another critical aspect of data security. Backups help if a drive on the server fails, but what would you do if the building (and server, client computers, and network cabling) burns to the ground? How will your company continue operations? What steps will you take? Who's in charge? Where will you go for expert assistance? If you don't have a solid disaster plan for your corporate network, you're making a very high-stakes gamble. We're going to discuss the elements of a good disaster plan so you can create one for your organization. It's not a difficult process, just one that requires you to think through various scenarios. The adage, "Hope for the best, plan for the worst," is applicable here.

SOME INDEPENDENT ADVICE

As with most policies and procedures in network administration, disaster planning should be done with a representative team from within your company. You might want to gather senior managers, Human Resources and other key personnel to help you determine the risks and the associated costs of those risks as well as your desired responses. There is always a trade-off between the cost of avoiding a risk and the cost of dealing with the risk after the fact. In most cases, the cost/benefit of avoiding the risk (disaster planning) is far superior to the cost/benefit of dealing with the aftermath. Involve key staff at your company so you're not out on a limb if or when disaster strikes. Once your disaster plan is finalized, distribute copies to key personnel – both management and those who may have specific duties in the disaster recovery process.

In fact, disaster planning should be one element in an overall business continuity plan developed by your senior management team so your business can continue to function or can quickly get back to a functional state if disaster does strike.

Every company's disaster plan will incorporate different elements based on the risks to that company. If your company is located in the Mississippi River valley, you might need to plan for floods. If your company is located in San Francisco, you might need to plan for earthquakes. Wherever your company is located, you also have to plan for things that could happen to any business, regardless of location including fire, localized flooding, power outages (and surges), storms, and even theft. The common elements in disaster plans include:

1. Risk assessment and prioritization

2. Legal considerations

3. Asset evaluation

4. Incident response

5. Plan testing and maintenance

Once you complete your disaster plan, you should keep a copy handy on-site in a binder as well as a copy of the plan in a safe location off-site. If your server room is destroyed by an errant fire suppression system, you can use your on-site copy of the plan, but if the building burns to the ground, you'll need to quickly access the copy of the plan kept in an off-site location. You should also distribute the plan to key members of your staff and/or organization and make sure that there is no single point of failure in your personnel planning either. If you have the only off-site copy of the disaster plan and you happen to go to Europe for a two-week vacation, your disaster plan is a disaster.

Risk Assessment and Prioritization

The first step in any disaster planning process is to identify potential risks. As mentioned a moment ago, if your company is located in Mississippi, your risk of earthquake may be very low, but your risk of flooding very high. If you live in the Midwest, your risk of flooding might be high along with your risk of tornadoes. Take a look at your geographic area and determine the risks your company may face.

In addition to geographic risk, you should also look at other risks. Is the building you're in well protected from fire, electrical problems, theft? Run through every possible risk you can think of (this is where working with a team comes in handy) and then prioritize those risks. Give each risk two priority numbers—the first number is how likely the risk is to occur. Use a rating system like 1 = very low risk, 10 = extremely high risk. Then, rate the risk again in terms of the cost to your business if that risk were to occur. Use the same relative scale such as 1 = very low cost, 10 = extremely high cost. Then, add the two numbers together and review your risk list. Organize the risks from highest likelihood/highest cost to lowest likelihood/lowest cost. You may decide that even though something has a low likelihood, its associated high cost makes it have a higher priority level. That's fine. This exercise is simply a way to get you to organize your risks and costs in a consistent and conscious way rather than simply listing risks and assuming they should (or should not) be considered. For instance, the likelihood of a major earthquake in most places in the U.S. is relatively low, even in California where small earthquakes are pretty common. However, as anyone who lives in California knows, the "big one" might just be around the corner and your firm should have a plan as to how it will respond in that event. As a company, you have to determine which risks are worth planning for based on likelihood, cost or a combination of the two.

Legal Considerations

Often-overlooked elements in disaster planning are legal considerations. First, you must ensure your plans do not violate any company policies or government regulations or laws. For instance, companies that work with patient health care data must comply with the Health Insurance Portability and Accountability Act (HIPAA) regulations. There may be other legal considerations such as the length of time you may be legally required to store e-mail, files, etc. For example, if your firm is a software development company, you may want to keep copies of your source code from day one to prove the software's development origins. There are many reasons you may need to keep records, so you should consult with your firm's CEO or owner and possibly your firm's legal counsel to ensure your plans cover the legal considerations.

Asset Evaluation

In Chapter 2, we suggested making a list of all your network equipment, jacks, locations, etc. This list can easily be kept up-to-date and can be inserted into your disaster recovery plan. You'll need this information for a number of reasons if disaster strikes. For instance, you may need this information for insurance and replacement purposes. You may also need this information so you can reconstruct your network if the building burns to the ground. Although your list may contain different (or additional) elements, you should at minimum consider:

- Data
- Computer equipment including computers, monitors, printers, and faxes
- Networking equipment including routers, switches, firewalls, and cabling
- Software including server applications and client applications
- Personnel
- Facilities

With regard to each of these categories, it's important to ask (and answer) the question, "What would happen if this asset was to go away?" In the case of personnel, you might look at unique skills that key members of the team bring to the company and ask what would happen if that person was to suddenly quit or become seriously ill. While this might fall outside the scope of your duties as a network administrator, you can help ensure these important issues are reviewed as part of the process.

Incident Response

If disaster does strike, what steps will you take? While the answer probably depends heavily upon exactly what type of disaster occurs, you can create general plans as well as specific plans based on risks you determined to be high likelihood of occurrence. You might create a designated incident response team so you can assign roles and responsibilities. Regardless of whether or not you create a team, avoid a single point of failure in any of your planning processes. In this case, make sure you're not the only person who understands and can implement a disaster recovery process. Train other members of your company should you be unavailable for any reason. Again, this is another good reason to distribute copies of your disaster plan to key members of your organization.

You might consider creating several accounts with Administrator privileges (if they do not already exist) and storing those passwords in a secure location. Make sure the location is extremely secure and make sure several trusted members of your company are aware of the location. This might include the company's

President and Vice President and/or Human Resources Director. What you don't want is for you to have the only Administrative access (and secret password) to the system in the event something happens to you. You also don't want to share the password for the built-in Administrator account. So, creating alternate accounts and storing those passwords removes the single point of failure issue while maintaining security.

Plan Testing and Maintenance

Once you've created your plan and identified key team members, you must test your plan and keep it up-to-date. A well-designed plan is useless if, when needed, it fails. You won't know if your plan will work until you test it. Of course, it's difficult (if not impossible) to create realistic tests based on disaster scenarios, but you can make sure that you have the basics down pat. Make sure you:

- Back data up regularly
- Verify backup data regularly
- Test restore function in controlled environment
- Keep needed tools and information in a safe place off-site
- Have a process in place for replacing hardware and software assets quickly
- Have a process in place for locating alternate work facility to recover normal work functions

Backing Up Data

As we know, unexpected events can cause minor or major data loss. Whether your system gets hit with a virus or power outage, partial or total data loss is a fairly common occurrence. Creating a backup plan and then consistently implementing that plan will help keep your network up and running, even in the face of data loss.

SBS contains a backup program that works just fine, but some companies opt for third-party back up programs. Either way you go, you should configure the software for regular backups. You'll be faced with a number of options, so let's go over backup concepts now. Though you may be familiar with these concepts, a brief refresher probably wouldn't hurt so you can make informed decisions as you configure your backups to meet your company's needs.

The first decision you'll need to make is which data should be backed up and how often. Your data typically falls into three categories: system data such as your system state data (how the server is configured), network applications and data such as Exchange or SQL Server, and user data. Typically, user data changes the most frequently and therefore may require more frequent backup schedules.

Once you've determined which data needs to be backed up, you'll need to determine an appropriate frequency. As with everything else, there's a balance between having solid backups and the amount of time it takes to create those backups. Most companies find that it's reasonable and desirable to conduct daily backups. These backups can be full, incremental, or differential, which we'll discuss in the next section. Depending on the type of backup routine(s) you choose, you'll also need to create a plan for restoring data from those backups. Different types of backup routines require different restore plans. We'll walk through that later in this chapter.

SOME INDEPENDENT ADVICE

Another great resource on backups and restores in Windows Small Business Server 2003 is the white paper published by Microsoft on the topic, found at http://download.microsoft.com/download/b/d/8/ bd8e1a40-d202-429a-8eb7-26300d62bcc9/BKU_BkupRstr.doc and another good one at www.microsoft.com/smallbusiness/gtm/securi- tyguidance/articles/backup_restore_sbs2003.mspx#XSLTsection12312112 0120.

Backup Concepts

Let's begin by talking about different ways you can back up your data. One of the things that occurs when you use a backup program (versus a regular old **copy** command) is that the backup program will adjust an archive attribute to flag the file as needing to be backed up (or not). This archive attribute is used to determine if that data has been backed up or not, allowing the backup software to backup all or just some of your data. You can create a *full* (also called *normal), incremental, differential, copy,* or *daily backup.* The type of backup is often determined by the amount of data that has to be archived as well as the capacity of the backup media.

A *full* or *normal backup* is just as the name implies. All critical data is backed up. This includes system state data that will help get your server back to its existing state should something go wrong, along with critical system files, server application files, and user data files stored on the server. The archive attribute is not used to determine which files to back up, but it is set for each file that is successfully backed up. By default, this is the type of backup SBS Backup performs. Although this is the default, we'll look at other types of backups so you're familiar with them, especially if you use a third-party program.

An *incremental backup* just backs up data that has changed since the last full backup or since the last incremental backup. You might choose to perform a full back up on Saturday nights and incremental backups on each weekday night, as an example. The incremental backup on Monday would back up only data that has changed since the Saturday night backup. Tuesday's backup would back up only files that had changed since Monday nights' backup and so forth. When a file is copied, the archive attribute is cleared. If a file is changed, the archive attribute is set, signaling the backup software that the file has changed and should be backed up.

If you end up needing to restore, you'll need the last good full backup and all the incremental backups between the last full backup and the most recent incremental backup. You would then restore first from the full backup and use the incremental backups from oldest to newest. Once you're finished, your system should be fully restored. This type of backup is the fastest to backup and the slowest to restore.

A *differential backup* just backs up data that has changed since the last full backup. In this case, performing a differential backup does not clear the archive attribute. Thus, when you perform a differential backup two days in a row, the second day's data will contain all of the changes made on the first day plus the changes made on the second day. If you need to restore, you would first use your last full backup and then apply the most recent differential backup and your system should be fully restored. This type of back up takes more time to back up but less time to restore.

A *copy backup* is similar to a normal backup except that the archive attribute is not changed. Selected files are simply copied to the backup media. This doesn't impact incremental or differential backups in any way. Copy backups are useful if you want to copy data from the server without impacting your backup routine.

Finally, you can perform a *daily backup* to back up all selected files that have been modified on that day. Files that have not been modified on that day are not backed up. As with the copy backup, a daily backup does not impact the archive attribute in any way and will not alter your backup routine (incremental or differential, especially) in any manner.

Backup Media

SBS supports backing up data to a permanent (or removable) hard disk or to a removable tape. That's it. If you have a writable CD-ROM or DVD drive, the SBS software does not support performing backups to these types of media. If your system doesn't have a tape drive, you will have to back up to an internal disk drive. While this does create a backup, it is still risky because the media cannot be removed to an off-site location. You can also back up to a network location, but this has the same challenges—no off-site storage. If any of the drives uses removable media, you'll be able to remove the media and take it off-site, always your best option. Most companies use tape drives as their backup media because tapes are relatively inexpensive. Two of the most commonly used tape formats are Digital Audio Tape (DAT) and Digital Linear Tape (DLT). All tapes store data in a sequential (serial) manner and as a result, backing up files can take a while. Depending on the disk capacity of your system and the capacity of a single tape (depending on the type of drive you have), you may need to swap tapes out during the backup routine. Some companies find that purchasing a tape autoloader is a good investment because tapes are swapped out automatically. Whatever hardware solution you use, make sure that it will support backing up your files. The last thing you need is for your "Saturday backup person" to opt to go out clubbing rather than head to the office for the weekly backup tape swap.

Managing Backup Media

Assuming you've got a tape drive and backup tapes, you'll need to figure out a system for managing the tapes. If you perform a normal backup on Saturday nights and incremental backups Monday, Tuesday, Wednesday, Thursday and Friday, you'll need 6 tapes. But…suppose you diligently do all your backups and on Saturday night, you go to perform you next full backup using last Saturday night's tape and the tape drive decides to shred the tape. Now, you not only don't have this week's full backup, you just lost last week's too. What happens if you actually DO need to restore? You guessed it. So, it's wise to crack open the old checkbook (or, more likely, the corporate account with your local computer supply company) and opt to purchase more tapes than you need. How many should you get? Well, as always, you'll need to strike a balance. Most companies find that they want to keep one full set of backups off-site in the event the building burns to the ground. They also want to keep one full set on-site in the event the server crashes but the building is fine. Some companies think it's just easier to manage three or four sets of six tapes each, for example. This way you can keep one or two backup sets (full plus incremental or full plus differential) on-site, and keep the oldest set off-site for safekeeping. This way, you always have a full set off-site in case of a major disaster.

SOME INDEPENDENT ADVICE

Make sure you test your tape media from time to time – tapes DO go bad and it's no fun to be in the middle of a backup and have a tape just halt with an error saying (in effect), "too many errors to continue." Test your tapes when you first get them and test them periodically thereafter. A good way to ruin your Monday morning is to come in and see the backup just sitting there awaiting a new tape.

Also keep in mind that while tapes are fairly hardy, they can wear out. The manufacturer typically provides specifications on how many times the tape can be read or written to and most companies toss the tape in the trash when it's between 50% and 75% of that lifespan because it's not worth the hassle of using a worn out tape. Keep in mind that older tapes sometimes write just fine, but if you need to read the tape for a restore, it might decide that's a great time to fail. Again, balance cost with risk of failure.

Finally, don't store your tape backups on-site in the server room. If the fire suppression system wipes out your server, there's a good chance your tapes are toast, too. Instead, store them in a secure but accessible location away from the servers. If you have a locked cabinet in your office, to which the HR manager or CEO has a key, that might be an ideal location for storage of on-site tape backups.

You should also carefully select your off-site location for several reasons. First, these tapes represent your company's entire set of data. The tapes should be kept in a secure location that is accessible to you (and another trusted member of your company) in the event of a disaster. They should be kept in a reasonable climate—protected from heat, cold, moisture, flooding, and fire. There are off-site storage companies you can use (make sure you provide them a list of authorized company representatives who can access the tapes) or you can store them at your house or the house of the CEO. Just make sure they are available when you need them and that they are stored securely to prevent unauthorized access (that includes your kids and pets).

Finally, keep your tape drive maintained by cleaning it periodically. Just like a VCR, the heads on a tape drive can accumulate dirt and particles from the tape causing read and/or write errors. Keeping the drive clean should be part of your normal routine to avoid problems with the tape drive or tapes. Most tape drives can use a cleaning tape specifically designed to clean the tape drive's heads.

The SBS Backup Utility

As mentioned earlier, you can use a third-party software program for your backups if desired, but SBS includes a backup program that will work just fine. The first time you access the backup utility, you'll be prompted to configure it, which we'll do here in a moment. Keep in mind that, depending on your backup hardware, your options may differ. Refer to the tape drive manufacturer's instructions if you have questions about the drive, the tape, its capacity, and maintenance. The SBS backup utility wizard will create a full system backup. For more flexible (and advanced) options, you can run the backup utility directly from a command line. For more on the details of the command line, open a command window and at the prompt, type in **ntbackup /?** then press **Enter**. The Command Line Help file will open. However, we'll restrict our discussion to the Backup Configuration Wizard.

The SBS backup utility has several helpful features including:

- **Backup Configuration Wizard** The wizard configures and schedules backups on SBS by using the NTBackup.exe program and the task scheduler. The default options will create a full system backup.

- **Single success and failure reporting** After each backup, the results are shown in the Manage Backup taskpad area. A status report for each backup is listed and this data can also be viewed in the server status reports.

- **Step-by-step restore document** This document provides specific, step-by-step instructions that will walk you through a restore, should that be necessary.

You can launch the Backup Configuration Wizard from the To Do List or you can launch Manage Backup function from with Server Management. Use the following steps to configure your server backup.

1. Open Server Management, select **Standard Management** and click **Backup**. If you have not configured your backups yet, you'll get a brief screen saying that you have not run the Configuration Wizard or backup has been disabled. To continue, click **Configure Backup** in the taskpad area to launch the **Backup Configuration Wizard**. On the Welcome screen, click **Next** to continue.

2. The second screen, **Backup Location**, prompts you to specify the location to which you want to save files. The recommended location is a tape drive, but you can select another location by selecting **Back up to a local hard drive or network share**. You can type in the location or click the **Browse** button to specify the location. Click **Next** to continue.

3. The next screen, Backup Data Summary, shows a summary of the data to be backed up. You can specifically exclude folders from being backed up by clicking **Exclude Folders**. After you exclude folders, you can click **Calculate Folder Sizes** to see the size of included and excluded folders. You may choose to exclude folders that rarely change or for which you have other backups. For instance, you may choose to exclude client application folders if you have those applications (and all updates) stored on CD-ROM or DVD already. Click **Next**.

4. Next, you need to configure your backup schedule. You have a variety of options from which to choose, though your default options are Monday through Friday at 11P.M. If you're storing backups on a removable disk drive (rather than tapes), you'll also be prompted for how many backups to keep in this location before overwriting the oldest copy. You'll also see a small reminder to make sure the disk you've selected has enough disk space. Click **Next** to continue.

5. If you're backing up to tape, the next screen is the Onsite Tape Changer screen, which allows you to select the person who will be responsible for changing the backup tapes and cleaning the tape drive. The person selected will receive an automated reminder at the specified time (based on your backup schedule you just configured in the last screen). You can also have that person sent a monthly reminder to clean the tape drive.

Although that's a good failsafe option, you should really clean the drive weekly if you're using the drive daily. Check the drive manufacturer's recommendations for the optimal cleaning interval. Select the account from the drop-down box, click **Next** to continue.

6. The next screen allows you to configure how you want to manage deleted files and e-mail. Since users often accidentally delete files and e-mails, these two options are of particular interest to most admins. Select desired settings for the two options available on this screen, **Retain copies of permanently deleted e-mail messages** and **Enable periodic snapshots of users' shared folders**. The second option enables users to locate and retrieve older versions of files as well as accidentally deleted files, as we discussed earlier in the book when discussing volume shadow copies. Click **Next** to continue.

7. The summary screen will be displayed. Click **Back** to go back and make changes or click **Finish** to complete the configuration.

You can use the Backup function in Server Management or you can manually launch the backup program by going to **Start | All Programs | Accessories | System Tools | Backup.** This will launch the Backup or Restore Wizard. For more experienced admins, you can access the advanced features by clicking the link for **Advanced Mode**. The Advanced Mode contains many additional backup options you may want to explore as you become more familiar with the backup function such as performing incremental or differential backups. You can customize the backup and restore settings from the Advanced Mode dialog box and you can also configure another useful feature, the Automated System Recovery Wizard.

Automated System Recovery

The *Automated System Recovery* (ASR) *Wizard* steps you through creating a two-part backup of your system (not your data files, your system files) – a floppy disk that has your system settings and the other media that contains a backup of your local system partition data. You can access this via **Start | All Programs | Accessories | System Tools | Backup.** On the Welcome screen, click the **Advanced Mode** link. In the Backup Utility dialog box, the Welcome tab is selected by default. On the Welcome tab, you have three options: **Backup Wizard (Advanced), Restore Wizard (Advanced),** and **Automated System Recover Wizard.** Click the latter button to create the ASR set. You will be prompted to enter the location of the backup media and the backup media name or filename. Once you enter that data and click **Next**, the system will create a backup of your system files and write them to a floppy disk. This disk, as well as your backup media, can then be used to restore your system if disaster strikes. It's important to keep them together as a set.

The ASR diskette is not a bootable floppy. It must be used in conjunction with the Windows Small Business Server installation media as well as the tape backup you made when you created the ASR. It's a good idea to keep two or three generations available—they're little, inexpensive insurance policies against big trouble.

The ASR diskette has just three files on it—Setup.log, Asr.sif and Asrpnp.sif. The first file points to the location of system files on your server, the second file contains information on disk, partitions and volumes on the system as well as the location of the backup media used, and the third file contains information on the various plug-and-play (PNP) devices on the system. Since each ASR diskette points to a specific system backup, it's important to keep the diskette matched up with the specific backup. Also, be sure to use freshly formatted media to avoid problems with the diskette or tape itself.

SOME INDEPENDENT ADVICE

Since it takes very little time, it's worth creating your first ASR set right after you finish configuring your SBS server. Save this as your absolute failsafe option. Then, create a new ASR set before you make major changes to your system. Create another new set again after you're sure everything's up and running properly again. The first will give you a fall-back option, the second and third options should be done every time there is a change to the system configuration such as adding or removing devices, changing disk partitions, etc. Since these are so quick and easy to create and save, archiving some of these can really come in handy if disaster does strike.

You can also use the links in the taskpad to perform common backup tasks such as:

- **Configure Backup** to configure your backup utility
- **Backup Now** to manually start a backup

- **Modify the Backup Schedule**

- **Modify Storage for Deleted Files and E-mail**

- **Configure My Documents Redirection** (covered earlier in the book)

- **Learn How to Restore the Server**

- **Restore Individual Files**

- **Restore SharePoint Files**

The **Configure Backup** link will step you through all the backup configuration options. If you're just interested in modifying specific settings, you can use the individual links provided, such as **Modify the Backup Schedule**. The information files provide step-by-step instructions for restoring files. You may want to print out the **Learn How to Restore the Server** file and add it to your disaster recovery plan. An updated version of this file is available on the Microsoft website as well.

Backup Status

After your backups have run, you should see status entries n the **Server Management | Standard Management | Backup** indicating success or failure, as shown in Figure 11.1. To view the information about the last backup, click the **View Last Backup Log** link. You can also look at other logs, as listed in the right pane, also shown in Figure 11.1. The log file is a text file that indicates what happened during that backup session. A sample is shown in Figure 11.2.

Figure 11. 1 Backup Status Message in Server Backup

Figure 11.2 Sample Failed Backup Log

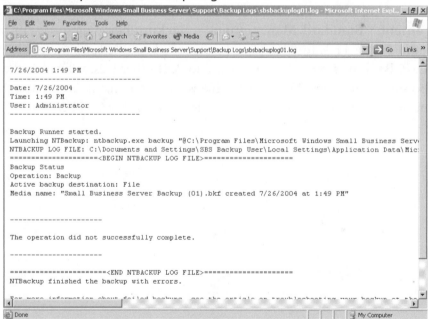

Recovery Console

One of the very handy recovery tools in Small Business Server is the Recovery Console. It's a more advanced tool, so it's probably for the more experienced admins out there. You can always access the Recovery Console from the SBS CD-ROM Disk 1, so you don't have to install it before disaster strikes. Since it provides an alternate method of accessing the system (read: security risk), you should think about whether or not you want to install the Recovery Console beforehand. Some companies do, some don't. Using the Recovery Console requires a strong understanding of how to do things like install driver files via the command prompt. If this sounds a bit out of your comfort zone, you don't have to use the Recovery Console, just be aware that this tool exists.

The Recovery Console is essentially a command prompt with muscle. It's secure, NTFS-enabled and can be used to copy files, start and stop various system services and perform other recovery actions when you can't boot the system using the Windows Small Business Server safe mode. You can install it using these steps:

1. Insert the first SBS CD-ROM in the drive. Close the autorun dialog box if it opens.

2. Click **Start | Run** and type in the command **d:\i386\winnt32\cmdcons**. If your CD-ROM drive has a different letter than D:, substitute your drive letter for the letter **d** in the command.

3. Click **Yes** to install the Recovery Console when the Windows Setup message appears.

4. If a Getting Updated Setup Files page appears, click the appropriate option then click **Next**.

5. The Copying Installation Files page appears and copies the needed files from the CD.

6. A message appears indicating the Recovery Console was successfully installed. Click **OK**.

The next time you reboot your system, one of the boot options will be the Recovery Console. If your system runs into problems and a Safe Mode boot doesn't help out, you can opt to use the Recovery Console. You can configure various recovery console settings by accessing the Recovery Console in **Start | Control Panel | System | Advanced** then click **Settings** in the Start up and Recovery box to display the Startup and Recovery dialog box. For more information about configuring or using the recovery console, query the Help and Support files or query **tools for troubleshooting** on the Microsoft website.

Restoring Your Server and Data

Though being an optimist is good for your long-term health (did you know optimists outlive pessimists by an average of 7 years?), being a realist is better when it comes to disaster recovery. It's great to *believe* you'll never have a disaster, never have a crashed disk, never have to restore your data. It's fine to hope you never have to restore as long as you're still fully prepared to do so. Let's assume for just a moment that some component in your server overheated and all the disk drives are toast (technical term meaning *kaput, finis, adios*). Ugly, unlikely, but possible.

Your server is down, disk drives fried. You've implemented your disaster recovery plan and you now have new disk drives in your server and you're ready to restore. Let's step through a restore process – remember, your steps may vary slightly, but these steps will give you a good idea of how to proceed. After we look at the full restore process, we'll step through how to do a partial restore, which is a common task when critical files are accidentally modified or deleted and someone needs to recover those files.

Full Restore

After a full system failure, you can restore your server from your last (successful) backup set. If the server itself was damaged or destroyed and you're restoring to new server hardware, you must ensure that the hardware is the same as the previous server including:

- Motherboard chipset
- Number of processors
- Hard disk size
- Drive letter of the boot partition
- SCSI Controller – you can restore to a computer using IDE controller even if the original drive(s) was SCSI

It is recommended that you attempt to purchase the exact same make and model server hardware as the original to avoid problems. If you have any external drives (USB, Firewire), disconnect them before starting your restore. You might also want to visit the Microsoft Small Business Server 2003 website and download or review any recent articles on restoring your system so you can be sure you're completely ready and up to speed.

BEST PRACTICES ACCORDING TO MICROSOFT

- If you upgraded from Small Business Server 2000, you need to create a floppy disk to use when you boot from the CD before you begin your restore.
- Copy the Winnt.sif and Winnt.bat from the folder \SBSSUPPORT\UpgradeRestore on the Windows Small Business Server 2003 Disk 3 to a diskette.
- In the Winnt.sif file, be sure that the TargetPath under [Unattended] is set to the same installation directory used before the restore. The Winnt.sif file can be opened in Notepad. The default Target Path in Small Business Server 2000 is TargetPath=Winnt.
- In the Winnt.bat, be sure the drive letter is the same as the drive letter of your CD drive, the default is D:.

For more information, query **system restore** in the Help files.

If you are restoring to new hardware, you should perform a *migration* rather than a restore. Steps for migrating are delineated earlier in this book and additional resources can be found online on the Microsoft website. As we stated earlier, migration is not an easy task, so you should consider hiring an outside expert to help you through the process. The steps for restoring your system include:

1. Install the operating system from the installation media.

2. Restore the server from your most recent successful backup.

3. Verify the success of the restore and rejoin client computers to the network.

Install the Operating System

Follow the normal operating system instructions as delineated in Chapter 3. Make sure you set your disk drives up with the same partition sizes (or larger) and same drive letters as your original system. This is where your system and disaster plan information regarding system configuration will come in handy (that's an understatement).

Restore the Server from Backup

After installation is complete, the server will restart. Press **F8** to access the **Windows Advanced Options** menu. If you get a logon screen, logon on and restart the computer. Press **F8** while the computer is restarting to access these options. Then, use the following steps.

1. Select **Directory Services Restore Mode (Windows Domain Controllers Only)**.

2. Log on using the Administrator account and password. In the Safe Mode dialog box, click **OK**. Note: If you have external drives, reconnect them at this time via **Start | Administrative Tools | Disk Management**. Configure the drives exactly as they were before. After configuring your drives, restart your computer, press **F8**, select **Windows Advanced Options**, then select **Directory Services Restore Mode**.

3. Ensure the backup media is in the appropriate drive and accessible to the system.

4. Click **Start | Run** and type **ntbackup** to open the Backup Utility or select **Start | All Programs | Accessories | System Tools | Backup**. Either way will launch the same backup utility.

5. When the Backup and Restore Wizard launches, click the **Advanced Mode** link on the Welcome screen.

6. In the Backup Utility dialog box, click **Tools** on the menu and select **Options**. In the Options dialog box, select the **Restore** tab and then select **Always replace the file on my computer**. Click **OK** to close this dialog box.

7. Click the **Restore and Manage Media** tab in the Backup Utility. Double-click the tape or file that corresponds to your last successful full backup.

8. To restore disk drives and system state, select the checkboxes for each. Do not check **Microsoft Information Store.** Note: Only select drives that were damaged or corrupted previously. If you restore a

working drive, you will overwrite any data on that drive and possibly lose more recent data.

9. Under **Restore files to**, make sure you select **Original location.** If you want to restore to an alternate location you can do so, but make sure you are doing so with good reason. Typically, you'll restore data files, not system files, to alternate locations, which we'll discuss just a bit later in the chapter. Click the **Start Restore** button to begin your system restore.

10. A warning box will appear, click **OK** to continue.

11. The Confirm Restore dialog box will be displayed. Click **Advanced** and select **Advanced Restore Options**, then ensure that the following boxes are selected:

- **Restore security settings**

- **Restore junction points, restore file and folder data under junction points to original location**

- **When restoring replicated data sets, mark the restored data as the primary data for all replicas**

- **Preserve existing volume mount points**

12. Click **OK** to close the Advanced options then **OK** again to begin your restore. Depending on the amount of data to be restored, this may take several hours. Use the duration of a typical full backup session to determine roughly how long your restore might take.

13. When complete, click **Report** to verify the system state and all files were recovered.

14. Close the Backup Utility and reboot the system. The system should be fully functional at this point.

Verify the Success of the Restore

1. After your restore is complete, you may see the **Continue Setup** icon on the desktop. If so, go ahead and delete this shortcut.

2. You may want to double-check your IP configuration information on your network adapters.

3. If you chose not to restore applications from backup, install these now.

4. On client computers, click **Start | Run** and type **cmd** to open a command prompt. Then, type in **ipconfig /renew** and press **Enter** to renew the IP configuration information for the client computer.

5. To verify the success of the restore, open Server Management and confirm system state, users, and computers are back to their previous settings (settings from the most recent successful full backup). Make sure you can connect to the Internet, send and receive e-mail, and check your company website (if it exists). This is not an exhaustive list of things you can check to ensure your system is back to full function, but is a good starting point.

Partial Restore of Files and Folders

There are essentially two ways to recover a folder, a group of files or even an individual file. The method you use depends on your particular configuration and other factors. In most cases, if you enabled **Shadow Copies on Shared Folders** and the file is in a shared location, you can recover using this feature. In other cases, you may not be able to recover using this method and you'll have to restore specific folders or files from your backup media.

Using Shadow Copies on Shared Folders to Restore Folders and Files

Windows Small Business Server 2003 uses volume shadow copy in the background to preserve previous versions of files. If a file is accidentally modified or deleted, you can recover the file by using this feature. We discussed it earlier in the book but will review it briefly here. To use this feature, you must have previously configured the **Shadow Copies on Shared Folders** shadow through the **Shadow Copies** tab of the local disk properties dialog box. To access a previous file, go to the client computer, right-click **My Documents** (or the shared folder location), select **Properties** from the shortcut menu and click the **Previous Version** tab. Double-click the most recent version of the folder that contains the file. Select the desired file then click **Restore**. Keep in mind that restoring an older version will overwrite the current version. If you restore an entire folder, it will revert to the state it was in when that shadow copy was created causing you to lose more recent data. If you do not want to lose current data, copy the data to a new location.

Using Backup Media to Restore Folders and Files

You may have to use your backup media to restore folders and files if you are unable to do so using the shadow copies just discussed. For more information, you can also open **Server Management | Backup** and read the help files on how to restore files or SharePoint files. Use the following steps to restore individual folders or files.

1. Insert the backup media that contains the desired folders or files into the drive.

2. Launch the backup utility via **Start | All Programs | Accessories | System Tools | Backup.** If the Backup Utility does not recognize your tape, the Recognizable Media Found dialog box appears. Select **Allow Backup Utility** to continue.

3. In the Backup or Restore Wizard, click **Next** to continue. On the Backup or Restore screen, select **Restore files or settings** then click **Next.**

4. The next screen gives you the opportunity to select which files or folders to restore. Select the desired folders/files and then click **Next.**

5. The summary screen is displayed giving you the opportunity to review your selections. If you're satisfied with your choices, click **Finish** to start the selective restore. If you want to change the location to which the files are restored (suggested if you want to preserve the existing files), click **Advanced.** Within the Advanced section, you'll have the option to change where and how files are restored as well as several advanced options.

Note that you can use a selective restore of a test folder to test and verify your backup and restore capabilities. Simply restore a selected folder to a different location (a test folder) and look at the files, folders, attributes, permissions, etc. for those files. While this doesn't guarantee your backups and restores are 100% reliable, it's a good quick test that can provide some measure of assurance.

Restoring Deleted E-mail

By default, the SBS Backup Utility is set to save 30 days' worth of e-mail on Exchange Server. If an e-mail is accidentally deleted, it can be recovered using the following steps:

1. Open Outlook 2003.

2. Click **Tools** on the menu and select **Recover Deleted Items.** This will open a dialog box in which you can select the item(s) you want to recover. Select the item(s) and click **Recover Selected Items.** The recovered items will show up in the folder from which it was earlier deleted.

You can also restore SharePoint files and list items. In the Backup section of Server Management, simply click the link labeled **Restore SharePoint Files** and follow the instructions in the wizard. We'll discuss SharePoint later in this book.

One More Time

In this chapter, you learned how to create a disaster plan by involving members of your company's management team and Human Resources department. You also learned not only the importance of performing backups but how to best back up your data to protect your critical corporate data. You also learned how to restore your data should you need to do so, whether you needed to restore an entire server or just a few folders or files.

☑ Disaster planning includes all information your company would need to continue business activities following a disaster. This is sometimes referred to as business continuity planning.

☑ The basic elements of a disaster plan include

- Risk assessment and prioritization

- Legal considerations

- Asset evaluation

- Incident response

- Plan testing and maintenance

☑ There are different types of backups you can perform, including full (normal), incremental, differential, copy, or daily. Copy and daily do not change the archive attribute and will not impact the files that will (or will not be) backed up during your scheduled backup session.

☑ The default backup using the Backup Wizard in SBS is a full backup. You must manually launch the backup utility to access other options.

☑ Backups should be done regularly based on how often data changes and how critical the data is.

☑ Backups are typically done using tapes but can be performed to other disk media. Backing up to removable media is not supported by the Windows Small Business Server 2003 Backup utility.

☑ You should create a rotation schedule for backups so that you always have two or three sets of recent backups available, the oldest one stored off-site for an absolute failsafe option.

☑ Clean the tape drive often to avoid tape read/write errors and discard tapes after they're reached their typical useful life. Check tape drive and tape manufacturer specifications for more information.

☑ If you need to restore an entire server, make every effort to match the original server hardware exactly. Subtle or slight differences between chipsets, BIOS versions, and other hardware components can make the restore either difficult or impossible.

☑ If you are unable to exactly match the server hardware, you may have to perform a migration rather than a restore.

☑ To fully restore a system you would install the SBS software again then restore from your most recent full backup. The final step involves checking the server to ensure your system is fully restored and functional.

☑ Individual files and folders can be restored using the shadow volume copy feature of SBS. To restore a file or folder, right-click the shared location and select the **Previous Version** tab. If this tab is not present, shadow volume copying has not been enabled.

☑ If you are unable to restore a folder or file using the shadow copy function, you can perform a selective restore from you backup media. If you want to preserve current (existing) files or folders, you can choose to restore to a different location using the Backup Utility.

☑ You can recover deleted emails that are up to 30 days old (or whatever setting you selected when configuring your backup program).

Chapter 12

Using Exchange Server and Outlook 2003

- Overview of Microsoft Exchange Server

- Working with Exchange Server

- Working with Outlook 2003

- Exchange ActiveSync 3.7

The End Result

By the end of this chapter, you'll have a solid understanding of Microsoft Exchange Server and the related client application, Microsoft Outlook. Although Exchange and Outlook are commonly thought of simply as e-mail applications (server and client), you'll learn in this chapter they have a broad range of capabilities that enable and support communication throughout the organization.

Overview of Microsoft Exchange Server

Microsoft Exchange Server is a feature of both the Standard and Premium editions of Windows Small Business Server 2003 (SBS). In this section, we'll look at exactly what Exchange Server is and what it can do for your organization. In the following section, we'll actually walk through configuring and managing Exchange Server.

Microsoft has alternately positioned Exchange Server as a simple e-mail server application and as a communication and collaboration tool. The reality lies somewhere in the middle. While you can use Exchange Server as a collaboration tool, it's fair to say it's a communications tool more than anything else. Collaboration in SBS is probably best handled by SharePoint Services, which we'll discuss later in this book. That said, Exchange Server is a server-based application that centralizes the configuration and management of e-mail, calendars, notes, contacts, distribution lists, and public folders. This provides users with a variety of communication tools that most companies come to rely upon pretty quickly once they discover the versatility and usefulness of these tools.

There are two primary places that you'll end up when working with Exchange Server. First, the Exchange Server application itself (accessed either through the Server Management console or via **Start** | **All Programs** | **Microsoft Exchange** | **System Manager**, which gets you to the same interface), provides a very powerful interface for managing all aspects of Exchange Server. For the most part, however, you won't go directly into Exchange to make changes once you've configured e-mail via the E-mail and Internet Connection Wizard. You'll find that using **Active Directory (AD) Users and Computers** is the place you'll work the most with Exchange Server – sort of from the other side of the fence. In any given user's Properties dialog box, you'll see a variety of Exchange-related settings. Once you get Exchange Server configured, you'll probably find yourself going into AD Users and Computers more often than in Exchange Server itself.

SOME INDEPENDENT ADVICE

Microsoft Exchange Server is a server application with enormous potential and complexity if you dig down into all the capabilities. Exchange Server is configured, by default, when you install SBS and run the Configure E-mail and Internet Connection Wizard. However, there are plenty of other settings you can configure if you want to really get your hands dirty in Exchange. The Exchange Server technical library can be accessed on the Microsoft website at www.microsoft.com/technet/ prodtechnol/exchange/2003/library/default.mspx. You can learn as much your heart desires by digging through the plethora of technical articles on this site, but be warned, you can get yourself into a world of trouble pretty quickly, so educate yourself before you start changing settings.

Exchange Server Components

Let's begin with reviewing the components that make up Exchange Server interface in SBS. When you open Server Management (**Start | Server Management**), navigate to **Advanced Management** and click **First Organization (Exchange)** or *DomainName* **(Exchange)**. If you expand this tree or look in the right pane, you'll see six options: Global Settings, Recipients, Servers, Connectors, Tools, and Folders, shown in Figure 12.1. Each of these provides a way to manage aspects of Exchange Server in your SBS environment. We'll go through each of these sections, but for the most part, you don't need to delve into these areas to successfully use Exchange Server in your organization. This section is provided primarily for background and reference for those interested.

Figure 12.1 Exchange Server Components

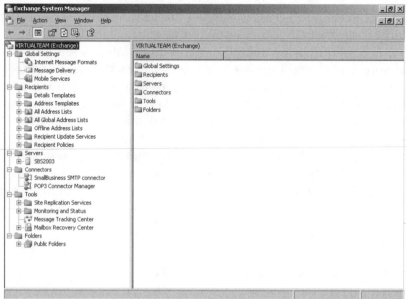

Global Settings

Global settings have an effect on all users. The three categories in global settings are Internet Message Formats, Message Delivery, and Mobile Services. In each of the properties of these settings, you'll see a **Details** tab that allows you to write and store notes. If you make modifications in these areas, it's a good idea to keep a few notes so you can easily understand when or why you made a particular change or implemented a specific setting. In troubleshooting, when something stops working, it's often the thing we did last, so this can be a great way to make notes about what you did in case you break something. It's also helpful for simply keeping track of what you're doing and why, even when things work great.

Recipients

In this section, you can manage details and address templates, all address lists, all global address lists, offline address lists, recipient update services, and recipient policies. This section is most often used if you want to generate dialog boxes used for setting up user information in different languages. Details templates control the appearance of address lists your Exchange users see when they look up recipient properties in the address lists.

Servers

In this section, you can manage details related to Exchange Server itself including queues (e-mail awaiting delivery inbound or outbound), storage groups, and protocols. The default settings here should be left as-is unless you've done your homework and you have a good reason for making changes. Queues, First Storage Group, and Protocols are located in this area.

Connectors

A connector is a component that enables communication or information flow between two systems. In the world of e-mail, this means that you can have connectors that provide messaging services between Exchange and other systems such as your ISP's (Internet Service Provider's) e-mail system. By default, Exchange Server installs two connectors—SMTP (Simple Mail Transfer Protocol) and POP3 (Post Office Protocol 3) connectors since these are the two most commonly used e-mail methods. You can add additional connectors, but for our purposes, these two will work just fine. If you right-click either the SMTP or POP3 connector, you can access its properties. The properties that can be configured vary with each type of connector. Figure 12.2 shows the properties of the default SMTP connector created when you install SBS and run through the E-mail and Internet Connection Wizard. Though you'll most likely use POP3, if you use SMTP, you should probably opt to use DNS (Domain Name System) to route to each address space rather than forwarding. Forwarding is a trick used by spammers and using this method will make all your e-mail look like it came from your ISP. In addition, if it's forwarded, your e-mail might be rejected since this is a common spammer tactic. For more information, contact your ISP about these settings or consult the Help files or Microsoft web site.

Figure 12.2 Properties of Default SMTP Connector in Exchange Server

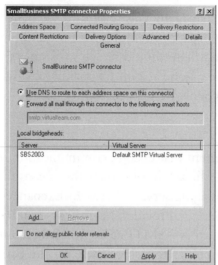

Tools

Under Tools, you can access Site Replication Services, Monitoring and Status, Message Tracking Center, and Mailbox Recovery Center. Site Replication works in conjunction with Active Directory to replicate (or copy) directory objects. In the Monitoring and Status node, you can set options related to receiving notifications (e-mail or script notifications) and viewing the status of various objects such as the SMTP connector or the POP3 connector. With Message Tracking, you can view the tracking history of an e-mail message. The Mailbox Recovery Center can be used to recover user mailboxes.

Folders

Public folders are one of the most popular features of Exchange Server (after e-mail, of course). Public folders provide a centralized place to store information of all kinds that users across the organization can access. You can create public folders for groups of users as well, and restrict access to them. These public folders can contain all kinds of files from simple messages to multimedia clips and custom forms. In some companies, creating separate public folders for various user groups makes sense. In other companies, the default public folders are just "out there" for all employees to use. If you use the latter method, you may want to work with your Human Resources department to create guidelines for proper public folders use. Is it ok for employees to post flyers for yard sales or free puppies? There is no right or wrong answer to how to set policies for public folder use, but you should consider setting up a few rules from the start and monitor public folders from time to time. You may run into legal issues if employees misuse public folders and post inappropriate materials. Since your company is hosting and managing these public folders, you should consult with your HR or legal counsel in creating your public folders policies.

Some Independent Advice

The version of Exchange included with Small Business Server 2003 is a full-blown version, so there's a tremendous amount you can do with Exchange in your small business. In this chapter, we're only covering the most common tasks and features. The default settings established when you installed SBS and when you ran the E-mail and Internet Connection Wizard will probably do just fine for you, so work with these default settings first and then make changes only when you find a setting doesn't suit your needs or when things aren't working as you'd like them to.

Working with Exchange Server

The good news here is that just by performing your basic SBS installation, you've configured a lot of the elements of Microsoft Exchange Server. There are many things you can do with Exchange and if it's something that interests you, there's a whole Exchange Server world awaiting you. Read up and understand what you can do and how to do it before you go jetting around in Exchange Server's settings, though. It's easy to lose your way and mess things up in a hurry. Since e-mail is the lifeblood of many organizations, you don't want to do anything to unnecessarily jeopardize this functionality.

In this section, we're just going to cover some of the more common tasks. This is by no means an exhaustive look at how you can work with Exchange Server, this is just meant to step you through some of the things you're likely going to want to do beyond the default settings.

By default, when you installed SBS, Exchange Server was installed. When you stepped through the To Do List and launched the E-mail and Internet Connection Wizard, you set up the Exchange Server settings related to e-mail delivery, etc. If for some reason you skipped this step or perhaps didn't configure it properly, a good resource to start with is your ISP. The ISP is how you'll get your e-mail in and out of your network (via your Internet connection), so talk with the ISP about how to configure your e-mail settings.

Also, when you added users, mailboxes were created for those users. If you locate a user on your server and right-click that user and choose **Properties**, you'll see the Exchange-related property tabs including **E-mail Addresses, Exchange Features**, and **Exchange Advanced.** If those tabs are missing, the user is not e-mail-enabled. When you create a new user, you can select to create an Exchange mailbox for that user. We'll look at both scenarios later in this section.

If you access Exchange via **Server Management | Advanced Management**, you'll see in the details (right side) pane, the following links: **Add a Distribution Group, Manage POP3 E-mail, Synchronize E-mail, Change E-mail Password**, and **More Information**. We'll focus on these tasks first, since they're the ones you're most likely to use.

Add a Distribution Group

If you recall from earlier chapters, distribution groups are groups of users that can be used for sending e-mail to groups within the company. Distribution groups have no security function and are used simply to contact groups of users such as Sales, Managers, Team Leaders, etc. Like security groups, you create a distribution group and add users to the group. Use the following steps to create and populate a distribution group:

1. Open Server Management and navigate to **Advanced Management | First Organization (Exchange)**. In the right pane, click on **Add a Distribution Group**. This will launch the Add a Distribution Group Wizard. Click **Next** on the Welcome screen. Alternately, you can access this same wizard via **Server Management | Standard Management | Distribution Groups**.

2. On the Distribution Group Information screen, enter the name of the group, a description, and the e-mail alias such as sales, marketing, managers, etc. The e-mail alias will be automatically entered based on the name you type in, but you can modify it if you want. Click **Next.**

3. On the Group Membership screen, click users in the left pane that you want to add to the group then click **Add**. The user will be shown in the right pane. If you add a user you want to remove, select the user in the

right pane and click **Remove.** When you're finished adding users to the distribution group, click **Next.**

4. On the Group Manager screen, you can select a user or group to modify members of this distribution group. While this is not required, doing so will help reduce your workload. The Group Manager has the ability to add and delete users from this group without having to involve you (the admin). Since distribution groups have no security function, you don't add any security risks by delegating this task. Click on the user or group within the distribution group to whom you want to provide this ability then click **Next.**

5. On the Group Options screen, you can select two options. The first is **Create a public folder to archive e-mail messages sent to this group** and the second is **Enable this group to receive e-mail messages from users outside your network**. The first option is self-explanatory. The second option allows outsiders to send e-mail to the e-mail alias created in step 2. Remember, however, that this e-mail address might be the target of spammers if you use defaults like marketing@somecompany.com. Spammers use these types of default addresses to get spam through corporate systems, as mentioned earlier. If you do not enable this feature, only users on your corporate network will be able to send e-mail to this alias. Click **Next.**

6. The final screen allows you to review your selections. Click **Back** to go back and make changes. To print, e-mail, or save the information (a good idea), click the appropriate link on the final page before clicking **Finish.**

Note that if you selected the first option in Step 5 to create a public folder to archive e-mail from this group, you'll see the group archive now listed in public folders. If it is not present, click the **Refresh** icon at the top of the window in the toolbar area. To view or modify current distribution groups, you can go to **Start | Server Management | Standard Management | Distribution Groups**. In the right pane, the groups are listed. To modify or remove a group, click the group and select either **Change Group Properties** or **Remove Distribution Group**.

Manage POP3 E-mail

There a two primary ways to manage e-mail coming into your company. Many people are familiar with using POP3 to retrieve e-mail from their ISP to their personal e-mail accounts at home, for instance. As you know, when you get an e-mail address from your ISP, messages sent to that e-mail address are received by the ISP's e-mail server and are held until your retrieve them with a POP3 e-mail client such as Microsoft Outlook.

In many companies, all e-mail is sent directly to the company's e-mail server where e-mail is then placed in the appropriate recipient's mailbox. This type of situation uses SMTP rather than POP3 and requires that your ISP configure special records called MX records. It takes a bit more configuration and requires that your e-mail server be up and available 24/7/365.

Some Independent Advice

SBS and Exchange Server in SBS support using a single, global POP3 mailbox for all your incoming corporate e-mail on your ISP. All e-mail can be received by one mailbox on your ISP and then routed to appropriate Exchange mailboxes on your end. There's no need to create or maintain separate POP3 accounts for each user on your ISP side. When POP3 mail is received by the POP3 Connector, it is automatically distributed to the corresponding Exchange mailboxes. For instance, an e-mail sent to JackieBrowne@somecompany.com can go into a global mailbox on the ISP and when received by Exchange Server, the POP3 Connector (when configured for routing) can route that e-mail to Jackie Browne's mailbox. If Rosie Black is in the Cc: line, the e-mail will also get forwarded to Rosie if the routing is set up. Essentially, you can set up routing for every Exchange mailbox so that e-mail received in your global mailbox at your ISP and sent to Exchange Server can then be routed to the appropriate recipients.

Other companies choose to implement SMTP mail and have e-mail come directly to their e-mail server. The ISP still provides Internet connectivity but e-mail is directly sent and received via the Exchange Server itself. If Exchange Server is installed (which it is by default in SBS 2003), you can use the E-mail and Internet Connection Wizard to specify how you will send and receive Internet e-mail. Based on the information entered in the wizard, an SMTP connector necessary for Exchange Server is automatically configured. You can also configure the POP3 connector, which we'll go over in this section.

Also, some companies use mailing lists such as Inquiries@somecompany.com. You might want to route all of these to Nick, for example, so you can set up a routing rule for these general e-mails to go to a specific person as well.

The decision as to how to proceed should be based on your expertise with e-mail configuration, your ISP and the services they provide, as well as your server availability.

One popular way for small businesses to handle their e-mail is by using their ISPs to manage the public side of their e-mail. SBS can automatically download e-mail from multiple individual POP3 mailboxes (located on your ISP) and distribute the e-mail into the correct Exchange mailboxes. This is done via the POP3 connector.

To configure and enable the Connector for POP3 Mailboxes in SBS, you need to add one or more POP3 mailboxes. If none are defined, the connector is not enabled. If you configured this in the E-mail and Internet Connection Wizard, you should be set. If not, you can go back and re-run this wizard preserving the settings you want to maintain by selecting the **Do not change this setting** option in the wizard screens. You need to point SBS to the location of the POP3 mailbox on your ISP. One you have designated this option, the Connector for POP3 Mailboxes is enabled and you can further configure it from within **Server Management** | **Advanced Management** | **Exchange** | **POP3 Connector Manager** or **Start** | **All Programs** | **Microsoft Exchange** | **System Manager** | **Connectors** | **POP3 Connector Manager.**

You can manage POP3 mailboxes including adding, deleting, or editing POP3 mailboxes using the POP3 Connector Manager found via either path mentioned above. We'll assume you went in via the first method, but the instructions are the same either way. In Server Management, you can click the link labeled **Open POP3 Connector Manager** or simply right-click the POP3 Connection Manager and select **Properties.** In the Properties dialog box, notice there are three tabs, **Mailboxes**, **Scheduling**, and **Troubleshooting.**

Add POP3 Mailbox

To add a POP3 mailbox, use the following steps from within the **Properties** of the POP3 Connection Manager (or by clicking **Open POP3 Connector Manager**, both achieve the same result).

1. In the POP3 Connector Manager dialog, make sure the **Mailboxes** tab is selected then click **Add**.

2. The POP3 Mailbox dialog box will be displayed, as shown in Figure 12.3. Enter the following information in the fields in this dialog box.

    ■ **E-mail server** This is the address of your ISP's e-mail server. This will typically look something like mail.yourISP.com.

    ■ **Port** This is the TCP/IP (Transmission Control Protocol/Internet Protocol) port number that your ISP uses for POP3 e-mail. The default value is 110, but you may need to change this if your ISP uses a different one (though many ISPs use this default value).

    ■ **User name** This is the ISP's account name for the POP3 mailbox, which may or may not correspond to the user's name in Exchange or on your SBS system.

    ■ **Password** and **Confirm Password** Enter the password for this account on the ISP side.

    ■ **Log on using Secure Password Authentication (SPA)** Some ISPs allow (or require) secure password authentication. If your ISP offers this options, use it to help maintain security.

    ■ **Mailbox type** You can choose between **User Mailbox** and **Global Mailbox**. You can tie this POP3 mailbox to a specific user or to a global mailbox used by multiple users (for instance, marketing@yourcompany.com would go to a global mailbox rather than a user mailbox if you wanted multiple users to access this e-mail).

    ■ **Exchange Mailbox** If you want to connect a particular POP3 mailbox to a specific user (that is, if you selected **User Mailbox** in the previous selection), select the Exchange mailbox from the drop-down box.

- **E-mail Domain** If you selected **Global Mailbox** instead of **User Mailbox**, you must specify the e-mail domain used as the return address for users of this mailbox.

- **Routing Rules** If each user of the global mailbox maps directly to an identical Exchange mailbox, you don't need to add routing. Otherwise, you'll need to add routing rules.

Figure 12.3 Dialog Box to Add New POP3 Mailbox

3. To add routing rules, click the **Routing Rules** button then click **Add.**

4. In the Routing Rules dialog box, enter the text n the To: or Cc: line that you want to "capture" and route. For instance, using the earlier example, this might be **Marketing**. Note that you can only route e-mail based on the To: or Cc: line, not on the Bcc: line or Subject: line. Routing Rules is only useful if you use the ISP to capture all corporate e-mail in a single mailbox.

5. Use the drop-down box to select the Exchange mailbox to which the e-mail will be routed then click **OK**. You can add additional routing rules, but you can only add one routing rule for each To: or Cc: line. For instance, you cannot route **Marketing** to two or three different mailboxes. However, if the same POP3 mailbox might also have **Sales** in the

Cc: line, you can add a routing rule for Sales that is forwarded to a different (or the same) Exchange mailbox.

6. You can **Add**, **Edit**, or **Remove** routing rules for this POP3 mailbox. When finished, click **OK** to return to the POP3 Mailbox dialog box.

7. Once you've entered and selected all the fields, click **OK.**

You can edit any POP3 mailbox by selecting it and clicking **Edit.** You can remove any POP3 mailbox by selecting it and clicking **Remove.** When you're finished, you can click **OK** to exit out of the POP3 Connector Manager Properties dialog box.

Setting a POP3 Delivery Schedule

By default, Exchange will download e-mail from POP3 mailboxes (your ISP mailboxes) once each hour, every hour, 7 days a week. You can modify this if your company has different needs. Often companies that live and die by e-mail want to receive e-mail more frequently than hourly. The minimum time you can set is every 15 minutes. To change the default schedule, open the POP3 Connector Manager and click the **Scheduling** tab (instead of the default Mailboxes tab) and use the following steps.

1. If you want to manually retrieve e-mail from POP3 mailboxes, you can do so at the top of the POP3 Connector Manager Properties dialog box (Scheduling tab).

2. If you want to modify the default schedule, set the parameters in the lower portion of the dialog. There are pre-set configuration values you can use or you can create a custom schedule by clicking the radio button for **Custom schedule** and then clicking the **Define schedule** button. This will open a new dialog box with a grid showing times on the top axis and days on the left axis. You can then create as customized a schedule as you'd like. This dialog box is shown in Figure 12.4.

Figure 12.4 Custom POP3 E-mail Retrieval Schedule

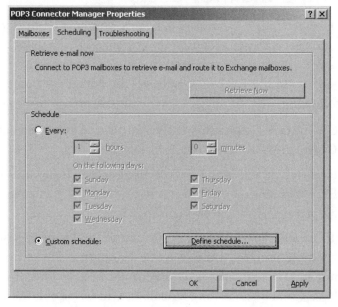

3. If you chose **Define** schedule, click **OK** after defining your custom schedule. If you chose standard scheduling options, click **OK** to close the POP3 Connection Manager Properties dialog box.

Synchronize E-mail

The **Synchronize E-mail** command available in Exchange is used to manually initiate the sending and receiving of e-mail to/from the Internet. Typically, e-mail will be sent and received according to the schedule you set. However, there may be times when you want to cause e-mail to be sent immediately, such as after troubleshooting an e-mail problem.

Change E-mail Password

If the SMTP Connector is configured to require a password, you can use this link to change the e-mail password. If the SMTP Connector is not configured to require a password, you'll simply get a message stating that you can't change the password because one is not configured. If you want to configure a password, run the E-mail and Internet Connection Wizard.

Enabling E-mail for Users

Most likely, when you created user accounts, you created mailbox-enabled accounts. However, if user accounts are not currently enabled to use Exchange mailboxes, you can enable them. Additionally, when you create new users, you can set them up to use Exchange right off the bat.

Use the following steps to check to see if an existing user is mailbox enabled:

1. Click **Start | Administrative Tools | Active Directory Users and Computers** to open the AD snap-in.

2. Right-click a user and choose **Properties**. If the user is not set up in Exchange with a mailbox, none of the usual Exchange-related tabs will be present, as shown in Figure 12.5.

3. To create a mailbox for the user, close the Properties dialog and right-click the user, this time selecting **Exchange Tasks** from the shortcut menu. This will launch the Exchange Task Wizard. If the user does not have a mailbox, creating a mailbox will be one of the options. If the user does have a mailbox, you can use this wizard for other Exchange-related tasks, including deleting or moving the mailbox or configuring other Exchange features.

4. After launching the Exchange Task Wizard, click **Next**. The first screen after the Welcome screen prompts you to create a mailbox, selecting an e-mail name as well as the Server and Mailbox Store. After entering the username and selecting appropriate server and mailbox store locations, click **Next,** then click **Finish**.

5. If you want to create a new user that is Exchange-enabled, from **Active Directory Users and Computers**, browse to the users in the left pane then right-click and select **New | User** from the shortcut menu. On the first screen of the New Object – User dialog box, enter the person's first, middle, and last name, full name and user logon name (remember to use your established naming conventions here). Click **Next.**

6. In the second screen of New Object – User, enter the password and re-enter to confirm it. Select password-related settings such as whether or not the user can change the password (etc.). Click **Next.**

7. The third screen prompts you to create an Exchange mailbox. You can probably just accept the default values, including the alias (e-mail name)

that is automatically entered based on the username you entered two screens back. Click **Next** then click **Finish.**

Figure 12.5 User Not Configured for Exchange E-mail

Managing User Exchange Tasks

You can access this within the Exchange Server System Manager console (**Start | All Programs | Exchange Server | System Manager**) or from within **Active Directory Users and Computers** since this is a user-side feature. Once in AD Users and Computers, you can manage individual user mailboxes by right-clicking the user and selecting **Exchange Tasks** from the shortcut menu. This will launch the Exchange Task Wizard. Within the wizard, you can add (if one does not exist), move, or delete (if one exists) a user mailbox. You can also configure Exchange features or remove Exchange attributes. Exchange features include mobile services and protocols such as Outlook Web Access, POP3, and IMAP (Internet Message Access Protocol). To modify the properties, if the option is available, click a service or protocol then click **Properties**. If **Properties** is disabled (grayed out), properties are not available for that selection. **CAUTION**: The **Remove Exchange Attributes** option is something you *should not* do unless you have a specific reason for doing so, such as instructions that include this as a step. This is a disaster recovery task and can cause serious problems beginning with the user being unable to send or receive e-mail.

For the most part, these are options you're not going to have to use other than to add or delete a mailbox.

Queue Viewer

Queue Viewer allows you to maintain and administer e-mail queues as well as messages in those queues. In Server Management, locate First Organization (Exchange) in Advanced Management. Expand that tree and locate **Servers |** **ServerName | Queues**. In the right pane, the various queues are listed. For any particular queue, you can right-click and select **Find messages** (in that queue), **Unfreeze**, **Freeze**, or **Force Connection**. For some types of connections, some of these options may not be available. If you select a queue and click the **Settings** button at the bottom of the right pane, you can change the refresh rate for the queue. You can use the **Find Messages** button after selecting a queue to find a particular message. This is the same command as selecting the queue, right-clicking and choosing **Find Message** from the shortcut menu.

Another important feature in this section is the **Disable Outbound Mail** button in the top left of the right pane. This can be used if your network has been hit with a virus that e-mails itself using your address lists. In this case, you can immediately stop the external spread of e-mail viruses by clicking this option. When the issue is resolved, you can Enable Outbound Mail using the same button (the name changes depending on the status of outbound mail).

Monitoring Server and Connectors Status

You can monitor server and connector status via **Server Management** or via **Start | All Programs | Exchange | System Manager**. In either case, locate and expand **Tools** then locate and expand **Monitoring and Status**. There are two options: notification and status. Notifications are used to alert an administrator that a server has entered a warning or critical state or that a connector is down. Notification can be set up by e-mail or through the use of scripts. Right-click **Notification** and select either e-mail or scripts then complete the dialog box options. If using a script, use caution, as the script runs with administrator privileges – so make sure you test that script in a safe environment and be sure of what it does before you use it on your live system.

You can get the status of all connectors and servers in the organization by clicking **Status** in the left pane. The servers and connectors along with their status will be listed in the right pane.

Message Tracking Center

If users report missing e-mail or if you suspect a problem with e-mail, you can use the Message Tracking Center to determine whether a message is waiting in a queue or whether it has been sent out. You can manually review message and tracking logs to determine the where e-mail is or whether it has been sent. Click the **Message Tracking Center** under **Monitoring and Status** in the left pane of either **Server Management | Advanced Management | First Organization (Exchange)** or in **Exchange Server System Manager.**

Creating and Managing Public Folders

We've looked at configuring e-mail both externally and internally, and reviewed some of the features of configuring and managing Exchange. Now, let's look at one very popular feature that is part of Exchange, but is not directly tied to the e-mail function: public folders.

Public folders are an interesting feature of Exchange Server, primarily because Microsoft isn't quite sure where they fit into the scheme of things. For instance, what's the difference between public folders, SharePoint Services shared resources, and network shared folders and files? Good question, and one that Microsoft probably can't answer very well. That's not to say that public folders aren't a useful tool, just that how they should best be used is a subject for debate and discussion. In this section, we'll try to give you some useful, real world guidelines on how to organize and manage public folders. In the end, you'll have to decide how your company can best use public folders.

With public folders, the best defense is a good offense, meaning that this is another place where solid planning before implementation will save you a lot of trouble on the other side. Let's start with a few guidelines—you can break these rules if you want, just be aware of the consequences of doing so.

1. Create a hierarchy that is easy for users to navigate and easy for administrators (you) to manage.

2. Determine what your top-level folders will be. Use this to create the rest of the hierarchy.

3. Create a logical and useful naming scheme and require that all public folders use this naming scheme. Names should give a good indication of the data stored in the folder.

4. Create written policies for what types of information should be stored in public folders (in conjunction with that, you should create related policies as to where and how to store other data that does not belong in public folders).

5. Include in your public folders policies information on what the default values should be for item retention, storage quotas, etc. Age limits and quotas are the only way to restrict what people can store in public folders, so set these up in a manner consistent with your server's capacity, your stated use of public folders, etc.

6. Determine who will administer public folders. This is often a task that admins overlook or skip over. It often makes sense to set up a separate administrative group that has permissions to manage public folders.

Create a Hierarchy

The hierarchy you create should be easy for users to navigate and easy for you to manage. Some companies find that setting up top-level folders by business unit makes sense. For instance, you may create top-level folders for Company (this might be the common folder to which all employees have access), Marketing, Finance, Human Resources, Operations, Customer Service, etc. Determining what the top-level folders should be is the first step in creating a logical and easy-to-navigate hierarchy for users. You can also suggest (or require) that the second-level folders also follow a common scheme. For instance, within each department's top-level folders, you might also create subfolders such as Operations, Policies and Procedures, Specifications, Work in Progress, etc. It's likely that based on the policies (we'll talk more about those in a moment), each department may store similar data in the public folders. If so, creating a common second-level scheme might make sense.

The hierarchy will depend on how your company is structured and what framework makes the most sense for you. However, by creating a solid structure before you start creating (or allowing the creation of) public folders, you'll create a much easier structure for you and the users.

Create a Naming Structure

A naming structure should be simple, short and meaningful. Public folders with names such as TCvrn4494 or Wrk88tyk are not easily understood or remembered. Using names like Customer Service, Training, HR Policies, Survey Forms, etc. will help users actually use public folders. Once you decide on a naming structure, publicize it and educate users as well as anyone you grant folder creation rights to and then keep an eye on folder names to ensure they stay within the guidelines.

Create Written Policies About Information Storage

What type of information should be stored in public folders? Well, if you ask Microsoft you might get a resounding "anything you want!" While that's true, you also need to look at a few constraints. Public folders make good storage areas for static data such as policies, procedures and forms. While Exchange data replication is not an issue when you're only running one instance of Exchange Server, if your company grows and you move to Windows Server 2003 and install other instances of Exchange Server, the public folder data replication can bog down a server and a network quickly. Because Exchange replicates all changes, not just incremental changes, replication can become a monstrous burden on your network. Plan for future growth by using public folders only for static data.

Determining the best location for company data is another consideration. You don't want users confused as to where to find information. Is it on a network share? Is it in public folders? Is it on a SharePoint website? Try to devise a clear, simple policy on what types of data should be stored where so users can easily locate needed resources. By creating a comprehensive plan for storage that includes public folders, you'll keep things simple for you and your users.

Create Policies On Managing Public Folders

In addition to creating policies on what should (and should not) be stored in public folders, you should also create policies regarding what the default values should be for item retention, storage quotas, etc. If you access the properties for the top-level folders, you can set rights for client permissions, directory rights, and administrative rights. In administrative rights, you can determine who has the ability to manage and administer the folder(s). As suggested earlier, you might want to create a group to which you assign these administrative privileges. Keep membership in the group small; the more people you have with administrative rights, the higher the likelihood of things getting messy (people misunderstanding or ignoring hierarchy, naming scheme, etc.). Note, this does *not* mean adding these folks to the Administrators group. Instead, create a new group, such as EXCHPFADMIN (Exchange Public Folder Admin), add a few trusted folks (who have been briefed on the rules, policies, hierarchy, etc.) and grant that group the permissions related to managing the top-level public folders. Users can create lower level folders and you should also have people whose job it is to monitor folder creation and use. For instance, you could have someone from each department be responsible for monitoring public folder use, scanning folders to ensure they contain appropriate information and are named according to established policies. While you don't need public folder vigilantes, you do need someone to watch over these because they tend to grow like weeds. As the network administrator, you probably don't have time to take on this watchdog role, so assigning others to monitor and report problems to you (or the small Exchange admin group) is a better way to go.

By default, the Everyone group can create a public folder. You may want to modify this so that the Everyone group has permission to create a public folder only in the top-level folder named Company (or whatever you might call a "catchall" group for the company). For instance, if you just want the customer service staff to access and create customer service public folders, you should remove the permission for the Everyone group. By default, only members of the Administrators group can create top-level folders. Do not modify this unless you want to watch your nicely designed hierarchy go down the drain.

To configure the settings for a particular public folder, right-click the folder to access the Properties dialog box. You might want to select the **Limits** tab and set storage, deletion, and age limits. You can choose to use the public store defaults (those set for the entire public folders store) or set specific settings for this folder.

Working with Outlook 2003

Outlook is to Exchange as steering wheel is to car. That is to say that Outlook is where users do all their tasks and "drive" their messaging functions such as e-mail, calendar, task list, and more. Outlook is the user-side application that you can use with or without Exchange. A lot of people use Microsoft Outlook at home to send and receive their Internet e-mail as well as to manage contacts and calendar and sync it up with their PDA (personal digital assistant). You don't need Exchange to do this for one or two home users, but when you get 60 or 70 people all running e-mail and related tasks, Exchange Server helps you, the admin, manage things.

In addition, Exchange Server provides two additional features you may want to look at: Outlook Web Access and Outlook Mobile Access. SBS ships with both the software and licenses to use Microsoft Outlook 2003. If you don't currently own Office or if you're using an earlier version of Office, you can still use the Outlook 2003 that ships with SBS.

Outlook Web Access

Let's start with what Outlook Web Access (OWA) is. It is an HTTP (Hypertext Transfer Protocol) virtual server installed and configured when you first set up SBS and Exchange Server. It is installed by default and will be running unless you specifically go in and disable it via the HTTP virtual server. OWA has most of the same features that Outlook has with a few minor exceptions, so we won't go into the features of OWA because they closely reflect the features found in a standard installation of Outlook.

You can enable or disable OWA on a per-user basis via Active Directory Users and Computers. In order for users to use Outlook Web Access from the Internet, the Exchange Server must have an Internet connection and a public IP address. Users must be part of the Mobile User Group. Use the following steps to enable or disable Outlook Web Access for a specific user.

1. Click **Start** | **All Programs** | **Administrative Tools** | **Active Directory Users and Computers**. Expand the tree to locate **Users**.

2. In the detail (right) pane, right-click a user and select **Properties.** Select the **Exchange Features** tab. In the details box under Protocols, click **Outlook Web Access**. If it is currently enabled, you'll only have the option to **Disable** it. If it's disabled, you can **Enable** it.

3. Click **OK** to close this user dialog box. This is shown in Figure 12.6.

Figure 12.6 Enable or Disable Outlook Web Access for User

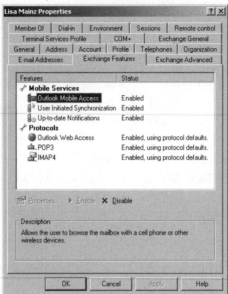

Outlook Web Access is managed like any other HTTP virtual server in Internet Information Server (IIS). While that may sound spooky, it's really not too bad.

Connecting to Outlook Web Access

Outlook Web Access is accessed via the Internet using a fully qualified domain name (FQDN) appended with the word **exchange**. For example, it might be https://somecompany.com/exchange. Or you may use the server's public IP address such as https://225.25.225.25/exchange. In either case, you'll reach the Outlook Web Access HTTP virtual server and begin the authentication process. You can also connect to Outlook Web Access within the Remote Web Workplace (RWW), which has a link called **Read my company e-mail** that will connect you with OWA. To test things out, you can also connect by opening a web browser and typing in **https://localhost/exchange**, as shown in Figure 12.7.

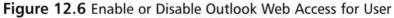

Figure 12.7 Connecting to Outlook Web Access

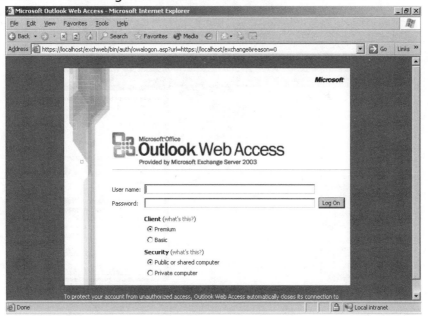

When you connect to OWA, enter your username and password. You can select **Basic** or **Premium** connection. If you're running over a slow connection, the Basic option will provide a faster response for you. If you're running over a fast connection, choose the Premium option to gain access to a few additional bells and whistles.

You'll also be prompted to select **Public or shared computer** or **Private computer**. Why, you ask? If you're working on a shared or public computer, OWA will time out more quickly than if you're working on a private computer. This is for security purposes.

Once logged in, you are presented with a fairly standard looking Outlook interface, shown in Figure 12.8, in which you can check e-mail, access Notes, Sent Items, Calendar, Contacts, Public Folders, and Options. When finished, click the **Log Off** icon on the upper right side of the screen.

Figure 12.8 Inside Outlook Web Access Session

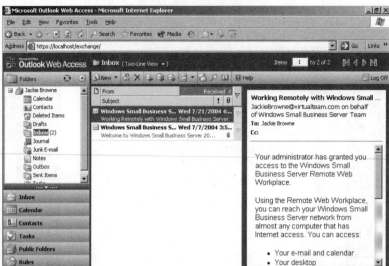

Outlook Mobile Access

Outlook Web Access allows user to connect to Outlook and Exchange Server features via the Internet. But what about users with PDAs who want to access e-mail? They need to connect wirelessly in a secure manner. Enter Outlook Mobile Access (OMA). As with OWA, OMA can be enabled or disabled on a per-user basis using the same steps delineated earlier for OWA.

OMA supports Wireless Application Protocol (WAP) 2.x as well as XHTML devices, full HTML browsers, and I-Mode devices such as cell phones and PDAs. OMA is configured in Exchange Server in the System Manager console. Locate **Global Settings**, right-click **Mobile Services** and select **Properties.** The mobile services that can be enabled and configured here are **ActiveSync** and **Outlook Mobile Access**. This enables or disables these features for all users (hence the *global* moniker). There are two checkboxes under Outlook Mobile Access. The first enables OMA, and the second allows unsupported devices. This is useful because not all devices have been okayed by Microsoft and yet they're still fine to use. If you want to disable this feature for specific users, access the Properties dialog box for that user in AD Users and Computers (right-click the username) and select the **Exchange Features** tab. This is shown earlier in the chapter in Figure 12.5

A user with a PocketPC wireless device or cell phone can connect by going to http://somecompany.com/oma. The same rules apply – your server must have an Internet connection and a public IP address to access this. Rather than typing **exchange** as you did to connect to Outlook Web Access, you use **oma** to connect to the wireless cousin. You'll be prompted to enter your username and password. You may get a message stating your device is not supported. If you selected the ability to use unsupported devices and you're using an unsupported device (we're assuming here that you're both the admin that set this up and the remote user testing things out), you'll get a message about an unsupported device. Simply click **OK** to continue. You can scroll down through Inbox, Calendar, Contacts, and Tasks.

Exchange ActiveSync 3.7

So far we've looked at Exchange and Outlook, in a sense two sides of the same coin. Now, let's close the chapter with a bit about ActiveSync, used to sync up to Exchange with a PDA or other similar device. You can synchronize using a cradle attached to the desktop, as many of you are familiar with, or you can synchronize using a wireless connection.

ActiveSync is enabled in **Exchange | Global Settings | Mobile Services | Properties**, as is Outlook Mobile Access. When you enable this here, you enable it globally. You can then enable or disable this on a per-user basis in the same place we've been looking at throughout the Outlook section of this chapter (**User Properties | Exchange Features**). In the global settings, however, you have three options. The first is to **Enable user initiated synchronization**. This setting allows users to synchronize their Exchange information with their mobile devices.

The second setting, **Enable up-to-date notifications**, allows users to receive notifications in order to keep their mobile device up-to-date. For instance, if your calendar changes or you receive a new e-mail, you can receive a notification.

The third setting, **Enable notifications to user specified SMTP addresses**, will only be available if you're using SMTP e-mail (most of this chapter assumed you were using POP3 e-mail, used by many small businesses). If you're using SMTP, you can select this checkbox to allow your users to use their own wireless service provider.

One More Time

We covered a lot of ground in this chapter. You should now have a strong understanding of Exchange Server in SBS and how to use it, manage it, and monitor it. We covered both the server side settings and the user side settings since both are important parts of the equation. Many small businesses use POP3 e-mail, so we focused our time on working with POP3 e-mail in Exchange. We also looked at two features of Outlook 2003—Outlook Web Access and Outlook Mobile Access—two features users will come to rely upon once they figure out how easy-to-use and reliable these features are. We also looked at ActiveSync, which can keep a mobile device like a PDA synchronized either through direct connection to the desktop via a cradle or via wireless connections.

- ☑ Features of Exchange include the ability to manage e-mail connections, message queues, global address lists, and many more features. The default settings in Exchange are a great starting point.

- ☑ You can easily and quickly get yourself into trouble by changing Exchange Server configuration without knowing exactly what you're doing. Make sure you know exactly what you're doing before making changes and document, document, document.

- ☑ Adding a distribution group is a simple task that allows users to send e-mail to an entire group instead of to multiple individuals.

- ☑ Distribution groups are in no way related to security groups.

- ☑ You can (and should) delegate distribution group management to a member of the distribution group. This eases your administrative burden and doesn't affect security since distribution groups don't involve security in any way.

☑ Working with POP3 e-mail is also relatively easy. You may need to contact your ISP for some settings including the port number (if the default 110 isn't used).

☑ Many small businesses use POP3 e-mail because it's easy to configure and manage in conjunction with your ISP.

☑ Queue Viewer allows you to view and manage your queues.

☑ Monitoring connection status is another tool provided in Exchange that you can use to monitor what's going on with your e-mail connectors (typically POP3 and/or SMTP).

☑ Since public folders is a very popular feature in many companies, setting up, configuring and managing public folders is an important task.

☑ Plan your public folder policies, naming conventions, and hierarchy before implementing public folders.

☑ Have your Human Resources department assist in developing use policies as well as monitoring use and content in public folders.

☑ Public folders can be created for separate groups within the company and their use can be restricted to these groups.

☑ Outlook Web Access is an easy-to-use web interface for accessing Outlook. Users can open a browser and enter the URL for the Exchange Server to access almost all the normal features of Outlook (with a few minor exceptions).

☑ OWA is enabled by default and can be enabled or disabled on a per-user basis in Active Directory Users and Computers.

☑ Outlook Mobile Access is another useful tool that provides access to Outlook for wireless users. As with OWA, OMA is enabled or disabled on a global basis and you can also enable or disable this feature on a per-user basis in AD Users and Computers.

☑ Exchange ActiveSync 3.7 enables users of PDAs and other similar devices to sync up with Exchange either by connecting the PDA to the cradle attached to the desktop or via a wireless connection.

Chapter 13

Managing Remote Connectivity

- Overview of Remote Connectivity
- Using Remote Web Workplace
- Understanding Certificates
- Wireless Access

The End Result

By the end of this chapter, you'll have a good understanding of the various methods used to connect to the network remotely. These include dial-up and Virtual Private Network (VPN) connections as well as wireless connections. You'll learn about certificates and how they fit into a remote access environment as well as how to effectively manage certificates in your network. You'll also learn about the Remote Web Workplace (RWW), what it is, and how it provides a great alternative to traditional remote access methods.

Overview of Remote Connectivity

If you configured Remote Access via the To Do List earlier, you've already seen some of the remote access options you have in Windows Small Business Server 2003 (SBS). In Chapter 9, we looked at the Routing and Remote Access Server (RRAS) console to look at network address translation and firewall settings (if you are using the internal SBS firewall). In this chapter, we'll look more specifically at the remote access part of RRAS.

Traditionally, remote access was accomplished via dial-up lines using a modem (or modem bank) on the server and a modem in the remote computer, such as a laptop or home computer. The remote computer would dial in to a specific phone number, the server would answer, and the two computers would establish a connection. This is a one-to-one connection meaning for each remote computer, there must be a distinct phone number or line on the server. Since this is a one-to-one connection and does not run across an open line, this type of communication is secure. Data sent and received can be encrypted if it is incredibly sensitive, but it's very difficult (but not entirely impossible) to intercept. Typically, this can only be done by physically tapping into the phone line. Too much work for too little payoff for a hacker and generally only successful in spy movies.

With the rise in the use of the Internet, a remote method of connecting via the Internet was established. This is called a *Virtual Private Network*. VPN connections use security protocols that create a highly secure, private connection between the remote computer and the server. The connection is established for that session and then released. Thus, it is a *virtual* private network. To use this type of connection, both the remote computer and the server must have access to the Internet. In order to create a secure connection across the very public and non-secure Internet, a private network is established between the two computers using security protocols and certificates. Certificates provide a secure electronic means of establishing the identity of an entity, be it person, computer, or website. We'll discuss certificates a bit later in this chapter.

The latest development in remote access comes in the form of a web interface provided by the SBS software that allows remote users to simply use an Internet browser and type in a URL (uniform resource locator) to access the corporate network remotely. This interface, Remote Web Workplace, provides several distinct advantages for small businesses in particular. First, it is highly secure and relies on the same security framework employed when users log in to the network from a local computer. Second, it is easy to manage and administer. We'll look at RWW in detail later in this chapter.

Dial-up Remote Access

Most servers these days come without a modem installed. In order to enable dial-up remote access, you'll need one or more modems in the server. If you don't have a modem, the only remote access option you'll be able to use is VPN. The Remote Access Wizard options will be based upon the presence (or absence) of a modem.

Assuming your server has one or more modems and associated phone lines, you can enable remote dial-up access. This requires three distinct steps – enabling remote access on the server, enabling remote access on the client computer, and adding users to the mobile users group. We'll look at configuring the remote client computer in just a bit since the process is the same for dial-up or VPN access. A quick note here about modems in your server – if you have them and you configure them for remote access, you cannot also use them a shared fax modems.

Configuring the Server for Dial-up Access

You may have already set up the server for dial-up access if you went through the Configure Remote Access Wizard via the To Do List. If you haven't, we'll run through the steps here briefly. As with all SBS wizards, most screens are self-explanatory, but you can always find more information via the **More Information** button (if available) or in the Help and Support files.

To configure the server for dial-up access, use the following steps:

1. In Server Management, click **To Do List** then select **Configure Remote Access** to launch the Remote Access Wizard. In the Welcome screen, click **Next.**

2. On the Remote Access Method screen, select **Enable Remote Access** and **Dial-in access (requires a modem)** then click **Next.** We'll configure VPN later in this chapter.

3. If the Client Addressing screen is displayed, specify that the DHCP server assigns IP addresses to remote clients. If you know what you're doing, you can also designate a range of addresses. Otherwise, allow DHCP to handle this. Click **Next.**

4. On the Modem Selection screen, select the modem(s) designated for remote users. Keep in mind that if there are not enough modems, remote users may have to wait to get a remote connection. Depending on how your business runs, this may be a problem. Click **Next.**

5. On the Dial-Up Phone Numbers page, enter the primary and alternate phone numbers remote users will use to connect to the server. Click **Next.**

6. The last screen is the summary page. Review your selections and click **Back** to make changes or **Finish** to make the desired changes.

7. If you haven't already enabled password policies, you'll be prompted to do so now. It's a good idea to implement these, so follow on the on-screen prompts or take a look in Chapter 3 for instructions on completing this task.

Virtual Private Networks

Virtual private networks are a bit more complicated to set up, but once done, you can communicate securely between a remote computer and the corporate network using the public resources of the Internet. For users that travel, this can cut down on phone bills that once accompanied remote dial-up access. Now all you need is a computer and an Internet connection. Figure 13.1 depicts the components and configuration of a VPN connection.

Figure 13.1 VPN Connection

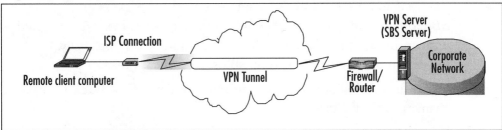

Typically, setting up VPN access requires several steps on both the server and client sides. However, SBS provides tools that configure the needed settings for both dial-up and VPN access for you, which we'll discuss in just a moment. First, let's look at setting up VPN on the server side.

Configuring the Server for VPN Access

Your server has to have an Internet connection in order to act as the VPN server. We're assuming you've already configured your Internet connection via the E-mail and Internet Connection Wizard. As with dial-up access, you configure VPN access on the server via the Remote Access Wizard. Use the following steps to configure your SBS server for remote access using VPN connections:

1. Click **Start | Server Management | Standard Management | To Do List | Configure Remote Access**. The Remote Access Wizard will launch. In the Welcome screen, click **Next**.

2. In the Remote Access Method dialog box, click **Enable remote access** (if it is not already selected) and select the **VPN access** checkbox. Click **Next.**

3. If the Client Addressing dialog box is displayed, specify that DHCP will assign IP addresses to remote clients. If you know what you're doing in the DHCP world, you can designate a range of addresses but only do so if you're sure you know what you're doing. Otherwise, let DHCP handle it for you.

4. In the VPN Server Name dialog box, specify the name of the server that will provide the VPN connection. This is either the full Internet name (Fully Qualified Domain Name, or FQDN) or IP address of your server. Keep in mind that the full Internet name is likely different than the

local name. For example, the local name might be *SBS2003.somecompany.local* and the full Internet name might be *SBS2003.somecompany.com*. The full Internet name is the one registered with an Internet registrar, not the local name you use internally. The server name is the name of your SBS server. Click **Next.**

5. In the final dialog box, review your selections and click **Back** to make changes or click **Finish.**

6. If you have not yet implemented password policies, you will be prompted to do so at this time. Click **Yes** to enable password policies or **No** to continue without implementing them. (**Hint**: The right answer here is **Yes** – to implement password policies, it takes about 20 seconds and you'll sleep better tonight knowing your network is safer).

Now that your server is configured for VPN (or earlier, for dial-up access), you need to configure client computers to connect remotely.

Configuring Computers for Remote Access

There are three ways computers can be configured for both dial-up and VPN remote access. The *Connection Manager* is a tool used when the computer is currently connected to the local network and will be used as a remote computer as is often the case with laptops. The second method entails creating and distributing a *Remote Connection Disk*, and is used when the computer is not part of the local network, as is the case when users want to connect to the network from their home computers. The third way is for the user to download the Connection Manager tool via the Remote Web Workplace. Setup for VPN can be tricky, so using these automated methods will reduce user frustration and help desk calls.

If the computer is currently connected to the network, you can install the Connection Manager automatically on the client computer to configure settings and provide instructions to users on how to connect remotely to the network.

Computer Currently Connected to the Network

To configure this for computers currently connected to the network, use the following steps:

1. Click **Server Management** | **Standard Management** | **Client Computers**.

2. Click the link **Assign Applications to Client Computers**. This will launch the Assign Applications Wizard. In the Welcome screen, click **Next.**

3. The next screen is the Client Computer dialog. In the left pane, the existing computers are listed. Locate the computers on which you want to configure remote access and click the computer then click **Add**. Continue this until you've added all computers that will use the Connection Manager. Click **Next** to continue.

4. The next screen shows the client applications you can add to the computers you just selected. If you want to add these applications, click to select them. If you do not, click the checkbox to clear the checkmark. There are two additional options: **During Client Setup, allow the selected applications to be modified** and **After Client Setup is finished, log off the client computer**. Choose these options if desired. There is also button you can click to **Edit Applications** and there are also **Advanced** options. These were discussed in Chapter 9 so we won't go into the details here. Click **Next** to continue.

5. The next screen is the Mobile Client and Offline Use dialog. Select **Install Connection Manager** (you can also opt to install ActiveSync 3.7 here as well). Click **Next**.

6. When you click **Next**, you'll get a Set Up Computer Wizard message box reminding you to configure remote access on the server. Click **OK**.

7. The final screen is the configuration screen in which you can confirm your choices. Click **Back** to make changes or **Finish** to continue.

8. To complete the installation, go to the client computer and log on. This will launch the Client Setup Wizard. If the computer is already logged on, log off then back on to launch the wizard.

Computers Not Connected to the Network

If the computer is not currently connected to the network, you can create a Remote Connection Disk (or two or three or forty) and distribute them to the users to bring home and install on their home computer (or a computer that is not currently connected to the network). Open Server Management and select **Client Computer** then click the link **Create Remote Connection Disk**. Follow the on-screen instructions for creating one or more diskettes. This includes specifying the drive letter for the floppy disk drive and the number of copies of the Remote Connection Disk to be made. Insert a blank floppy into the server's drive and click **Finish**. Once you've created one diskette, you can copy these contents onto other media such as a CD-ROM, USB flash drive (sometimes called key or pen drives), or other removable media. The contents are less than 600KB. When the user inserts the diskette in the computer, he or she can browse to the floppy disk and double-click the Setup.exe program. Users should be running Internet Explorer 5.0 or higher.

Downloading Connection Manager from Remote Web Workplace

The third option for client computers is to download the Connection Manager from the Remote Web Workplace. This option, like the creation of the Remote Connection Disk, is used for client computers that are not currently connected to the local network. Once users connect to the Remote Web Workplace website (more on that in the next section), they can click the **Connect My Remote Computer to the Network** link. This will download and install the Connection Manager in the same manner as if they had inserted a diskette. This is useful if the client computer doesn't have a diskette drive (a configuration that is becoming more common) or if the user simply wants to get set up quickly from a remote location.

Configuring Users for Remote Access

As you can see, none of the steps involved in setting up remote access is difficult. It just takes planning, so you make sure that you identify the users and computers that require remote access and then set up the server, client computers, and users appropriately. Setting up users is the final step we need to review in this process. You may have already set up users for remote access. If so, you're set. Remember, you should avoid granting remote access to users unless they actually need it. By restricting remote access to business necessity, you maintain tighter network security.

Users are typically granted remote access by adding the user account to the Mobile User group. Use the following steps for this task.

1. Open **Server Management** | **Standard Management** | **Security Groups**.

2. Locate **Mobile Users** in the right pane. Click this group then click **Change Group Properties**. This will open the Mobile Users Properties dialog box.

3. Click the **Members** tab. At the bottom of the dialog box, click **Add.**

4. In the Select Users, Contacts, Computers or Groups dialog box, type in the user names you want to add to this group. Click **Check Names** to verify you've selected the correct users. Click **OK.**

5. In the **Members** tab, you'll now see the names of the user you added. Click **OK** to add the users to the Mobile Users group or **Cancel** to exit without saving these changes.

An alternate method is to access **Users** in **Server Management**, locate the user account and click **Add User to a Group**. In this case, when the Select Users, Contacts, Computers or Groups dialog box is displayed, you would enter **mobile users** and click **Check Names** then click **OK.** If you just want to add one user, this method is fine. If you want to add multiple users, the method delineated above is the easier method.

Using Remote Web Workplace

One last topic we'll discuss in this chapter on remote connectivity is the **Remote Web Workplace** (RWW). RWW allows users to connect to the corporate network using a secure, easy-to-use interface. There are two distinct tasks related to implementing RWW—enable and configure RWW, and configure user access. Configuring the RWW requires you to enable the internal firewall for SBS.

To connect to a remote desktop on the local network using Remote Web Workplace, the remote computer must be running Windows 2000 Server or Windows XP Professional. A remote computer running any other operating system must use a VPN or dial-in connection as discussed earlier.

Enable and Configure Remote Web Workplace

You may have already configured this when you went through your To Do List and configured E-mail and Internet options. If not, use the following steps to enable and configure RWW.

1. Click **Start | Server Management | To Do List** and select **Connect to the Internet** to launch the E-mail and Internet Connection Wizard. On the first screen, click **Next** to continue.

2. On the Connection Type screen, click **Do not change connection type** then click **Next**.

3. On the Firewall screen, select **Enable Firewall**, then click **Next**. On the Services Configuration screen, select services you do want to provide or disable services you do not want to provide (including VPN) and click **Next**.

4. On the Web Services Configuration screen, click **Allow access to only the following Web site services from the Internet**. Select (at minimum for RWW) **Remote Web Workplace.** If you would like users to be able to also access other applications listed, check those as well. Click **Next**.

5. On the Web Server Certificate screen, you can select **Do not change current Web server certificate** if you already have a certificate or you can select **Create a new Web server certificate**. If you select the latter option, you can accept the default name, which should be the full domain name. Although SBS does not provide full Certificate Services, it can create a self-signed server certificate for use with a secure website. We'll discuss certificates briefly later in this chapter. Click **Next** to continue.

6. On the Internet E-mail screen, if you've already configured this, select **Do not change Internet e-mail configuration**. Otherwise, click **Enable** or **Disable** and follow the on-screen prompts (or refer to Chapter 3 for more details). Click **Next**. On the final screen, review your choices, then click **Finish**. The system will configure the options you just selected and when that is complete, click **Close**. Note: If you haven't already configured password policies, you will be prompted to do so. Click **Yes** (recommended) to configure password policies or **No** to skip it. See Chapter 3 for information on setting these policies.

Configure User Access

This is actually pretty much a no-brainer. By default, all templates for creating users include the ability to connect to the Remote Web Workplace, so if your user accounts already exist, they can already connect to the RWW. You can disable this feature on a per-user basis by selecting the user properties and removing them as a member of the Remote Web Workplace Users group.

Clients can access the RWW by opening Internet Explorer and typing in the corporate URL. Note that this assumes the user has access to the Internet at some remote location, such as home or other location away from the office. The URL the user should type in is:

https://*registereddomainname*/remote or https://*companyexternalIP address*/remote. For example, it might be https://virtualteam.com/remote or https://166.24.14.9/remote. When the user enters this URL in the address space in the browser, he or she should be directed to the Remote Web Workplace website on the SBS server.

Remote Web Workplace User Features

Once the user logs onto the RWW, he or she will have several features available for use, depending on how the SBS server is configured. Each is a link that users can click to access the feature, if you installed it in the E-mail and Internet Connection Wizard. We'll look at each option briefly.

- Read My E-mail
- Access the Desktop of My Computer at Work
- Use My Company's Shared Application
- View My Company's Internal Web Site
- View Server Usage Report
- Connect My Remote Computer to the Network
- Information and Answers

Read My E-mail

If you configured Outlook Web Access when you ran the E-mail and Internet Connection Wizard, users will be able to use a web-based version of Microsoft Outlook to check and manage e-mail, use their calendar, contacts, and other Outlook folders, as well as receive notification of e-mail and meeting reminders.

Access the Desktop of My Computer at Work

If a user's desktop is running Windows XP Professional (or later), the users can access their desktop features remotely by selecting their computer from the **Computers** list and then clicking **Connect.**

Use My Company's Shared Application

If you have one or more servers configured to share applications, users can connect to those shared applications via RWW by clicking the **Use My Company's Shared Application** link. This is generally not an application such as Word or Excel that is installed on every desktop, but a single installation of a company-wide application such as an inventory program or a financial program.

View My Company's Internal Web Site

The **View My Company's Internal Web Site** link is available if you selected SharePoint Services when you were setting up e-mail and Internet connections. SharePoint Services includes the ability for users to share content, post news, post information about important dates and events, and copy events into their own Outlook calendar. Users can share internal and external contacts, review and manage shared tasks (good for project management), and review documents online. Finally, SharePoint Services lets users share information via discussions, create and manage online surveys, and create custom lists and configure the display of those lists.

View Server Usage Report

The **View Server Usage Report** link will only be available if you have run the Monitoring Configuration Wizard. We'll do that later in this book when we explore monitoring, so this option may not be configured on your system. Once configured, if a user has proper permission to do so, he or she will be able to view usage reports for the server. This is typically used by network administrators or those assisting in network administration, rather than typical users.

Connect My Remote Computer to the Network

Remote users can connect their computers to the corporate network by using a VPN connection. Clicking the **Connect My Remote Computer to the Network** link will install Connection Manager on their home or mobile computer. Connection Manager automates the process of establishing a virtual private network connection to the SBS server for a secure, remote connection, as discussed earlier in this chapter.

Information and Answers

This is the equivalent of Help and Support on a desktop computer and provides RWW users with help, information and answers to questions about using the RWW features.

Remote Web Workplace Administrator Features

Network administrators can use RWW to perform a variety of tasks on the network from a remote location. This includes accessing server and client computer desktops (must be running Windows XP Professional or later), monitoring help desk, administer the company's internal website, view server performance and usage reports, use Outlook Web Access, download the Connection Manager, and view client help (help available to client computers). In order to use these features, you must be a member of the Domain Administrators group.

BEST PRACTICES ACCORDING TO MICROSOFT

- Many companies do not want to maintain multiple modems and phone lines for remote user access and rely upon the Internet for remote connectivity.
- The easiest way to establish remote connectivity is via the Remote Web Workplace. It is secure, easy to use, and easy to administer.
- There may be cases where the Remote Web Workplace does not meet users' needs. In these cases, users can connect to the network via the Internet by establishing a secure VPN connection.
- Users should always sign out of the Remote Web Workplace when finished to prevent unauthorized access.

SOME INDEPENDENT ADVICE

The Remote Web Workplace is a very useful tool to enable users to connect to corporate resources in a secure manner from a remote location.
The RWW uses the Hypertext Transport Protocol Secure (HTTPS) protocol,
which is why you were required to configure a certificate when setting it
up. The HTTPS protocol creates a secure connection between the remote
computer's browser and the web site it's connecting to. Using this
secure protocol, user data can be passed back and forth between the
remote computer and the network. This is an easy-to-use tool and it
makes your life as an administrator much easier. We recommend using it
if users require remote access.

Understanding Certificates

A public key certificate, typically referred to simply as a *certificate*, is a digitally
signed file that binds the value of a public key to the identity of some entity
(whether that's a server, a client computer, a user, or a software application) and
that entity's private key. *Public Key Infrastructure*, or PKI, relies on the use of both
a public and private key combination and certificates are one way of implementing PKI.

Certificates are typically used for a variety of things including Web user
authentication, Web server authentication, and secure e-mail. The entity that
receives the certificate is referred to as the *subject* of the certificate. The issuer and
signer of the certificate is known as the *certification authority* (CA). SBS can create
a self-signed certificate (meaning that it verifies itself, which in some instances is
not an acceptable level of verification) or you can purchase third-party certificates from public CAs such as Verisign or Thawte. These certificates come at a
cost, but there are some instances when a certificate from a third-party is either
desirable or required. A certificate has a finite life span. When issued, it is valid
only during a certain time period and contains *Valid From* and *Valid To* dates.

When users log on remotely by establishing a VPN connection, the VPN
server can present a server certificate to establish its identity. The client computer
can proceed with the connection because the client computer knows, via the
server certificate, that it has established a connection with the desired VPN server
and not some unknown server out there on the Internet. This is just one

example of how certificates can be used to verify identities and establish secure connections.

Windows Server 2003 provides a service called Certificate Services, but SBS does not include this feature. A web certificate can be created by SBS or a third-party certificate can be implemented when you set up Remote Web Workplace. See Step #5 in the "Enable and Configure Remote Web Workplace" section earlier in this chapter. For more information on certificates and certificate services, you can query the Help and Support files (query **web server certificate** and select **Add or change a Web server certificate** in the Small Business Server Topics section) or check on the Microsoft Small Business Server 2003 website. Since you may run into various needs for certificates as you work with secure communications, it's important to have at least a baseline understanding of certificates.

Wireless Access

Wireless access is not exactly remote connectivity, but depending on where you place your wireless access points, it can start to cross that line. For instance, one secure way to implement wireless access is to place wireless access points (WAPs) outside of the corporate network and firewall. By doing so, users would need to establish connections using VPN. We're not going into the specifics of configuring wireless networking here, but we will look at some of the components.

Let's look a few facts about wireless that are not always well advertised or highlighted.

- Wireless access is much slower than wired access. The published specifications should not be taken at face value. There are many mitigating factors and you should assume you'll get 50-75% of the published speed.

- Wireless access is prone to disruption of service. Sometimes just turning on a nearby appliance can interrupt wireless communications.

- Wireless access requires the implementation of wireless security measures.

- Wireless communications that are not secured are incredibly easy prey for hackers. In fact, some people in high-density neighborhoods can typically access one or more wireless networks provided by their neighbors.

Wireless is an excellent choice for surfing the web at your local coffee shop or even for your home network. Wireless is most useful in situations where you don't want to run wires (like a local coffee shop) or where it's just impossible or cost-prohibitive to run wires. In these cases, wireless is great because it offers connectivity where it would otherwise not be possible. That said, it's still slower than wired networking and configuration can be tricky because there are different generations of wireless equipment that don't always play well together. You also have to take extra steps to configure secure wireless access, otherwise you'll simply open a big door for hackers to walk on through.

In time, wireless technologies will certainly provide the kind of speed, reliability, and security we all want. For now, implement it judiciously. And, it takes planning, persistence and some level of technical expertise, so make sure you do your research. Since many small companies either lack the real business need (beyond the "isn't this cool" factor) or the technical expertise to implement wireless access in a secure manner, we're not going to go into tremendous detail on this aspect of connectivity. In this section, we'll provide you with a framework so that if you decide to implement wireless access, you'll have a roadmap you can use in researching and designing your plan.

SOME INDEPENDENT ADVICE

Home users implement wireless networking all the time and for the most part, that works just fine. However, not only do most home users forget (or neglect) to implement wireless security measures, it's shocking to realize that many businesses don't use wireless security either. There's a practice called *war driving* where people with laptops and wireless network adapters simply drive around looking for an open network. With alarming regularity, war drivers report the ability to find open networks in homes and businesses. If you're going to implement wireless in your company, you should really take time to research the ins and outs of wireless – from the networking components (and interoperability issues) to security protocols and more. Microsoft has some excellent wireless networking resources on their website including www.microsoft.com/resources/documentation/WindowsServ/2003/all/deployguide/en-us/Default.asp?url=/resources/documentation/WindowsServ/2003/all/deployguide/en-us/dnsbm_wir_overview.asp?frame=true or go to www.microsoft.com/resources/documentation/WindowsServ/2003/all/deployguide/en-us/Default.asp and expand **Deploying Network Services** and locate **Deploying a Wireless LAN**.

You can also go to the Microsoft site and use the search phrase **Windows Server 2003 Deployment Kit** and you should be able to find this resource. Since we can't cover everything on wireless in this chapter, make sure you read up on this topic before implementing wireless. If you want an excellent book on the topic, pick up **Designing a Wireless Network**, ISBN: 1-928994-45-8.

Wireless Infrastructure

Let's start with the basic components. First, any client that wants to connect using wireless technologies must have a wireless network interface card. The wireless network interface card (or integrated wireless adapter) communicates with a wireless access point, which is connected to the network in some manner. There are various wireless hardware standards and not all versions work well together, so do some research before buying your wireless equipment. For instance, there is 802.11a, 802.11b, 802.11g, 802.11a/g, and more.

Next, the ideal placement for your wireless access point(s) outside of your network and firewall. This will require users to establish VPN connections, but will prevent casual users from jumping onto your network. Many routers these days come with wireless access points built in, so this would be a viable option. If you're using an external firewall, it might also have a WAP. If you're using the built-in SBS firewall, you should consider installing a router with a WAP between the server and the ISP Internet connection and run your wireless network from that access point. Again, read up on the various configurations but we'd strongly recommend against installing wireless access points within the network boundaries.

Wireless Components in Windows Server

Now that we've covered the hardware, let's look at the Windows Server components needed to create secure wireless network access.

Active Directory (AD) is the component that keeps track of both legitimate users and users who have been granted remote access privileges. You can also use *group policies* to implement many aspects of wireless security and GPOs are part of Active Directory. You also need *DHCP* (Dynamic Host Control Protocol) to automatically assign IP address configuration information to wireless clients and *Domain Name Service* (DNS) to provide name resolution services. Both are already enabled in SBS and while you may want to make a few minor modifications in DHCP for wireless access, you're pretty much set in this area. So, AD, DHCP, and DNS are required for wireless access and those are already in place in SBS.

In order to secure the wireless network, you will need to either implement a wireless security protocol or implement a PKI. Security protocols, discussed briefly below, are typically suitable for small to medium businesses. PKI is a more secure solution, but more complex to implement and manage. It relies on certificates, which are digitally signed and secured files verifying and guaranteeing the identity of the certificate holder. PKI is not technically required in wireless networking, but if you want the tightest security currently available, PKI is the only option.

The final component involved in creating secure wireless access with PKI is the use of RADIUS (Remote Authentication Dial-In User Service). This service is called *Internet Authentication Service* (IAS) in the Microsoft world. IAS uses security protocols for remote access that make it virtually impossible to intercept, spoof, modify, or hack into wireless data transmissions and wireless access points.

PKI and IAS provide the highest level of security for wireless access and if your company routinely deals with sensitive data, this should be the security method you use. If you are working with financial records, health care records, or other sensitive data, using anything less secure could create both a security and legal problem for your company. While this may sound dire, many people underestimate the ease with which someone can gain access to a wireless connection so it's important to use appropriate security measures.

Wireless Security Overview

There are several different ways wireless access can be secured. It's outside the scope of both the chapter and book to discuss these protocols in depth, but we'll mention them here and if you're interested, you can research these further on your own. The Microsoft website has excellent technical articles on these protocols and on wireless security you can peruse. The current methods supported include:

- 802.11 identify verification and authentication
- 802.11 Wired Equivalency Privacy (WEP) encryption
- 802.11 Wi-Fi Protected Access (WPA)
- 802.1X authentication and security

802.11 Identity Verification and Authentication

The least secure method of identity verification and authentication is 802.11 because it uses *open system authentication* and *shared key authentication*. Open system verification is really not secure because it only verifies identity between the wireless client and the wireless access point, not the Active Directory database itself. Second, a shared key is also not very secure because the key is shared by all wireless access points and, in practice, it's rarely changed. It's like writing down your password, photocopying it, and handing it out to a few "trusted" associates and asking them not to lose it or share it. This method might be fine for a home network with little security risk, but it's not acceptable for a corporate environment. Of course, if you're working at home with sensitive data (your online brokerage account or files from work), this might still be an unacceptable level of risk.

802.11 Wired Equivalency Privacy Encryption

This specification is an improvement over simple 802.11 verification and authentication because it uses data encryption between the wireless client and the wireless access point. Data is kept safe and confidential through the use of WEP encryption.

WEP uses either 40-bit or 128-bit (and a third variant, 152-bit) encryption, which sounds pretty secure, but serious flaws in the WEP encryption scheme have been uncovered showing that it is easily hacked with one of several commonly available tools (Airsnort among them). WEP is probably fine for home wireless security, but is generally not a great choice for corporate security. In some cases, using WEP is acceptable if you do *not* use a static key and if the key is re-negotiated frequently. Even though WEP can be cracked, if the key changes and is re-negotiated frequently, it would make it difficult for all but the most sophisticated, persistent hacker to get in, so WEP can be a viable options if properly configured.

802.11 Wi-Fi Protected Access

The *Wi-Fi Protected Access* is an extension of WEP. WPA requires the shared key be changed using a protocol called *Temporal Key Integrity Protocol* (TKIP). This addresses the major weakness of WEP. WPA was proposed as a stop gap solution before the stronger 802.1X options were available. If you're using WEP and want to get stronger encryption, you can implement WPA. Alternately, you can go right to 802.1X options now available.

802.1X Authentication and Security

This specification is a standard developed for authenticated access to Ethernet-based networks and wireless 802.11 networks. This standard supports centralized user identification, authentication, and dynamic key management. Unlike open system or shared key authentication (WEP), IEEE 802.1X enforces verification of user-based credentials for a wireless computer or user before allowing access to the wireless network and, depending on the authentication method used, dynamically determines encryption keys for wireless communication. This specification can use a variety of protocols including Extensible Authentication Protocol (EAP) and other variations such as PEAP (Protected Extensible Authentication Protocol), EAP with MS-CHAPv2, or PEAP with EAP-TLS (transport layer security). If you want to use 802.1X authentication, you'll need to do some research on all these variations and determine which is most appropriate for your organization. 802.1X also supports the use of RADIUS, which is implemented in the Microsoft world as Internet Authentication Server. IAS provides an even stronger mechanism for wireless access (and is used for other things as well), but is more complex to configure, implement and manage.

As you can see, there are a number of ways to implement wireless security and it's outside the scope of this book to discuss the exact methods of implementation. However, if you use the information in this chapter as the framework for creating your wireless access security and implementation plan, you should be able to create a plan that provides wireless access in the most secure manner possible. Whatever you do, don't go wireless until you understand the inherent benefits, risks, and costs. Also, devise a security and monitoring plan that will ensure your network stays safe. Your biggest worry shouldn't be whether or not your corporate competitors can get into your network, it's those random teenage hackers that get in and muck around just for the fun of it that really pose you biggest threat.

SOME INDEPENDENT ADVICE

Microsoft has some great technical papers on implementing wireless networking in a secure manner. Use these as the basis for creating your wireless strategy. Although using PKI and IAS is the most secure solution, it is also the most complex and is typically appropriate for large organizations. You can create a relatively secure solution using PEAP with passwords. That solution is very well documented in this article on the

Microsoft website.
www.microsoft.com/technet/security/guidance/peap_0.mspx. Remember,
web content is dynamic and the link might change. Query on **wireless
security peap** to find this article if it moves.

One More Time

In this chapter, you learned the three elements of establishing remote connectivity: configuring the server, configuring the remote computer, and granting remote access privileges to users. Users can dial in or establish secure VPN connections across the Internet. They can also use the Remote Web Workplace, which makes it easy for users to connect remotely and easy for you, the administrator, to manage.

☑ The server must contain modems if users want to establish remote dial-in connections. The server must have a public Internet address for users to establish a VPN connection.

☑ Client computers connected to the network can be configured for remote access via the **Assign Applications to Client Computers** link in **Server Management | Standard Management | Client Computers**.

☑ Client computers not connected to the local network can be configured via the Connection Manager, which can be copied to diskette (and then to other media such as CD or flash drive) or downloaded via the Remote Web Workplace.

☑ The Remote Web Workplace is a useful tool to enable users to connect to corporate resources in a secure manner. This reduces user and remote computer configuration and eases the administrative burden as well.

☑ Certificates are used in a variety of settings where strong security is needed. Certificate Services are not available in SBS, but you may need to work with certificates in some scenarios.

☑ Wireless networking, though not technically remote connectivity, comes with many of the same challenges are remote connectivity and must be actively managed.

☑   Wireless networking should employ some sort of security whether that's WEP, WPA, or the more secure (and complex) options available via the 802.1X specification including PEAP, EAP-TLS, and others.

☑   There are a number of ways wireless networking can be achieved and it's important to fully understand the costs, considerations, benefits, and risks before implementing wireless networking.

Chapter 14

Using SharePoint Services

- Overview of SharePoint Services
- SharePoint Components
- Customizing the SharePoint Website
- Advanced SharePoint Administration
- Backing up and Restoring SharePoint Files

The End Result

By the end of this chapter, you'll understand what SharePoint Services is, how it can be used by your organization, and what the components of a SharePoint website are. You'll also know how to modify and manage the SharePoint website and you'll have a good understanding of some of the advanced features available to you in SharePoint Services.

Overview of SharePoint Services

SharePoint Services is a feature in Windows Small Business Server 2003 (SBS) that you may not be familiar with. It's a great addition to the SBS family and a tool you might find indispensable once you become acquainted with the various components and the ease with which you can work with them. SharePoint Services essentially installs a default internal website for your company when you install SBS. The default website has a number of components that make sharing information and collaborating with others easy.

SharePoint Services is a website that has a number of built-in, pre-defined components. Most of the components can be added, removed, modified, or re-arranged to suit your needs. In this chapter, we'll look at the various components and what you can do with them. We'll look at the individual components in the next section in detail.

The SharePoint website can be administered in two ways. In the Server Management console, click Internal Web Site to access management options. You can also access, modify and administer the site directly via http://companyweb/default.aspx. In this chapter, we'll work directly from within the website, but you can use the Server Management console as well. Users can access the site locally or via Remote Web Workplace. Of course, Microsoft recommends using Internet Explorer 6.0 (or later), but any browser will work. If you are using Internet Explorer, you should use the latest version to take advantage of enhanced security and usability features. The default website contains numerous features and we recommend you get used to the default settings before modifying anything. Once you're familiar with the features of the website, you can modify to your heart's content. Figure 14.1 shows the default website and its features. The SharePoint website (http://companyweb) should not be confused with the default SBS website (http://<SBSServername>).

Figure 14.1 Default SharePoint Website

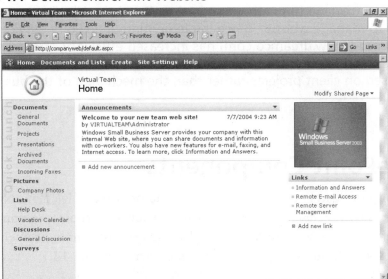

SOME INDEPENDENT ADVICE

Let's look at a real-world example to get a better idea of how SharePoint Services can become a useful tool for your small or medium business. There's a small, innovative graphic and web design company called Dreamco®. The head of the firm, Greg, constantly looks for new tools to help his company become more efficient. He believes that providing tools for his staff that improve performance frees them up to be more creative and the proof is in the results the company generates. Greg brings in a number of interns each year to not only to provide real-world training for local university students, but also to generate a constant flow of new energy and ideas to the company. These interns, along with Dreamco's full time staff, collaborate on projects that may be for local and national clients. Staff work flexible hours, either at home or at the office. To facilitate collaboration, file sharing, and project management, Dreamco implemented SharePoint Services.

On their SharePoint website, Greg's posted the company's policies and procedures, the work schedule (that includes all on-going and planned projects), a company calendar that shows people's availability and vacation schedules, announcements, and a discussion forum. Staff that are working on the same project can check files out (to avoid two people working on the same file at the same time), and can post comments in a discussion thread to record questions and notes related to a particular project. They can also work with task lists, access their contact list, and manage forms they use in their business. All this from a single, easy-to-manage website. Since implementing SharePoint Services, Dreamco (www.dreamco.com) has increased efficiency, streamlined processes, and freed up their very talented staff to be more creative and focused on client projects rather than the mechanics of the business.

SharePoint Components

In the world of SharePoint, the various elements are called *Web Parts*. Not too catchy, but certainly descriptive. A Web Part is a single-purpose component that you can place on the website to present data, images, lists, announcements, etc. Let's discuss the default components, shown earlier in Figure 14.1.

Top Navigation Bar

The top navigation bar is common to all pages in the website and includes the following links: **Home**, **Documents and Lists**, **Create**, **Site Settings**, and **Help**.

- **Home** The main page of the website that can be customized to meet your company's needs. We'll talk about how you can customize it later in the chapter. The default components are the top navigation bar, the Quick Launch link bar on the left side, and the details pane on the right. By default, the details pane shows announcements and links only.

- **Documents and Lists** This page shows all the libraries, lists, discussions boards, and surveys on the site. Clicking on any of the items listed displays a new page dedicated to that topic. For instance, under **Document Libraries** is a link called **Projects**. If you click that link, you'll access the Projects page where you can store company proposals, project plans, etc. You can create new folders, upload documents to this area, and more. In the left Quick Launch link bar area, the choices change depending on the topic in the right part of the page (details).

- **Create** You can use this link to create a new page for your website based on any one of several templates, or you can create you own. The default choices include adding a new page to the document, form, fax, or picture libraries, create new links list, announcements, contacts, events, tasks, issue, Help Desk tickets, web pages, web parts, surveys, and more.

- **Site Settings** These are settings for the entire site including managing users, configuring the site and site administration. You can customize the site in Site Settings, including changing the site title and description, applying a theme, modifying content, and customizing the home page. You must be part of the Administrative or Web Designer site group to make these changes. Site groups define security settings and are discussed a bit later in this chapter. If you are not part of either of these two groups when accessing the Site Settings section of the web, you'll be prompted for a username and password. If you do not have sufficient privileges, you'll be denied access to this feature.

- **Help** Clicking **Help** opens the Microsoft Windows SharePoint Services 2.0 Help HTML Help files. Items are grouped by type such as **Startup and Settings**, **Managing SharePoint Sites**, and more. You can also access a glossary, troubleshooting help, and an index here. You might want to spend some time surfing around in these help files – you'll no doubt stumble upon some great information you might otherwise miss.

Quick Launch Link Bar

On the Home page, the Quick Launch link bar is located on the left side of the screen and contains a variety of links by default. These are **Documents, Pictures, Lists, Discussions and Surveys**. If you click a link in the Quick Launch bar, the details are displayed in the right pane. Depending on what you select in the Quick Launch area, the details in the right pane as well as subsequent options in the Quick Launch bar will vary. For instance, Figure 14.2 shows the screen after clicking the **General Documents** link under **Documents** in the Quick Launch bar.

Figure 14.2 General Document Options

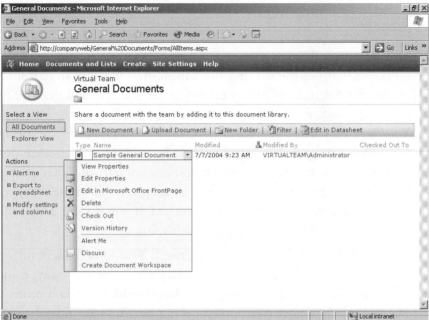

About Site Groups and User Rights

Before we discuss the various features in SharePoint in detail, it's important to understand how user permissions are set and how that impacts available options. *Site groups* are used to manage security on a SharePoint website. There are five site groups defined by default. As with other SBS settings, the default settings are typically all you need to manage your site. While you can customize permissions, it's best to start off using the default permissions and see how things go. These default site groups are *Guest, Reader, Contributor, Web Designer* and *Administrator*.

As with other types of rights or permissions in Windows, these rights are cumulative. *Guest* has very limited access to web content including restrictions on pages that can be accessed. This site group cannot be accessed via Site Settings like the other site groups and access via the Guest permission is based on granting specific access to lists or documents by way of the per-list permissions for that object. *Reader* has read-only rights. *Contributor* has all of the Reader's rights plus a few more, and so on. Therefore, while a user *can* belong to more than one group, there's really no need for it. Keep it simple. Users are added to the site groups in the **Manage Users** section of the website found under **Site Settings**. We'll discuss this more later in this chapter when we look at how to modify various site settings. User rights consist of 20 individual rights and these are defined in various combinations in the four site groups. Some of the permissions include **add and customize pages**, **add/remove web parts**, **apply themes and borders**, **manage lists**, **view items**, and **view usage data**. For a complete list of permissions and their descriptions, click **Help** in the top navigation bar, click **Index**, click the **Index** link, click **S**, then scroll down until you locate **Site Group**.

Available options are dependent on which site group a user belongs to. For instance, if a user is a member of the Reader site group, he or she will not be able to add items to announcements or upload documents. If a user is a member of the Contributor site group, he or she can add items to announcements or to the calendar, upload documents and modify how the website is viewed. If you change a user's site group, the new permissions will be enforced when the user goes to a new page on the website (or refreshes the view on the current page). Any features select that are not available to the user will prompt the user for username and password.

Working with SharePoint Information

One of the really nice features of the SharePoint website is that it is very intuitive and user-friendly. There are links and drop-down boxes that provide choices specific to the selected item. From the user interface, you can add items, check out items (check out as in library check out), get alerted to changes, import and export files, and join discussions. The following discussion of options assumes you have Administrator privileges. Other site groups will have different options.

Adding Items

The default items on the main page are announcements and links. You can add a new announcement, for instance, by simply clicking the link labeled **Add new announcement** (this option is visible in Figure 14.1, shown earlier). When the new announcement window opens, your choices are well defined. The window for adding a new announcement is shown in Figure 14.3. It's pretty clear that you can enter a title and the announcement, you can format the body of the announcement, and you can set an expiration date, if desired (a very nice feature to avoid old, tired announcements from being abandoned on the site) and click **Save and Close**, **Attach File**, or **Go Back to List**.

Figure 14.3 Add New Announcement Window

If you want to add a document, select the category from under **Documents** in the Quick Launch bar. If you want to add a new item to the shared calendar, click the **Calendar** under **Lists** in the Quick Launch bar, etc. If you want to add new elements to the site, you can click **Modify Shared Page** in the upper right portion of the screen. We'll look at modifying the site elements later in this chapter.

Checking Out Items

Another very useful feature of this site and one the Dreamco folks use extensively (mentioned in the Some Independent Advice earlier in the chapter), is the check out feature. Document, pictures, any kinds of files on the site can be checked out. This is especially helpful when you have multiple users working on documents. If the documents are kept in this central location and must be checked out before working on them, you can avoid the all-too-common problem of someone overwriting or duplicating someone else's work. This provides a document management system that is perfect for small businesses. To check out a document, users simply click the down arrow to the right of the file name and select **Check Out** from the options, shown earlier in Figure 14.2. Documents are checked in using the same method. Users can also view version history, another nice document management feature. When you check a document back in, you have the three options: *check in document; check in changes saved to this document, but keep the document checked out; discard changes and undo check out.* You can also record comments that are preserved.

Alerts

You can be alerted to various changes to the website documents. The options are to be alerted via e-mail to all changes, added items, changed items, deleted items, and web discussion updates. You can choose to have alerts e-mailed immediately, or as a daily summary or weekly summary. Depending on your user permission levels, your alert choices may differ.

Import and Export Files

On many of the different pages on the SharePoint website, you have the option of exporting the data to a spreadsheet or datasheet. This will export the data to Microsoft Excel, if present on the local user's computer. You can also import Calendar items and Contacts from Outlook or export these items to Outlook.

Discuss Pages and Documents

There are two key discussion features in SharePoint website. First, you can discuss documents by clicking the down arrow to the right of a document and selecting **Discuss** from the pop-up menu shown in Figure 14.2. This feature is available for a number of different types of files such as documents, projects, presentations, and more.

You can also use the **Discussions** link on the Quick Launch navigation bar to create and participate in threaded and unthreaded discussions. Threaded discussions are newsgroup-style discussions on topics relevant to your team or company. This is another very useful tool for collaboration. Creating a threaded discussion on a client project, for instance, keeps all the discussions on that topic in one virtual area and helps everyone by keeping a record of discussions, comments, ideas, problems, and solutions. Unthreaded discussions are not connected to others and become a sort of general discussion area.

Sites and Subsites

You can subdivide the SharePoint website into multiple sites, and each site can have subsites. This is a more advanced feature we won't go into tremendous detail on, though we will briefly touch on it. You should be aware of this option whether or not you choose to use it. It is a useful feature if you want to create separate sites for each department in your company, for each specific client project, or however that division might make sense for your company. We'll discuss the steps to do this in the next section. Sites and subsites are created and managed via **Site Settings** on the top navigation bar.

Customizing SharePoint Website

The elements on the SharePoint website are called Web Parts. These parts can be added, deleted, and moved around to customize the site to suit your needs. Remember, it's a good idea to work with the SharePoint default site for a while to get a good feel for what the features are and how your team might want to utilize these features. Once you're familiar with the default site, go ahead and start customizing it.

There are two main ways to modify the default site. You can make changes to the Shared View on the home page by clicking the link *Modify Shared Page*. We'll discuss shared views and personal views in a moment. You can also modify the default site and gain access to a few more design options by clicking **Site Settings** on the top navigation bar. The default settings are shown in Figure 14.4. As you can see, the major categories are **Administration**, **Customization**, and **Manage My Information.**

Figure 14.4 Default Site Settings in SharePoint Web Site

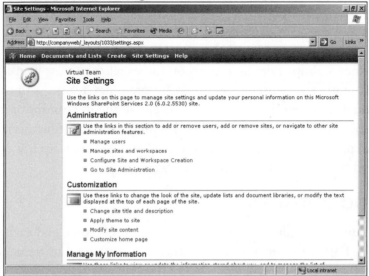

Shared View vs. Personal View

There are two types of views available, *shared views* and *personal views*. Shared views are created (or modified) by members the Administrator or Web Designer site group and apply to all users immediately. Individual users who are part of the Administrator, Web Designer or Contributor site group can modify settings to create a personal view of the site content. The personal view does not effect the shared view. Members of the Reader group must use the shared view and cannot create a personal view.

Administrators and Web Designers will have a link in the upper right corner that toggles between *Modify Shared Page* and *Modify My Page* depending on which option is active. This can be changed by clicking the down arrow to the right of the text and selecting either *Shared View* or *Personal View*. Changes made to the Shared Page will effect all users and will be implemented immediately. If a user is a member of the Contributor group, he or she will simply have a link labeled *Modify My Page*. If the user is a member of the Reader group, no link will be present.

The Modify *Shared* Page option allows you to add Web Parts, design the shared page, modify My Web Parts and toggle between Shared View and Personal View. The Modify *My* Page option allows you to Add Web Parts, Design this Page, and Modify My Web Parts. Modifying My Web Parts allows the user to change how the available Web Parts are viewed (what a list will look like, how it's displayed and more) but does not allow the user to *choose* Web Parts.

Administration

The administrative section in Site Settings allows you to **Manage users**, **Manage Sites and Workspaces**, **Configure Site and Workspace Creation**, and **Go to Site Administration** (different than this Administration).

- **Manage Users** In this section, you can add and remove users and edit their membership in site groups. As you now know, membership in site groups is how security is managed in SharePoint services.

- **Manage Sites and Workspaces** In this section, you can create new sites, document workspaces, and meeting workspaces. As mentioned just a moment ago, you can create separate sites and subsites for various departments, projects, or other organizational units to fit the needs of your company. A site is the defined area and the workspace is what's in that area. An analogy would be that the site is the folder and the workspace is made up of the files within that folder.

- **Configure Site and Workspace Creation** This is a very small section that allows you to enable workspace creation by others. You can select which of two site groups (Contributor and Web Designer) are allowed to create sites and workspaces. You may want to keep this group to a minimum to prevent the website from becoming disorganized and redundant.

- **Go to Site Administration** Site Administration contains more detailed settings than the Administration section we just reviewed. Some of the tasks overlap, such as managing users. Other tasks are available only in this section including more advanced user management options, site management and statistics, site collection galleries and site collection administration. A *site collection* is a group of websites on a virtual server that have the same owner and that share administrative settings. Each site collection contains a top-level website and may contain one or more subsites. There can be multiple site collections on each virtual server. These are more advanced concepts that you should work with only after you've become familiar with the layout, structure, and administration of the default site.

Customization

Customization is the major section of **Site Settings**. You must be part of the Administrator or Web Designer site group to modify these settings. In this section, you can **change the site title and description**, **apply a theme to the site**, **modify site content**, or **customize the home page**. Themes are collections of colors, images and fonts that can be applied to a site or to individual pages, much as you can use themes in Microsoft PowerPoint or FrontPage (and elsewhere). In the **modify site content** section, you can customize all the pre-set items such as general documents, general discussions, Help Desk, vacation calendar, etc. You can also create new content by clicking the **Create new content** link. Just FYI, if you click this link, you'll end up in the same place as if you clicked the **Create** link on the top navigation bar. There are numerous predefined elements you can then create through the use of the templates provided. The **Customize home page** link allows you to add, remove, and move Web Parts.

Since you're a quick study, you've probably noticed by now that you can get to different functions and features in one of several ways. This follows the typical Microsoft model that provides a number of different ways to achieve the same result, giving you the flexibility to work with the tools in the way that makes the most sense for you. Take some time clicking through your options on the website to become familiar with how you access various features. Some features only have one way in, others have several.

Manage My Information

This information is based on your user login, so your options may differ based on your account and your site group membership. If you're logged on using an account with Administrator privileges, you'll see **Update my information**, **My alerts on this site** and **View information about site users**.

Advanced SharePoint Administration

We've touched on the topic of administering your SharePoint website and we'll go into a bit more detail here. However, some of these concepts are somewhat advanced, so proceed with caution. It would be worth the effort to surf around in these screens to get an idea of what you can do in the administrative areas, but be sure not to make changes you don't fully understand. The Help files in SharePoint are fairly good, though they don't always go into the level of detail you might like. There is additional information on SharePoint Services on the Microsoft website at www.microsoft.com/technet/prodtechnol/windowsserver2003/technologies/sharepoint/default.mspx. Be sure to look through this website for information, tips, tricks, and updates from time to time.

Another important concept to understand is that, up until this point, we've been focused on the SharePoint website located by default at http://companyweb. There is also the default SBS website, located by default at http://*SBSServerName* (*SBSServerName* is the name of your SBS server), which is the Small Business Server site. This is the location of **My Company's Internal Web Site (http://companyweb)**, **Network Configuration Wizard** (to connect computers to the network automatically), **Remote Web Workplace** (to connect to the SBS network over the Internet), and **Information and Answers**. This site is shown in Figure 14.5. When you delve into advanced administration, there are places where you'll be presented with options as to which site(s) to manage. Understanding the differences between these two sites is important when you start making changes.

Figure 14.5 Default Small Business Server Website

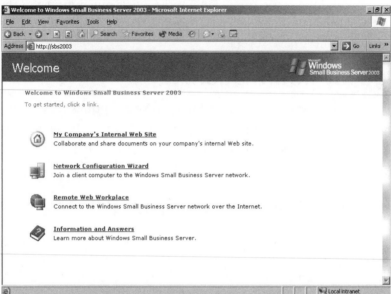

The SharePoint site can be administered from a higher level through Internet Information Server (IIS) virtual server management console, accessed via **Start | Administrative Tools | SharePoint Central Administration.** The Central Administration console looks more like SharePoint services (essentially a web page) than a typical server management console. Within this tool, you can manage **Virtual Server Configuration**, **Security Configuration**, **Server Configuration**, and **Component Configuration.** We've listed all the options, but we'll only discuss the ones you're most likely to use. Other options can be explored at your leisure. Remember, don't change settings unless you know what you're doing in here because you're impacting all sites and services on your SharePoint Services server.

Virtual Server Configuration

Virtual Server Configuration links provide the ability to configure settings across all sites on a server or create a new top-level website. A virtual server is a distinct "section" of a physical server. In this case, each virtual server is a distinct website.

By default, there are three virtual servers created in SharePoint: companyweb, default website, and SharePoint Administration. They all reside on the same server but are seen as three distinct websites. The links to perform these four administrative tasks are:

- Extend or upgrade virtual server
- Create a top-level website
- Delete site collection
- Configure virtual server settings

If you've created site collections that are no longer needed or wanted, these can be deleted. Choosing the **Delete site collection** link will allow you to specify which site collection you want to delete. Doing so will delete the site, all of its subsites, and all of the content that is a part of that site collection. Sound dramatic? It is. Later in this chapter we'll discuss backing up and restoring SharePoint files and list items, so you have a bit of a failsafe option here.

When you click the link to configure virtual server settings, you are given options as to which virtual server (website) to configure. Once you select that virtual server, you'll be provided with another fairly extensive list of administrative options. You may want to go into this area and modify default settings for managing settings for Web Parts Pages. You can improve both security and performance by modifying users abilities to connect web parts or to access the Online Web Part Gallery. If you modified settings and you want to undo, this section provides a **Restore Defaults** button. Don't make any changes until you've worked with the SharePoint default options for a while.

Security Configuration

As with the Virtual Server configuration, the settings you work with in this section apply to security settings across all virtual servers. Security Configuration includes links to perform these five administrative tasks:

- Set SharePoint administration group
- Manage site collection owners
- Manage website users
- Manage blocked file types
- Configure antivirus settings

As we've discussed numerous times throughout this book, Windows Server 2003 and, by extension, Small Business Server 2003 are more secure right out of the box than any previous Windows Server operating system. That said, you may still want to modify some of the default security settings. At the risk of being repetitious, only do so after you've given the default settings a good test period. You may find you don't need to make any changes at all. You can specify which security group should have full Administrator privileges in SharePoint. You can also manage website users for sites and subsites in this section (providing users access to the Training subsite but not the Finance subsite, for instance). Another helpful feature you'll find here is the ability to manage blocked file types. You may recall a similar list when we discussed setting up e-mail earlier in the book. Files using the extensions on the list cannot be saved to or retrieved from any site on the server. While this might be a good thing in some circumstances, if your company regularly deals with a particular file type on the blocked list, that wouldn't be such a good thing. You can remove blocked file types by removing them from the list by simply highlighting then and pressing the **Delete** key. You can add blocked file types by typing in the extension and clicking **OK**. Certain file extensions, such as .exe files, are executable and are the favorite flavor of hackers and authors of those insidious worms and viruses. As with other settings in SharePoint, changes take effect immediately.

The last, and probably most useful feature in this section, is the **antivirus settings**. You can specify when you want documents stored on this site to be scanned for viruses. This is one area you probably do want to delve into and set up because the default settings are may *not* adequate. Microsoft provides a list of antivirus software vendors whose products work with SharePoint (though whatever you have now may work just fine). No antivirus software is included with SBS or SharePoint. Access the Microsoft list at http://directory.partners.extranet. microsoft.com/AdvSearchResults.aspx?sharepoint=4.

Server Configuration

Server Configuration includes links to set and update server connections including e-mail, databases and Web servers. These links are:

- Configure default e-mail server settings
- Manage Web server list
- Set default content database server
- Set configuration database server

- Configure HTML Viewer
- Configure virtual server for central administration

The default settings for e-mail that get configured here will be used for all sites to e-mail alerts, invitations, and administrator notifications. You can create, configure, and manage additional databases in this section. SharePoint services relies upon SQL Server (which we'll discuss a bit later in this book). You can modify security settings for your databases, but unless you know what you're doing, it's best to leave these settings as you find them.

Component Configuration

The last section in the Central Administration console contains links to manage components that work across all virtual servers including search, usage analysis, and quotas. These links are:

- Configure full-text search
- Configure usage analysis processing
- Manage quotas and locks
- Configure data retrieval service settings

One of the tools you might want to use in this area is the usage analysis processing. In this section, you can enable logging, set the file location, and define the number of log files to create. You can also enable usage analysis processing, which allows you to see how your website is used, the number of visitors, and other site usage details. Quotas and locks are also managed here and you can set site storage limits to prevent your SharePoint website from taking over your disk drives. You can also set a warning level so you're notified before the quota kicks in. These are hard quotas and will prevent additional data from being added when the quota limit is reached.

There is one last note in the Advanced Administration section. You can use Microsoft FrontPage 2003, included with the SBS product, to completely customize your default SharePoint website. Don't worry if you're not familiar with FrontPage; we'll take a quick look at in toward the end of this book. Although we won't go into the specifics of how to use FrontPage 2003 (either here or at the end of the book), it is worth mentioning that you can install FrontPage 2003 on a client machine. FrontPage and Outlook are the only two components included with SBS that you *can* (and should) install on a machine other than the SBS server. Installing FrontPage 2003 on a client computer and then opening the default website in FrontPage 2003 allows you to use the FrontPage editing capabilities to get as creative as you want. There are two sites created by default by SBS that can be modified – one is the default SBS site (http://*SBSServerName*) and the other is the default SharePoint site (http://companyweb). You cannot edit the SharePoint website with previous versions of FrontPage. There are features in SharePoint not supported by earlier versions of FrontPage, so you have to use FrontPage 2003, included in the Premium edition of SBS. You can purchase FrontPage 2003 separately or bundled with the Microsoft Office suite if you don't have the Premium edition of SBS.

Backing Up and Restoring SharePoint Files

When you back up your server, the SharePoint files and databases will be backed up (unless you specifically exclude them in the Backup Wizard, which would not be a good choice) so you can always restore files based on your latest backup. Another option, for more experienced net admins, is to enable the recovery of individual SharePoint files. That way, if a user accidentally deletes a file that was modified a number of times in between backups (for instance, several important modifications during one work day), you can restore just that file or list. This is a feature similar to shadow volume copy, which we discussed earlier in this book. Be forewarned, however, that this is not for the faint-of-heart. Step-by-step instructions can be found on the Microsoft website in a document on backing up and restoring SBS, www.microsoft.com/windowsserver2003/sbs/techinfo/productdoc/default.mspx. Access the site and select *Backing Up and Restoring Windows Small Business Server 2003*. You can also query on the file name, **BKU_BkupRstr.doc** in the **Search** box, or you can query the SBS Help and Support files with the phrase **enable recovery of individual SharePoint files**. One more note about backing up SharePoint; if you're using a third-party backup utility, make sure it's capable of backing up SQL data stores. SharePoint uses SQL data stores to manage site documents.

One More Time

It should be clear after reading this chapter that SharePoint Services is a very powerful, flexible, and easy-to-use tool that enables (some would argue it encourages) collaboration. Whether you use this site to work with employees

who aren't always in the office or use it to help teams manage collaborative projects, you'll certainly be able to get up and running quickly using the default settings. Once you've become familiar with the features of SharePoint Services, you
can customize the site (and create layers of subsites, each of which can be customized) to meet the needs of your organization.

☑ SharePoint Services creates a default website located at http://
   companyweb. This site contains a number of default features that enable
   you to start sharing documents, calendars, announcements, contacts, and
   more.

☑ SharePoint contains a two primary navigations bars. The top navigation
   bar is always visible on each page and includes **Home**, **Documents
   and Lists**, **Create**, **Site Settings**, and **Help**.

☑ The left navigation area is called the Quick Launch link bar. This area's
   contents change depending on your selection.

☑ All types of documents can be uploaded, checked in, checked out,
   modified, and shared via the links on the document pages.

☑ The various components of the website are called Web Parts. These can
   be added, deleted, moved, and modified to customize your site.

☑ Site groups are used to manage security within the SharePoint
   framework.

☑ Users, security, and other site-wide settings are accessed via **Site
   Settings** on the top navigation bar.

☑ Advanced SharePoint administrative features are accessed via **Start** |
   Administrative Tools | **SharePoint Central Administration**. This
   launches a management console that looks more like a SharePoint
   website than a traditional management console, but provides higher-level
   (and more advanced) administrative options than SharePoint Site
   Settings.

☑ You can customize both your default SBS website
   (http://*SBSServerName,* where SBSServerName is the actual name of
   your SBS server) and the default SharePoint website (http://
   companyweb) using FrontPage 2003, the website creation tool that is
   included with the Small Business Server 2003 software.

☑ Outlook 2003 and FrontPage 2003 are the only two applications that come bundled with SBS that can be (and should be) installed on a computer other than the SBS server.

☑ FrontPage 2003 comes with the Premium edition of SBS. Earlier versions of FrontPage cannot be used to edit SharePoint websites.

☑ If using a third-party antivirus program or backup program, check that its compatible with SharePoint.

☑ The Backup Wizard will back up your SharePoint site according to the backup configuration settings. However, you can also enable the recovery of individual files and lists. This enables you to recover files and lists without resorting to a restore. Download the document from the Microsoft website or query the SBS Help and Support files for **enable recovery of individual SharePoint files** for more information.

Chapter 15

Monitoring, Tuning, and Troubleshooting

- Monitoring the SBS Server
- Advanced Monitoring Tools
- Troubleshooting Basics
- Tuning and Troubleshooting the SBS Server

The End Result

By the end of this chapter, you'll understand the tools available to you to monitor, tune, and troubleshoot your Small Business Server (SBS) 2003 server. You'll understand how and when to use the tools as well as the importance of regularly monitoring your server. You'll also understand basic troubleshooting techniques and learn about several troubleshooting tools you can use to diagnose and repair problems on your SBS server.

Monitoring the SBS Server

Monitoring and reporting are critical tasks you should make time for every day. Monitoring is a key defense against network monkey business, potential hardware and software problems, and hacker attacks, to name just a few issues. Monitoring can help you spot existing or potential hardware problems, software configuration problems, and bottlenecks. *Bottlenecks* are areas of the server (or any computer) where things grind to a halt and cause slow response times and user frustration. Some bottlenecks are the result of the aforementioned problems; some are due to growing demand for resources. Some problems are painfully obvious; others develop slowly over time. Either way, monitoring server performance and usage will help you resolve issues and prepare for upgrades before things come to a complete halt. Though monitoring is really a daily task, keeping an eye on things is generally all that's required. If you notice something unusual, you can dig deeper. Think of monitoring as your network neighborhood watch.

One of the key concepts to understand about monitoring is that, as with auditing, you must strike a reasonable balance. There are literally thousands of things you can monitor in Windows, and a vast majority of them are rather useless to you. Our focus will be to show you the tools and different options and then help you determine what type of monitoring configuration will be most useful. Once you determine what you want to monitor, you can establish *baselines*. These are your "normal" settings, against which you can compare unusual results to determine if the problem is a blip, an early warning, or a serious threat.

A wealth of information is available on monitoring and reporting in the SBS Help and Support files as well as the Help files accessible via the specific tool and on the Microsoft Web site. You can quickly overwhelm yourself with data and details, so our focus will be on setting up basic monitoring that will cover most situations.

To begin, you'll need to configure monitoring in SBS. We'll head back into the To Do List in Server Management to launch this wizard. The wizard steps you through setting up alert notifications and server performance and usage reports. Follow these steps to configure monitoring on your SBS server:

1. Click **Start | Server Management | Standard Management | To Do List**. In the right (details) pane, click the link labeled **Configure Monitoring** (or the Start arrow to the right). This will launch the Monitoring Configuration Wizard. Click **Next** in the Welcome screen.

2. The first screen (after the Welcome screen) is Reporting Options. There are three check boxes, one under *Performance Report* and two under *Usage Report*. Choose your desired options here. Under Performance Report, you can choose to **Receive a daily performance report in e-mail**. This report contains status information about services, performance counters, and alerts for your SBS server. It's recommended that you select this option. The second option, under Usage Report, is **View the usage report in Server Management**. This report holds information about users' Internet, e-mail, and fax usage as well as information on remote connectivity. This is also a recommended setting. If you select this option, a third option will be enabled, **Receive a usage report in e-mail every other week**. By default, the Domain Administrators group has access to monitoring and usage reports. You can configure additional groups to have access in just a moment (two screens ahead in the wizard). For more information on the details of what's included in a Performance or Usage Report, click **More Information**. The Performance and Usage Reports are also available in Server Management any time you want to view them. These options provide a more automated way for you to get this information, making your life just that much easier. Click **Next** to continue.

3. The next screen, E-mail Options, provides a text box where you can enter one or more e-mail addresses to which the reports should be sent. Multiple addresses are separated by a semicolon. Enter the desired address(es) and click **Next**.

4. The Business Owner Usage Report dialog is next. Here you can specify if you want others in your organization to view usage reports on their intranet. By default, members of the Domain Administrators group can view these reports, but you can extend permission to others. Select users

from All Users in the left pane, then click **Add**. The users will be added to the right pane in *Owners or authorized users,* as shown in Figure 15.1. When you have finished adding users, click **Next**.

Figure 15.1 Enabling Business Owners to Receive Usage Reports

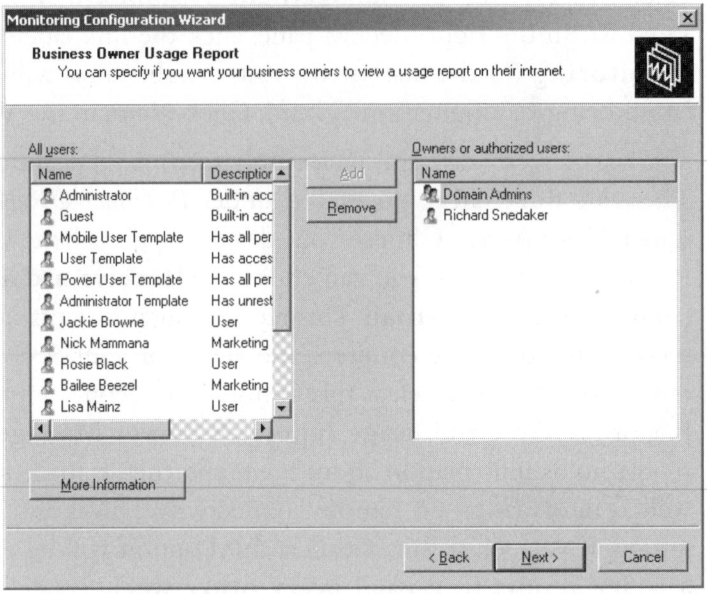

5. The next screen is **Alerts**. You can specify if you want to receive immediate notification for performance alerts via e-mail. Enter the desired e-mail addresses, separated by semicolons. There is a long list of performance-related alerts you could conceivably receive. Click **More Information** in this screen to view the entire list.

Even if you don't understand what all these things are, you should opt to receive these alerts. If the event triggers an alert, you can research the meaning of the alert and figure out what your next steps should be. Later in this chapter, we'll look at some troubleshooting resources you can use to begin to unravel the mystery of some of these alerts. One option is to contact Microsoft support (paid support) for assistance in resolving problems related to alerts. A partial list of these alerts is shown in Figure 15.2. Click **Next**.

Figure 15.2 Partial List of Performance Alerts

<figure>

Service	Description
DHCP Server	Performs TCP/IP configuration for DHCP client computers, including dynamic assignments of IP addresses, specification of the WINS and DNS servers, and connection-specific DNS names. If this service is stopped, the DHCP server will not perform TCP/IP configuration for client computers.
DNS Server	Activates Domain Name System (DNS) client computers to resolve DNS names by answering DNS queries and DNS dynamic update requests. If this service is stopped, DNS name resolution will fail, and DNS updates will not occur. This can prevent users from accessing the server and the Internet.
Error Reporting Service	Collects, stores, and reports unexpected application crashes to Microsoft. If this service is stopped, then Error Reporting will occur only for kernel faults and some types of user mode faults.
Event Log	Activates event log messages issued by Windows-based programs and components to be viewed in Event Viewer.
Fax	Allows users to send and receive faxes, utilizing fax resources available on the computer running Windows Small Business Server 2003. By default, service and performance alerts for Fax are not enabled. If you install and configure a fax modem, you can enable the Fax alerts by using the Alert Notifications configuration tool.
IPSEC Services	Provides end-to-end security between client computers and servers on TCP/IP networks. If this service is stopped, TCP/IP security between client computers and servers on the network will be impaired.
Kerberos Key Distribution Center	Allows users to log on to the network using the Kerberos authentication protocol. If this service is stopped, users will be unable to log on to the network.
Microsoft Exchange Information Store	Manages the Exchange mailbox and public folder stores. If this service is stopped, mailbox stores and public folder stores on the computer running Windows Small Business Server 2003 will be unavailable.
Microsoft Exchange Management	Manages Exchange management information that uses Windows Management Instrumentation (WMI). If this service is stopped, Exchange management information using WMI will be unavailable.
Microsoft Exchange POP3	Provides Post Office Protocol version 3 (POP3) services to client users. If this service is stopped, client computers will be unable to connect to the computer running Windows Small Business Server 2003 by using the POP3 protocol. This alert is disabled by default.
Microsoft Exchange Routing Engine	Provides Exchange routing services using link state information. If this service is stopped, messages will not be routed by the computer running Windows Small Business Server 2003.
Microsoft Exchange System Attendant	Provides monitoring, maintenance, and Active Directory lookup services, such as monitoring of services and connectors, defragmenting the Exchange store, and forwarding Active Directory queries to a Global Catalog server. Most Exchange services depend on the Microsoft Exchange System Attendant service and will stop if this service is stopped. Additionally, if this service is stopped, then monitoring,

</figure>

6. The final screen displays a summary of your selections. Review these selections, click **Back** to go back and make modifications, or click **Finish** to implement your choices. Remember, as with most (if not all) of the Summary dialogs in SBS, you can click the link to print, save, or e-mail the information you just configured. This is a useful tool for keeping track of what you've configured.

7. Once you click **Finish**, you'll see the wizard configuring the data store, data collection alert thresholds, and reports. When the progress bar indicates it's complete, click **Close** to finish this process.

Once you've granted permission to access the report to various users, they will receive an introductory e-mail message explaining what the report is and how to access it. The usage report is accessed via http://*SBSServername*/monitoring, where *SBSServerName* is the actual name of your SBS server (in our example, it's SBS2003). You can choose simple or extended reporting for any desired time frame and then click **Create Report** to generate the report based on your selected parameters. To understand more about server usage reports, you can search for "understanding the server usage report" in the Help and Support section of your SBS server. These report on usage, not performance issues, and can be helpful in understanding and tracking how users are accessing the intranet.

Once you've finished configuring monitoring via the wizard, you can access **Monitoring and Reporting** in the Standard Management tasks in Server Manager. Once this option is selected, you'll see options in the details pane that include links in the taskpad area as well as details in the right side of the pane. After monitoring is configured, performance data is collected hourly, so initially there will be a short announcement stating that no performance data is available. You can toggle between viewing the performance report and the usage report in this pane by alternately clicking the link labeled **View Usage Report** (visible when you're viewing Performance Report) or **View Performance Report** (visible when you're viewing Usage Report). Once enough data has been gathered, you can view and print the server performance report.

The information included in the Performance Report in this screen (right side or detail pane of Monitoring and Reporting) is extensive and includes:

- Server Summary
- Server Specifications
- Performance Summary
- Top 5 Processes by Memory Usage
- Top 5 Processes by CPU Usage
- Backup
- Auto-started Services Not Running
- Critical Alerts
- Critical Errors in Application Log
- Critical Errors in DNS Server Log
- Critical Errors in File Replication Service Log
- Critical Errors in Security Log
- Critical Errors in System Log

Though this information is recorded and stored in log files, it may also be e-mailed to you if you chose that option when you were configuring monitoring.

By regularly reviewing the information in these reports, you'll find that after a while, you can easily spot unusual patterns that could indicate the beginning of a network attack, a hardware failure, or a software configuration issue. You should also use this information to establish baseline values for key counters (memory, CPU, and disk usage) so you'll begin to get a feel for what's normal and what's not. Figure 15.3 shows a sample Server Performance Report, as displayed in **Server Management | Standard Management | Monitoring and Reporting**.

Figure 15.3 Sample Server Performance Report

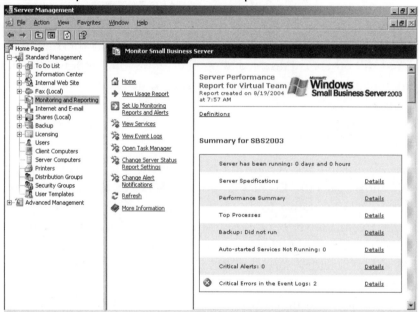

In the Monitoring and Reporting area in Server Management, you can also reconfigure monitoring by launching the Monitoring Configuration Wizard from the link labeled **Set Up Monitoring Reports and Alerts**. Also available from this taskpad are links to View Services, View Event Logs, Open Task Manager, Change Server Status Report Settings, and Change Alert Notifications. We'll look at each of these briefly.

View Services

Clicking the **View Services** link opens the Services Management console. This console can also be opened via **Start | Administrative Tools | Services**.

Here you can see the status of a service or explore the descriptions of the services. Click once to select the service to display the description, click twice or right-click to access the service's properties. Services can be sorted by any column heading; click once to sort in ascending order, click again to sort in descending order. If you access the service's properties dialog, you can start, stop, pause, and resume a service. *Use extreme care with this feature.* Avoid stopping, starting, pausing, or resuming a service unless you're absolutely sure of what you're doing. If you accidentally disable a critical service, you can cause your network and/or server to come crashing down around you.

If you're in your monitoring section and click **View Services**, you will probably want to look at a particular service highlighted in your performance alert or report. Locate the service and first look at the Status and Startup type. Some services are started by default when the system starts; others are started manually, and still others are disabled altogether until you configure them. If you're responding to an alert, you might be able to determine the cause of the problem here.

View Event Logs

Also in the Monitoring and Reporting taskpad is the **View Event Logs** link. Clicking this link opens the Event Viewer. Like Services, the Event Viewer can be accessed via Administrative Tools. Unlike Services, you're apt to stay out of trouble in the Event Viewer because you are looking at events that have already occurred and been recorded. The Event Viewer contains these logs: Application, Security, System, Directory Service, DNS Server, and File Replication Service. We'll look at each one briefly so that you understand what each is used for and how each might help you monitor the health and well-being of your server.

The default view of the Event Viewer console is shown in Figure 15.4. To view the details of an event in any of the logs, click the category (application, security, etc.) then double-click the event or right-click and select **Properties** from the shortcut menu. For more information on any of the events, review the information in the Description box. In some cases, a great deal of information as well as troubleshooting steps are included here. For more information, you can click the link typically provided in the Description box. This link will bring you to the Microsoft Web site for more information on that particular event. Event log information can be very useful in troubleshooting, especially if you're working with a consultant or with a Microsoft support engineer who might be able to pinpoint the problem using log file details.

Figure 15.4 Event Viewer Management Console

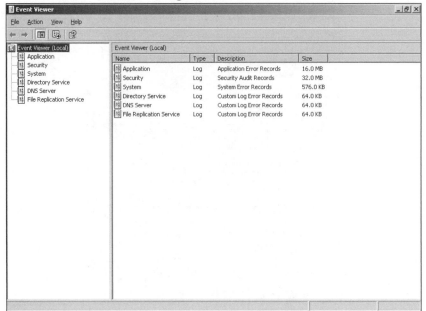

Event Types

Before we discuss the specific event logs, it's important to understand event types. There are five types of event: information, warning, error, success audit, and failure audit. An *information event* provides information on successful events such as "The DNS server has started." A *warning event* is not necessarily significant but might indicate a potential future problem. These warning events tell you there is something wrong that might or might not correct itself. This could be a configuration issue or some other event that might require your attention. Figure 15.5 shows a warning event from the DNS Server log file on an SBS server. An *error event* is really the most critical type, and each error event should be thoroughly investigated and resolved. An example of a DHCP error event is shown in Figure 15.6.

A *successful audit event* is just that—the event you chose to audit for success occurred. This might include a user successfully accessing a particular file that you want to keep an eye on, or it could be a successful remote connection. A *failure audit* tracks those selected events that fail. You could be auditing failed logon events, for example, and each time an attempted logon fails, it is logged as a failure audit event. These audits can be extremely useful for early spotting of attempts to hack into your network (assuming you review your logs regularly).

Figure 15.5 Warning Event Details

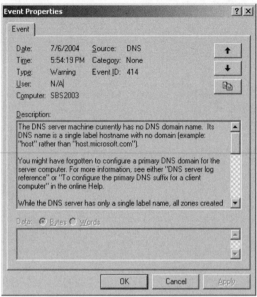

Figure 15.6 Error Event Details

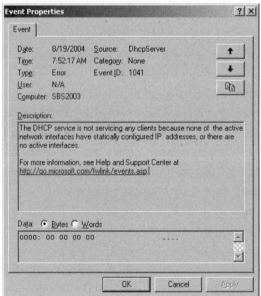

Event Log Properties

For each of the log types, you can define various parameters for that file. Right-click the log in the console tree and select **Properties** from the shortcut menu. On the **General** tab, you can set the maximum size of the log and specify whether or not the events are overwritten or stored for a particular length of time. By default, when a log file is full, the oldest event is deleted first. Although you can customize these settings, the default settings will work just fine. Once you're familiar with your network, its configuration, and the typical volume of events being logged, you can make modifications as needed in the log file properties.

Event Logs

As mentioned earlier, the event logs are Application, Security, System, Directory Service, DNS Server, and File Replication Service. Each log file stores events related to that category. Perhaps the most important log file to view with regularity (and consistency) is the Security log. This might be your first glimpse into a potential security breach, and you can use the events in the log file to determine what's happening, when it's happening, and often what to do about it. Let's look at what each of these log files contains.

The Application Log

The Application log contains events logged by applications and programs on the server. You don't have much control over this log in the sense that whomever developed the application or program decided which events to log. You can review this log and look for consistent, recurring, or repeated problems with a particular program.

The Security Log

This log is, of course, where you view security-related events. These events include valid and invalid logon attempts as well as other resource access and usage events. The security events logged here are configured by the Administrator (as opposed to the application developer mentioned in the previous section). If you enabled logging for successful or failed access of a sensitive file or folder or for logon failure, you'll see such events logged here. Check this log regularly. You can catch irregular patterns and perhaps spot an attempted hack before it becomes a serious problem.

The System Log

The System log captures events logged by the Windows system. These are not events you can configure for logging; these are events that the Windows system tells you about. These events might include the failure of a driver to load or another component that should have started during system startup. Any odd behavior is noted here. This log can be a good place to spot problems early on. If a printer driver fails to load, for instance, you might want to reinstall the driver or look for an updated version for that printer before your users tell you the printer is acting squirrelly.

The Directory Service Log

The Directory Service log is one of two log files you'll find only on a computer running the Windows Server 2003-based operating system configured as a domain controller (which in your case is your SBS server). This log file logs events that occur within the Active Directory service. These events might be a bit more enigmatic to you, but you should check this log anyway. If you do notice problems here, you'll need to do some research to determine both cause and resolution. The answers aren't always obvious with problems of this nature; this is where having an expert consultant available to you can really make your life easier. Often, searching the Microsoft Web site using the exact text of the error message yields excellent results, and the text can be very helpful when you're working with a consultant or Microsoft support engineer to resolve the issue.

The DNS Server Log

The DNS Server log is the other log file you'll only find on a computer running the Windows Server 2003-based operating system configured as a domain controller. The DNS server log records events concerning the DNS service. Typically, this log will generate a fair amount of activity, including information events stating that the DNS service has started.

The File Replication Service Log

The File Replication Service log contains events related to replicating domain-type information. If you are running only one domain controller (recommended)—the SBS server—most of the replication events logged will be information events.

Open Task Manager

Since it's been so many pages since we started looking at this console, let's refresh our memories. We're working in the Server Management console and we've been looking at the options available in Monitoring and Reporting. We started with View Usage Report, then View Services, and we just looked at View Event Logs. The next option available in Monitoring and Reporting is Open Task Manager. You can also access Task Manager by pressing **Ctrl + Alt + Del** and clicking the **Task Manager** button.

Task Manager provides information about the processes and programs running on the computer. You might be familiar with Task Manager because it's available on nonserver computers such as Windows XP and earlier versions of Windows. Five tabs are available, each providing different slices of information about your server. The tabs are:

- **Applications** This tab shows the status of programs running on the computer. You can start, end, or switch to an application from this tab. If an application status indicates "Not responding" you can terminate the application by clicking **End Task.**

- **Processes** A *process* is an executable program or a service. On the Processes tab, you can view the processes running, the username, CPU usage, and memory usage. In some cases you can spot problems by viewing memory usage. If a process takes up too much CPU time or too much memory, you can terminate it by clicking the **End Process** button. Although you might not know exactly how much is too much (CPU time or memory), you can often spot potential problems, or other indicators combined with these may confirm your suspicions. *A word of caution here:* Some processes are required for the system to run, so don't terminate a process you're not completely familiar with or your server could come to a grinding halt. If it's a process you are familiar with, such as Word (winword.exe), you can usually end the process without dire consequences, though whenever possible you're better off doing so from the Application tab and not the Processes tab.

- **Performance** You can view various performance-related counters on this tab, including graphs of CPU usage and Page File (memory-related) usage as well as CPU and Page File history. You can view total memory, available memory, system cache, and other memory-related values here. It's worth becoming familiar with this area so that you can spot normal and abnormal activity here.

- **Networking** On this tab, you can view the graphical representation of network performance. Again, becoming familiar with normal and abnormal activity here is worthwhile. You can view the quality and availability of your network connection.

- **Users** The Users tab (if present) displays the names of users connected to the computer as well as connection (session) status and names. The Client Name specifies the name of the client computer that's connected. The Session provides a name for you to use in, for example, sending another user a message. *The Users tab is not available on computers that are members of a network domain.*

Change Server Status Report Settings

Using the Change Server Status Report Settings link in the taskpad of Monitoring and Reporting, you can create or edit existing server status reports. To run and send a report, select it from the list and click **Send Now**. You can also create new reports by clicking the **Add** button, edit existing reports by clicking **Edit**, **Remove** existing reports, and **Close** the Server Status Reports dialog.

Change Alert Notifications

By clicking the **Change Alert Notifications** link in the taskpad of Monitoring and Reporting, you can configure numerous alert options. In the Alert Notifications dialog, you can access Services, Performance Counters, Event Log Errors, and E-mail Address tabs.

BEST PRACTICES ACCORDING TO MICROSOFT

- Set up a monitoring configuration so you're automatically kept up to date. Regularly review reports.
- Keep records of performance and usage data for historical comparison and troubleshooting.
- For more information on setting up a monitoring configuration, query Help and Support using the phrase "setting up a monitoring configuration." The result will show up in the Help Topics section.
- Keep your monitoring "overhead" low by using graphs only for short-term, real-time viewing. Avoid sampling data more often than needed. Frequency of data collection adds to monitoring overhead and can slow down your system. Avoid adding too many counters or objects for monitoring. The more you select, the slower things go. Monitor only critical items; see the Help file referenced for details on recommended monitoring configurations.
- Analyze your data and establish baselines. If you don't know what "normal" looks like, you'll have a hard time spotting potential or new problems.
- Set alerts for key thresholds.
- Monitor performance and tune system settings as needed to improve performance.
- Use monitoring data to help plan ahead. If CPU usage increases or memory load increases, or if disk utilization is too high or rising quickly, you can plan to upgrade before you hit the wall. This data can also be very useful in making the business case for needed upgrades.

SOME INDEPENDENT ADVICE

The process of configuring and monitoring the SBS server is greatly simplified by the use of the Monitoring Configuration Wizard as well as the performance and usage reports available in Server Management in Monitoring and Reporting. Use these tools regularly. There are numerous other monitoring tools you can use once you become proficient with the standard SBS tools. Become familiar with the Help files, and read articles on the Microsoft Web site. Although the day-to-day tasks of SBS administration are fairly simple and routine, becoming well-versed in these performance and usage tools will pay off in the long run. Think of it as your insurance policy. You hope you'll never need to use it, but you'll always be glad you have it. In this case, the premium you pay is a few minutes of your time each day to make sure everything looks good. Hey, you were going to read the paper while you had that second cup of coffee—why not read the performance and usage reports instead?

Advanced Monitoring Tools

You might want to explore two other useful tools once you've gotten a handle on the basic performance and reporting options provided in SBS. As with many things in SBS, the user interface is designed to simplify the tasks so that you don't have to be a seasoned IT admin to manage an SBS-based network. The underlying tools often have layers of depth (and complexity) that are "hidden" to the SBS admin but that can be accessed via other interfaces that are part of the Windows Server 2003 operating system. Let's look at a few of those tools now.

Performance Console: System Monitor and Performance Logs and Alerts

If you go to **Start | Administrative Tools | Performance**, you'll open the Performance management console. You can access both System Monitor and Performance Logs and Alerts in this console.

   If you select System Monitor in the left pane, you'll see a graphical representation of system activity (the default setting) in the right pane. There are a number of icons on the tool bar in the right pane that you can use to change the view. Your best bet is to read the associated Help files to get a solid overview of the System Monitor tools and configuration options. If you right-click in the detail pane and select Properties, you can view and modify counters, data views, and more. By right-clicking you also can add counters for monitoring. We'll discuss counters in a bit more detail in the next section. One thing to keep in mind is that viewing graphs is good for real-time monitoring, but it does take up system resources. Logging data will reduce the overhead but will not give you that real-time look. Each method is appropriate in different circumstances, and with practice, you'll be able to determine the best method for your situation.

Also in the Performance management console is the Performance Logs and Alerts section, which you configured using the wizard earlier in this chapter. There are additional options here, such as setting up a trace event log, but a trace event log is not likely to yield information useful to a network admin (with possibly a few exceptions), so the configuration you did earlier is just fine and you don't need to work with Performance Logs and Alerts in this manner, since the wizard walked you through the key elements.

Health Monitor

Health Monitor is another tool that replicates some of what we've discussed. We mention it here so you're aware of this tool and so that you can use it if it makes sense for you. As with the Performance console, we won't go into step-by-step instruction but will provide an overview for you. If you have time and interest, you might want to explore the capabilities of this tool. You might find Health Monitor more useful than System Monitor. You can access Health Monitor via **Start | Administrative Tools | Health Monitor**.

Once you've opened this management console, you have the standard navigation tree in the left pane and the details in the right pane. You can monitor multiple computers from here, but the default is the SBS server. Health Monitor keeps track of the selected computer(s) and performs basic fault detection, performance monitoring, event notification, and automated actions. Sound familiar? Health Monitor can be configured to monitor:

- Performance monitor counters, including system- or application-level information such as processor usage, network activity, etc.

- Windows Events, including information about hardware, software, system, and security events written to the Windows Events Log

- Windows Services, which tracks whether various system services are running

- Processes, which tracks whether various processes are running

- HTTP Addresses, which keeps track of whether the site can be accessed and whether Web forms are being processed correctly

- Windows Management Instrumentation (WMI)

- Ping (ICMP) Monitor responses
- TCP/IP Port Connections
- COM+ Application Statistics

If this list sounds intimidating, don't worry. You can stick with the Monitoring and Reporting options presented earlier in this chapter via the Server Management | Standard Management console. This is a great example of how the pre-defined wizards and settings in SBS help guide you through what can quickly become a technical jungle. These two tools (System Monitor and Health Monitor) are mentioned so you are aware that there are advanced tools you can use, should you choose to learn them. Otherwise, stick close to home by using the tools in the SBS Server Management console. If you're troubleshooting a problem with a Microsoft technician (or other technical expert), you may be instructed to open System Monitor or Health Monitor, and at least now you'll have heard of them.

Troubleshooting Basics

Successful troubleshooting is a combination of technical knowledge, methodical approach, creative art form, and a little bit of luck. The more you have of the first two things, the less you need of the last two. In this section, we'll look at some general troubleshooting techniques you can use to troubleshoot any problem— whether it's your SBS server or your malfunctioning garbage disposal at home. After reviewing these basic troubleshooting techniques, we'll discuss tuning and troubleshooting your SBS server. Tuning and troubleshooting go hand in hand, so we'll talk about them together in the next section.

Troubleshooting Basics

Everyone has had to troubleshoot some sort of problem at one time or another. Some people seem to be naturally better at this than others. However, regardless of your current troubleshooting skills, you can improve them by increasing your technical knowledge and following some basic troubleshooting guidelines. These steps are written with your server in mind, but they apply to just about any troubleshooting you do:

1. **Repeatedly ask "Why?"** This should help you get to the root cause. With computers, one problem can cause another, which can cause another. If you start troubleshooting the third problem, you not only

won't get to the root cause, you could inadvertently cause a fourth problem along the way. Ask "Why is this happening now and not earlier?" "Why is this symptom showing up here in this manner?" and so on. Don't jump to conclusions, and don't just leap in and start "fixing things." Chances are you'll do more harm than good. Step back and look things over, ask why, and then go to step 2.

2. **Ask "What just changed?"** Often the last thing that was done is the thing causing the problem. If you just modified a setting on the server, undo that setting (if possible) and see if that resolves the problem.

3. **Cut the problem in half.** Always look for ways to cut the problem in half. If a user reports a problem printing to a network printer, try printing from another computer. In cutting the problem in half, make sure you can tell yourself what the result will tell you. For instance, if you print from another computer and it works, what will that tell you? If you can't determine what the result will tell you, you won't be able to figure out the next step once you see that result. Some things don't further the resolution but simply provide extraneous (and sometimes confusing) information. If you've successfully cut the problem in half, cut the problem in half again and continue until the problem is resolved.

4. **Look for the simple solution.** To paraphrase Occum's Razor (Occum was a mediaeval philosopher), whenever there are two or more explanations or solutions, the simplest one is often the right one. This applies to troubleshooting. Although you might encounter some very difficult and complex problems, in most cases the simplest explanation or solution is the right one. Is the cable *really* plugged in? Did you pull it out and plug it back in, to be sure? Is the cable itself bad? Did you swap it out with a known good one before deciding that the network interface card or the entire computer was malfunctioning? Always try the simple things first and don't overlook them. Sometimes it's worth doing them even if they're not on the top of your "suspect list," simply because it *is* easy to try them and you can then eliminate the easy things first. It takes far less time to reseat or swap out a cable than it does to replace a NIC or reconfigure a server. Of course, don't swap out a cable if the problem is clearly unrelated to the cable, but don't overlook the obvious. Continue to seek out the root cause (which is often something

simple)—don't just do the easy thing because it's easy, do it because it will further your goal of cutting the problem in half.

5. **Gather evidence.** You've configured your performance monitoring and reporting, look through these tools to gather evidence that can help you find the root problem.

6. **Make only one change at a time.** We've mentioned this before, but if you change two or more things at a time, you have a chance of either not knowing what fixed a problem or, worse, creating a new problem.

7. **Use parts you *know* work.** One common mistake that will have you chasing your tail for hours, days, or even weeks introducing a new problem in the midst of fixing the original problem. If you're going to start swapping out parts, make sure you're working with known good parts. A new part can introduce a new problem and have you running in the wrong direction. If a new part does not appear to resolve the problem or the problem seems to change after the introduction of a new part, take out the part, replace it with the original part, and test again. If necessary, get a second new part and test again.

8. **Write things down.** Troubleshooting is usually done under some pressure, and as you investigate problems and try to resolve them, you're very likely to forget exactly what you did and when. Approach troubleshooting calmly and document everything you do or think about doing. If you have ideas about the problem that are not appropriate to do immediately, make a note of it for later. Write down every change you make and the results of that change. You might need to retrace your steps; having carefully written notes to refer to will help. Furthermore, when it's all over, you should recap the problem, its symptoms, and how you resolved the problem. This will be helpful information for you in the future.

9. **Look for subtle details with intermittent problems.** Often problems that appear to be intermittent aren't as random as they might at first appear. Try to evaluate every detail, even if the detail doesn't initially seem relevant. For instance, does the server lock up after it's been on for 20 minutes? Thirty minutes? You might not be able to say exactly when the server *will* lock up, but you might be able to say that it does not happen until at least one hour after the system boots up, for instance. That's helpful information, even if it doesn't specifically pinpoint the

problem. Does the server only hang 30 minutes after a particular application is launched and that application is only launched every few days? This might appear to be an intermittent problem when in fact it's quite predictable in the right circumstances.

10. **Understand cause, effect, and relationships.** Just because two things happen at the same time does not mean one caused the other. So, although we just finished saying that you should try to connect the dots in intermittent problems, you should avoid jumping to conclusions about cause/effect relationships. Using the previous example, if the server locks up 30 minutes after a particular application is launched, that's good information, but it does not conclusively tell you that the application is responsible for the lockup. It's something worth investigating, certainly, but don't jump to conclusions without additional evidence.

SOME INDEPENDENT ADVICE

One of your most valuable troubleshooting tools is often a simple second opinion. Sometimes when we have to state our case to another person, he or she can help us see the error in our thinking, the assumptions we're making, or the things we're overlooking. It's a great idea to join a computer group, either in your area or online, to develop a circle of trusted associates to whom you can go for a second opinion. Always trust your own judgment and assessment, but do use others as sounding boards to help you sort out problems. There are also countless technical advice newsgroups, discussion threads, and websites out there, but beware—not all the information you get from these sources is good (you know that, but it never hurts to be reminded). If you find information you think is good, verify that with other trusted sources before implementing a recommended solution. After a while, you'll be able to determine the reputable sources and avoid the less reliable ones.

If you're linked to a site via the Microsoft Web site, for instance, you should have a higher degree of confidence than if you find "George's House of Sure-Fire Computer Fixes" through a search engine. Finally, you should identify a go-to expert in your area that can help you if your system really runs into trouble and fixing it appears to be outside your expertise. You may have developed a relationship with a local firm or expert consultant when you were installing SBS, especially if you were migrating. If not, you might want to take time to talk to local firms, get recommendations, and build that expert list before you run into trouble.

There are many resources available to you if you run into problems, but having a trusted second (third, fourth) opinion can help you verify your information, assumptions, and decisions to help avoid making mistakes.

For troubleshooting tips specific to the SBS, check out the Help and Support files on your server. In the Help contents in the left side of the screen, locate and click "Troubleshooting Windows Small Business Server 2003." Also notice that in the right side of the pane, you can access Support (online), tools, and error and event log messages as well. In the troubleshooting information are detailed instructions for troubleshooting users and groups, client computers, mobile devices, e-mail, monitoring, backup and restore, Internet access, your intranet, shared network resources, remote access, and licensing issues. That's a pretty extensive list, and if that's not enough to keep you out of trouble, you can look on the Microsoft site as well. Also, Microsoft technical support staff are generally quite helpful. Although you have access to the same technical resources they do for the most part, they have something you might not have: experience troubleshooting a variety of problems. They take calls and answer e-mails all day long, and that builds expertise quickly. You might find this is an excellent choice to assist you in identifying and resolving server problems.

SOME INDEPENDENT ADVICE

Many areas on the Microsoft site can be useful for troubleshooting. Some you might know about, others might be new to you. For instance, by now you're probably aware of the Microsoft Small Business Server 2003 site. It's part of the Windows Server 2003 family and can generally be accessed any time there's a link to Windows Server products. The URL for this site (currently) is www.microsoft.com/windowsserver2003/sbs/default.mspx.

There's also the Knowledge Base, which contains thousands of constantly updated technical articles on every topic you can imagine. These articles are sometimes "how-to" articles, but most often they step you through identifying, troubleshooting, and resolving specific problems. These articles can be referenced directly by number, and the entire Knowledge Base (sometimes called the "KB") can be queried as well. If you have a specific error message, enter the text of the message with quotes to get specific results. The KB, along with hints on how to best

use it, can be accessed via http://support.microsoft.com/default.aspx?
scid=fh;EN-US;KBHOWTO.

If you haven't used the KB often, you would benefit from reading
some of the documents on ways to query for best results. Querying is
really an art form, and the more you know about how the search engine
works, the better the results of your query.

In addition to the SBS site and the KB, there's also a whole other
world called TechNet, which is an area some people know nothing
about. TechNet is built from the ground up for IT staff to provide in-
depth technical (rather than user-based) information. You can find a
wide range of articles, tools, discussion groups, and more on every technical topic related to Microsoft, ranging from simple to very complex.
TechNet can be accessed via www.microsoft.com/technet/default.mspx,
and the general support site is located at http://support.microsoft.com.

Tuning and Troubleshooting the SBS Server

Tuning the server is really a process of monitoring and adjusting. We discussed
basic monitoring earlier in this chapter. In this section, we're going to look at specific items you can monitor and what they indicate so that you can use them as
tools for improving server performance over time. Through monitoring these elements, you can tune your system or use the information to troubleshoot problems.

Since the SBS server is tasked with running the server operating system,
managing security, providing network services, and providing key functions such
as e-mail, Internet connectivity, and more, you can imagine that server hardware
gets a good workout. The three elements that have the greatest impact on server
performance are CPU, memory, and disk. Everything the server does touches
one, two, or all three of these components, and if one isn't pulling its weight (or
if something is hogging system resources), the server will slow down, and user
response time will be sluggish. To avoid this, you can monitor these key components, establish baselines, and set alerts telling you when these thresholds are
exceeded. That way, if your CPU, memory, or disk capacity is regularly being
overwhelmed, you can take necessary steps to resolve the issue.

One other note on troubleshooting the server: If you open Help and
Support, you'll see a wealth of self-help information you can use to troubleshoot

specific problems. In the left column, you'll see a link for Troubleshooting Windows Small Business Server, which provides specific step-by-step instructions for numerous issues, including those related to users and groups, client computers, mobile devices, e-mail, monitoring, backup and restore, Internet access, your intranet, shared network resources, remote access, and licensing. Also on the main page of Help and Support are resources for support, tools, and event and event log messages as well as top issues. We've mentioned this before, but it bears repeating because this vast array of resources is the best place to start troubleshooting any issue you run into. If these don't work and you've dug around on the Microsoft Web site, a call or e-mail to Microsoft support or your local expert tech is probably in order.

Monitoring Memory Usage

It's important to understand how your server uses memory under normal circumstances so you can spot bottlenecks in this area.

Paging is the process of temporarily placing information from memory on the disk drive to make room for other information in system memory. The *page file* is where this data is stored on the disk drive. A *page* is a fixed-length block of data. When memory is needed, pages of data are moved to the disk drive. Some paging is normal, especially during bursts of activity, but frequent paging indicates that the system needs more memory. A *page fault* occurs when information needed by a program is not found in memory and must be pulled back in from the disk drive. Page faults slow things down and can indicate memory problems or disk problems.

It's also important to understand that some programs don't manage memory very well. Some use memory and don't release it properly, leading to what's commonly referred to as a *memory leak*. A memory leak shows up as progressively less and less available memory. The symptoms are a progressively slower system, an application that locks up, or a halt condition (when memory and paging files are full).

It's a good idea to check to see that all the system memory is actually available before doing anything else. Although a memory problem usually results in a system halt or "blue screen", checking to make sure all your memory is available is a fast and easy step to take. If you have multiple memory modules in your system, it's possible that one segment is malfunctioning without giving you other indications. Check memory availability in Task Manager (that's just one of several places) on the Performance tab. Memory is displayed in kilobytes, not megabytes or gigabytes, so you'll have to do the conversion and keep in mind that it won't be exact. For instance, 1GB of RAM might be displayed as 1046512. That's fine—just make sure your 1GB doesn't look like 522684.

You can set counters that track various events, and some of these counters will help in tracking down memory-related problems. Details of each counter (and all the other available counters) are outside the scope of this chapter, but Table 15.1 lists the key counters and briefly describes what they track and how they might be used. Remember that the monitoring set up through the Server Management Monitoring and Reporting Wizard will do just fine, so there's no need to go into System Monitor and tweak these settings until (or unless) you become comfortable with what they do, what they indicate, and what you'll do with the information they give you. If you're working with a technical expert, he or she might ask you to configure certain counters to assist in identifying the problem. The expectation is not that you'll go in and work with these counters right away, but we'd be remiss if we didn't mention them, since they can be very helpful in troubleshooting.

Table 15.1 Commonly Used Memory Counters

Counter Name	Description and Use
Memory/Pages/Sec	Displays the number of pages written to or read from disk to resolve hard page faults. If this value is above 20, you should check paging activity more closely. A high value here could indicate a paging problem (vs. an actual memory problem).
Memory/Committed Bytes	Number of bytes of virtual memory committed at any one time. Monitor this along with Memory/Available Bytes over time if you suspect a memory leak.
Memory/Pool Nonpaged Bytes	There are some things (certain critical system data) that cannot be paged out to disk and are therefore *nonpaged*. If this value is high, it means you have a lot of memory being chewed up by things that cannot be moved (paged) out to disk. You might need additional RAM on your server to address this. A high value here could also indicate that an internal system process (kernel mode) has a memory leak (some earlier Windows operating systems had these kinds of problems that seem now to be resolved).

Continued

Table 15.1 Commonly Used Memory Counters

Counter Name	Description and Use
Memory/Available Bytes	When available memory runs low, the system borrows it from other processes and applications that aren't using their full allocation. This can result in paging and slower performance. If you see this value decreasing and paging increasing, you might need more server memory.
Paging File/% Usage (all instance)	If you suspect that the paging file could be the cause of your slowdown, review this along with Memory/Available Bytes and Memory/Pages/Sec. The acceptable threshold for this value is 99%. The paging file is named *Pagefile.sys* and can be increased if this counter hits 100%.
Physical Disk/% Disk Time *and* Physical Disk//Avg. Disk Queue Length	These two values can indicate a need for more RAM on the system. They can be used in conjunction with Memory/Pages/Sec to determine if the problem is likely a lack of memory.
Physical Disk/Avg. Disk Sec/Transfer	This counter displays the average disk transfer in seconds. To determine if there's excessive paging going on (an indicator that you need to add memory to your server), multiply this value times the Memory/Pages/Sec. If the result is >0.1, paging is taking up more than 10% of the disk drive's access time (monitor this over time), so you might need more memory.
Server/Bytes Total/Sec	This counter monitors the number of bytes per second sent to and from the network. This can be a good indicator of how busy the server is. If this value creeps up and remains high over time, you might need to add memory or processing power to your server or move applications to other servers (other than those bundled with the SBS server, which must reside on the SBS server).

With these counters, we've only just brushed the surface of a very deep topic. However, you can begin looking at these counters and establishing baselines for your server when you're not in troubleshooting mode. These counters can be added in a number of ways in several places. Perhaps the easiest is to access the Performance management console (**Start | Administrative Tools | Performance**), select **System Monitor** in the left pane, then right-click in the right pane and select **Add Counters**. The **Add Counters** dialog will be displayed, and you can select from a number of options. Figure 15.7 shows how to add a physical disk counter.

Figure 15.7 Adding a Counter in System Monitor

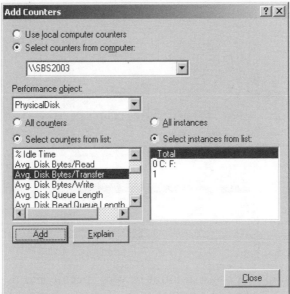

When you've selected the counter you want, you can click **Explain** to learn more about it or click **Add**, which will immediately add the counter (there's no confirmation dialog). If you add something you don't want, locate it in the bottom of the right screen, right-click, choose **Properties**, then choose **Remove**. The System Monitor screen after adding the counter is shown in Figure 15.8.

Figure 15.8 System Monitor with Added Counter

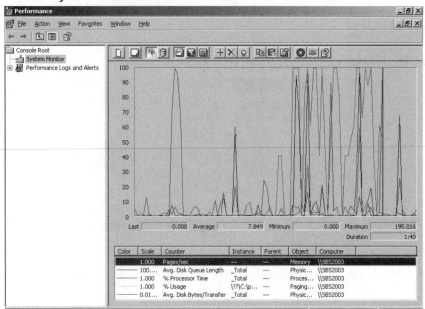

Also keep in mind that a vast amount of very specific and useful performance data is included by default in the SBS Performance Report available in **Server Management | Standard Management | Monitoring and Reporting**. This should always be your first stop for checking server status. Don't get wrapped around the axle with System Monitor, Health Monitor, counters, and all those tools. These are more advanced tools that you may or may not choose to explore right away.

Monitoring Processor Activity

Several processor activity counters might also be useful to you at some point. Again, we'll list them and give some general guidelines, but start with Performance Report in SBS before jumping into these counters. Table 15.2 describes some of the more commonly used counters for process activity.

Sometimes the solution to a problem is as simple as moving an application or service to another server. For instance, if you installed one or more printers on your server and users are connecting to these printers through the SBS server, you might want to create a new print server on a computer other than your SBS server. This will reduce the load on the SBS computer. You might find at some point that usage is simply overwhelming the computer's CPU and it could be time to upgrade your hardware.

Table 15.2 Processor Activity Counters

Counter Name	Description and Use
System/Processor Queue Length (all instances)	Sustained queue length of more than 10 items could indicate that your system processor (CPU) is the cause of the bottleneck.
Server Work Queues/ Queue Length	A queue length greater than four over a sustained period of time could indicate that your CPU is the holdup.
Processor/% Processor Time (all instances)	Use this counter to determine if the processor is busy more than 85% of the time over a period of time. If so, you might need a faster processor.

Monitoring Disk Activity

The last major area we'll cover is disk activity. Many more counters are available, but if you learn about memory, CPU, and disk, you'll be hitting the high percentage counters. Table 15.3 describes some of the more useful disk activity counters and what they might indicate.

Table 15.3 Disk Activity Counters

Counter Name	Description and Use
Physical Disk/% Disk Time	Indicates how busy the server's disk drives are. If the % rises steadily over time or remains above 90% for a sustained period, you need more disk capacity. If you're using RAID disks, though, you could see readings above 100% that are still okay; refer to your RAID documentation before taking action.
Physical Disk/Current Disk Queue Length (all instances)	Again, if you have RAID, the rules are different. If you don't have RAID, this queue should not exceed 1.5 or 2 times (over a sustained period) the number of drives you have in your system. If so, you might need more or faster disks.

Continued

Table 15.3 Disk Activity Counters

Counter Name	Description and Use
Physical Disk/Avg. Disk Sec/Transfer	If this number is high over time, it might indicate that the disk drive has a lot of errors and it's taking the disk controller longer than it should to actually transfer the data. A value of 0.3 seconds or more could indicate a problem.

Of course, you should perform standard disk management tasks including error checking and defragmenting from time to time to check the basic health of your drives.

One More Time

In this chapter, we began by looking at the tools provided in SBS for monitoring, reporting, and alerting you to problems. We also briefly looked at two advanced tools, System Monitor and Health Monitor. We discussed the basics of troubleshooting and defined 10 steps you can take to increase your troubleshooting skills. You learned a bit about counters, how they're used, and how they might be helpful in tuning and troubleshooting your server. Though these are more advanced tools that you should use only after you've become proficient at the basic tools, it's good to know they exist.

- ☑ Begin by configuring monitoring by running the Monitoring Configuration Wizard, accessible via **Server Management | Standard Management | Monitoring and Reporting.**

- ☑ After configuring Monitoring and Reporting, view the Server Performance Report and Server Usage Report regularly.

- ☑ If you configured alerts in the Monitoring Configuration Wizard, you'll be alerted via e-mail when thresholds are met or exceeded. Review these alerts and take action as needed.

- ☑ The default settings for alerts is fine to begin with. Modify these default settings and thresholds by accessing the Services, Performance Counters, Event Log Errors, and E-mail Address tabs in the Alert Notifications dialog, accessed in Monitoring and Reporting (click the link **Change Alert Notifications**).

☑ You can view the status of services, but use caution in this section. Don't disable or stop a service if you aren't absolutely sure what the impact will be.

☑ Event logs should be reviewed regularly. They give you a good snapshot of what's been going on in your system and can be used to spot problems early, especially various network attacks. In some cases, the events you've chosen to audit (discussed elsewhere in this book) will be logged here if they occur. In other cases, events are generated by the operating system and can notify you of an existing or potential problems.

☑ Task Manager, accessed in Monitoring and Reporting as well as by pressing **Ctrl + Alt + Del**, can give you a good quick snapshot of applications, processes, memory, network activity, and CPU usage. Applications that are "Not Responding" can be terminated on the Application tab.

☑ Two advanced tools you should be aware of are System Monitor and Health Monitor. Both can be used to monitor, check, and troubleshoot system status and health. Counters can be added to monitor very specific events. A complete discussion of this topic is outside the scope of this book.

☑ In troubleshooting anything, you can take a number of common steps to increase your chances of success. These 10 steps will help you take a systematic and logical approach to solving problems.

☑ There are three key areas on the Microsoft website you should be familiar with: SBS Home, the Knowledge Base, and TechNet. These three areas will provide you with a wealth of troubleshooting tips, tricks, how-to articles, and step-by-step problem resolution.

☑ Develop a strong network of technical associates to whom you can go for a second opinion. Often a second opinion helps you avoid mistakes or confirms your decisions. Use caution with online resources, however, since some are more reliable than others. You can contact Microsoft technical support via phone or email or you can work with a local technical expert to resolve more difficult problems.

☑ Many server problems begin with memory, CPU, and disk usage. Regularly reviewing your Server Performance Report and Server Usage Report in SBS Server Management will help you establish a baseline of normal settings. Comparing these reports over time will help you spot trends.

Chapter 16

Premium Edition Features

- Internet Security and Acceleration (ISA) Server 2000

- SQL Server 2000

- FrontPage 2003

The End Result

By the end of this chapter, you'll have an understanding of the Premium Edition features in Windows Small Business Server (SBS) 2003. You'll understand how they're used and how to install and configure these advanced components of SBS. You'll understand ISA Server and SQL Server. FrontPage 2003 is the last Premium Edition feature, and we'll discuss how to use this application to create and edit websites, including the default sites used in SBS. By the end of this chapter, you'll also have several resources you can use to learn more about these features.

Internet Security and Acceleration (ISA) Server 2000

Many companies opt to use an external firewall devices of some sort rather than a firewall on the server itself. By separating the firewall and server functions, you can create a more secure environment. However, many small companies opt to use the firewall included with SBS. It's a trade-off among cost, expertise, and security. Many smaller companies are at less risk than well-known companies that are obvious targets of hackers, but there is a risk just being connected to the Internet. Ultimately, the decision is yours, and there are pros and cons to both configurations.

The firewall component in the Standard SBS edition does a good job, and the firewall provided in the Premium Edition via Internet Security and Acceleration (ISA) Server 2000 is even better. If you opt to use an internal firewall and you purchased the SBS Premium Edition, you should strongly consider using the ISA firewall rather than the standard SBS firewall. It takes a bit more configuration than the standard SBS firewall, but it also provides much more security. A note about installing ISA (and SQL Server, for that matter) is appropriate at this point. These applications are typically installed on dedicated machines. In the SBS world, they must be installed on the server. Both are rather hefty applications that can bog your server down quickly. Before installing either ISA or SQL Server, make sure your server hardware is up to the task. Using both of these will definitely hammer your server, so make sure your sever has a super fast processor (or two) and plenty of RAM (2GB or more).

The ISA Server 2000 is one of two additional server applications included with SBS Premium Edition (the other is SQL Server, which we'll discuss later in this chapter). ISA Server provides two primary functions. As an enterprise-strength firewall, it provides more advanced options and better security than does the default SBS firewall. It uses network address translation and packet filtering to provide strong security. It also provides Web caching. *Caching* is the process of temporarily storing information. The ISA Server caches information from frequently accessed websites and stores it on the ISA server. When users request information from one of these sites, the information is provided from the ISA Server's cache. This speeds up the response for the end users. During periods of lower activity, the ISA Server will go out to these frequently accessed sites, refresh the data, and cache it again to keep the information up to date. This process is called *active caching*. The ISA Server can also provide *reverse caching*, assisting Web servers in providing information from a corporate Web site to Internet clients.

ISA Server uses three basic techniques to provide security. First, it relies on the use of *network address translation* (NAT), discussed earlier in this book. NAT provides address translation so that the internal network addresses are protected from the Internet. Second, ISA provides *packet filtering*. Packet filtering is the process of capturing packets that try to pass through the firewall (into or out of the network) and examining them. If they meet certain criteria, they can pass through. If they do not meet the criteria, they are discarded. Default packet filtering is enabled when you configure your settings with the E-mail and Internet Connection Wizard. Other more advanced packet filtering is done through the ISA Management interface and is not covered in this book. Finally, the ISA Server provides caching, the acceleration component of ISA.

There are several important things to know about ISA Server (well, a lot more than several, but these next four are critical) *before* you install it. First, once you install it, remote users may not be able to access your SharePoint Web site (http://companyweb) without some reconfiguration on your part. If users are accessing the site from behind an ISA Server, a second part of the reconfiguration is required. While neither step is complex, it requires going step by step through the reconfiguration to restore these services. That's good to know before you install ISA. It's possible that patches, updates, or fixes will be released to address this issue, so check out connectivity before you "fix" something that's not broken.

You may also experience problems with e-mail getting through to your Exchange Server since that, too, is sitting "behind" the firewall. If you experience e-mail problems, you'll need to look up the exact issue you're having on the Microsoft support site. Applications, such as Outlook Web Access, configured through the E-mail and Internet Connection Wizard will be configured properly in ISA. Though Outlook may be properly configured with ISA, it won't matter if your Exchange Server can't send and recieve e-mail.

Another important thing to know is that clients must have the ISA Firewall client installed. The process of installing ISA will place a copy of the Firewall client software on the server, and you must then add that to client computers. We'll talk about that process in just a moment, but it's another important step to know about before you install ISA. This firewall client only works on Windows-based clients. For alternate clients, look up instructions for using the SecureNAT client on the Microsoft ISA site. Also note that you should *not install* the Firewall client on the ISA Server itself. If you need direct Internet connectivity from the computer running ISA Server (meaning that you're sitting at the SBS computer), you may need to take additional steps; you can find instructions on the Microsoft site or on the Internet—those by Dr. Thomas Shinder are reliable and accurate, others might or might not be reliable.

If you upgraded from Windows Small Business Server 2000 and had previously installed ISA Server 2000, you do not need to (nor should you) install ISA Server again.

One final note: As with other components of SBS, ISA Server 2000 cannot be installed on a computer other than the SBS Server. However, some companies elect to get a standalone version of ISA Server (ISA Server 2004 is now available) and run that on a separate computer. You can use ISA when it's installed on another server; you just can't install the version of ISA that comes with SBS Server on a different machine. If server performance is an issue, an stand-alone version of ISA may be a viable option for your firm.

If all these caveats haven't scared you off, then you're probably ready to proceed. Just make sure you've done a good, full backup before you start. The ISA Server firewall is a very secure firewall, but with that security comes a fair level of complexity. If everything works on your SBS server after installing ISA Server, you're good to go. If it doesn't, it could take some more advanced technical skills to resolve the issues. Keep this in mind as you evaluate your options.

SOME INDEPENDENT ADVICE

For more information on reconfiguring your settings to enable access to SharePoint Services after installing ISA Server, read the Knowledge Base article on how to reconfigure things if remote clients need to access the SharePoint site from behind an ISA Server. The error message is "Blank Page or Page Cannot be Displayed When You View SSL Sites Through ISA

Server," and the Knowledge Base article is 283284, www.microsoft.com/?id=283284. The steps for re-establishing connectivity to your SharePoint site through Remote Web Workplace are included in this chapter. Be prepared to fix these issues, but also remember that there are patches, updates, and fixes coming out all the time that might address them, so you might not have to deal with them. That's another good reason to keep your system software up to date.

Installing ISA

Here's how the ISA installation works. First, ISA Server setup assumes that you have two network interface cards (NICs) in your SBS server—one to your internal network and one to the Internet (via your ISP). Once you begin installation, you'll be prompted to enter your private IP addressing scheme, since ISA uses NAT (discussed earlier in the book). After configuring NAT and completing installation, ISA will launch the E-mail and Internet Connection Wizard. You're probably familiar with this wizard, since we stepped through it in Chapter 3. If you step through the wizard this time and make your selections, ISA will configure itself properly. For instance, ISA will figure out what to block and what to allow based on the Web access choices you make within the wizard. So, initial configuration of ISA is automatic and relatively painless. If you want to modify what can and cannot come through the firewall, you can relaunch the E-mail and Internet Connection Wizard and make changes from within that interface. That way, ISA Server configuration will be handled by the system based on your choices in the wizard. (Remember the caveats from earlier in this chapter, though: You could lose remote access capabilities to your SharePoint Web site, and you might lose Internet connectivity to your Exchange Server as well.)

To use ISA Server, you must install this feature from the Premium DVD or CD-ROM (it's not automatically installed when you install SBS). Choose a time when users are not on the system. Make sure you close all applications, including virus protection, and disconnect the computer from the Internet before starting Setup. Select **Install Internet Security and Acceleration Server 2000** from the Welcome screen. You can also access installation instructions for ISA Server, SQL Server, and FrontPage 2003 on the Premium Edition DVD or CD-ROM. Browse the disk and locate the file *premiuminstallationsteps.htm*. This file can also be accessed once you've launched the Setup Wizard on the main screen by clicking **How to Install**. You might want to read this information before installing any of the three Premium applications.

When installing ISA, you have three options. You can install just the firewall functionality, you can install just the cache mode functionality, or you can install both using integrated mode. If your server is going to act as the firewall, you should use the ISA firewall. If you have an external, third-party firewall, you could use the cache mode only. For this example, we've selected the integrated mode. Once you've made your choice, ISA will then take a stroll through your system and stop any services it needs to stop to properly install ISA. You might get one or more messages; take note of the message contents. Click **OK** to continue (or **Help** for more information) in the message dialogs that are presented.

You'll be prompted to set up a cache on one or more disk drives. This is where ISA Server will store content from frequently accessed websites. You can accept the default values for both drive (although if you have two or more drives, you should select a drive *other than* the C: drive) and maximum cache size (100MB). Click **OK** to continue.

The next screen prompts you to enter the IP address ranges that span the internal network address space. If you're using private addressing for your network, as recommended in Chapters 2, 3, and 9, this range probably begins with 192.168.X.Y. You can construct a table (essentially, use internal information to answer this question for you) by clicking the **Construct Table** button. Two check boxes are available: *Add the following private ranges: 10.x.x.x., 192.168.x.x., 172.16.x..x-172.31.x.x and 169.254.x.x.* and *Add address ranges based on the Windows 2000 Routing Table.* In this example, we chose the second option and selected the NIC that is attached to the internal network (which also displays the internal addresses), as shown in Figure 16.1.

Figure 16.1 Constructing a Local Address Table

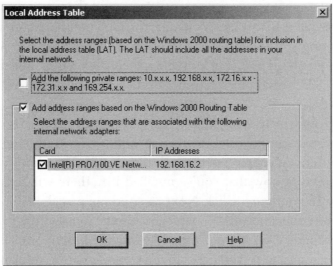

Click **OK** twice (the second OK is to configure a message stating that if your internal information is wrong, so too is your LAT). You should now be back to the IP address range dialog, which now is populated with your internal IP ranges, as shown in Figure 16.2. If you have ranges that were not automatically populated, you can enter them here. Click **OK** to continue.

Figure 16.2 Internal Address Ranges

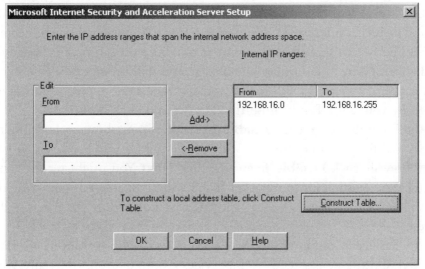

You might briefly see a message about Setup stopping services, then it will continue with the usual types of messages. Setup will then start or restart services it stopped (pretty nice that it cleans up after itself). The final Setup dialog is a message prompting you to launch the ISA Server Getting Started Wizard; this is a good idea, so go ahead and check the box, then click **OK**. After that, you'll get a message that ISA Setup completed successfully, and you have to click **OK** to close that dialog.

Next, the Configure E-mail and Internet Connection Wizard will launch. ISA Getting Started window will be open as well (underneath) and you can return to that after you've stepped through this wizard. This should look pretty familiar to you except now that you've installed ISA, there will be additional options for you to configure. Click **Next** to continue past the Welcome screen.

Choose your connection type, then click **Next**. Some settings might require you to re-enter them, even if you formerly configured them. You should have this information available to you, so grab your configuration information so that you can complete this wizard.

Depending on the connection type you selected, your options will differ. If you chose Broadband, select how you connect to your ISP using the options in the drop-down box (for more information on these options, see Chapter 3). Click **Next** to continue.

In the Network Connection screen, select whether your Internet connection is using DCHP or an assigned, static IP address. If using an assigned address, enter the IP configuration information (IP address, subnet mask, default gateway) here, then click **Next**. If your system has two NICs installed, you'll be prompted to identify which is connected to the internal network and which is connected to your ISP. The system should easily figure it out, but you can make changes here if needed. Click **Next** to continue. The next screen will prompt you to enter the default gateway, preferred DNS server, and alternate DNS server (information provided by your ISP). Enter those IP addresses and click **Next**.

In the Firewall dialog, click **Enable firewall**. If you chose cached mode for your ISA installation and do not want to enable the firewall because you have an external firewall, click **Disable firewall**. Click **Next**. You might receive a message indicating existing custom packet filters will be disabled. If you created any custom filters, this applies to you. Click **OK** to acknowledge the message if it's displayed.

In the Services Configuration dialog, select services you want to enable, then click **Next**. On the next screen, Web Services Configuration, select any Web services you want to make accessible through your firewall, and click **Next**. The next screen, Web Server Certificate, prompts you to either create a new Web server certificate if you're going to use Secure Sockets Layer (SSL) or to point the server to a third-party certificate. If you're not sure, you can use the server certificate to start with. Select the appropriate option, and click **Next**.

The next screen begins the configuration of Internet e-mail, which is probably already set up. If so, select **Do not change Internet e-mail configuration;** otherwise, select **Enable Internet e-mail** or **Disable Internet e-mail**. If you select the Enable option, you'll have to step through all the e-mail configuration options (see Chapter 3 for details). Click **Next** after making your selection. The final screen is the summary page that shows you the selections you've made. Click **Finish** to implement these settings. The wizard will configure the settings, including network, firewall, secure Web site, and e-mail configuration settings. When the process is complete, click the **Close** button.

Configuring ISA

If you recall, at the end of our ISA setup we selected an option to open the Getting Started Wizard. If you selected that option, you should have the ISA console open on your server. If not, click **Start | All Programs | Microsoft ISA Server | ISA Management**. If you open it in this manner, you can access the Getting Started Wizard by clicking **Internet Security and Acceleration Wizard** in the left pane and selecting the **Getting Started Wizard** in the right pane. The Getting Started Wizard (GSW) has its own navigation in the bottom of the right pane, as shown in Figure 16.3. Using this navigation, you can step through the GSW options shown in the middle of your screen (the left side of the right pane). The GSW is used not only to learn about various options (click **Help** on any screen) but to assist in configuring ISA. If you're unfamiliar with ISA, this is absolutely the best way to get your feet wet. If you're familiar with ISA, you can navigate around ISA using the left navigation pane.

For more detailed instructions on configuring and using ISA, consult the Help files within the ISA Management console or, as always, the Microsoft website at www.microsoft.com/isaserver. Remember that some of the information in both in the Help files and online might not apply to you since your SBS server has a few restrictions that a full Windows Server 2003 installation does not.

Figure 16.3 ISA Getting Started Wizard

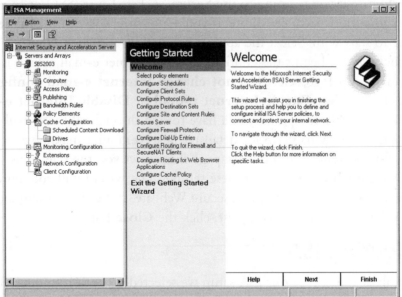

Installing the ISA Firewall Client

Once you've installed and configured ISA Server, you'll need to install the ISA Firewall client on client computers. Remember, even though the firewall client is placed on the SBS server, it should not be *installed* on the SBS server. Installing it on client computers is relatively easy, and you can use the steps listed here:

1. Browse to the **C:\Program Files\Microsoft\ISA Server\Clients** folder (assuming your Program Files folder is on your C: drive).

2. Right-click the **Clients** folder, and select **Sharing and Security** from the shortcut menu. Select the **Security** tab.

3. Click **Add** to add users. In the Select Users, Computers, or Groups dialog that opens, type **Domain Users**, click **Check Names**, then click **OK**. Click **OK** again to close the Properties dialog.

4. Next, go to **Server Management | Standard Management | Client Computers**. Click **Assign Applications to Client Computers**. This will launch the Assign Applications Wizard. Click **Next**.

5. In the center of the dialog, click **Add All** to add all client computers. Click **Next**. Remove any client computers that are not running Windows XP or Windows 2000 by selecting them in the right pane and clicking **Remove**. You'll have to browse to the Setup.exe file on the SBS server to install the client software for client comuters running older versions of Windows.

6. In the next dialog, Client Applications, click **Edit Applications**. This will launch the Set Up Client Applications Wizard. Click **Next**.

7. In the Available applications dialog, click **Add**.

8. In the Application Information dialog, type a descriptive name such as **ISA Server Firewall Client**. In the *Location of setup executable...* box, type "*<servername>*\mspclnt\setup.exe", where *<servername>* is the name of your SBS Server. The entire string should be in quotation marks. Then click **OK**.

9. You might receive a warning message. Click **Yes**. If you forgot to use quotation marks, click the **Edit** button to return to the Application Information dialog to make changes. Otherwise, click **Next**.

10. Click **Finish** to close the Set Up Client Applications Wizard.

11. In the open dialog in the Assign Applications Wizard, you should now see ISA Server Firewall client (or whatever name you gave it) and it should be selected. If it's not selected, select it now. Click **Next**.

12. In the Mobile Client and Offline Use page, you can add Connection Manager and/or ActiveSync if you haven't done so in the past. If you

have, don't add them again (you'll end up with multiple installations on the client computers —not tragic but unnecessary). Click **Next**.

13. Review the Summary page, and click **Finish** to implement this change.

14. You'll receive a notice stating, "To finish setting up the client computer(s), including network configuration and application deployment and configuration, go to the client computer(s), start Internet Explorer, and type http://SBS2003/ConnectComputer in the Address bar." Click **OK**.

15. Since we're assuming that computers have already been configured and connected to the network, you most likely won't need to perform the actions identified in Step 14. Instead, the next time users log on, they'll see a shortcut placed on their desktops to install the Firewall client. Double-clicking the shortcut will install the Firewall client. Instruct your users (typically done via email) that they should double-click the icon on their desktop to install the firewall. Note that this automated setup only works on client computers running Windows 2000 and Windows XP. Users of older operating systems will need to connect to the shared installation point (see Step 1) and run setup.exe.

Restoring Remote Access to SharePoint Web Site

We mentioned earlier that installing ISA Server could disrupt remote access to your corporate SharePoint site. Although this indicates ISA is doing its job, it will require some reconfiguration on your part. The steps are included in this section, but it's also recommended that you query the exact symptoms you're experiencing on the Microsoft website to see if there are additional tips, tricks, patches, or updates that address this issue. At the risk of stating the obvious, check to see if remote access users can access the SharePoint site through Remote Web Workplace *before* you go monkeying around with these settings. It's entirely possible that you won't run into this issue, and these instructions could become moot—don't fix something that's not broken.

WARNING

The following steps include editing the Registry. Incorrect editing or changes in the Registry can completely disable your system. When you make changes to the Registry, they are effective immediately. You will *not* be prompted to save or reject changes when you exit out of the Registry. There is *no* **Edit | Undo** function. Before making any changes to the Registry, perform a full backup on your system. Although the changes to the Registry in the next section are few, one false move and it could be all over, so beware. Furthermore, if you find terminology in this section that you don't understand, you can query the Help files in ISA Management. You also might want to wait to perform this step until after you've finished reading the ISA Server Getting Started information (mentioned earlier).

Use the following steps to restore connectivity to your SharePoint Web site via Remote Web Workplace:

1. Create a new protocol definition for Inbound TCP/444. In **ISA Management | Policy Elements | Protocol Definitions,** click the **Create a Protocol Definition** icon in the right pane and follow the on-screen instructions. Call this protocol definition **Companyweb Inbound**. The port number is **444**, the protocol type is **TCP**, and the direction is **Inbound**. In the Secondary Connections dialog, keep the default of **No**.

2. Create a server publishing rule to publish the new protocol by opening **Publishing | Server Publishing Rules** in the ISA Management console.

3. Click **Publish A Server** in the details pane to open the New Server Publishing Rule Wizard. In the name box, enter **Publish Companyweb**, then click **Next**.

4. In the Address Mapping dialog, enter the internal and external IP addresses of your Windows Small Business Server, then click **Next**.

5. On the Protocol Settings page, select **Companyweb Inbound** (or whatever you named it) from the drop-down box. Click **Next**.

6. On the Client Type page, select **Any Request**. Click **Next**.

7. Review the selection in the Summary page, then click **Back** to make changes or **Finish** to complete this task. The results appear as shown in Figure 16.4.

Figure 16.4 Publish Companyweb Server in ISA Management

8. Next, open the **Internet Information Services Manager** from **Start | Administrative Tools | Internet Information Services (IIS) Manager**.

9. In the Internet Services Manger console, open **Web Sites** in the left pane, then select **companyweb**. Right-click **companyweb** and select **Properties** from the shortcut menu. Companyweb Properties is shown in Figure 16.5.

Figure 16.5 Companyweb Properties

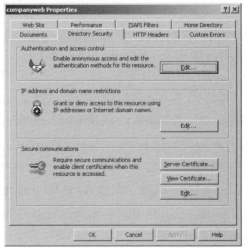

10. In the Properties dialog, click the **Directory Security** tab, then click **Server Certificate** to open the IIS Certificate Wizard. Click **Next** in the Welcome screen.

11. In the Server Certificate dialog, click **Assign An Existing Certificate**, then click **Next**. If Assign An Existing Certificate is not an option, choose **Replace the current certificate,** then click **Next**.

12. In the Available Certificates dialog, select the certificate for your fully qualified domain name (FQDN) from the list, then click **Next**. This step is shown in Figure 16.6.

Figure 16.6 Certificate for Fully Qualified Domain Name

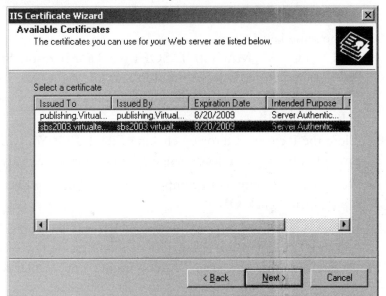

13. If the **SSL Port** dialog appears, type **444** in the SSL Port box, then click **Next**. You can verify this setting in the **Properties** of companyweb on the **Web Site** tab.

14. Click **Next** again, and click **Finish** to complete this task.

15. Next, you'll need to edit the Registry. *If you didn't read the caution at the beginning of these steps, please go read it now.* If you've read it and you're ready to go, pay close attention to the following steps. Accuracy is key here.

16. Click **Start | Run**, and in the Open box, type in **regedit**, then click **OK**.

17. Locate (by expanding the tree in the left pane) **HKEY_LOCAL_MACHINE\SOFTWARE\Microsoft\SmallBusinessServer\RemoteUserPortal\KWLinks**. In the right pane, locate the name **STS**. Double-click to open the Value dialog. Notice the current Value data is 0. Replace the 0 with a 1, then click **OK**.

18. Next, locate and click the **AdminLinks** just above KWLinks in the left navigation pane. The full navigation path is HKEY_LOCAL_MACHINE\SOFTWARE\Microsoft\SmallBusinessServer\RemoteUserPortal\AdminLinks. In the right pane, locate the name **STS** and double-click it to change the value data from 0 to 1, then click **OK**.

19. In the same key, HKEY_LOCAL_MACHINE\SOFTWARE\Microsoft\SmallBusinessServer\RemoteUserPortal\AdminLinks, in the right pane locate the **Help Desk** name. Double-click it and change the value data from 0 to 1, then click **OK**.

20. Close the Registry Editor by clicking **File | Exit**. You will not be prompted to save or reject changes; the changes are already made.

21. Next, open a Command Prompt window by clicking **Start | Run** and typing **cmd**. Click **OK**.

22. In the command prompt window, type **iisreset** then press **Enter**. This will stop and restart the IIS service. It might take a few seconds, so be patient. You'll see a message, "Attempting to stop....Internet services successfully stopped. Attempting to start....Internet services successfully restarted." Type **Exit** to close the command prompt window.

23. In the Server Management console, locate **Advanced Management | Computer Management (local) | Services and Applications | Services**. In the right pane, locate **Microsoft ISA Server Control**. Right-click Microsoft ISA Server Control and select **Restart** from the shortcut menu.

Hopefully you survived this procedure and your remote access users can now get to SharePoint Serivces via the Remote Web Workplace. If you have clients behind an ISA firewall that need to access the company web, you might also need to do some additional configuration. These steps can be found in the Microsoft Knowledge Base article 283284 online.

There's a lot more to know about ISA Server, but the information included here should give you a running start. Be sure to read the Getting Started information and check regularly for updates.

SQL Server 2000

SQL Server 2000 is the second server application available only in the Premium Edition of Windows Small Business Server 2003. It is also installed from the Premium DVD or CD-ROM. SQL (typically pronounced "sequel") stands for the Structured Query Language used to work with databases. SQL Server is an enterprise database application and has a powerful set of features. If you're familiar with a database program such as Microsoft Access, you can think of SQL Server as Access on steroids (which is not a banned substance in the software application arena). Along with the extra strength comes extra server load. We mentioned this in the ISA section but it bears repeating (especially if you're not installing ISA Server) that the installation of ISA and/or SQL Server on your SBS server could slow things down dramatically. These two applications are often installed on other computers when used outside of the SBS environment. When bundled with SBS, these two applications cannot be installed on a computer other than the SBS server, but you have to make sure your server has the muscle to handle either or both of these applications. Make sure you have a lightning-fast processor (or two) and plenty of RAM (2 to 4 GB should do it).

As with ISA Server 2000 installation, there are a few things to note before you install SQL Server. If you choose to install SQL Server, you must also install the Service Pack 3a, included on the Premium disk. This service pack addresses a serious security problem, including protection against the Slammer worm. Read the information in the *premiuminstallsteps.htm* file on the Premium DVD or CD-ROM for more information. This file can be accessed on the Welcome screen of the Setup Wizard by clicking **How to Install**. In addition, the release notes are located on the Premium disk under SQL2000\Readme.txt. Read this file before installing. The release notes on Service Pack 3a are located on the Premium disk under SQL2000_SP3\SP3readme.txt.

We'll step through installing SQL Server and the service pack in this section. As with ISA Server, we won't cover many of the features of SQL Server.

Discussion of this server application could take up one or two volumes. There are many excellent books and resources on SQL Server, and if you like working with databases, you should definitely read up this product. It provides powerful database capabilities to your organization and can be used as the underlying engine for an e-commerce site, for internal applications such as warehousing or scientific data collection and analysis, and much more. The uses are almost limitless, but it takes a lot of know-how to put SQL Server to good use.

Installing SQL Server

Use the following steps to install SQL Server on your SBS server. As with other applications bundled with SBS, you must install SQL Server on the SBS server, but there's no rule that says you have to install it on the C: drive. If you have multiple drives, install SQL Server on another drive to free up your C: drive for other system data, if possible. Also keep in mind that even though this application is being installed on your SBS server, it is the same version of SQL Server you'd use on any other server. As such, some of the options and information in the Help files might not apply directly. For instance, when installing, you'll have the option of installing on the local computer or a remote computer. However, SBS setup requires that you install SQL on the local computer. Choosing unsupported options will cause the installation to halt, fail, or not complete successfully. You should be logged on using an account with Domain Administrator privileges (as is the case with all installations you perform on the server). Now use the following steps to install SQL Server:

1. Insert the Premium DVD or CD-ROM disk into the drive, and **autoplay** should start the Setup wizard. If it doesn't, browse the disk, locate the **setup.exe** file, and double-click it.

2. On the main screen, click **Install Microsoft SQL Server 2000**. You might receive a warning that SQL Server 2000 SP2 and below are not supported by this version of Windows. Click **Continue**. We'll install SP3a afterward and that will take care of this issue.

3. On the Welcome screen of the SQL Server 2000 setup, click **Next**.

4. By default, **Local Computer** is selected. Accept this default and click **Next**.

5. In the Installation Selection dialog, select the option you want from among the three presented. You can click each of the options to read a

brief description of what each does. We'll assume you just want to install SQL Server, so accept the default option (**Create a new...**) and click **Next**.

6. On the User Information screen, enter a name and company, then click **Next**.

7. Click **Yes** to accept the End User License Agreement (EULA) displayed.

8. The next screen prompts you to enter your CD key. Locate the yellow sticker on the back of the SBS software and enter that key now. Note that there are different keys for the Standard and Premium software. The key requested is the key on Case 1. If you get a message stating that the system was unable to validate the key, try the other key. Click **Next**.

9. In the Installation Definition screen, choose the desired option from among these three choices: *Client Tools Only, Server and Client Tools*, or *Connectivity Only*. By clicking each option, you can read a brief description of what it does. Select your choice (we'll select **Server and Client Tools**), then click **Next**.

10. In the Instance Name screen, leave **Default** checked and click **Next**.

11. In the Setup Type screen, you can choose *Typical, Minimum*, or *Custom* installation. **Typical** is the default, which we'll use. You can also set the **Destination Folder** here and you should point these to a drive other than your C: drive to offload some of the work to another drive. Click the **Browse** button for both Program Files location and Data Files location. If desired, you can install the Program Files on the C: drive (to keep all your Program Files on one drive) and point the Data Files to another drive. Click **Next**.

12. In the Services Accounts dialog, accept the default **Use the same account for each service. Autostart SQL Server Service.** In the Service Settings section, accept the default Domain User account (or enter the desired account with Administrative privileges), enter the account password, verify the domain, and click **Next**.

13. In the Authentication Mode dialog, accept the default **Windows Authentication Mode**. The Mixed Mode is provided for backward compatibility and is less secure and is therefore not recommended. Click **Next**.

14. The Start Copying Files dialog will let you know Setup is ready to start copying files. You may be prompted for licensing mode information before the installation will proceed. If you want to make changes to the preceding configuration information, click **Back**; otherwise, click **Next**. Setup will complete in a few minutes. Click **Close** to close the Setup wizard.

15. Next, you'll need to install Service Pack 3a. Open the Premium disk again, double-click the **Setup.exe** file, and select **Install SQL Server 2000 Service Pack 3a** from the options. Click **Next** in the Welcome screen. Click **Yes** in the End User License Agreement screen.

16. In the Instance Name, accept **Default** and click **Next**.

17. In the Connect to Server dialog, **Windows Authentication** will be selected by default since we selected this option earlier. If you chose Mixed Mode, you can select *SQL Server system administrator* and enter the system administrator (sa) password. Otherwise, click **Next**.

18. In the next screen, you'll be prompted to enter an *sa password* even if you're using Windows authentication. Enter a strong password (and make a note of it, then store it in a safe place) and enter it a second time to confirm it, then click **OK**.

19. The next screen deals with backward compatibility. Click **Continue**.

20. The Error Reporting screen gives you the opportunity to elect to send fatal error reports (should they occur in the future) to Microsoft for analysis. If you want to do this, click the check box; if not, leave the checkbox cleared. Click **OK**.

21. Setup will gather information and you'll again get the Start Copying Files dialog (see step 14). Click **Next**. Various components will be set up. When the process is complete, you'll be prompted to back up your databases and restart the computer.

SQL Server is not integrated into the SBS server management console, so you'll have to work with SQL Server through its own management console. This console can be opened via **Start | All Programs | SQL Server | Enterprise Manager**. For more information on SQL Server, refer to the SQL Server Books Online, accessed from **Start | All Programs | SQL Server | Books Online**, shown in Figure 16.7, or by clicking the question-mark icon on the menu from within Microsoft SQL Server Enterprise Manager. This is a great place to start to read up on SQL Server, but keep in mind that some options might not be viable or available for SBS.

Figure 16.7 SQL Books Online

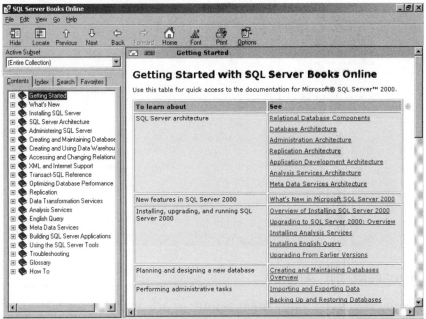

Backing Up SQL Server Databases

Backing up your SQL Server databases should be part of your regular backup routine, and backup, restore, and disaster recovery procedures should include (or be updated to include) your SQL Server data. Recovering from a lost or corrupted database without good backups is virtually impossible, and chances are that if you're using SQL Server, you really *need* those databases to run your business. If you are using a third-party backup utility, you may need to purchase a SQL Server backup option separately. Check your backup software to see if it includes this capability or if you can purchase it as an add-on. You can access the native backup features in the SQL Server Enterprise Manager console. In the left pane, expand **Microsoft SQL Servers | (local)Windows NT) | Management | Backup**, shown in Figure 16.8. Right-click **Backup** and select **New Backup Device**. After configuring the backup device, you can back up by selecting **Backup a Database** from this same shortcut menu. The best way to backup SQL databases in SBS is to place SQL into simple recovery mode. Check the Help files for more on this topic.

Figure 16.8 Backup Utility in SQL Server 2000

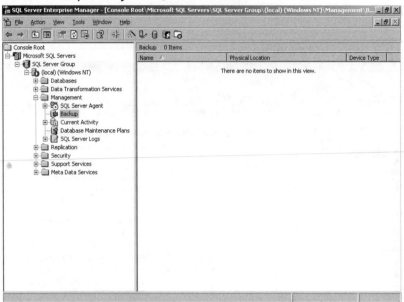

SOME INDEPENDENT ADVICE

As with ISA Server, many great resources are available for SQL Server 2000. You can start on the Microsoft Web site at www.microsoft.com/sql/default.asp. You can also read information, including case studies on the use of SQL Server in small and medium businesses, at www.microsoft.com/sql/smb/default.asp. There are lots of great books on SQL Server; choose one that suits both your technical level of expertise and your organization's needs. Since SQL Server is often used as the foundation for other applications, a mountain of information is available that's specifically focused on developers; you'll want to avoid those resources (unless you *are* a developer) and look for resources that will help you understand and implement SQL Server in your organization. There are also a lot of highly competent independent consultants who can help you with SQL Server.

FrontPage 2003

FrontPage 2003 is the third and final Premium Edition feature of SBS. Unlike the others, it is not a server application and should be on a computer other than the SBS Server. The application comes on its own disk, and installation follows the standard Microsoft application installation process.

FrontPage 2003 (FP) is a Web authoring application. You can create websites from scratch, edit websites, or edit the default SharePoint website. In fact, if you want to edit the SharePoint site, you cannot use earlier versions of FrontPage—you must use FrontPage 2003. Numerous features in SharePoint sites are not supported in earlier versions of FrontPage. After you install FrontPage 2003, you can select from among SharePoint templates. You can also choose to create and edit packages, including creating Web Log (blog) sites.

FrontPage is an easy-to-use program that lets you quickly and easily design and edit websites. One thing to keep in mind is that just because you have a web authoring application, it doesn't necessarily make you a web designer, any more than having Excel makes you an accountant. Making a few changes or additions to your SharePoint site is one thing; creating an entire corporate presence on the web is another. In today's competitive environment, you should have a website that is clean, concise, easy to navigate, and pleasing to look at. It's worth the investment to hire an experienced web designer to do this for you if you don't have the in-house talent. Take a look at other companies' sites, especially those of your competitors, to get an idea of what's going on out there. Check out the sites that have received awards (www.webbieawards.com) to see what's good and what the trends are. A poorly designed site can do more damage to your business than not having a site at all. These days it's pretty much a requirement to have a website, even if it's just a corporate presence site (sometimes called "business card" site) letting visitors know a bit about your company and how to contact you.

For more information on FrontPage 2003, check out the Microsoft website (part of the Office section) at office.microsoft.com/home/office.aspx?assetid= FX01085802.

SOME INDEPENDENT ADVICE

FrontPage 2003 can be used to create websites hosted by another company. This can be a great option because hosting companies are very good at security, backups, and maintaining server availability, since that's the business they're in. Hosting plans are very inexpensive and can be hosted on Windows, UNIX, or Linux platforms. If you plan on using FrontPage 2003's special features, your hosting company will need to support FrontPage Server Extensions. That means they'll have to install those extensions for your site in order for certain FrontPage features to work. Most web hosting companies do support FrontPage Server Extensions (most at no extra charge) and their sites typically will let you know all that and more. Once you create your site in FrontPage 2003, you can use FTP to transfer the files to the hosting company's server or you can publish the site to the IP address or domain name. Your hosting company will provide specific instructions on how to do this.

One More Time

In this chapter, we looked at three additional features included in the SBS Premium Edition. Internet Security and Acceleration (ISA) Server 2000 is a full-featured firewall and web caching server application. It provides enhanced security over the standard internal SBS firewall and, through its caching capabilities, can provide faster web access to users. When installing and using ISA Server, you should be aware of several caveats, as discussed in the chapter. SQL Server is the second Premium application bundled with SBS. SQL Server is a full-featured database application. It provides enterprise-level data collection, analysis, and management features. FrontPage 2003 is the third and final application that is part of the Premium Edition of SBS. FrontPage 2003 should be installed on a client computer and used to author and edit websites. FrontPage 2003 is required to edit SharePoint sites; earlier versions of FrontPage cannot be used with SharePoint.

- ☑ Internet Security and Acceleration Server 2000 uses network address translation, packet filtering, and caching to secure and accelerate Internet access.

- ☑ ISA Server setup will configure needed settings by launching the E-mail and Internet Connection Wizard when setup is complete.

☑ The easiest way to manage ISA settings is by launching E-mail and Internet Connection Wizard. Changes made from within this wizard will be reflected in ISA Server.

☑ ISA Server must be installed on the same computer as SBS. Make sure your server has enough horsepower to handle running SBS Server and ISA Server.

☑ Once you install ISA, remote users might not be able to access the SharePoint site via Remote Web Workplace. If this occurs, query the Microsoft Web site for the specific cause and solution or use the steps included to modify settings to re-establish connectivity.

☑ You can manage ISA Server via the ISA Management console.

☑ The ISA Firewall client must be installed on clients. This can be done automatically for Windows 2000 and Windows XP clients through Client Computers in Server Management and by selecting Assign Applications to Client Computers. Clients using earlier versions of the Windows operating system will have to connect to the shared Clients folder and run setup.exe.

☑ SQL Server is a full-featured database application. It is very powerful but somewhat complex and will likely require additional research on your part to implement it successfully in your company.

☑ SQL Server must be installed on the SBS server. You can (and should) point the data files (and possibly the program files as well) to a location other than the C: drive to help balance the load. Make sure your SBS server has enough CPU power and memory to run this application. A very fast processor (or two) and 2-4GB of RAM are ideal.

☑ SQL Server SP2 and below is not supported in SBS 2003, so you must also install Service Pack 3a, which is included on the Premium disk.

☑ FrontPage 2003 is a web authoring tool you can use to author and edit websites.

☑ FrontPage 2003 should be installed on a client computer, not on the SBS server.

☑ If you want to edit your SharePoint website with FrontPage, you must use FrontPage 2003. Earlier versions of FrontPage are not compatible with SharePoint features.

Index

Syngress: *The Definition of a Serious Security Library*

Syn·gress (sin–gres): *noun, sing.* Freedom from risk or danger; safety. See *security*.

CYA: Securing Exchange Server 2003 and Outlook Web Access

The down and dirty guide to configuring, maintaining, and troubleshooting essential Exchange Server 2003 features. Network engineers operate in high-stress environments where competitive business demands often run counter to "best practices." Design and planning lead times are non-existent and deployed systems are subject to constant end-runs. But at the end of the day, they are held accountable if things go wrong. They need help. They need to guarantee they've configured their network professionally and responsibly. A highly portable, easily digestible road-map, ensuring that the reader has in fact covered his a**.

ISBN: 1-931836-24-8

Price: $$39.95 US $59.95 CAN

The Best Damn Windows Server 2003 Book Period

Susan Snedaker

Windows Server 2003 is certainly Microsoft's most robust, and complex, enterprise operating system developed to date. Any one of the component "services" in Server 2003 has more features and functionality than existed in the entire Windows NT 4 operating system! In addition, the audience of system administrators has now evolved to a highly professional, skills certified community of IT professionals with a need for the tens of thousands of pages of Microsoft documentation and web-based support to be distilled into a concise, applied format. This is the book that meets the needs of today's Windows Server 2003 professional.

ISBN: 1-931836-12-4

Price: $59.95 US $79.95 CAN

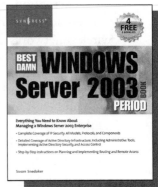

CYA: Securing IIS 6.0

Networking professionals responsible for configuring, maintaining, and troubleshooting Microsoft's Internet Information Server 6.0 will find this book indispensable. They operate in high-stress environments where competitive business demands often run counter to "best practices." Design and planning lead times are non-existent and deployed systems are subject to constant end-runs. But at the end of the day, they are held accountable if things go wrong. They need help. They need to guarantee they've configured their network professionally and responsibly. They need to CYA.

ISBN: 1-931836-25-6

Price: $$39.95 US $59.95 CAN

SYNGRESS®